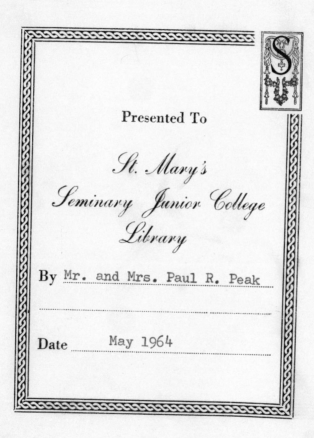

Presented To

St. Mary's
Seminary Junior College
Library

By <u>Mr. and Mrs. Paul R. Peak</u>

Date <u>May 1964</u>

HENRY MOORE TELLER

Henry Moore Teller

HENRY MOORE TELLER

Defender of the West

by Elmer Ellis

ILLUSTRATED

The CAXTON PRINTERS, Ltd.
Caldwell, Idaho
1941

Printed and bound in the United States of America by
The CAXTON PRINTERS, Ltd.
Caldwell, Idaho
55590

TO THOMAS CLARKSON ELLIS
AND HORACE BAGLEY
IN GRATEFUL MEMORY

PREFACE

MY REASONS for writing a biography of H. M. Teller are found in an abiding interest in the part which the West has played in national affairs. While the accidents of the search for hitherto unused manuscripts might have led to another statesman, it has been a frequent subject of self-congratulation that the fortunes of the chase led to Teller; for all of my subsequent study has indicated that he was the ablest representative of the West during the period of his activity in Washington. Teller's vision was not limited to his section; for his strong nationalism forced him to see beyond mere local interests. Moreover, he always treasured the common touch that distinguishes real statesmen in a democracy. The idealism of his youth was never lost in the warm competition of business, law, and politics. Teller is one of the small group of political leaders of whom it can be said that political experience made him increasingly sensitive to the needs of the underprivileged. Although disappointed in the trend of politics and increasingly legalistic in his point of view after 1896, he never lost his faith in the democratic processes, or in the ability of the common man in America to create a great society.

My aid from others in writing this biography has been unusually large and significant. In 1930, I completed a thesis on "The Public Career of Henry M. Teller," under the direction of Louis Pelzer. To him, to George R. Davies, to W. T. Root, and to the late Benjamin Shambaugh, all of the University of Iowa, my debt is very great for a wide range of suggestions. In the various drafts that the narrative has assumed since that time, the following have kindly read and criticized one or more chapters: the late Charles S. Thomas, of Denver, Chapters X to XXVI; the late James H. Teller, of Denver, Chapters I to XXVI; the late Chase Withrow, of Denver, Chapters III to VI; Allan Nevins, of Columbia University, Chapters I to XXVI; Fred A. Shannon, University of Illinois, Chapters I to X; Leroy R. Hafen, Colorado State Historical Society, Chapters III to VI; Frank F. Stephens, University of Missouri, Chapters XX and XXI; E. E. Dale, University of Oklahoma, especially Chapter X; Leland H. Jenks, Wellesley College, Chapter XX; Charles Bent, Jr., Morrison, Illinois, Chapter II; W. E. Weaver, Morrison, Illinois, Chapter II; John H. Nankivell, of Den-

ver, Chapter III; L. E. Atherton, University of Missouri,
Chapters I to XXVI; and Willoughby Johnson, University
of Missouri, Chapters I to XXVI.

In many ways my greatest debts are to librarians and
their excellent institutions. The libraries of the State University of Iowa and the State Historical Society of Iowa
and their staffs bore the brunt of my first extensive research
on this subject. Besides these, the following have been especially helpful: the Library of the State Historical Society
of Colorado; the Historical Collection of the Colorado University Library and its administrators, the Department of
History of that institution; and the Western Collection of
the Denver Public Library. The Manuscripts Division of
the Library of Congress—including extraordinary helpfulness from T. P. Martin and the late J. F. Jameson—has
provided materials that were essential to the completion of
the book. The staff members at the Iowa State Historical,
Memorial and Art Department at Des Moines, the University of Chicago Library, the St. Louis Public Library, the
Library of Alfred University, the Pettigrew Museum at
Sioux Falls, the Library of the Ohio State University, the
Library of the Ohio State Historical Museum, the Widener
Library at Harvard, the New York Public Library, the
State Historical Society of Kansas Library, the Hayes
Memorial Library of Fremont, Ohio, and the Yale Univer-
sity Library, have all been very helpful and obliging. Most
of all, the University of Missouri Library and the Library of
the State Historical Society of Missouri have suffered continuous and burdensome demands upon their services with
patience and unfailing helpfulness.

Suggestions and advice upon specific points have been
made by a number of friends: my former teacher, Orin
Grant Libby, University of North Dakota; George F. Howe,
University of Cincinnati; the late James F. Willard, University of Colorado; A. T. Volwiler, Ohio University; Jeannette P. Nichols, Philadelphia; James Barnes, Temple University; W. J. Burke, formerly of the New York Public
Library, now with Charles Scribner's Sons; George M.
Stephenson, University of Minnesota; James C. Malin, University of Kansas; Roger W. Toll, of Denver; Henry Steele
Commager, Columbia University; Lynn I. Perrigo, University of Kansas City; the late Frank J. Cannon, of Denver;
and L. E. Hardy, of Rushford, New York.

The late Mrs. G. E. Teller, of Sacramento, a daughter

of Senator H. M. Teller, was unusually helpful, going to a
great deal of trouble to locate important manuscripts and
writing for my use a long and valuable series of answers to
specific questions regarding her parents. Her keen appreciation of the problem and her willingness to help without
asking for restrictions of any kind, were highly gratifying.

Thomas F. Dawson deserves credit for the care with
which he preserved the sources on Teller's career. After
Dawson's retirement as Executive Secretary of the United
States Senate, he became Historian and Curator of the
Colorado State Historical Society. In the library of that
institution he placed his own correspondence with Teller,
as well as a large group of highly valuable documents from
Teller's files. Then he assiduously gathered reminiscences,
newspaper clippings, and other materials, obviously intending to write a biography of his former employer. His accidental death in 1923 prevented that. His writings, manuscript and published, especially his *Life and Character of
Edward Oliver Wolcott,* indicate his viewpoint on most questions of importance. He was in an ideal position to know
what was going on in both Colorado and Washington, as he
knew everyone and inspired confidence. His death before he
had written his life of Teller has meant a great loss to the
political history of the United States.

Ruth Clapper Ellis has assisted me in all the labor of
gathering materials for this book, and has prepared the
manuscript for publication.

ELMER ELLIS

University of Missouri
February, 1941

CONTENTS

ILLUSTRATIONS

HENRY MOORE TELLER

CHAPTER I

THE BACKGROUND
1830-58

ON A HOT June day in 1896, the Republican National Convention, assembled at St. Louis, had just cheered the reading of the platform as submitted by its committee on resolutions. The chairman recognized a Colorado delegate to present a minority report. The announcement of his name started a small demonstration of applause among scattered groups of delegates representing the Rocky Mountain states, but the large blocks from the East and Middle West sat angry and silent, apprehensive of what was about to happen.

The minority report in the form of a substitute plank providing for the free coinage of silver was read by the secretary of the convention. Its sponsor, a white-bearded old man in a frock coat, appeared on the platform where he looked small and helpless beside his two companions, the chairman of the convention and the head of the committee on resolutions. He began to speak in a tone of sadness and regret, absent-mindedly addressing the chair as "Mr. President!" He had no hope, he said, of influencing the decision of the convention, but wanted to justify himself and his colleagues in the action they were about to take.

I believe that the adoption of the gold standard in the United States will work great hardship.... I believe that the whole welfare of my race is dependent upon a rightful solution of this question.... I believed that the Republican party stood for the great masses of men; that its legislation was intended to lift up and elevate and hold up and sustain the unfortunate and distressed and give all American citizens equal opportunities before the law. That is why I became a Republican. ... I do not believe that these blessings can be had on a gold standard.

You will doubt my judgment ... but shall I doubt it? ... I must answer to my conscience and not my neighbors'....

When the Republican party was organized I was there. It has never had a national candidate since it was organized that my voice has not been raised in his support. It has never had a great principle enunciated in its platform that has not had my approbation until now. With its great leaders, its distinguished men of forty years, I have been in close communion and with many of them on terms of close friendship. I have shared its honors and its few defeats.... Yet I cannot before my country and my God, agree to that provision that shall put upon this country a gold standard and I will not.[1]

---

[1] Thomas F. Dawson, *Senator Teller* (Washington, 1898), pp. 15-21. The order of phrases in one sentence has been changed.

Tears coursed down his cheeks before he finished, but fire and passion had replaced the meekness that was in his voice when he began. As he sat down the chairman of the committee on resolutions moved that the substitute plank be tabled, and the motion carried by a ratio of nearly eight to one—only the Far West and scattering votes from border and Southern states were in the negative.

"This pronounced defeat of the silver forces," wrote one reporter, "threw the gold standard delegates into a paroxysm of delight; Negroes from the South, Harvard graduates from New England, Wall street representatives from New York, and the 'influenced' delegates from the central West, together with McKinley rooters from everywhere, shouted and clapped their hands, stood in their chairs and waved handkerchiefs, flags and canes."[2]

After the reading of a statement of reasons for withdrawing from the convention, the delegate from Colorado walked off the platform and down the main aisle toward the door. The band struck up a martial air, and the convention arose to sing, yell, and catcall at the retreating figure. As he proceeded on his way, he was joined by other delegates from the Rocky Mountain states, having twenty-two behind him when he reached the door. The great West, formerly a firm upholder of the Republican Party, was now leaving it.

Henry Moore Teller was the leader of the bolt.

Starting out in life as a Democrat, he later became a Republican, then a Silver Republican, and then a Democrat again—a circle that it took fifty years to complete. Few characters in American politics have been buffeted by fate as he was; few maintained themselves in positions of influence with more persistence. He lived in Washington for thirty years as a member of the Senate representing Colorado, and for three years as a member of the Cabinet.

His ancestry was one of those curious mixtures common to Americans. His paternal grandfather, Rem Remsen Teller, was of old New York Dutch descent diluted by an admixture of French. His paternal grandmother was Catherine McDonald, just one generation removed from Belfast, Ireland. Dutch had been as commonly spoken as English in the home where Henry Teller's father, John, had grown up. On the maternal side Henry Teller was of New England ancestry. His grandmother Moore boasted of descent from

---

[2] St. Louis *Republic* June 19, 1896.

that ideal of Puritans celebrated by Saint-Gaudens' statue, Deacon Samuel Chapin. His grandfather, Willard Moore, had operated a woolen mill at Windham, Vermont, until a disastrous fire induced him to try his fortune farther west. Henry's mother, Charlotte Chapin Moore, was born in Vermont and grew to womanhood there and at Saratoga, New York.[3]

Allegany County, in western New York, was a hilly, timbered country that still had most of the characteristics of a pioneer region when Henry Teller was a boy. It had been missed by the streams of westward-moving pioneers, and remained as an island of frontier within a generally populated area. Few of the farms in this region were pretentious, and the average was unquestionably poor. Even during Henry Teller's boyhood many of them consisted of little more than a clearing within a large tract of timber. The farm of John Teller was one of the poorest.[4]

Henry M. Teller was of the first generation to be born in that part of New York. He was the oldest boy of the family, born May 23, 1830—a sister, Sarah, being a year older. Four years after Henry, came his brother Willard, and three years later, Addison. Then came three girls, Katherine Julia, Caroline Susan, and Mary Elizabeth. The last of the children, James Harvey, was born in 1850, after Henry had reached an age that seldom found him at home.

Male children were then a distinct asset to their parents and began early to bear a share of the toil of planting and gathering crops, removing timber, and caring for the livestock. At times when work was not pressing at home, they were allowed to "hire out" to a neighbor and earn a little money for themselves. Country schools were held in the winter when there was little work to do on the farm, and the Teller boys attended as often as their duties at home would permit. Their parents were confirmed believers in the ability of an individual to improve his economic and social status through education, and consequently the boys received every encouragement to procure all the training that parents poor in purse could give them.

Probably the event in a typical week most enjoyable to the boys was the Saturday afternoon trip to the post office. This was located in the village store, and as mail—consist-

[3] Teller family Bible; James H. Teller, "Recollections," MS. in the library of the State Historical Society of Colorado; Sarah Teller Barnum to Mrs. Dean, Feb. 9, 1909, quoted in the Emma Teller Tyler "Recollections."

[4] Interview with J. B. Chaffee in 1883, clipping in Dawson Scrapbook.

ing chiefly of newspapers—came but once a week it was an
event to be looked forward to. Here the boys of the neighborhood gathered on Saturday afternoon and evening to get
the mail, make a few purchases, and spend an enjoyable few
hours in the all too rare companionship of rural life. The
following day no unnecessary labor was done. The family
went to church and read and talked over the contents of the
newspapers, thus enjoying the two great interests these
people had outside their daily work—politics and religion.
The church supplied the center of the latter, and the newspapers, together with stump speeches around election time,
the former. The significance of these weekly newspapers in
the intellectual life of the rural population can hardly be
overestimated. They were the chief source of information
from outside the community, and, as they were published for
the purpose of supporting certain political programs and
leaders, they helped to make those the common currency of
thought and discussion. As Henry Teller remembered it
many years later, a man selected his paper according to his
politics.

"If a man was a Democrat, he got the old New York
Evening Post. If he was a little off color and did not want
to be a full Democrat, he could take the New York *Herald*.
If he was a Whig, he took the *Times*, or Greeley's paper
when that came on."

Presumably the papers coming to the Teller home during
Henry's boyhood were Democratic, since that was the
family's politics, but Greeley's New York *Tribune* eventually
replaced them. John Teller was a Democrat, but he became
an Abolitionist, and, as the latter sentiment overcame the
old political attachment, the *Tribune* became the family
newspaper. Its arguments for abolition, temperance, and a
protective tariff became the subjects of weekly discussion,
and when Henry Teller left home and began to subscribe for
a paper of his own it was naturally Greeley's well-known
publication.[5]

John and Charlotte Teller had joined the local Methodist
Church soon after their marriage, and their home was
dominated by the moralistic religion peculiar to recently
occupied farming regions in America. John Teller was a
man of extremely strict principles, a regular attendant at
church, and a supporter of causes. At the time of his father's

―――――――
[5] *Congressional Record*, 59 Cong., 1 Sess., p. 2064; *ibid.*, 60 Cong., 1 Sess., pp. 6064-
66.

death in 1879 Henry wrote: "I have since his death gone over his life as I can remember it & I am more than ever impressed with the even character of his life. 53 years a member of the Church & during all that time I know his fellow members had no cause of complaint or to criticize his conduct. And he was not like some men who go through the world thus easily because they never antagonize anyone for he was a man of strong convictions & never was afraid to declare them. A strong Churchman & yet not a bigot. . . . I do not think anyone ever pointed at him as preaching one thing and practicing another."

An old friend recalled that he "was always an earnest and inflexible temperance man, and an honest and outspoken Abolitionist. The words he spoke for liberty were bold, timely, and pointed. He meant what he said and said what he meant. In him the poor hunted fugitive from the house of bondage ever found a firm, fearless, and generous friend. Never was needy human brother or sister—black or white— sent away from the door of John Teller, unaided. He was eyes for the blind, feet for the lame, bread for the hungry, and money for the poor."

Of his later years it is recalled that he would not work his horses on Sunday to the extent of driving to church, but walked instead. Even when his grown children refused to follow his example and with their mother drove to church, John Teller walked. The mother, though less insistent upon the formalities, joined her husband in his enthusiasms. Her "strong mentality" was often remarked, and she maintained a lively interest in all current happenings, being even in her old age an omnivorous reader of newspapers and magazines dealing with public affairs. Both parents were in harmony in these matters, and the family grew up in an atmosphere where public questions, religion, and reform were the common talk of the household.[6]

The work on the farm was hard and promised little more than a laborious and uninteresting life. Furthermore, it was then difficult for a young man to secure a farm in that region. To continue a life of farming it would be necessary to join those migrating westward, of whom many were from Teller's neighborhood. The other way out was by means of education. This qualification usually led to the ministry or to the law. The great statesmen of the day who were the sub-

---

[6] H. M. Teller to Harriet B. Teller, Nov. 10, 1879, Tyler MSS.; clippings from the Girard *Cosmopolite* and *Whiteside Sentinel* in the Tyler Collection.

jects of discussion and argument were generally lawyers. Considering the interests that surrounded the three older Teller boys at home, it is small wonder that two of them later joined that profession. But the way to the bar was neither direct nor easy. Some education beyond the country school was necessary, and this was expensive. About the only way in which a bright boy could earn the money to secure an education was to teach a country school and use his small earnings to attend an academy in one of the neighboring towns. This was a road that many boys followed; and as soon as they were old enough—possibly as young as fifteen— Henry and Willard Teller began to teach rural schools in Allegany and Cattaraugus counties.[7]

Schoolteaching occupied only part of the year, the remainder being spent in doing farm work and hauling lumber to the Erie Canal for shipment. Tiring of this, in the spring of 1852 Henry Teller decided to see some different country. He worked his passage on a lumber raft down the Allegheny and Ohio rivers to Cincinnati. After visiting with relatives he went on to Paris, Kentucky. He spent some time between Paris and Louisville, possibly teaching school for a while near the latter city. Family tradition records that his Abolitionist leanings were intensified by this short stay in a slave state.

After a few months he became ill and started back to New York. He worked his way to Erie, Pennsylvania, where he remained for a time with his Uncle Henry Teller, after whom he had been named. Uncle Henry was a prominent farmer, a member of the state legislature, and was immersed in politics. Between him and his namesake there was always a deep friendship. At this time Uncle Henry loaned his nephew enough money to pay for transportation back to Granger. Young Teller had had enough of aimless wandering.

That same fall, John and Charlotte Teller, despairing of maintaining a secure living on their farm, left it and moved to another, near Henry Teller in Pennsylvania. Instead of accompanying their parents, Henry and Willard enrolled in Alfred Academy in the town of the same name, not far from the old home.[8]

The town of Alfred had been settled by Rhode Islanders,

[7] Interview with H. M. Teller in the New York *Sun*, Nov., 1910, clipping in the Tyler collection.

[8] Interview with H. M. Teller in the Denver *Post*, May 26, 1911.

who brought with them many of the nonconforming characteristics that have distinguished the descendants of Roger
Williams' colony. For the most part they were Seventh-Day
Baptists with a puritanical outlook and a great faith in education. They soon established a school by subscription and
donated labor. This became an accredited academy ten
years before the Teller boys entered it, and a university some
years later. Officially it was nonsectarian in 1852, but the
faculty were recruited largely from the membership of the
Seventh-Day Church—most of them in fact being ministers
of that church. The Academy was largely a teacher-training
school for southwestern New York, and the year was conveniently divided into seasonal quarters so that needy students could teach in the winter, do farm labor in the summer,
and attend school the other two quarters. In the year 1852-
53 there were 163 "gentlemen" and 98 "ladies" in attendance.
Some of the faculty had been students at Oberlin and prided
themselves that Alfred was still more "advanced." Peda-
gogy, the classics, and science were not the only types of
education offered by the institution. It was a recognized
center of the popular forms of radicalism of the day. Its
president was described by his successor as "somewhat radical, even eccentric." The professor of Natural Science, who
at that early day bore the given name of Darwin, was described by a fellow teacher as "the fiery radical, the ready
talker, who in his chapel speeches made every heart to throb
and every face to glow."

Temperance was then a subject of much contention, and
Alfred had long been "dry" under a type of local option—a
situation brought about by the faculty of the Academy.
Women's rights and vegetarianism also had their advocates.
But most important of all causes was the abolition of Negro
slavery. Had not the professor of History, Metaphysical,
Political, and Moral Sciences assisted escaped slaves to
secure passage to Canada?

Alfred Academy possessed several literary and debating
societies, but it does not appear that either of the Tellers
joined them. Probably it was because these organizations
spent so much energy upon parliamentary rules—upon one
occasion seventy-two speeches were made on a single point—
that the more practical-minded Tellers never took an active
part. Public speaking, however, they did cultivate. Their
entrance into the Academy coincided with a great revival of

the art of elocution and reading under a special teacher from Boston.[9]

Either before or after this year at Alfred—or possibly both before and after—the Teller boys attended the Academy at Rushford in the same county. This institution was similar to Alfred, except that it was smaller. The principal of the school, Ira Sales, A.M., Ph.D., was a favorite with Henry Teller, and in later years when the professor's health prevented further teaching, his former pupil found a place for him in the Geological Survey. The courses offered the students consisted of languages—Latin, Greek, and German—mathematics of a large variety, several sciences, history, philosophy, and English literature. The Tellers belonged to a literary group called the Philomathean Society, under whose auspices visiting notables sometimes addressed the students. Among these were Horace Greeley, Frederick Douglass, and Horace Mann. Rushford, like Alfred and indeed all western New York, was alive with movement and change chiefly of a religious and moralistic nature. Elizabeth Cady Stanton and Susan B. Anthony appeared there advocating women's rights. Mormonism began a short while before Henry Teller was born, and a few members of that faith still remained long after the larger group had moved West. Spiritualism likewise became prominent, and the phenomenon of the "Rochester knockings" was a topic of warm discussion during the boys' student days. Temperance societies flourished, revivals were common and intense, and the ordinary political campaigns were extremely emotional. Most important of all questions was abolition, preached and practiced at Rushford as at Alfred, with an occasional escaped slave to help on his way to Canada to lend reality to the problem. These were times that made a young man's mind naturally turn to public affairs.[10]

It was obvious to Henry Teller that he must soon select a life career. Teaching a country school was in itself no easy task, and the remuneration was small. The one great compensation for this life was that one could make some progress toward a better position. As Henry Teller gained age, experience, and education, he secured better positions,

[9] *General Catalogue of Matriculates and Graduates of Alfred University, 1836-1896* (Westerly, R. I., 1896), pp. 5-8, 21; *ibid.*, Part II, Jonathan Allen, "A Memorial of President William Colgrove Kenyon," p. 6; A. A. Allen, *Life and Sermons of Jonathan Allen* (Oakland, Calif., 1894), pp. 18, 38, 41, 55, 56, 58.

[10] *The Rushford Centennial* (Rushford ?, 1908), pp. 59-65, 94-96, 126-32, 321, 503; Jerome C. Smiley, *Semi-Centennial History of the State of Colorado* (Chicago and New York, 1913), II, 4.

until he became principal of a town school. This paid a better salary and gave distinction of a kind, but still it held no future for an ambitious young man.

It seems he had been reading law to some extent for several years. In 1856 he secured a teaching position at Angelica, the county seat of Allegany County, and at once arranged to read systematically in the office of Martin Grover, an able and honored lawyer, who later became one of the judges on the New York Court of Appeals. Grover was an unusual lawyer, and his influence was large in giving Henry Teller a sound legal education.

Henry Teller was twenty-six years old when he went to Angelica as a schoolteacher. He had grown up to be a moderately tall, slender young man, whose most striking characteristic was a great shock of stiff, dark-brown hair, allowed to grow longer than was the current fashion and combed straight back. He was quiet and studious, as became a young teacher. He attended the Methodist church of his parents, although he did not maintain a membership in it.

Henry Teller was intensely interested in politics. It was hard for young men in the fifties not to be, and his father and Uncle Henry had an interest that was contagious. Following the family Democratic tradition, Henry had cast his first vote in a presidential election for Franklin Pierce in the fall of 1852. Then followed a period of change in political affiliations all over the country, stimulated by the Kansas-Nebraska Bill of 1854. The abolition sentiment in the North, which had never accepted the Fugitive Slave Law of 1850, was now fanned to a white heat of indignation. In western New York, "anti-Nebraska" Democrats repudiated their national party. Allegany County was a focal center of this movement. A caucus of antislavery men, which met at the town of Friendship in May, called a convention at Angelica for October. This meeting was attended by the insurgent Democrats, Whigs, and Free-Soilers. They nominated candidates for the county offices, and under the old Jeffersonian name of Republican Party carried the election for their ticket. These meetings were the origin of that party in New York, and, it was claimed, in the nation. Henry Teller, presumably, was present at the Angelica convention, which he referred to in later years as the birth of the Republican Party. His father, like most practical-minded antislavery men, was an ardent follower of the new faith, and young Henry was no less enthusiastic. Two years later these fac-

tions became the national party, with the arresting program
of "No extension of slave territory." The new party nominated John C. Frémont for the presidency, and Henry Teller
began a lifelong political career by advocating his election.[11]

But politics, law, and teaching did not take all of his time.
There was an academy for girls at Angelica, and no young
man of Henry Teller's disposition could help being somewhat interested in its students. Among them was an attractive girl of nineteen years named Harriet Bruce. She was
the daughter of Packard Bruce, a farmer near the town of
Cuba, in the same county. In her old age, Harriet Bruce,
then Mrs. Teller, left this recollection of Henry Teller at
Angelica:

"I was attending a young ladies' academy and Mr. Teller
was there engaged in the dual capacity of studying law and
teaching school, although not the school I was attending.
Naturally an eligible young man, such as Mr. Teller was at
the time, attracted the attention of the girls, and as now, we
made free to discuss the young gentlemen who came under
our observation, Mr. Teller included. I recall very well that
we pronounced against his hair. He had plenty of it, a head
full and very black, which he combed back as far as the
stiffness would permit. This was the predominant feature as
we saw it. We commented freely, and when someone proposed to introduce him to me I said: 'The first thing I will
say to him will be to tell him to cut his hair.' But I didn't
say it. We found plenty of other things to say."

This acquaintance became a serious romance in the
following year, and when Miss Bruce finished her academy
course, Henry Teller, accidentally no doubt, secured a teaching position at Cuba, her home town. Continuing to read
law under the future Judge Grover, and to earn his meager
salary as a teacher, Teller also carried on his courtship of
Miss Bruce.

Not long after Teller had moved to Cuba an acquaintance
of his returned from a trip to Illinois and sent word to Teller
that Hiram A. Johnson, a lawyer of Morrison, Illinois, was
looking for a young man to become his partner. After some
preliminary correspondence Johnson asked Teller to become
his associate. This he agreed to do, reserving only time
enough to take the New York bar examinations. It was not

---

[11] James H. Teller, "Recollections"; Emma Teller Tyler, "Recollections"; Dawson, *Teller* (Washington, 1923), p. 10; Francis Curtis, *The Republican Party* (New York, 1904), I, 202, 210; Frank S. Smith to William E. Chandler, Oct. 1, 1884, Chandler MSS.

necessary to take these, as the regulations in the newer states made it relatively easy to secure admission to the bar, but there was added prestige if a lawyer had been admitted in one of the states with higher standards. For this reason Teller journeyed to Binghamton, New York, where the supreme court was meeting, successfully met the requirements, and on January 5, 1858, was admitted to the bar.

Teller and Harriet Bruce were now engaged, but the question of marriage was postponed because of a lack of necessary money to provide double transportation to Illinois and to start housekeeping. Calling in brother Willard to take over his school at Cuba, Henry Teller left his home community on what may well be called the beginning of his life's work.[12]

---

[12] Dawson, *op. cit.*, pp. 7, 17; Mrs. H. M. Teller, "Senator Teller as a Young Man."

CHAPTER II

THE YOUNG ATTORNEY AND POLITICIAN
1858-61

LATE in the winter of 1858, Henry Teller arrived at the little town of Morrison, Illinois,[1] a village fairly typical of new prairie towns brought into being by the construction of a railroad. Although that part of Whiteside County bordering upon the Mississippi River had been settled for a longer period, Morrison itself had grown up with the building of the railroad less than three years before. A census taken the fall after Teller arrived gave it a population of 455. The land about it was soon occupied by farmers, who could make a living in this region now that it was supplied with transportation facilities. The people were largely New Yorkers and Yankees who had moved West, although there were enough foreigners to bring this comment on a session of court from a local Republican newspaper, "The balance of the afternoon was occupied in 'making Democrats' or in other words naturalizing Irishmen."[2]

Conditions in western New York, particularly, were such in the forties and fifties that many settlers and professional men moved West to become leaders in the newer states.[3] When Teller was in the Senate in 1877, he was to find that he had five colleagues, representing five different states, all of whom had as boys worked on near-by farms in Allegany County.[4]

Morrison was experiencing a boom when Teller came. The county had voted to move its seat of government from the neighboring town of Sterling to Morrison, the actual transfer taking place shortly after Teller arrived. From the standpoint of legal business the removal of the county seat made a great improvement in the town. Hiram A. Johnson and his first partner had formerly been its sole attorneys, but now other lawyers established offices, until the local bar had as many as nineteen members, all but two or three of whom actually lived in Morrison.[5]

---

[1] Teller was admitted to the bar on Jan. 5, Dawson, *op. cit.*, p. 7. There are no numbers of the *Whiteside Sentinel* between Dec. 24, 1857, and April 14, 1858. The Johnson and Teller card is carried in the latter issue.

[2] *Whiteside Sentinel*, Oct. 14, 1858, Oct. 18, 1860.

[3] Out of six biographies of "founders" of Morrison in the history of Whiteside County, five of the subjects are from New York and one from Vermont. Charles Bent, *History of Whiteside County* (Morrison, 1877), pp. 322-24.

[4] *Independent*, May 7, 1908.

[5] Bent, *op. cit.*, p. 307; *Whiteside Sentinel*, Oct. 13, 1859.

Hiram A. Johnson seemingly had lived there since the founding of the town. He had married a local girl, and, as one of its two established attorneys, he was a man of importance in the community. He dominated the Douglas faction of the Democratic Party in Whiteside County. He was a popular and able lawyer, and Teller's association with him did a great deal to establish the younger man locally. The two men were not alike personally. Johnson was a breezy, rather boisterous type, who enjoyed his boon companions and their indulgences in a way that Teller, with his background and personality, could not or would not imitate. The older lawyer was an adventurous individual with more than a touch of the gambling spirit in his make-up that made him a most stimulating associate for his sober and less venturesome partner.[6]

There is no doubt, if one may judge by the reports of court cases, that the firm of Johnson and Teller secured far more than its share of law business. This ranged over the entire field of law, but in the civil cases it was generally concerned with property in land. It is a fair estimate that the firm was concerned in fully half of the court cases in Whiteside County, although one of its competitors did the bulk of what lawyers call the paper work. Johnson had formerly been satisfied to run the simple card, "Attorneys and Counsellors at Law and Collecting Agents," but after Teller's arrival their card became the most elaborate of the local firms', reading:

JOHNSON AND TELLER

ATTORNEYS AND COUNSELLORS AT LAW,

AND SOLICITORS IN CHANCERY

Will practice in all Courts of the 22nd Judicial District, and in the Supreme Court and United States District Courts of the State of Illinois.[7]

Law was the vocation but not the only interest of either Teller or Johnson. The three years Teller spent in Illinois were three of the most strenuous and significant years in all American political history, and both men were in the midst of the contest. The attempt to bring Kansas into the Union

---

[6] Bent, *op. cit.*, p. 511; notes from Chase Withrow, Denver, 1929. Mr. Withrow read law in the office of Johnson and Teller in the early sixties.

[7] *Whiteside Sentinel*, Nov. 26, 1857, April 14, 1858. The same card was run in the Sterling *Republican and Gazette*, July 28, 1860. W. A. Davis, *History of Whiteside County, Illinois* (Chicago, 1908), I, 327.

with a slave constitution caused another political upheaval. A few months after Teller arrived in Morrison the local Democratic convention, brushing aside the opposition of a few administration men, adopted resolutions condemning the "Lecompton swindle," as the slave constitution was called, and sent Johnson and two other delegates to the state convention at Springfield, pledged to support Stephen A. Douglas for senator. Not long after this the Republican county convention met, and Teller, a delegate from Morrison, was placed on the committee on resolutions, although he had been in the community less than six months. Delegates were selected to attend the state convention. The chief contest in 1858 in Morrison, as over the country, was the Lincoln-Douglas campaign for the Senate. Even the details of the Republican state convention were given publicity by the local Republican press.[8] Among other things, its special correspondent wrote:

At 7 o'clock in the evening we had been promised a speech from Lincoln. Everybody and his wife were determined to hear that effort, if somebody had to be squeezed a little. At that time a long legged, longer armed, big nose, bigger mouth, swarthy black-eyed individual who possibly may have seen sixty summers approached the speaker's stand, accompanied by great cheering. This was Abraham Lincoln, the homeliest man in Illinois. In a moment the fire broke out and we forgot the person, and became charmed by his clear and convincing eloquence.

In the ensuing campaign, the famed Lincoln-Douglas debates did not come to Morrison, but they were followed with close interest. Johnson took an active part in the campaign for Douglas, but we have no record of any political activity by Teller beyond his participation in the county convention.

But the agitation did not die down with Douglas' victory. One of the minor routes of the Underground Railroad passed through Whiteside County. Violation of the Fugitive Slave Law was open and unashamed. Early the following year the local paper noted:

We learn that two fugitive slaves passed through this county on the U. G. R. R. a short time since. They were both females and chattels of a prominent Judge in Nebraska.

Later it noted that in the past few weeks there had been a "thriving business" on the same route, some ten persons hav-

_____
[8] *Whiteside Sentinel*, April 14, May 26, June 24, Sept. 16 and 17, 1858.

ing passed through. The Harpers Ferry raid was watched
with considerable interest. On the day of John Brown's
execution public meetings of protest were held in many
towns in northern Illinois, and the Morrison paper published its first extra—a mere handbill, containing the telegraphed dispatch of that event. Near the first of the year a
"Lyceum or Debating Club" was formed,[9] and the first debate scheduled was upon the subject: *"Resolved*, That we
should desire and encourage the formation of a Sectional
Party."

As the election of 1860 approached, interest increased.
In the Republican county convention to select delegates to
the state convention, Teller worked with the successful faction in the main contest and helped name delegates pledged
to Richard Yates for governor. Again he was on the resolutions committee. The fight in the convention was protracted
and bitter, and it was only by continuing the contest far into
the night by long speeches that the Yates faction won. Later
another convention was held to select delegates to the Congressional convention. This gathering, the "largest and
most noisy" ever held in the county, was more hotly contested than the earlier meeting. A Republican editor predicted that the local organization would end if harmony
were not soon restored. The convention split and two sets
of delegates were chosen, Teller being one of the majority
group that was eventually seated in the Congressional convention. Here the Whiteside delegation voted for the incumbent, who was defeated by a Chicago candidate with the
solid support of that large delegation.[10]

When the Republican National Convention assembled at
Chicago, Teller was present with a group of faithful Republicans from Morrison to witness the event and help create
an atmosphere favorable to the Illinois candidate. Judging
by his description of this scene later, it must have impressed
Teller as few things in his life had. The nomination of
Lincoln secured, he returned home to prepare for the campaign—a contest between Lincoln and Douglas as far as
Illinois was concerned. It officially opened in Whiteside
County with an address by Teller before the Morrison Republican Club. This is the first speech of his on record, and
the summary in the local Republican newspaper is worth
quoting:

---

[9] *Whiteside Sentinel*, Feb. 17, Nov. 10, Dec. 2, 8, 14, 1859.
[10] *Whiteside Sentinel*, April 26, May 17, June 28, July 12, Aug. 2, 1860; James H.
Teller, "Recollections."

The meeting of the Club on Saturday evening was well attended, and evinces that the true spirit of Freedom is awakening an interest in our community, which is destined to make its influence felt at the ballot box in November. At the appointed hour H. M. Teller, Esq., proceeded to address the meeting in plain, common sense speech, in which he defined the principles of the several political parties, clearly proving that the Republican is now the only party contending for the true principles of government as laid down in the constitution and adopted by the "fathers" of the Republic. He quoted from Washington, Jefferson, Monroe, Madison, Jackson, Clay and others, to show that the opinions entertained by them were substantially the principles now advocated by the Republican party; that on the great questions of Freedom & Slavery Abraham Lincoln entertained the same views as those entertained by every pure patriot and statesman from Washington's time down to the present day. The empty professions of Douglas and his squatter sovereignty doctrine were portrayed in their true colors. Douglas was as much in favor of the extension of slavery as Jeff Davis or any other fire-eater of the South. In his speech in the Senate on the 16th & 17th of May last, he maintained that by his exertions in repealing the Missouri Compromise, territory had already been secured to slavery, equal in extent, to five times the size of the State of New York. This is the beneficent fruits of the workings of "Popular Sovereignty" as declared by Douglas himself. Are northern freemen prepared to see slavery further extended over our free territories? If so vote for Douglas and his squatter sovereignty humbug. That will effect it just as essentially as to elect Breckinridge and Lane.

Later in the campaign Teller spoke in various parts of the county in the interest of the Republican ticket. But the campaign locally was not so warm as might have been expected. The county was too predominantly Republican to make much of a contest. When the votes were counted in Whiteside County, Lincoln had 2,713, Douglas, 1,110, and Breckinridge and Bell between them received 25.[11]

This contest was only an introduction to a larger one. As the time of Lincoln's inauguration drew near and the secession movement in the South progressed, the people of the North began to awaken to the realization that it was no ordinary crisis that Lincoln would have to meet. In order to strengthen his hand in dealing with the problem, public meetings were held to discuss the issue and agree upon a line of action. Late in February, Teller and the four other members of the Republican county central committee issued the following notice:

The Republicans of this county will meet in Convention at Morrison, on Saturday the 9th day of March next, at two o'clock P.M. to

---

[11] *Whiteside Sentinel*, Aug. 30, Sept. 8, Nov. 8, 1860; James H. Teller, "Recollections"; Dunham Wright, "A Winter in Estes Park with Senator Teller," *The Trail*, July, 1920.

confer together upon our duty in this our great peril as a Nation. Come, let us council together, and renew our devotion to the great principles of the founder of our Republic. Each town in the county is requested to send the same number of delegates as at the County Convention held last fall.[12]

No report of that meeting exists, and Teller was not to take part in what followed. Other events had so shaped his course that this was to be his last public act as a citizen in Illinois.

The years Teller spent at Morrison were years that meant hard times for the frontier farmer. The effects of the panic of 1857 were still felt in curtailed credit and low prices. In these years, "times are hard" was a regular complaint of the editor of the Morrison paper, although, Western-like, he usually added that there was "unmistakable evidence on every hand of a bright and prosperous future for Morrison." This lack of prosperity was not personal to Teller, as his law practice brought in a good income for a beginning lawyer. He was even able to acquire a tract of cheap land, which eventually became valuable. His younger brother, Addison, came from the East and began farming operations, and a few years after Henry Teller left, his parents came to Morrison and farmed the land belonging to him.[13] But the general depression kept communities such as Morrison from increasing in population and wealth as rapidly as the inhabitants wished.

To the disappointed and superambitious came a new hope. Late in 1858 gold was found in the foothills of the Rocky Mountains, in what is now east-central Colorado. This news spread rapidly over the frontier, hopeful news to some, but bad news to others. In a new community with a large share of foot-loose people, such news as a gold strike can quickly reduce its population. Those who have invested effort and capital in such communities fight hard to keep their population. This was the case at Morrison. In January, 1859, editorials and news items appeared in the local press casting doubts upon possibilities of gold in the "Pike's Peak Region." On March 10 it noted that teams were passing through on their way to Pike's Peak, and that a party was forming in town and would be on its way in a few days. A month later appeared an account of the "Pike's Peak Hum-

[12] *Whiteside Sentinel*, Feb. 28, 1861.

[13] *Whiteside Sentinel*, Dec. 24, 1857, May 6, 1858, March 15, 1860; Mrs. H. M. Teller, "Senator Teller as a Young Man." A. J. Teller is listed among the judges of the contests at the county fair in the March 15, 1860, issue of the *Sentinel*.

bug." But in the fall when some of the local people wrote
back and some returned, the confession was made that it
was a real strike. Then the movement quieted down for the
winter. But by the middle of the following March the editor
sorrowfully noted that it seemed that Morrison was to be
"drained" of population by those going to Pike's Peak.[14]

Among this group who left in the spring of 1860 was
Hiram A. Johnson. Always willing to gamble, always looking for a big strike, the lure of the gold fields was too much
for even a successful small-town lawyer. Some eight weeks
after he had been in "the new Eldorado," Johnson wrote a
letter from Nevada City to the editor of the Morrison paper
to set at rest all rumors regarding it. This was a straight
statement of conditions and prospects.

> But here, as everywhere else in a mining country, mere surface
> men, and surface work, can never succeed, and I am glad that it is a
> discriminating country. All who come here are not deserving of
> success. A man must have capital, work hard, and be exceedingly
> lucky, or come short of success. I tell you, of all the places I ever
> saw, this is entirely the worst place for the gentleman of leisure.
> Hard fisted, big hearted, bold, adventurous men may come here, hoping
> to better their circumstances, while others had better remain where
> they are as their board will cost them entirely too much in this country.

When Johnson was describing the type of men who
would be successful in the gold fields he was no doubt giving
a self-portrait; for he was enthusiastic over his own prospects and did not return to Morrison for the election. During
the winter of 1860-61 he repeatedly urged Teller to join him,
but the latter was reluctant to make the move. There was no
good reason for his leaving Morrison, as he had an assured
position at the bar and fine political prospects in a small
way; he was acquiring some property and earning more
money than he ever had before. The national political situation was so threatening that he must have disliked to get
out of touch with the regular sources of information. He had
many good friends, especially among the younger men, and
these, with his political and fraternal connections, tended
to keep him in Morrison. It was hard to leave all this for the
uncertainty of a mining region so far from the centers of
population as was the "Pike's Peak Country."[15]

---

[14] James F. Willard, "The Gold Rush and After," in *Colorado: Short Studies of Its
Past and Present* (Boulder, 1927), pp. 101-21; *Whiteside Sentinel*, Jan. 27, April 14,
Aug. 11, Sept. 1, 1859, March 15, 1860.

[15] *Whiteside Sentinel*, Aug. 9, 1860; T. M. Marshall, *Early Records of Gilpin County*
(University of Colorado Historical Publications, edited by James F. Willard), (Boulder,
1920), II, 132; W. A. Davis, *History*, I, 327, II, 638; *Portrait and Biographical Album,
Whiteside County*, (Chicago, 1885), p. 325.

Johnson's enthusiastic urgings finally won, however, and Teller agreed to go for a trial of a month, regretting his promise after he had made it. Putting off his departure as long as he could, he finally left Morrison by rail for St. Joseph, Missouri, about the middle of April. From St. Joseph an irregular stage ran to Denver City, whence other stages went into the mining country. For six days and nights, with rests only when horses were changed at the stations, Teller rode across the bleak, empty plains to Denver City. On the trail he passed slow-moving bull trains hauling supplies to the new settlements and gold seekers in their own wagons trekking westward. And less frequently—perhaps because it was spring—he would meet a disappointed gold seeker returning home, admitting the second alternative in the slogan, "Pike's Peak or Bust."

Teller was not impressed favorably as he rode the weary route westward.[16] Pausing in Denver City only briefly, he pushed on by coach through Golden City, reaching the Gregory "diggings" on April 27. Here he arrived to try his fortune in the gold country. He was none too sure that he would not soon turn eastward and join those who declared they had "seen the elephant" and were going back to "America."

---

[16] James Burrell, "History of Gilpin County," in W. B. Vickers, *History of Clear Creek and Boulder Valleys* (Chicago, 1880), p. 205; Dawson, *Teller* (1923), p. 10.

CHAPTER III

HENRY M. TELLER found himself in one of the most peculiar communities in America when he arrived in Colorado. There were other mining camps, to be sure, but none like this one. Because Gilpin was the smallest county in the Territory and dominated it throughout the early territorial period, it was affectionately referred to as the "Little Kingdom of Gilpin." It included several smaller mining camps, but those in Gregory and Nevada gulches were its heart and soul.

This gulch—the two were really one—branched off from Clear Creek Canyon and extended about two miles in a westerly direction. It was narrow and crooked, and extraordinarily steep. Along the bottom of the gulch, eagerly seizing upon any chance level ground, were buildings— miners' cabins of logs, roughly built stores, saloons, and stamp mills. These extended throughout the entire length of the gulch, thinning out in some places and crowding close together in others. The first large grouping of buildings was at the place where the gulch stream emptied into Clear Creek. This was the town of Black Hawk. Farther west, without any noticeable dividing point in the buildings, was a larger aggregation named Central City, where Johnson and Teller located. Still farther up the continuation of the Gregory, called Nevada Gulch, was Nevadaville, the least of the cities that made up the gulch settlements. In this gigantic gully were to be found the majority of the white people in Colorado in 1861, exclusive of the Mexican residents in the southern part.

The sides of the gulch rose steeply to a great height. These were dotted with mine shafts, each with its pile of dirt and rock. The pines that had once covered part of its barren walls were cut away in the immediate neighborhood of the camps. The gulch was obviously a one-street settlement, except at Central City, where side gulches made a cross street possible. Above the buildings on the main street was ranged a row of houses looking out over the roofs of those below, and kept level by a foundation of poles on the gulch side. Later these were connected with the street by long flights of wooden stairs.

It was not a beautiful sight. The unpainted buildings were, for the most part, made of rough-hewn logs. The landscape had once had a type of barren, mountainous beauty, but this had been ruined by mine shafts, ugly buildings, and areas of cut-over trees. To a visitor with an eye for beauty, nature seemed "to be suffering from an attack of confluent smallpox."[1]

But people were there, and more were coming. The Gregory diggings had been the first real strike in the region, and for several years remained the principal gold-producing region of the world. It was discovered in 1859, and during that and the following year miners had flocked into it in great numbers. So famous did it become that Horace Greeley made a trip from New York to inspect it, and stayed long enough to give the first public speech ever made there, warning the assembled prospectors against speculation, gambling, drinking, and other vices. In the spring and summer of 1860 it was estimated that five thousand people were coming each week. There were not so many the next year when Teller came. Claims were so extensively taken up by that time that there was little for the newcomers unless they were able to buy out someone. Hence they drifted on to newer camps, and with them drifted the bulk of the "bummers" and other vagrants who lived off the abundance of a new strike without the exertion of productive labor. The large number that remained were typical of the better class of Western miners. Although the gulch towns had all the usual pleasure resorts of such places, these did not dominate the community. Denver was a better place for a miner's periodical celebration, and, in comparison, Central City and Black Hawk were sober villages. Central was neither a Leadville nor a Cripple Creek.[2]

Colorado had become a territory about a month before

---

[1] In 1861 the temporary town of Mountain City was between Black Hawk and Central City, but was soon incorporated in the latter. Johnson and Teller were established there in 1861. Lynn Irwin Perrigo, "A Social History of Central City, 1859-1900" (unpublished thesis, University of Colorado, 1936) ; Bayard Taylor, *Colorado: A Summer Trip* (New York, 1867), p. 54 ; Frank C. Young, *Echoes from Arcadia: The Story of Central City, as told by one of "The Clan"* (Denver, 1903), pp. 5 ff. ; Albert D. Richardson, *Beyond the Mississippi* (Hartford, 1869), p. 335 ; O. J. Hollister, *The Mines of Colorado* (Springfield, Mass., 1867), p. 142.

[2] Frank Fossett, *Colorado, Its Gold and Silver Mines* (New York, 1880), pp. 140, 143, 290 ; Samuel Cushman and J. P. Waterman, *The Gold Mines of Gilpin County* (Central City, 1876), p. 25 ; T. M. Marshall, *Early Records of Gilpin County*, p. 1 ; C. B. Goodykoontz, "The Exploration and Settlement of Colorado," in *Colorado: Short Studies of its Past and Present*, p. 72 ; Young, *Echoes*, p. 29 ; Perrigo, "Social History of Central City," Chapter 8.

Teller arrived, but it had been existing politically for over two years. First, an attempt had been made to repeat California's experience, and a constitution was drawn up for the "State of Jefferson," but the miners voted it down. An extralegal government was maintained under the name of the "Territory of Jefferson" until Congress made it a legal entity under the name of Colorado Territory. Local government had rested on a similar basis. When the miners in Gregory Gulch had found that a degree of public order was necessary, they called a meeting, organized a mining "district," adopted laws that supplied all the needs of such a primitive community, and set up a government to enforce them. And all this without a shadow of authority, except that they were American citizens not under "any active or protecting branch of the central government." Other districts followed suit, and soon all the gold region was under local governments, conditioned by popularly adopted constitutions written down in copybooks, and codes of law similarly recorded, covering every subject from the method of recording mining claims to the penalty for murder. The laws were to be applied in "miner's" or "people's" courts, consisting of a judge elected at a general meeting of the district, and the usual jury. Appeals in some cases could be taken to the general meeting of the district itself, and its judgment was final in all cases. This practice of trial by public meeting was not entirely forgotten after the territorial courts were established, and its methods frequently resembled those of Judge Lynch. The law to be applied in any case was that adopted by the district. Characteristically enough, some districts refused to allow the use of their courts to collect debts contracted outside the district— Eastern creditors were not looked upon with favor—and some refused to allow lawyers to appear in court. The latter was not true of most districts, however, and there was still room for a legal practice under the rule of these primitive tribunals. Eventually the territorial legislature replaced these with a general system, but the old courts continued to function for some time, and Teller's first legal work in Colorado was in them.[3]

There are innumerable tales, probably losing nothing in their transmittal, that give a picture of some of the diffi-

---

[3] F. L. Paxson, "The Territory of Colorado," *American Historical Review*, XII (Oct., 1906), 60-61; T. M. Marshall, "The Miners' Laws of Colorado," *American Historical Review*, XXV (April, 1920), 426-39; T. M. Marshall, *Early Records of Gilpin County* (Boulder, 1920).

culties the careful Illinois lawyer met in adjusting himself
to the informalities of the miner's courts. On what must
have been one of his first cases he went to Nevadaville with
a client to appear before a court presided over by one John
Jones, late of Missouri, and never before of the bench or the
bar. Jones saw Teller coming with a lawbook under his arm.
Stopping the court proceedings immediately, he called out:
"See here, young man, you can't bring no luther-kivered
book in this here room."[4] And that was not the end of his
initiation. Appearing for a defendant, he filed a demurrer
to the plaintiff's complaint, and, on hearing, made an ex-
haustive argument of two hours' length, only to have the
judge say: "Mr. Teller, I wish you to understand that no
demurrers are allowed in this court; you will have to file
an answer." All his explanations of the practice in the
States availed him nothing.

A somewhat different experience was in store for him
when he appeared in a slander action for a woman who
was seeking to recover damages against a man who had
boasted publicly that he had enjoyed her favors. The case
was heard before a shirt-sleeved judge holding court in a
barroom. In his appeal to the jury, one of the defendant's
counsel attempted to read a letter that the judge had ruled
was not in evidence. Before he had it unfolded, the judge
audibly cocked one of the two guns he carried in his belt
and announced that the counsel could not read the letter.
Whereupon the counsel "covered" the court and stated that
he "thought" he would. The crowd left precipitately, but no
shooting resulted; the sheriff and his deputy came to the aid
of the judge, prevented the reading of the letter, and Teller
won his case.[5]

Another notable trial in which Teller played a part did
not require his legal talents. A Mexican of bad reputation—
it was easy for a Mexican to get a bad reputation in most
mining camps—was caught red-handed robbing a sluice box
of its precious deposit. That was the one capital crime in
a mining camp, as stealing horses was among ranchers. At a
public meeting he was tried, found guilty with apparent
unanimity, and sentenced to be hanged immediately. At the
scaffold Teller's request that the prisoner be given a chance

---

[4] Hal Sayre, "Reminiscences." MS. in Colorado State Historical Society Library.
The name Sayre was "Sayr" in his early days in Colorado, but a final *e* was added
later, and that spelling is followed here.

[5] Peter Wikoff, "The Bench and Bar of Denver and Colorado," *Magazine of Western
History*, IX (March, 1889), 608-10.

to pray was granted. When the thief refused the opportunity, Teller himself offered up a respectable petition. In
this manner the story began that Teller had tried to get a
greaser into Heaven who was not good enough for the
Kingdom of Gilpin.[6]

The regular legal business was very profitable in spite of
the irregularity of many proceedings. Litigation was frequent, fees were high, and profits were greater than they
had been at Morrison. There was a vast stimulation in
living in a community in which the element of uncertainty
played such a great part. Political opportunities were
equally attractive, with extraordinary possiblities of advancement. It was clearly a place where a young man of
ability and ambition could go far. Teller soon gave up any
ideas he may have had about returning to Illinois.

After a strenuous spring and summer Teller became ill
with what was known as "mountain fever," but which may
have been only a digestive disturbance brought on by his
diet since leaving Illinois. As yet there was little food produced locally, and almost all miners' supplies, except the
sandy flour and "Taos Lightning" whiskey that came from
New Mexico, had to be hauled overland from "the River."[7]
But whatever the cause, Teller became seriously ill, and, after
a session in the local "hospital," he and another patient were
moved into an empty cabin and cared for by a young man
named Dunham Wright. Teller recovered strength slowly,
and his doctor suggested a lower altitude. In December he
and young Wright started for a lonely farm near Fort
Lupton, intending to spend a part of the winter season there.
Soon after their arrival they accepted an invitation to join
Joel Estes, who was wintering a herd of cattle in the park
that now bears his name. Here Teller and Wright spent most
of the winter, Wright helping with the cattle and Teller
hunting and cutting wood for the fire. Late in the winter
Teller was strong enough to ride horseback to Central City
and prepare for the business that was expected with the
opening of spring.[8]

It was now four years since he had left the town of Cuba

---

[6] Clipping, undated, from Chicago *Times-Herald*, in Dawson Scrapbook; Peoria
Journal, Aug. 13, 1895, clipping, Tyler MSS.

[7] Irving W. Stanton, *Sixty Years in Colorado* (Denver, 1922), p. 50; Young *Echoes*,
pp. 48-50.

[8] Dunham Wright, "A Winter in Estes Park with Senator Teller," *The Trail*, July,
1920; H. M. Teller interview in Denver *Post*, May 26, 1911. Some doubt is thrown upon
the details of Wright's account by Enos A. Mills, *The Story of Estes Park* (Longs Peak,
Estes Park, 1911), pp. 7, 8.

Mrs. H. M. Teller shortly after her marriage.

and Harriet Bruce to whom he was engaged. Miss Bruce was living with her widowed mother, and marriage would break up their household. This was particularly distasteful to Mrs. Bruce, and it was partly at her insistence that the marriage had been postponed. It seemed highly desirable to the younger people that it not be delayed any longer.

In the spring, therefore, Henry Teller went back across the plains to Morrison and on to Cuba. He found conditions greatly changed from the last time he had been in the East. The Civil War was in progress, and brother Addison was in service, as were the brothers of his fiancée and most of his former companions. In the midst of this atmosphere, Henry Teller and Harriet Bruce were married on June 7, 1862. Mrs. Teller has left this reminiscence of that occasion:

> The wedding took place in our home, but it was not a very joyous occasion. Mr. Teller had suffered a serious illness soon after coming to Colorado and his recovery had been slow. At the time of the wedding he was almost without color and as thin as a rail. My sister had just died of galloping consumption and my own health was so precarious that I was believed to be coming down with that fatal disease. I was as pale as the bridegroom, and people generally remarked that never had they seen such a hopeless looking couple so far as health was concerned. To our friends the proposed journey more than half across the country, much of it by stage over barren and uninhabited plains, seemed a desperate undertaking. Many were the predictions that neither of us ever would again see New York State.

But the toilsome journey was made, and the newlyweds arrived in Denver on the third of July.[9] Pioneer Colorado was not settled by the fainthearted; even the stage journey across the plains was as effective a barrier to the timid as a long sea voyage would have been.

Henry Teller now became a permanent fixture in the life of Central City and the entire gulch. He had immediately taken a prominent part in its community life as had also his partner, Johnson, but the younger man was soon crowding his senior partner out of the leading place. He was active in various businesses, at the law, and in politics. He soon became the recognized leader of the gulch towns.[10]

The national situation, which had developed into war soon after Teller reached Colorado, could not help but influ-

[9] Mrs. H. M. Teller, "Senator Teller as a Young Man"; *Colorado Republican and Mountain Herald*, July 3, 1862.

[10] "Mr. Teller is a very pleasing speaker—a lawyer of fine ability and a highly respectable gentleman." Central City *Miner's Register*, Aug. 13, 1862. When a flood occurred at Denver, the telegraphic call to Central City for aid was addressed to Teller and two others. *Ibid.*, May 25, 1864. He was high man in a vote for members of the Territorial Central Committee of the Union Party. *Ibid.*, March 12, 1864.

ence affairs there. The people were interested, but were not inclined, at first, to be extremely partisan toward this still distant struggle. As most of them—except the Mexicans in the south—were Northerners, they naturally favored that side. There were enough Confederate sympathizers, however, to give them sufficient courage to raise their flag over a building in Denver, and to try to arm a group of men. But these bold steps were quickly halted, and there was no danger afterward of the Territory going over to the Confederacy.[11]

Probably as disappointing as anything else was the lack of reliable news from the war front. Rumors that Washington had been captured and that Jefferson Davis was dead were typical of those that reached the mountain towns in the fall of 1861.[12]

Back at Morrison, Teller's former Republican associates had formed companies to go to the aid of Lincoln's government. Had Teller remained there he in all probability would have had the privilege of going to the front as captain of one of the companies. His political standing would have insured that. Possibly he hoped to accomplish the same thing in Colorado on even a larger scale, or perhaps he was moved merely by a desire to raise troops for the government, and had no intention of attaching himself to them. At any rate, he wrote the following letter on May 24, 1861, some five weeks after he reached Gregory Gulch.

Hon. Simon Cameron
Secretary of War
    Sir: Here in these mountains we have hundreds anxious to contribute to the support of the Government and to assist in maintaining the integrity of the flag of our country. If we organize companies will the government accept our services? If we had the assurance that volunteers would be accepted there would be no lack of men inured to toil and hardships ready to enlist for the war.

Yours, respectfully,
HENRY M. TELLER

Secretary Cameron replied immediately that his Department had "no desire at present to raise troops at so great a distance from the scene of action."[13]

In spite of its distance "from the scene of action" it was

    [11] James Teller, "Recollections"; Stanton, Sixty Years, pp. 60, 61.
    [12] Diary of J. W. Hawley, especially entries of Aug. 29 and Sept. 19, 1861.
    [13] The War of the Rebellion, A Compilation of the Official Records of the Union and Confederate Armies, Series III, Vol. I, 232, 246.

not to be expected that Colorado would keep entirely aloof from military affairs. The Confederate movements in New Mexico, the Indians, and the suspected Southern sympathies of the Utah Mormons would prevent that. The first governor, William Gilpin, began to raise troops with great zeal. Believing that his office gave him authority, he enlisted a regiment of the toughest miners in the Territory—paying wages and buying supplies by issuing orders on the United States Treasury. These troops were quickly dispatched to the South to defend the Federal forts in the Territory of New Mexico against the Texan forces under General H. H. Sibley. In the subsequent engagements, which ended successfully for the Union troops, the man who covered himself with honor was Major J. M. Chivington.

Chivington is one of the curiosities of American history —a frontier edition of one of Cromwell's Roundheads. Coming to the mining region as a pastor of the Methodist Church, he had become well known for his vigorous preaching. When offered the chaplain's place in the newly raised regiment he refused, asking instead for a fighting commission. Changing what might have been a defeat into a Federal victory by a rashly bold exploit, he was placed in command of his regiment as a reward. He later proved to have all of the contradictions of character that would allow a Methodist pastor to attend the open house of a new gambling establishment, and to find it necessary to call on subordinate officers to "cuss" the men in ranks when the drill was not satisfactory. His subsequent military activities did not disgrace him with the miners. It was only when he married his son's widow that local sentiment turned definitely against him.[14]

When Gilpin's orders on the United States Treasury were not paid, it wrecked the finances of the Territory. Some $375,000 worth had been issued and were chiefly in the hands of the local merchants. Eventually they were paid, but Gilpin was removed, and John Evans, the founder of Evanston, Illinois, took his place as governor. Evans continued to raise troops, all of which saw service either in protecting the frontier or in fighting Confederates.[15]

Teller could, no doubt, have secured a commission in one of these regiments had he so desired. He was ill when the first regiment was raised, but fought his first political battle

[14] H. H. Bancroft, *History of Nevada, Colorado, and Wyoming* (San Francisco, 1890), p. 421; James Burrell, "History of Gilpin County," in Vickers, *Clear Creek and Boulder Valleys*, p. 42; Hal Sayre, "Reminiscences."

[15] Edgar C. McMechen, *Life of Governor Evans* (Denver, 1924), p. 102.

in defense of Gilpin's recruiting activities. Afterward he made it his duty to keep up a war spirit among the gulch miners, and to encourage enlistments. War meetings were held frequently, at which local orators competed in explaining the issues connected with the struggle. Teller was the most popular of these speakers, who were recruited chiefly from the bar. The gulch press almost invariably praised his speeches as the best of the evening. One of the first press comments indicates the trend of Teller's opinion in the summer of 1862.

It was equally surprising to hear H. M. Teller—who had always been classed among the ultra Republicans (if not an abolitionist) denounce the Phillipses, the Garrisons, and kindred disunionists of the North.[16]

The cause of the Union was in Colorado, as in the East, closely bound up with party politics. By 1864, Teller had become the dominant leader in the pro-war Republican Party in Gilpin County.

The troops raised in 1862 and 1863 were mustered into Federal service, and the greater part was sent from Colorado to oppose the Confederates in Missouri and Arkansas. This cooled the patriotic ardor of the Coloradans considerably, as it left them without troops with which to oppose probable Indian attacks.[17]

To provide for protection against this danger, the legislature of 1862 passed a law dividing the Territory into two military districts. The governor was made commander in chief of all the territorial forces, and given power to appoint a major general for each district, and subordinate officers sufficient for the troops raised. When the Indian menace became threatening, and the Federal Government was unable to supply troops, Governor Evans put the territorial law in force and appointed H. M. Teller major general in command of the militia.

This appointment was due to Teller's position in the mountain towns. These settlements were never in any danger from an Indian attack. There were from five to seven thousand people there, almost all of whom were young men, possessing arms and accustomed to their use. It would have been a simple matter to defend their mountain position

---

[16] *Miner's Register*, Sept. 1, 12, 22, Oct. 26, 1862. (This newspaper was later titled variously *Daily Miner's Register* and *Daily Central City Register*. Succeeding references will be given simply as *Miner's Register*.)

[17] John Evans to H. A. Johnson, Nov. 22, 1862, Teller-Orahood MSS.

against any body of Indians that could have assembled. This was not true of Denver and the transportation routes to the East. If these lines were broken for any length of time, mining operations would have to cease. It was not difficult to get the people of Denver to prepare to defend themselves, but the immediate necessity in case of any attack would be to bring down a maximum number of miners to Denver's aid. What was more natural than that Teller, a popular local leader in Gilpin County, and also a man of abounding energy, should receive this appointment?[18]

Although Indian danger was in the air all through the winter of 1863-64, there was no call for extensive preparations. A regiment of United States cavalry under Chivington's command was in the Territory, and that seemed to be ample protection. Some local military companies, however, were formed and drilled. A real Indian scare was necessary to bring on effective action. It came early in June, when a report of an impending Indian attack on Denver threw the inhabitants of that city into a panic. The excitement in the gulch rivaled that in Denver. "Companies were organized, and in less than an hour, over one hundred men were ready to march to their immediate assistance." The report proved false, but it greatly stimulated military activity. Governor Evans instructed Teller to hasten the organization of militia for active duty. As an aid to enlistments the Governor proclaimed that the ownership of all property taken from hostile Indians would be transferred to the captor, adding that "any man who kills a hostile Indian is a patriot."

Teller called a meeting of Gilpin County citizens on the sixteenth of June at Central City, placed the situation before them, and issued a call for volunteers. The enlistments were not numerous, there being no pay for the recruits, or even horses to mount them. But a number offered themselves and began drilling. No sooner were these preparations made than the news reached Denver that a family living within twenty-five miles of that place had been murdered by Cheyenne Indians. The mutilated remains of this family were exhibited in Denver and served to frighten the citizens into action.

All through the summer the Indians remained active, finally stopping all transportation to the East. Measures for defense were increased. Samuel E. Browne, attorney general

---

[18] *Colorado, General Laws*, 2nd Legislative Session, pp. 83-89; Smiley, *History of Colorado*, I, 415; W. F. Stone, *History of Colorado* (Chicago, 1918), I, 89.

of the Territory, working under Teller's direction, succeeded in raising a full company, which became the most important unit of the militia. It was not an easy task, as enlistments were few even in Denver. On August 1, the *Rocky Mountain News* disgustedly concluded, "About ninety-nine hundredths of the citizens of Denver who are able to bear arms are constitutionally opposed to doing so." Authority was finally received for raising Federal troops for home defense, and with the Federal treasury behind them, these efforts were more successful.[19]

The situation became more tense, and in August an attack was again anticipated at Denver. Teller brought all available forces from the mountain towns to Denver, and prepared to assist with its defense. The character of these forces is well indicated by Teller's laconic inspection report on Tyler's Rangers, mustered in on August 15, 1864, and mustered out October 14 of the same year. "Discipline—Good. Instruction—Fair. Millitary Appearance—Good. Arms—Good, found by themselves. Clothing—Poor, found by themselves. Accoutrements—Various, found by themselves." The Gilpin County Commissioners voted one thousand dollars to be used in arming and equipping the militia, "to be disbursed by the order of H. M. Teller." The pressing danger that was felt at Denver is evident in the following telegram which Teller sent to Central City:

> Government can arm a full regiment. Martial law has been declared here by Chivington. Get all 100 day men you can. Tyler's company has arrived and will march tomorrow morning. I will get what arms I can for home defense. Indians all around the country. Recruiting is going on briskly here now.[20]

The bulk of the militia was being used to defend Denver, while the United States forces were patrolling the stage lines and scouting for Indians. It must not be supposed that because he was a major general of the militia Teller was in command of all these military operations. The governor was legally and actually commander in chief of the militia, and he was present and active. Then Colonel Chivington was in command of the Federal troops—which were kept in Colorado, declared a local editor, in "actual dis-

[19] *Miner's Register*, June 16, 17, Aug. 13, 14, 1864; *Daily Mining Journal*, July 27, Aug. 13, 15, 1864; Smiley, *Colorado*, I, 415-19; Jerome C. Smiley, *History of Denver* (Denver, 1903), p. 404; Stone, *op. cit.*, I, 90-92.

[20] John H. Nankivell, *History of the Military Organizations of the State of Colorado, 1860-1935* (Denver, 1935), p. 38.

obedience to orders." In the case of military operations on an extensive scale Chivington would probably have taken command of all forces. But the militia was a necessary factor in assuring Denver of its safety. The editor of the *Rocky Mountain Daily News* wrote of the Gilpin County help:

Gen. Teller, Major Kinney, Capt. Tyler, Capt. Sayr, and other prominent public spirited men from the mountains, who came down here, together with their companies have so inspired our valley boys with bravery, and thereby so aided this expedition against the redskins ... they ... have made the name of mountain men immortal for the enterprise and the *animus* with which they have entered into this engagement *en masse* and regardless of their business and pecuniary relations.

The military preparations were so effective under the spur of danger that on the twenty-third of August the same paper was able to comment:

Denver is at last thoroughly military in every respect. Every able bodied citizen over the age of sixteen is enrolled.... Business is suspended except for two hours each day—from eleven to one o'clock—and nearly all work has ceased.

But the city was never attacked and the excitement gradually quieted down. Governor Evans opened unsuccessful peace negotiations with some of the Indian leaders. Even after these had failed, the populace was confident that no attack would be made on Denver. The stage routes to the East were reopened, although mail was still coming by way of California in the middle of November.[21] Teller did not resign his commission until 1867, but his active military experiences were ended. He had seen no actual fighting; he had worn no uniform. His work had been that of raising troops, inspiring them to activity, and preparing Denver for a possible Indian attack.

The war, unfortunately, was not over, and no agreement had been reached with the Indians. Colonel Chivington, hearing in November that there was a large encampment of them on Sand Creek, led his troops there and attacked the camp, killing a large number of men, women, and children. The Colorado public, aroused over the atrocities of the Indians and the immediate danger to themselves, hailed this event with joy and gratitude. The Indian power was

---

[21] *Rocky Mountain Daily News,* Aug. 17, 20, 24, 1864; *Miner's Register,* Aug. 13, 23, Nov. 16, 1864; *Daily Mining Journal,* Aug. 18, 19, 20, 1864.

effectually broken and the danger removed, or so they thought. But such was not the reaction in the East. Spurred on by the judicial officials of the Territory—whom Governor Evans and the bulk of the territorial bar were then trying to have removed—a committee of Congress investigated the attack and made a report that put Chivington and Evans in a very unfavorable light. What Teller thought of it at that time we have no means of knowing. Opinion in Colorado, however, was stimulated to defend its troops by the character of the attack upon them in the Eastern press. Chivington was replaced by Colonel Thomas Moonlight, who defended the actions of his predecessor. He spoke at a war meeting in Central City, at which three cheers were given for the "Sand Creek Killers." In commenting on this affair, the editor of the *Miner's Register* expressed a gruesome opinion commonly held in Colorado and, for that matter, on every American frontier:

> Colonel Moonlight's speech on Thursday night contained one feature, with which we were unusually pleased, and that was his statement that "nits make lice," and that his plan of conducting an Indian war would be to kill all ages and sexes; in other words he should make the war one of extermination.... Extermination is their final doom, and we do not care how much it is hastened. We hope our boys will spare none.

A Congregational missionary in the community described local sentiment as, "Let them [the Indians] be exterminated, men, women, and children together." He even admitted that his personal opinion had changed since he had been in the West. "We who have seen live Indians know that, as a whole, they are a filthy, lazy, treacherous revengeful race of vagabonds.... The grace of God may indeed be sufficient for them; and yet, humanly speaking, there seems to be no better destiny in store for them, than to fade away before the white man."[22]

When the Civil War ended the following spring, there was rejoicing in the mining camps. It was immediately proposed to have a "celebration, an oration, a procession, and two wagons of beer" in honor of the event. The day selected for the festivity was handicapped by a bad snowstorm, and other misfortunes followed. The salute of thirty-six guns which was to have opened the day was halted by a premature

---

[22] *Miner's Register*, Feb. 3, 11, 1865; McMechen, *Evans*, p. 136; Smiley, *Colorado*, I, 425; Colin B. Goodykoontz, "Colorado as Seen by a Home Missionary, 1863-1868," *Colorado Magazine*, XII (March, 1935), 60-69.

discharge that disabled the artillerists. A more disastrous accident was narrowly averted when, loaded with rifle powder and mud, the lone cannon exploded. The procession was ruined by the snowfall, but the oration of the day was given, and Teller was selected to extol the victory of the government that he had so often upheld from the platform. It was a long speech, and one of the local papers reported it at length. In it he reviewed the causes of the war, finding the chief one in the slaveholders' enmity to democracy. There were four lessons, he found, that the war had taught. The chief one was that slavery had to be abolished—the war could not have been won on the single cause of union. The other three were that the Negro had a high grade of ability, that citizens had individual rights in peacetime that were nonexistent in time of war, and that Europe had been taught we would brook no interference from abroad. He closed with a plea for nationalism.

Let us abandon the idea of State or Territorial sovereignty, and claim only the sovereignty of Americans, claim to be what we are, citizens of America instead of citizens of this or that locality.

Then there was singing—"Columbia the Gem of the Ocean." A local pastor spoke, and then Willard Teller, who had recently joined his brother at Central City, and still others followed. It was several Fourths of July all in one, in spite of the snow. "Many persons," noted a local editor, "undoubtedly had occasion to think of Mike Dougherty's song, 'Think of yer 'eds in the morning.' "[23]

The war spirit was aroused once more when the news of Lincoln's assassination reached the gulch. General Fitz-John Porter, who had come to the gulch as manager of a mining company after being cashiered from the Union army for cowardice, took alarm at the temper of the miners and remained shut up in his cabin all that day. A miner was reported, probably incorrectly, to have spoken approvingly of the assassination. A mob gathered for a lynching party, and a deputy sheriff hurried the intended victim to the Central City jail for protection. The word went about for a public meeting at the Montana Theater to decide upon a course of action. It would have been difficult for a sheriff to have stood out against the judgment of that meeting, especially as that had been the legal and accepted type of trial a few years

---

[23] *Miner's Register*, April 11, 14, 1865; *Daily Mining Journal*, April 13, 14, 1865.

before. Teller secured the platform, and by an appeal for law and order influenced the meeting to turn the prisoner over to the Federal authorities. The following day the sheriff took his charge to Denver by the stage, and the prisoner lived to remind Teller of the affair some years later.[24]

---

[24] Denver *Post*, Dec. 9, 13, 1903; clippings in the Dawson Scrapbook; Peoria *Journal*, Aug. 13, 1895, clippings in Tyler MSS. (an eyewitness's recollection).

CHAPTER IV

PROFESSIONAL AND FINANCIAL SUCCESS
1861-66

TELLER'S character had not changed with his removals from New York to Illinois and finally to Colorado. He was still the strict moralist of his college days, and lived a personal life that was highly satisfactory to a Calvinist. He continued to be at least a near Abolitionist, although his Union sentiments during the war kept him from the extreme position assumed by many of them. His temperance ideals were never concealed, even in a mining town where they could not have been popular. During his residence in Morrison, he had joined the Good Templars, a temperance group. He helped to organize a branch of that organization at Central City, and gave the address at the first anniversary meeting of the group at Nevadaville.[1]

In spite of his rather Puritanical personal life, Teller was not lacking in the social graces, and took a distinct pleasure in the company of others. Central City was blessed with a theater, in which fairly able companies played the romantic dramas of the period, as well as a number of the classics, introducing, it is said, considerable profanity in the dialogue in order to please the miners. Teller attended these occasionally, and on at least one occasion subscribed to a benefit for a favorite actor. When a masquerade ball club was formed to hold such entertainments regularly, he was made president of the organization.[2]

Chiefly, however, he found his social life in the Masonic fraternity. He had been initiated into this lodge while in Morrison, and its emphasis upon fraternity, personal morality, and good works had found a ready disciple in Teller.[3] After helping to organize a lodge in Central City, he took a prominent part in all of its activities and functions. In 1864 he became grand master of the territorial body and was re-elected in 1868 and for the five years following. As no other member ever held that office for more than one year, this was a rather notable feat of leadership. It was remarkable primarily for his attempts to improve the quality of the

---

[1] *Whiteside Sentinel*, Nov. 15, 1860; Hall, *History of Colorado*, III, 418; *Miner's Register*, Jan. 23, 1863; Stone, *Colorado*, I, 689, 690. This organization was a real force in the gulch towns. See Perrigo, "Social History of Central City," pp. 285 ff.

[2] *Miner's Register*, Dec. 15, 1863.

[3] Secretary of Dunlop Lodge, No. 321, C. W. Barnes to writer, Nov. 4, 1929.

membership of the organization. In his annual addresses to
the fraternity he urged that merely "good" men should not
be admitted, but only men of affirmative character. "The
interests of the fraternity," he advised, "require the frequent
use of the blackball." More members were not necessary, he
insisted, but better morals were. When the evil of intem-
perance manifested itself in certain of the lodges, he advocated expulsion where reform was not successful. On a trip
in the winter of 1863 to Mrs. Teller's home in Cuba, New
York, he became a Knight Templar. In this branch of
Masonry he was equally active, being eminent commander
of the local group for its first ten years, and first grand
commander of the Colorado organization. Eventually the
Central City Masons built a fine stone temple within a few
steps of Teller's office, and the work of the organization became an essential phase of Teller's personal life.[4]

Teller was not a professional "joiner," and never associated himself with another fraternal order, although many
organizations flourished in the gulch towns. Significant of
the difference between the two brothers, Willard Teller
never joined the fraternity his brother led. He was a silent,
introverted individual, who resembled Henry in many ways,
but differed from him chiefly in that he did not enjoy the
company of others. Although an able lawyer—there were
many who said he was the most able member of the firm—
and a successful public speaker, he never became popular. He
was gruff and brusque in his manner toward everyone. He
had little respect for popular opinion, and was extremely
forthright where Henry was diplomatic and charitable. On
public and personal questions, however, the two brothers
were generally in agreement. Willard, like Henry, gave
temperance lectures, testified before a grand jury in an attempt to force the local saloons to close on Sunday, and
united strong Abolitionist and Union sentiment with many
of the ideas that were later to characterize the Liberal Republicans and the Mugwumps. Destined to play second fiddle
to his older brother all his life, he permitted his bad temper
and sharp tongue to keep all but a very few people at a distance. He "has no more blood in him than you can get out
of a terrapin," J. B. Chaffee was to say in what was generally a very laudatory comment. In contrast, Henry's ap-

4 *Proceedings of Grand Lodge of Ancient Free and Accepted Masons of the Territory
of Colorado*, Reports 1 to 15, particularly Reports 4 and 10; *Proceedings of the Grand
Commandery of the Knights Templar of Colorado at Its Thirty-ninth Annual Conclave*
(Denver, 1914), p. 37.

Henry Moore Teller in 1862.

proachableness, democratic manner, and easily opened purse predestined him for the political career that was denied the younger man because of the lack of these qualities. On formal occasions, Teller continued to be addressed as "General," but to most Central City people he was simply "H. M."[5]

Henry Teller's income and wealth increased rapidly in Colorado, partly from his legal work and partly from business enterprises. His receipts for 1862, his first full year in Colorado, show an income of $1,823, and those for 1863, $11,594.[6] With this wealth he expanded his investments in Colorado property. He built a large home in Central City, probably the finest dwelling in the gulch, where he entertained the notables who visited that city.

Mrs. Teller was an ardent church worker, taking an active part in the affairs of the local Methodist organization. Teller himself did not join a church, although he attended services with Mrs. Teller regularly, and acted as a trustee of the local church. It would appear that something in his past experience had antagonized him toward sectarian religion, and he went through most of his life without church affiliations. Mrs. Teller made their home the headquarters of Methodist activity. The Rev. B. T. Vincent, who for a time filled the pulpit in Central City and then was transferred to Denver, was such a frequent visitor that he and Mrs. Vincent seemed like uncle and aunt to the Teller children.[7]

The Civil War had caused a great boom in the sale of securities in the Eastern markets. Late in 1863 the speculators began to use gold-mine stock for investment and manipulation. The Coloradans had long been proclaiming the inexhaustible richness of their mines, and that propaganda formed a fine background against which to sell mining stock. Market manipulators, and, no doubt, some conservative investors, formed companies, bought up mining properties, and proceeded to sell stock. A great boom was on that winter and the following spring, which changed the business of the gulch towns from mining to selling mining

---

[5] Notes from Chase Withrow. Dawson interview with S. K. Linscott, Oct. 24, 1921, MS. in Colorado State Historical Society; Perrigo, *op. cit.*, pp. 282, 426; clipping from Richmond *Enquirer*, 1882, Dawson Scrapbook.

[6] These income tax receipts are in the Teller-Orahood MSS.

[7] Stanton, *Sixty Years in Colorado*, p. 141; Isaac H. Beardsley, *Echoes From Peak and Plain* (Cincinnati and New York, 1898), p. 289. Teller was on the board of trustees for Colorado Seminary, later Denver University, a Methodist institution, in 1868. *Ibid.*, p. 393.

claims. The avidity of the Eastern speculators, anxious to turn their greenbacks into property, coupled with the optimism of local agents, led to the organization of companies to mine property that was very unpromising. Almost all producing mines changed hands, and no end of questionable claims were sold. To the local mine owners and businessmen it was too great an opportunity to be overlooked, and they soon engaged in the promoting business. The local newspaper accurately described the situation which lay back of it.

> The lode claim fever never raged higher than at present. It costs but fifty cents to secure a life title to one hundred feet of any lode claim not previously taken up in the mountains. By the judicious outlay of $100 any man may secure near two hundred such claims. . . . Colorado now affords a greater field for speculation than any other country in the mining world.[8]

Johnson and Teller went into it along with the rest, and Teller, who had a growing reputation as a mining lawyer, became the agent of many Eastern companies. Johnson gave up his law practice in 1863 and opened an office in New York City to sell Colorado mining properties. The boom lasted until April, 1864, and then collapsed, leaving most of the mines in the hands of distant corporations. But the speculative fever remained. In 1865 the surveyor general reported that,

> Many companies are doing nothing, some waiting for better times, some waiting for machinery, some experimenting on new processes, some fooling away their money by trusting their affairs to ignorant men, and some who never intend to mine outside of Wall Street.[9]

The companies that held title tried to realize upon their mines by working them, but all too frequently they sent out managers from the East without the experience or force of character necessary to make even a good mine pay. Mining was no longer a poor man's business, as gulch mining had played out. The lodes were becoming progressively harder to work, because of the difficulty encountered in reducing the ore. In the East, machinery was made which manufacturers promised would solve the reduction problem, but none was found that was a complete success. Many of the new class of managers gambled their capital upon these expensive toys, only to have to discard them later. It was not many years until almost all the foreign corporations had with-

[8] *Miner's Register*, April 7, 1864.
[9] Quoted in the *Congressional Globe*, 39 Cong., 1 Sess., p. 2137.

drawn or sold out, leaving an experience of innumerable mistakes to guide the local miners, as well as many a tale to amuse them. A contemporary described these mine managers as

... that numerous class of company's agents, the "jolly dogs"—usually nephew of the president, or son of the head director—excellent masters of the billiard cue, with uncommon pride in high boots and spurs, whose champagne bills were charged to "candles," and whose costly incense to Venus appeared on the books as "cash paid for mercury." It was a charming farce to witness a General Fitz John and staff of assistants, all finely mounted, reviewing the corps of masons on the stone "folly" or riding to and from the mine, but was it business?[10]

Johnson and Teller had engaged in active mining before the boom began. Afterwards they incorporated and enlarged their holdings. With this mine, the Croydon, was a small stamp mill, used in reducing the ore. Teller, as manager of the company, carefully refrained from investing in other expensive machinery as most companies were doing.[11]

The Croydon Company gradually acquired near-by properties, and Teller came to own an increasingly large share of the company. Johnson never returned to the practice of law after he left Colorado. He continued to sell mining property in New York for a time and then went on to London. After some successes there he was ruined by the panic of 1873. H. M. and Willard Teller bought his Colorado property, including his share in the law firm. The Croydon property became the center of Teller's mines. After he went to the Senate, he, in partnership with Hal Sayre, secured several surrounding mines, and united them into one. These were worked under Sayre's management. Teller had other mining properties in Boulder and Clear Creek counties, but by some accident the only mines he secured were gold mines. He never owned a silver mine. His list of properties in the seventies reads like vast holdings, but most of them were claims that never became producing mines.[12]

Several of Teller's associates became wealthy through their mines. Often it was by sheer chance that a man—as in the case of Horace A. W. Tabor—became possessed of a great fortune. If a mine owner happened to make an extraordinary find of rich ore upon his property he became rich. If not,

---

[10] Cushman and Waterman, *The Gold Mines of Gilpin County*, p. 33.

[11] *Miner's Register*, March 30, 1863; *Daily Mining Journal*, Jan. 18, 1865.

[12] *Colorado Directory of Mines* (Denver, 1879); *Colorado Mining Directory* (Denver, 1883). The Hal Sayre MSS. contain a very large number of letters from Teller relating to their mutual interests.

and if he had bought his property intelligently, he probably made a little money in good years and none at all at other times. Teller belonged in the latter class. Although some of his mines were still in operation at the time of his death, it is very questionable whether in the long run he made more than expenses out of them. The profit from one was sunk in developing others that never paid.

Above all other businesses, Teller was interested in, and devoted himself to, the law. Western lawyers of the period were of many varieties and qualities, but their reputed superior knowledge of "Colt on revolvers" over "Coke on common law" was only a local jibe. Undoubtedly there were many odd individuals among the Western lawyers, as there were among Western people generally. Men with mental or physical peculiarities tended to drift into the newly established communities, where their talents were in such demand that their oddities were overlooked. A friendly newspaper's comment upon an able attorney who had been sent to Washington as the territorial delegate indicates the resignation with which such men were tolerated:

> Judge Bradford is filling his position very well. If he could be persuaded to brush the hayseed from the arctic overshoes he wears instead of boots, it would be greatly to the credit of Colorado.

Many were too well acquainted with John Barleycorn to keep a respectable reputation in a well-established place, and far more were highly adventurous men, who came West to try their hand at mining, and remained to practice their profession.

Among such colleagues Teller soon distinguished himself. His experience at Morrison had been a good training ground, and, as the Colorado territorial government modeled its law after the Illinois code, he was at home from the first. Teller had a factual mind, with great liking for exactness and precision. As mining was the principal business of the region, he set out to become an expert on the phases that would be useful to a lawyer in dealing with mining cases. That meant the study of technical books, together with the personal investigation of working properties. In such activity Teller showed his abilities in their best light. He derived an intense satisfaction from studying a case and becoming familiar with all its ramifications and details. He could so completely absorb himself in the law and evidence that he was greatly feared by opposing council. "A most persistent and uncompromising adversary," as a colleague was later to describe him. In argument he was vicious in his attack. Using no weapons but well-organized argument and a bit of salty sarcasm, he was usually able to win his cases. His manner in the courtroom was in decided contrast to that outside, where he was the most mild-mannered of men.[13]

Lawyers had no easy time in Colorado Territory. Court buildings were primitive, hotel accommodations few, and transportation from one county seat to another very poor. At least once the court and bar drove from place to place carrying camping equipment with them and preparing their own meals. Teller enjoyed traveling, and liked nothing better than to sit beside the driver of the stagecoach during the daylight hours of a trip. There were localities, however, that one could reach only, as one of Teller's colleagues put it, "by mounting the hurricane deck of a mule."

But the difficulties of the legal profession went deeper than these inconveniences. The common law was not made to fit a mining community in which property was acquired by priority of possession. A new legal development had to take place in order to adapt that law to fit these conditions, and that could only be done with a progressive and intelligent bench and bar. Unfortunately, the bench was not capable of this expansion in the early territorial days. The Republican politicians at Washington viewed the new territory as a convenient place to dump the henchmen they were obligated to provide for but who were too inefficient or corrupt to be allowed to hold office nearer home. Since many politicians were lawyers, they could qualify technically for the bench, and Colorado received a job lot of broken-down wirepullers to man its courts. The first chief justice, B. F. Hall, was forced to leave the Territory under a cloud not long after he was appointed.[14]

Then there was a Judge C. L. Armour, formerly of Maryland, and a man of ability, whose talents never found a worthy outlet. At first Teller welcomed Armour as a relief from the usual run of Federal appointees, but his petty exhibitions of the small tyrant soon turned all the bar against him. He was given to excessive drinking, and his condition on the bench was such that a clever lawyer was known to quote from Hoyle, pretending, successfully, that it was the

[13] George Q. Richmond, "The Men with Whom I've Smiled," *Colorado Magazine*, I (May, 1924), 146; *Miner's Register*, Feb. 6, 1866; E. T. Wells, "Colorado Bar," in Stone, *History of Colorado*, I, 790.

[14] Moses Hallett to Hiram A. Johnson, June 30, 1862, Teller-Orahood MSS.

law. Finally, in order to protect themselves, the territorial
legislature gerrymandered the judicial districts in order to
put Armour in a specially created jurisdiction, sometimes
known as the Botany Bay of Colorado Territory—the two
Mexican counties of Conejos and Costilla. But Armour's
hide was as thick as his name would indicate, and in the
words of a local historian,

...with sublime indifference he refused to visit his adobe castles in
Spain or resign his office, but smilingly smoked his imported cigars
[imported by bull train from Missouri], sipped his toddies of which
he was fond, drew his salary, of which he was fonder, and held out his
term as a gentleman of elegant leisure.[15]

It was before a bench characterized by such a lack of
judicial character that the old law had to be adapted to the
new conditions. The common sense of public opinion determined that old concepts must change to meet these conditions, but the judges, solidified mentally in the antiquated
forms, could change only very slowly when at all. Under
the old law running water was not real property, but such
a concept could not last in a mining community such as
Gilpin County. This had long been recognized, and one of
the early miners' meetings had picturesquely resolved that
"all water claims be held as real estate and not jumpable."[16]
Most of the legal adjustments were not so great as that
regarding riparian rights, and better success attended the
efforts made to establish them. The second fall that Teller
was in Colorado he was on what was one of the most important cases that had been tried in the Territory up to that
time. It involved the question of whether one miner could
work his property in such a manner as to injure neighboring
property—in this case so that a mine drained into its lower
neighbor. This case attracted a great deal of attention and
employed the leading legal talent in the mining country.
Johnson and Teller were the senior counsel for the plaintiffs,
and helped to set the precedent that mining in such a manner
made one liable for damages.[17]
The most important of the new legal concepts which
Teller helped to establish was that regarding ownership of
the lode. From the beginning of deep mining in Colorado
there had been controversies over the ownership of a lode

15 Stone, *History of Colorado*, I, 734.
16 Henry A. Dubbs, "The Unfolding of Law in the Mountain Region," *Colorado
Magazine* (October, 1926), 142-51.
17 *Miner's Register*, Aug. 4, 1862.

or vein of ore. The old common law ruling would have made the ownership go with that of the surface without the turning of a hairsbreadth. Against that concept was the practical proposal that the owner of the apex of the vein— the edge or crest of the vein nearest the surface—should be able to work it to any depth or distance within the length of this claim, even though the vein extended over the side lines and entered adjoining lands. And so the famous cases of the apex versus the side line,. and vice versa, began in Colorado court circles.

One of the most striking of these cases, although not important judicially, was that between the New York Mining Company, of which Fitz-John Porter was manager, and the Smith Parmelee Gold Mining Company. The latter had been mining a vein at a lower level than the New York Company. After a time the New York Company had sunk its shaft into the region where Smith and Parmelee were mining. Immediately, Porter went to Chief Justice Stephen S. Harding, assuredly the "most unsatisfactory occupant of the Colorado Bench" in its history, and secured an injunction preventing his competitors from working that vein. Then Porter, with judicial approval, put his men to work mining the vein in question. Whichever concept of the law was to prevail, this amounted in effect to a complete transfer of property by means of a court injunction. Teller was called in by the Smith-Parmelee people and went over the mine carefully, as he always did in preparing a case. While in the disputed region underground, Teller saw, or thought he saw, Judge Harding himself among a party from the New York Company who were also examining the mine.

The effect of the injunction was to arouse the gulch towns as no other law case had done. It was obvious that, could the court dispossess one miner to the benefit of another without a trial, there was no safety with a person of Harding's character on the bench. Probably acting upon Teller's advice, Smith and Parmelee caused fires to be built in their tunnels in such a way that the smoke and sulphur fumes would be drawn through the shaft in which the New York Company was working the disputed vein, and effectively prevent work there. The community was aroused to a high pitch of excitement. Arms were being collected, and it looked for a time as though the government would return to the primitive days of the miners' meetings. The bulk of the people were with Smith and Parmelee, although each side was supported by a local newspaper.

Porter again appealed to Harding, and the managers of the Smith-Parmelee Company were brought before the court on a charge of contempt. The *Daily Mining Journal*, which was defending Harding and Porter, gives a summary of Teller's argument at the hearing.

> He claimed that Judge Harding had no right to issue an injunction which restrained the defendants from working or occupying the disputed territory and gave the complainants possession; that he should resist any action on the part of the Judiciary, so far as was in his power, which was in direct violation of law or justice. He did this in behalf of the people whose rights were being tramped upon by such action on the part of those who were sent here to represent the majesty of the law. A Judge who would make such a decision could not expect, nor should he ask the people to sustain him. He wished to obey the law, wished to prevent the effusion of blood, but if it was necessary, he would buckle on his armor and go out to fight in defense of the law and rights of the citizens.

Other reports relate that Teller accused the judge of being in the pay of Porter, and when Harding ordered Teller's arrest for contempt of court the sheriff refused to carry out the order. The two papers carried on a publicity war, the editorials in the *Journal* being answered in part by letters in the *Register*, signed "Law and Order," the *Journal* insisting that "Law and Order" was none other than Teller himself. By some curious reasoning Judge Harding finally held the managers of the Smith-Parmelee Company for trial for violating the injunction. But the judge's conduct had been so unjudicial he was unable to maintain himself. As Samuel Bowles, of the Springfield *Republican*, who was in the gulch during the trial, put it, "There could be no contempt too great for such a court as that." The bar of the Territory had been persistently urging Harding to resign, and after this case he left the Territory and did not return. Tradition holds that later when Porter had bankrupted the New York Company and its books became public property, payments to Judge Harding were found included among its expenses.[18]

But this did not settle the apex question. It was to be fought over for several years and continued after Colorado gained statehood. In many of the important cases Teller

18 *Daily Mining Journal*, May 23, 24, 25, 26, 31, 1865; Samuel Bowles, *Across the Continent* (New York, 1865), pp. 60, 61; Albert D. Richardson, *Beyond the Mississippi* (Hartford, 1869), pp. 335, 336; W. F. Stone, "The Colorado Bar," in Smiley, *Colorado*, I, 653; notes from Chase Withrow.

appeared for the apex rule, and eventually that became the law.[19]

Teller's relation to this issue was typical of his professional work. Few important civil cases came up in Colorado Territory where he was not represented as counsel. Frequently he was called in on cases in the neighboring territories of Utah and New Mexico, where his reputation had spread. Even as far west as San Francisco, members of his own profession who specialized in mining law knew Teller as an uncomfortable opponent. Very few lawyers established the professional reputation that Henry Teller was able to achieve in his first ten years at the bar. He was firmly planted on the road to legal distinction by 1870.

---

[19] Stone, *Colorado*, I, 302, 752 ; notes from Chase Withrow.

CHAPTER V

POLITICAL FAILURE
1862-68

TELLER had many interests, and in many lines of endeavor he played a leading role. Above all others his training and his talents had fitted him for politics—politics not in the sense of the local log-roller, making deals and trades for the income and prestige of local office; but politics founded upon solid economic interest and definite political beliefs regarding the manner in which government should be run, along with a vigorous ambition to control the throttle.

On reaching Colorado he immediately became active in in politics, repeating his experience at Morrison. The first territorial election was held a few months after he reached there, and he gave his support to the Republican candidate for delegate to Congress, although there is no evidence of his political activity in that contest. When the regular election came about in the fall of 1862, the national party situation was so confused by the Civil War that in Colorado a group containing most of the dominant politicians, both Republican and Douglas Democrats, organized as the Administration Party and nominated the sitting delegate, Hiram P. Bennet. Teller and the Republicans of abolitionist leanings refused to go along with them, and former Governor Gilpin became their candidate for Congress. The issue between these two groups was chiefly Gilpin's administration as territorial governor, particularly his attempt to raise troops to aid the Federal Government, and the record of Delegate Bennet in Washington. The Democrats with suspected Southern leanings also picked a candidate, choosing J. M. Francisco from the Mexican section of the Territory. A three-cornered campaign resulted. In Gilpin County it was a battle of oratory, chiefly among three champions: Teller for Gilpin; his partner, Hiram A. Johnson, for Bennet; and James M. Cavanaugh, the delight of the Irish of Nevadaville, for Francisco.

Political meetings became a regular institution, with competitive oratory the main attraction. Anyone could call a meeting, and, especially if it were Saturday night, be assured of a large audience. The crowd usually took control of the meeting and ran it as it wished, "calling out" the speakers it favored, and howling down those whom it did not want. Usually the assembled miners were not particular about the politics of the speaker, and would applaud anyone who made a likable speech with an abundance of humorous thrusts at the opposition. The first meeting was early in August, with the delegate himself to lead off. The report, in a paper favorable to him, includes this description of Teller's argument:

> At the conclusion of his speech, H. M. Teller, Esq., was called out, and occupied the stand for an hour or more. Mr. Teller is a very pleasing speaker—a lawyer of fine ability, and a highly respectable gentleman. He is ultra Republican, and supported Mr. Bennet when he ran on the Republican ticket. Now he opposed his reelection: he favored the maintenance of strict party lines, and charged those who endeavored to ignore them with demagoguery; he reviewed Bennet's congressional career, endeavoring to depreciate his labors in behalf of the Territory, and belittle him in the eyes of the audience. His effort, though able and eloquent, resembled throughout, the argument of a lawyer pleading a desperate case before a jury. He seemed to feel that Gilpin was his client, and Bennet the prosecutor, and he determined to leave nothing undone which could influence them in favor of the former or prejudice them against the latter. His plea, though ingenious, we do not think will secure a favorable verdict.

Later, Cavanaugh attacked both Gilpin and Bennet and supported Francisco and the Democracy. Hiram Johnson followed for Bennet, and others carried the debate well into the following morning.

This meeting was typical of all those held during the campaign. Rallies were held frequently either at Nevadaville, Central City, or Blackhawk, with Teller, Johnson, and Cavanaugh the principal speakers. The audience was composed of miners, for the most part, and varied little from one town to another. Outside of those parts of the speeches devoted to "mere politics," the debate centered on the issues that concerned Colorado Territory, the Bennet supporters claiming that the delegate had been influential in securing the homestead law, the Pacific Railroad law, better mail service, extinction of the Indian land titles, and a branch mint in Colorado. Teller's attack centered upon the failure to secure a railroad law that would bring the route through Colorado. His defense of his candidate was the patriotism and legality of Gilpin's efforts to raise troops for the support of the Union.

If the Bennet press accounts of the political meetings can be credited, Teller was more popular with the audiences than any of his competitors—even more so than the humor-

ous Cavanaugh. But when the votes were counted, his candidate was last, and Bennet returned to Washington.[1]

The following spring found the Gilpin and Bennet men
of the fall before united into one group upon the issues of
the war. During the winter the question of the support of
the war policy of the Government became the chief political
issue. It became the "unconditional Union" men versus the
"unterrified Democracy." In the local election of 1863 Teller
was active in the county and district conventions and led the
fight for the ticket. At the principal Union meeting he gave
the main address, committing what his opponents called
sacrilege by a comparison between Jackson's attitude toward
nullification and Lincoln's attitude toward secession. He
defended the war powers assumed by the national Government as a wartime necessity. The Administration Party
carried its ticket in the county by a handsome majority.

By the end of this campaign Teller had achieved what
was probably the dominant position in his political organization in Gilpin County. At the county convention held in
March of the following spring, he was sent as a delegate to
the territorial convention and placed on the county central
committee of five. When the territorial convention met,
striking evidence of his hold in the larger unit of organization was given by the one formal ballot for members of the
territorial central committee. The six high were considered
elected, and Teller had the largest number of the votes.[2]

Prophetically, the second highest was Jerome B. Chaffee,
who was to be Teller's chief competitor in territorial politics.
Curiously, Chaffee also came from western New York.
Relatives of his there had married relatives of Teller's, and
their fathers had for a brief time worked together on the
Erie Canal. Chaffee was an able manager with a great talent
for political organization. Engaging first in mining, he made
a small fortune, and then branched out into other kinds of
business, soon becoming one of the wealthiest men in Colorado. In the early sixties he was a resident of Gilpin County
and represented it in the legislature, but soon removed to
Denver, and for several years the competition between the
two men was the usual condition of Colorado politics.[2] Each
man played the game by a different system. Chaffee was in

[1] *Miner's Register*, Aug 11, 13, 15, 18, 20, Sept. 5, 8, Oct. 8, 25, Nov. 2, 1862;
Hollister, *The Mines of Colorado*, p. 128.

[2] *Miner's Register*, Feb. 25, Aug. 11, 15, 18, 29, 31, 1863, March 9, 12, 1864.

[3] J. F. Willard, "J. B. Chaffee," *Dictionary of American Biography* (New York
1929), III, 590.

most ways a typical American politician, who rose from a
small office to a large one by serving the organization
well, eventually becoming its leader. Teller, on the other
hand, outside of unopposed membership on the city council
and school board in Central City, never held a public office,
and never aspired to one except the United States Senate.
Frequently, almost regularly, he held a position of leadership
within the Republican Party organization, but with this his
office holding ended. He never worked up from the bottom
through the local party organization. Even in contests that
became extremely bitter, others did the work of rounding up
voters, and organizing the caucuses and conventions. Teller
gave direction and form to their activities by work on resolutions, platforms, and, above all else, from the stump.

Territorial politics, like more fundamental economic
questions, was dividing the Republican Party into two con-
testing groups. The most important of these, the "Denver
crowd," soon came under the leadership of Chaffee. The
other, the "Golden crowd," was usually under Teller's direction. The bone of contention between them was the location
of the commerical center of the state and the control of the
political offices. The fight became most bitter in connection
with railroad construction, but it permeated every political
controversy as well. Denver, favored by geography, was
the center of the one group, and Golden, a few miles west of
Denver, was the other. Outside these cities themselves people
were more or less divided on the issue, and that was the case
of the gulch towns.

The political question that more than all others disturbed
Colorado in the territorial period was the proposal to make
Colorado a state. This arose in the decade of the sixties not
because of local demand, but because of the national situation. The leaders of the Republican Party in Washington,
with the purpose of strengthening their hold upon the electoral college and of getting constitutional amendments ratified, decided in 1864 to create three new states—Nevada,
Colorado, and Nebraska. An enabling act was passed for
Colorado by providing for a constitutional convention in
July and a popular referendum in October to ratify or reject
the proposed charter. Later, the date of the election was
changed to September in order to bring the state government into operation in time to take part in the national
election and add the new state's electoral votes to Lincoln's
total. It was only natural that H. M. Teller with Governor

John Evans, a Federal appointee, should assume the lead in carrying out locally the wishes of the national organization.[4]

On the governor's call, conventions were held in each county to select delegates to the constitutional convention. In Gilpin County, Teller was high man on the informal ballot, and he and five others were chosen. On July 4 the constitutional convention met at Golden, the legal capital, but adjourned to meet again the day following at Denver, the actual capital. Teller was appointed chairman of the judicial committee, and served also on the finance and compensation committees, playing a prominent part in all the proceedings.

The convention produced a typical state constitution of its period, except for the salary schedule of the state officials. Sparsely populated and poor in taxable property as Colorado was, the statehood leaders correctly foresaw that the chief argument of their opponents would be the probable influence of statehood upon the annual tax bill. In anticipation of the campaign they included one of the lowest salary schedules any constitutional convention of the time seriously considered. It provided such incomes as one thousand dollars for the Secretary of State, four hundred dollars for the attorney general, and three dollars a day for the members of the legislature when in session. This was probably a tactical error, as it made the prospective state offices unattractive.

The most serious difficulty the Republicans had to meet was presented by the brief time between the vote on accepting statehood under the constitution just framed and the presidential election. Between the September vote and the national election in November an election of state officials would have to be held, and the machinery of the state government brought into operation. To overcome this difficulty they decided to hold the election for state officials at the same time as the vote on the constitution, and the confusion of issues that resulted went a long way toward defeating statehood.

One of the great sources of strength that a statehood movement could be expected to have would be the support of the politically ambitious. To these the territorial status had been one long fast day. As one of them later complained, "Decrepit and windbroken politicians who clamored for the support of the general government were preferred to the

---

[4] Elmer Ellis, "Colorado's First Fight for Statehood," *The Colorado Magazine*, VIII (Jan., 1931), 23-30. The numerous annotations in this article are not repeated here.

first class native timber to be found here in exhaustless quantities." However, if the prospective offices were passed around before the vote on statehood was taken, the "exhaus- less quantities" of politicians not among the elect would have nothing to spur them on to action.

At the "Union Administration" convention a slate of candidates was nominated for all the state offices. Those opposed to statehood also held a convention and nominated candidates. The disadvantage of holding the election at this time was evident when those Republicans disappointed in the outcome of their convention either refused to aid in the statehood campaign or came out directly against it. Chaffee, for instance, declared for statehood so tardily that the anti- state convention seriously considered making him one of its candidates.

To the disappointed Republicans in opposition were added nearly all Democrats who could see no advantage either local or national in statehood. The citizens of Mexi- can descent in the southern counties also were unanimously opposed to any change that would leave them under a local government in which they were a minority. The majority of the territorial officials, whose terms would end if statehood carried, were also opposed. It was generally understood that if statehood carried, Evans and Teller would be the Republican candidates before the legislature for the United States Senate, although the convention had taken no action. This gave the "antis" grounds for charging that the state- hood movement was merely an office seekers' scheme, and urging the temporary unpopularity of Evans and Chiving- ton—the Republican nominee for Congress—as a reason for opposition. Statehood, they urged, would raise the taxes to unreasonable heights to provide support for its institutions. Possibly with more effect, they warned that if statehood carried, the Federal military conscription law would apply to the new state and make many voters subject to the draft.

Teller, who escaped the criticism heaped upon Evans, gave vigorous leadership to the statehood campaign. He declared in a public statement:

The minority magnify our poverty and declare we are unable to support a healthy state. Whoever heard that a healthy vigorous Territory would make a "sickly state"? How much do the minority think they benefit Colorado by such kind of stuff? Will it induce immigration or capital to proclaim through the press and ballot box, that Colorado cannot support an economical State Government? A rich country indeed, if we cannot pay for governing ourselves. If the minority are the only friends of Colorado, well may she say: "Save me from my friends."[5]

Beginning in August, a series of rallies was planned in order to stimulate statehood sentiment. At Central City, Teller opened the campaign with a "stirring, strong, and argumentative speech," attempting to show that a state government would not add greatly to the taxes. When the "anti-states" held a rally of their own there was enough pro-state sentiment present to dominate the meeting and to "call out" Teller to reply to the previous speakers.[6]

Teller did not confine his efforts to Gilpin County, but also spoke at rallies in Denver. In a speech in Union League Hall in that city, Teller—of whom it had been said, "No man in Colorado is more careful of his position"—declared that he was attorney for at least three fourths of the mining companies organized to operate in the Territory, and that they all favored statehood. He argued that the changed status would give Colorado adequate protection at Washington. With two members of the Senate and with electoral votes as well, such unfriendly legislation as the Pacific Railroad Act, which had left Colorado off the transcontinental route, would have been prevented, and the proposed Federal tax on mining profits could be fought with real weapons. He did not overlook the argument that statehood would end the terms of certain unpopular territorial officials now active against the proposed change.[7]

But the campaign was a losing fight from the beginning. The real reason for statehood—national politics—could hardly be used publicly. In a vain attempt to save the cause, Evans announced that he would not be a candidate for the Senate in case statehood won, but the opposition never let up its attacks upon him and Chivington. When the ballots were counted, it was announced that statehood had been defeated 1,520 to 4,672. This closed a campaign that "in bitterness, acrimony, and unscrupulousness on both sides, never was equalled in any other political campaign during Colorado's territorial period." Teller had failed in his first attempt to lead a significant political movement. As success would probably have sent him to the United States Senate,

[5] *Miner's Register*, July 20, 1864.
[6] *Ibid.*, Aug. 6, 16, 17, 1864.
[7] *Rocky Mountain News*, Aug. 16, 27, Sept. 3, 1864; *Miner's Register*, Aug. 18, 26, Sept. 3, 1864.

and thus satisfied his greatest ambition, it was a hard blow to him personally.

Immediately following this election occurred one of the strangest reversals in Colorado's political history. A few days after the defeat was admitted, the *Rocky Mountain News* recorded the rumor that some of the former anti-state leaders were organizing a new statehood movement, which they expected to control. Whatever the conferences were that went on behind the scenes, the following spring a call for a constitutional convention was published on the authority of the central committees of both parties, and that of the anti-state committee as well! No authority now existed to form a state government, as the enabling act only provided for the one election. With no national election in prospect, it may well be doubted that the Republican leaders in Washington would go out of their way to make Colorado a state. But it was argued that Congress having once agreed to it, the National Government would not refuse admission because of technicalities.

The new leaders of the statehood movement—largely the Denver group with Chaffee playing a leading part—profited by the experience of the year before and did not make the same mistakes. The charter formulated did not differ greatly from that of the year before, except that the usual salaries were attached to the state offices. The campaign began with many more prospects of success than the one of 1864.

Teller and his friends offered no public opposition to the constitution or to statehood. On the other hand they offered little encouragement, perhaps because the movement was in the hands of enemies of the Golden crowd. An appeal for statehood by the mining companies, which included Teller's signature, was used to secure support for the movement.[8]

When the votes were counted it was announced that statehood had carried 3,025 to 2,870, but fraud was openly alleged, and irregularities were common. This majority of 155 for statehood, one year after the same issue had been overwhelmingly defeated, had a suspicious appearance that did not pass without notice. There was no question of the lack of legal form in the election. It was not held in one county, and another did not know of it until the forenoon of

---

[8] Hall, *Colorado*, I, 366-69; McMechen, *Evans*, pp. 145 ff.; *Miner's Register*, Sept. 1, 2, 1865.

election day. Yet returns for these counties were manufactured somewhere.

As soon as the results were definitely known, the party committees issued calls for conventions to nominate candidates for state offices. During the statehood campaign, the Denver group had secured control of the party machinery in the Territory, and now began to use it in securing a legislature to its liking. Chaffee was an avowed candidate for the Senate, and, no doubt, the Republican candidates would be from the controlling faction who were not friendly to the Central City leader. "Mr. Teller is objectionable to men of conservative views because of his well known radicalism," declared the *Daily Mining Journal* of Blackhawk.[9]

The bait of the nomination for representative was held out to him as a consolation prize, but he refused it. He could not, after the defeat of the year before, contest the Territory with the Denver group, but he could and did challenge their control of the party in Gilpin County. In the local and county conventions it was a straight fight between Teller and Chaffee. The Teller group was able to show a two-to-one majority in the county convention, and the Chaffee delegates bolted and placed a ticket of their own in the field. This division of the Republicans served to return Democratic members to the legislature from Gilpin. Nevertheless, the Republicans won, and the entire "state" administration was in the hands of the Denver Republicans. When the legislature met, Chaffee and Evans were elected to the United States Senate, Chaffee having fifteen votes in the Republican caucus to Teller's eight. The Central City editor summed up the result:

> Jerome B. Chaffee is not, perhaps, so brilliant a man as Henry M. Teller, though his quiet, unassuming manners, gentlemanly deportment, liberality of ideas, and general influence among the grand circle at Washington, will effect more good for Colorado than a more showy man could hope to do.[10]

President Andrew Johnson refused to recognize the "state" of Colorado because of its failure to conform to the enabling act, and turned the matter over to Congress. When no partisan advantage was to be gained by admission, Congress, in the early spring of 1866, was not so anxious to allow it as it had been in 1864. Nevertheless, a bill to admit

---

[9] Oct. 26, 1865.
[10] *Miner's Register*, Dec. 19, 1865.

Colorado under the government recently set up was brought in, supported chiefly by Western senators and generally opposed by Easterners. Some of the latter objected to it because of Colorado's small population, and some because of the lack of Negro suffrage. Senator Ben Wade, who had supported the bill of 1864, and later supported this one, talked of rotten boroughs, and the bill was defeated.

Under ordinary circumstances the contest would have ended here. But 1866 was not a normal political period. The growing bitterness between President Johnson and the Radical Republicans was rapidly coming to a head. Shortly after the vote on the Colorado bill, the President vetoed the Civil Rights bill. The majority of Radical Republicans was large enough to pass this over his veto, but it was barely sufficient in the Senate. Anxious to increase their majority, the Republican leaders soon saw their error in refusing admission to a state whose senators might add two to their majority. A reconsideration was moved and the following contest found most of the Republicans now in favor of statehood, Charles Sumner being the outstanding exception. This genius of consistency wanted Negro suffrage in the Constitution before he would vote for admission, and was willing to charge that "there were known and avowed arguments and there were arguments whispered in this Chamber, that these men should be admitted because we need their votes." The statehood bill now passed both houses to the delight of its Colorado friends. Although Chaffee and Evans assured President Johnson that they had not "sold out to the radicals," he vetoed the bill on the grounds that the population did not entitle Colorado to admission. As it had not received the necessary two-thirds majority on its original passage, it was useless to attempt to pass it over the veto.[11]

As the lines between the President and his opponents became drawn more tightly, the congressional leaders made another attempt to admit Colorado the next year, and thus add Chaffee and Evans to the Senate. In order to unite more of the Republicans behind statehood for Colorado, they now brought in a new bill with a provision that its sponsors claimed would insure Negro suffrage. It passed with large majorities, and again met with the presidential veto. Senator Wade now held the vetoed bill up until absences in the Senate made it a strategic moment to pass the bill over the

---

[11] House of Representatives, 40 Cong., 1 Sess., *Report of Committees*, No. 7, "Impeachment Investigation," p. 27.

veto. The strategy was ineffective, however, as it again failed to receive the necessary two-thirds majority.

In the meantime the fight over statehood had been revived in Colorado, if indeed it can be said ever to have died down after the election. The "Denver crowd" was the chief force behind the demand for admission and controlled the state administration, which needed only congressional approval to become the government of Colorado. The "Golden crowd" had generally come into direct opposition to statehood. Their antagonism had been growing, and soon after the results of the election of 1865 became known, Willard Teller had written letters to friends in the House of Representatives, urging them to oppose admission, while H. M. Teller went to Washington in the spring of 1866 to lobby against the bill, and thus counterbalance the efforts of Chaffee and Evans, who were on the ground urging its support.

This shift of position on Teller's part after his vigorous support of statehood in 1864 did not pass unnoticed by his enemies, who naturally charged it to disappointment over the election of senators. The pro-state attacks upon him were vigorous, and in his absence were replied to by Willard, who insisted that neither he nor H. M. had approved the second statehood movement. They "believed its agitation so soon after its defeat of last year was conceived in political aspiration and born in political trickery." The corruption that was evident in the 1865 campaign for statehood made it a "farce and a swindle," although Willard admitted that he might not have come out in opposition "had better men than 'Granny' Evans as you used to call him and *Joey Bagstock* Chaffee" been elected.[12]

Unquestionably Teller's defeat for the Senate played a large part in his opposition, as well as the natural resentment he felt toward those who helped defeat the original movement, only to turn around and successfully carry through a second one. Other factors, however, were also present. There was no longer the pressing demand from the national administration for action on the plea of national preservation. Colorado had changed also. In the spring of 1864 it had been at the height of its mining boom, and its future prospects looked extremely favorable. By 1866 the realities of Colorado's future development were more appar-

---

[12] *Daily Mining Journal*, March 10, 13, 19, 1866.

ent, and the lack of any necessity for immediate statehood
was evident to all. Colorado opinion reflected this change. If
there was an actual majority for statehood in 1865, it is
unlikely that there was in the few years following. Several
attempts were made to get the territorial legislature to petition Congress for admission. Although such bills passed
one house on some occasions, the only one that passed both
was associated with a proposition to extend the boundaries
of the proposed state north to include that part of present-
day Wyoming containing the Union Pacific Railroad. Party
conventions did not think it a popular move to vote an
endorsement.

The failure of the first statehood bill had served to revive
interest in the territorial government. Evans had been replaced as governor by Alexander Cummings, a politician of
questionable reputation from Pennsylvania. Like most of
the territorial officials who stood to lose by statehood, he
lent aid to those in opposition. The election of 1866 was
an opportunity for Teller to re-establish his influence over
the Republican Party organization. He and Willard were
both active in the preliminary and state conventions, H. M.
being on the Territorial central committee. The principal
contest was over the nomination for delegate. Chilcott, the
member of the house under the "state" organization, was
named.[13] He was pro-state, but had refused to follow
Chaffee and Evans in their efforts to secure admission. The
Democrats, now increased by some Union men supporting
President Johnson under the name of the "Administration
Party," nominated A. C. Hunt. Both Tellers were active in
support of Chilcott, and in electing a new territorial House
of Representatives. When the votes were counted it was
found that the contest had been very close. Governor Cummings gave Hunt a certificate of the election, and a majority
of the state canvassing board gave one to Chilcott, both of
which were forwarded to Washington.

To the delight of many Coloradans, this contest was soon
followed by the appointment of Cummings to an internal
revenue collectorship in Pennsylvania, and by his resignation as governor of Colorado. The feeling with which this
news was received is evident in the following headlines in
the Central City paper:

---

[13] Miner's Register, July 13, 15, 1866.

GLORIOUS NEWS!
GOOD-BYE TO CUMMINGS!
*He is sent to curse Pennsylvania,
Let the Lord be Praised!*[14]

President Johnson appointed A. C. Hunt to the consequent vacancy in the governorship of Colorado, a situation
that was extremely unpleasant to the statehood group in
Colorado, and to Chaffee and Evans in particular.

Teller was at this time chairman of the executive committee of the Republican Party in Colorado. Chaffee and
Evans planned to make a fight in the Senate against Hunt's
confirmation. After some deliberation, Teller, in his party
capacity, requested the Republican members of the Senate to
confirm Hunt. Immediately he was subject to attack by the
friends of Chaffee and Evans. An open letter was published
in the Colorado press signed by prominent Denver Republicans, as representatives of the caucus of that city, protesting against the action, which they declared was contrary to
the wishes of the party. Teller replied immediately, denying
that the signers of the letter represented more than a secret
cabal. He refused to defend Hunt, and declared his support
of Delegate Chilcott:

> I did not approve of the appointment of Governor Hunt as the best
> that could be made, but as the best likely to be made.... If you desire
> to continue the contest between ... Hunt and Chilcott ... and thus
> to deprive the people of both delegate and Governor for a considerable
> time I cannot act with you.... Your request that I retract what I have
> said in favor of Mr. Hunt's confirmation, I prefer not to consider. Not
> recognizing my responsibility to the caucus you profess to represent,
> it merits and shall receive no attention from me.[15]

Hunt became the new governor.

Early in 1868 a final attempt was made to bring Colorado
into the Union under the constitution and officials of 1865.
The Senate Committee on Territories held hearings at
which Chaffee and Evans submitted statements. Teller went
East in order to present evidence against admission. He
arrived too late to go before the committee, but just in time
to watch an excited House of Representatives vote articles
of impeachment against President Johnson. "In all my experience in the far West," Teller recalled later, "I never saw
so disgraceful a scene as the House of Representatives then
presented."

---

[14] *Ibid.*, April 25, 1867; Hall, *Colorado*, I, 408.
[15] *Miner's Register*, July 17, 1867; Hall, *Colorado*, I, 408.

Partisan Republican though Teller was, he was too conservative a lawyer to approve that action. "I had greater fear at that hour," he recalled, "for the perpetuity of the institutions of the United States than I ever had at any other time."[16]

With that trial pending it was difficult to get anyone interested in the statehood question. By some means Teller met Senator Roscoe Conkling and presented his case to him. The New York senator won Teller's lifelong gratitude by taking the lead in opposing statehood. To counteract the extravagant claims made by Evans and Chaffee in regard to the Territory's growth, Teller drew up a statement of his case in the form of a memorial to Congress, which Conkling presented to the Senate. His argument was that the formation and adoption of the constitution had been a questionable procedure, that Colorado's population and wealth had not increased as expected, and that the people were against statehood. He estimated the number of people quite accurately as "not exceeding thirty thousand," in contrast to the seventy-five to one hundred thousand that Evans and Chaffee claimed. As to the popularity of the constitution and statehood, he challenged the submission of the question to a popular vote. "This is all we ask. The people of Colorado feel competent to decide this question."

The impeachment trial intervened, and when it was over, the bill could be considered upon its merits. Although it had many supporters, Conkling effectively used Teller's challenge of a referendum to rally the opposition. This attracted so much support that it became apparent the bill could not pass without such an amendment. Its advocates seemed to feel that it would be voted down if submitted to a referendum, so they failed to push the bill further.

The publication of Teller's memorial rekindled the fires of controversy in Colorado. To the "state" press, Teller's truth-telling was an unpatriotic attack upon the prosperity of the Territory. Never before nor after was he the subject of such denunciations as that on the front page of the *Rocky Mountain News* of Denver:

In former days he did have some respect, where now is man so mean as to do him honor? The brand of Cain is upon him. . . . Let the curse of every citizen be upon him. Let him be a dead man among us, so vile, so corrupt, so offensive, that the very mention of his name

---

[16] *Congressional Record*, 53 Cong., 1 Sess., 1674.

will excite loathing. Let the guilt of his own base acts be made to weigh so heavily upon him that he will only be too glad to escape where he cannot even hear the name of the territory he has so abused.[17]

The implication in Teller's argument that Colorado was not prospering greatly was open to the same objections he had made to the "anti-states" in 1864. A memorial was presented to Congress signed by a number of political workers denying the truth of Teller's statements. Another was presented by a public meeting at Golden approving his statement. The "anti-states" claimed that three fourths of the people agreed with Teller.

In spite of a demand that the Republicans repudiate him for his memorial, Teller presided over the Republican territorial convention of that summer. Both he and Willard were active on the stump during the campaign, and the Republicans won, although the split within their ranks resulted in a very small majority. It was presidential year also, and in his speeches H. M. Teller emphasized national issues, which were then dividing the parties in the nation rather than local matters. Particularly he attacked the opposition of the Democrats to the resumption of specie payment for greenbacks. But emphasizing national issues did not bring the factions together, and the fight was very warm in Gilpin County.[18]

After the election of 1868 H. M. Teller withdrew from active participation in politics. Many factors were undoubtedly influential in bringing this about. His law practice, mining interests, and, above all, the affairs of the Colorado Central Railroad, were demanding more time than he could give them. With U. S. Grant's election to the Presidency, Chaffee and his friends had complete control of the Federal patronage, a political factor that was extremely powerful in a territory. This made any attempt to compete with them hopeless from the beginning. Furthermore, the growing power of Denver, and the relative decline of the gulch towns, both economically and politically, left little to struggle over besides personalities and a lost cause. The control of the "Denver crowd" over the Republican organization seemed inevitable, and in subsequent elections it was able to choose its leader, Chaffee, as delegate to Congress regularly. It was hardly in Teller's nature to surrender, and he simply dropped

[17] *Rocky Mountain News*, March 14, 1868.

[18] *Ibid.*, April 6, 1868; *Daily Colorado Tribune*, July 8, 15, 1868; *Miner's Register*, Sept. 5, 6, 1868; Stanton, *op. cit.*, p. 146.

territorial politics for other interests that were then demanding his attention.

Only at home in Gilpin County was the Republican organization faithful to Teller, and ready to follow any suggestion he might make. But he made no demands upon it, confining his political activity to advocacy of the party ticket at election time. If the "Little Kingdom" had a king, his name was still Teller, but more and more the emphasis in Colorado politics was being placed upon the adjective in the title of his realm.

CHAPTER VI

THE REWARDS OF LABOR
1864-76

TELLER'S retirement from active competition in territorial politics left him with more time and energy to devote to professional and business affairs. His activities in these fields kept him before the public about as effectively as had politics.

During the later sixties mining in Colorado was a depressed industry. For this condition there were two principal causes: the difficulty of extracting gold from the ore, and the lack of cheap transportation to the East. Professor Nathaniel P. Hill, late of the faculty of Brown University, solved the first problem by introducing European reduction methods into his mill at Blackhawk. But the problem of cheap transportation remained unsolved, and upon it hung many developments other than mining, as it was essential also to the success of farming and ranching.

The agitation for a transcontinental railroad had interested Coloradans from the beginning of settlement, and they had used all the little influence that a new region possesses to bring the road through the Territory. But they had failed, and the transcontinental route had gone through Wyoming to the north, leaving Colorado off the line of travel and distant from cheap and rapid transportation.

To be left off the line of transportation meant stagnation, particularly at a time when mining was not prospering. When Grenville M. Dodge remarked that "Denver was too dead to bury," he was stating the predetermined condition of a city remote from a railroad. Hence projects were organized for the purpose of securing branch lines connecting various Colorado cities with the transcontinental railroad. But where the Territory had been a unit in attempting to secure the transcontinental route, the proposal of a connecting road immediately split Colorado into contending factions over the question of which city would be most advantageously connected with the railroad. It was mainly a controversy between Golden and Denver. The former had the advantage of being close to the important mines in Gilpin and Clear Creek counties, and had the Territory's industries remained confined to this region, Golden might have become the metropolis. But as other regions of greater importance developed, Denver's ultimate success was assured. While all this is easy to see in the clarifying atmosphere of retrospect, it was not so plain in the sixties. Arrayed upon the two sides were the property interests of those in the two towns, everyone trying to raise the value of his property by increasing the commercial importance of its location.

Identified with the local interests of Golden was an interesting and able group of men. The most notable of this group were W. A. H. Loveland and E. L. Berthoud. Loveland was the promoter of the group, and for persistence and never-say-die spirit, Colorado never saw his equal. Berthoud was the engineer, fortunately with wide experience in railroad building behind him.

Loveland had long been fascinated by the possibilities of railroading in Colorado, and as early as 1861 had sponsored the preliminary survey of a route west from Golden to Central City. When the transcontinental railroad project had first been agitated, Berthoud had surveyed a route from Golden across Colorado, using the pass that bears his name, and this was the route that Colorado had presented for the consideration of the Union Pacific.

Before it was definitely known that the Union Pacific would use the Wyoming route, the territorial legislature chartered a railroad company, later known as the Colorado Central. This charter provided for the building of railroad lines in four directions from Golden, and would provide an outlet for the gulch towns. The directors included the Golden group, Teller, and several Eastern capitalists, most of whom were from Boston. Included among them was John A. Dix, then president of the Union Pacific.[1]

Many other projects were planned for the prospective metropolis by members of the Golden group under Loveland's inspiration. Among other enterprises, the "Colorado Iron, Engine and Mill Manufacturing Company" was incorporated to do a general iron-mill business. Teller, Loveland, and other local men were its incorporators. There was more than a touch of Beriah Sellers in some of their plans. When Bayard Taylor came to Golden in June, 1866, Loveland told him that they planned to manufacture rails for the transcontinental railway from the local coal and iron ore. His enthusiasm was infectious enough to inspire Taylor to

---

[1] *General Laws of the 4th Legislative Session*, pp. 108-16; Vickers, *History of Clear Creek and Boulder Valley*, p. 195; Smiley, *Denver*, pp. 583, 584; Smiley, *Colorado*, I, 502-04; G. M. Dodge, *How We Built the Union Pacific Railway* (n.p., n.d.) p. 110.

predict that "the quiet of Golden City will not endure much longer; and the day may not be far off when the smoke from its tall chimneys, rising up behind Table Mountain, will be seen in Denver."[2]

The railroad was the important thing, and when the Union Pacific selected the less mountainous Wyoming route for its through line, near panic struck all Colorado. However, its mines and its population would make substantial railroad traffic; its coal would supply the locomotives with cheap fuel; and the Union Pacific was interested in Colorado connections. There followed negotiations with both Denver and Golden interests in which the main Colorado controversy was whether the proposed branch should connect with the Union Pacific by a line to Denver via Golden or to Golden via Denver. Fearing that Golden might get the shorter haul, and safe in the knowledge that the Kansas Pacific would reach Denver anyway, the Denver group rejected the offer of the Union Pacific and proceeded to build a line of its own to Cheyenne, to be known as the Denver Pacific. The Union Pacific then made an agreement with the Colorado Central which made it close to a subsidiary of the greater company. Both as an incorporator of the Colorado Central and as an important property owner of the gulch towns, Teller was closely identified with these proceedings. As he was soon to become the Union Pacific's legal representative in the Territory, a third interest tied him in with the Colorado Central Railroad.[3]

At first the Union Pacific placed one of its own men, T. J. Carter, in charge of construction and management. It is clear that neither Teller nor Loveland got on very well with him. Moreover, the Union Pacific was without a consistent policy toward the Colorado road, and its construction lagged badly. By the time the Colorado Central was ready to build seriously, Denver was about to gain double rail connections with the East by means of the westward-building Kansas Pacific and with the Union Pacific at Cheyenne by means of the Denver Pacific. Carter then laid out the Colorado Central from Golden to a connection with the Denver Pacific at a point some distance from Denver. This would give the Golden-centered road a direct connection with the East without using Denver as a transshipping point, or at least it made that possible if the Denver Pacific co-operated. It was

---

[2] Taylor, *Colorado*, p. 51.
[3] *Daily Mining Journal*, July 12, 1865; *Miner's Register*, Nov. 6, 1868.

planned, as a contemporary put it, "not so much to connect the two cities as to separate them." Thus the contest between the Denver and Golden interests continued, with the previous removal of the territorial capital to Denver but the forerunner of general victory. However, that result was not predetermined in 1870; in fact, the result depended primarily upon the competition of Eastern railroad interests. In the struggle among these groups, Colorado interests were little more than pawns which exercised but slight influence upon the result.

The interests of property owners in the mountain towns, as well as in Golden, were discouragingly dependent upon distant market places. Should the controlling capitalists suddenly combine the Kansas Pacific and Union Pacific railroads, they would probably unite the Golden road with Denver's, and the resulting lack of competition might leave the mountain towns dependent for many years upon primitive transportation to the railheads at Golden or Denver. Rumors in 1871 that the Pennsylvania interests, already large holders of Kansas Pacific stock, were buying into the Union Pacific was a threat of sheer disaster to the Golden group. Moreover, the board of directors of the Union Pacific itself was split on the desirability of competing with the Denver-centered roads. President Carter was involved in these factions. As he had brought in the entire responsible personnel of the Colorado Central Railroad from the East, the local promoters of the road were merely helpless observers of the maneuvering of the great railroad interests. There can be little doubt that this helpless condition was fully appreciated by the local groups, all of whose property interests were dependent upon the decisions made in Boston and New York.

There is no clear record of exactly how it happened, but it is clear what happened. The Golden crowd, with help from an Eastern stockholder or two, captured control of the Colorado Central at a stockholders' meeting in May, 1871. Teller was elected president in place of Carter, and Loveland was made vice-president. With the control in its hands, the Golden crowd could at least threaten to join with the Kansas Pacific and thereby frighten the Union Pacific board who were not favorable toward a consolidation with that road.[4] As this faction of the Union Pacific was at least

---

[4] Oliver Ames to Teller, March 8, 1872. Teller-Orahood MSS.; Samuel Donald Mock, "Railroad Development in the Colorado Region" (unpublished thesis, University of Nebraska, 1938), pp. 328-32.

temporarily dominant, Teller was able to drive a bargain with it that secured the main thing the Golden crowd wanted: the active extension of its own railroad. But this was secured only after a long period of negotiations and threats, with the Union Pacific entering into a traffic contract with the Denver Pacific and threatening to buy it.

By 1872 Teller's understanding with the Union Pacific was completed, although its terms are not entirely clear. The Golden crowd was left in control of the Colorado Central, and building was commenced again to connect the gulch towns with Golden and the Kansas Pacific. Apparently no guarantee was made that the Colorado Central would be connected directly with the Union Pacific, although building in that direction was to commence also. In addition a traffic agreement which was very favorable to the Colorado Central was put in force. In return for these concessions the Colorado Central group had to give up two things to the Union Pacific management. One was control of the construction company which was to do the building, and the other was to make the treasurer of the Union Pacific, secretary-treasurer of the smaller corporation.

Teller began the construction of a narrow-gauge line up Clear Creek canyon toward the gulch towns. He carried bond elections in Gilpin, Weld, and Boulder counties. These county bonds were exchanged for stock in the road, and then sold by the company to secure capital for building, a regular way of financing railroads of the period. The successful conclusion of these bond elections, usually against organized opposition from Denver-centered roads, was a political feat of no mean proportions, and involved a campaign of speeches, advertisements in the press, and even watchers at the polls.[5] With the bond issues assured, building operations went forward as fast as the Union Pacific management would permit. Within the management of the larger road, factional quarrels frequently delayed or interfered with the work, but Teller insisted on direct control of operations. He replaced with Colorado men many of Carter's employees who had been brought in from the East. It seems clear in fact that a sectional conflict went on within the corporate structure, with the Union Pacific management wanting to

---

[5] A bill of Teller's to the company, Sept. 21, 1872, indicates that $1,371.40 was spent by him in the campaign, $1,007.14 of which was furnished by two Eastern stockholders. The detailed accounting shows that most of it went for traveling expenses for himself and others. Teller-Orahood MSS.

send out its own selections for personnel, and Teller insisting upon finding them in Colorado. When Union Pacific
officials wanted one of his men discharged, Teller refused.
"I think it is the old trouble," he confided to one of the
Golden crowd. "He is a Colorado man & that is what is the
matter."[6]

When he assumed control, Teller had succeeded in reducing overhead enough to show an operating profit the first
year, and even paid off some of the debts that hung over the
company.[7] Construction was pushed until the panic of 1873.
stopped it by shutting off Eastern capital. By this time
narrow-gauge lines had been completed to Blackhawk and to
Floyd Hill up North and South Clear Creek canyons. Substantial building had been done on the main line designed to
go from Golden to Boulder to Longmont to Greeley and eventually to connect with the Union Pacific near Julesburg, in
order to give the system a short route to the East. That more
had not been completed was due solely to the hesitancy of
the Union Pacific in furnishing the rails and in marketing
bonds sufficient to complete the road. By April, 1873, the
road was in operation from Golden to Longmont on the
main line. The mines of the gulch towns had a good outlet
to the East, and had easy access to the farming and local
mining areas on the Colorado Central main line.

The connection with Blackhawk was a great personal
achievement for Teller, since it was, in a way, a solution of
the other economic problem of the gulch towns—cheap transportation. The fact that many residents of the Little Kingdom had from the beginning declared that the idea of building a railroad up Clear Creek Canyon was "undiluted nonsense" added savor to the achievement. When the first train
arrived in Blackhawk on December 15, 1872, it was one of
the gala occasions in the gulch.[8] It gave a new spurt to
mining activity there, and carried out a promise Teller had
made to secure railroad service for the Little Kingdom.
Still it was not complete, as he had promised that the road
would reach Central City also. The steep grade from Blackhawk to Central gave the Union Pacific engineers reason to

---

[6] Teller to C. C. Welch (copy), June 27, 1874. Teller-Orahood MSS.

[7] Teller to Oliver Ames (copy), Nov. 29, 1871. Teller-Orahood MSS. Mock denies
that there was an actual operating profit. Pp. 229-30.

[8] Vickers, *op. cit.*, pp. 195-97; Perrigo, "Social History of Central City," p. 406;
Stone, *Colorado*, I, 342-43.

hesitate, and it was with great difficulty that Teller kept them committed to the extension up the gulch.[9]

In 1873, Teller could point to an operating profit each year since he had been in charge, with increased income and decreased overhead as compared with the record of his predecessor.[10] As a matter of fact, the road was strategically located to tap the mining area. In contrast, the allied Denver and Kansas Pacific roads, lacking feeders, were bankrupt as soon as the panic checked the flow of new capital, and they went into receivership the following year.

The general policy of the Union Pacific after 1873 prevented resumption of construction on the Colorado Central. Jay Gould, who had now become the main factor in its management, had his eyes upon the bankrupt Kansas Pacific, control of which would remove the Union Pacific's reasons for completing the Julesburg line of the Colorado Central. It seems very clear that these negotiations were the cause of the Union Pacific's refusal to permit completion of the Julesburg line in 1874 and 1875.[11]

By 1875 the Union Pacific directly and indirectly held the majority of the stock in the Colorado Central, and when its arrangements with the Kansas Pacific were satisfactory, it proposed to unite the Colorado Central with the Kansas Pacific.[12] With Teller presiding at a stockholders' meeting this proposal carried, along with a proposition that reduced the paper value of the stock to its real value. The chief objection to this was to come from Golden, which bade fair to lose its "center" to Denver, and with it the railroad shops and transshipping profits.

Whether the local directors liked it or not, there seemed to be nothing that could be done to prevent the consummation of the plan. But Loveland found a way: at the stockholders' meeting the next year the committee on credentials, a distinctly Golden group, threw out enough Union Pacific votes represented by proxies to give the Golden group control.[13] Loveland was elected president, and took actual control of the road by force and stratagem. When the Union Pacific appealed to the courts to recover control, the judge who was to issue the order was kidnaped. Then internal

---

[9] Teller to Oliver Ames (copy), Nov. 22, 1871; Ames to Teller, Sept. 9, 1874. Teller-Orahood MSS.

[10] *Report of the Colorado Central Railroad* (Golden, 1873); Teller-Orahood MSS.

[11] T. E. Sickles to Teller, March 4, 20, April 27, 1874, Feb. 10, 1875. Teller-Orahood MSS. See also McMeechen, *Evans*, pp. 146-71.

[12] Denver *Daily Times*, May 1, 10, 12, 1875.

[13] Denver *Daily Tribune*, May 22, 1876, is the most detailed account.

quarrels developing between the boards of the larger roads temporarily ended Gould's desire to unite the Colorado Central with the Kansas Pacific. This gave Loveland an opportunity to make an advantageous compromise that postponed consolidation for a few years and permitted construction to continue.[14]

Teller's part in these dramatic movements is far from clear. His own papers are lacking for these two years, and the newspapers give disappointingly meager information. Although Loveland was backed by intense public sentiment in Golden and Boulder, there seems to have been no resentment against Teller for his part in all of this. He was elected to the Senate soon after Loveland seized control, but even at Washington he continued to be an active force in the company, being appealed to from time to time by all local factions and by the Union Pacific to use his influence upon the others to secure certain desired ends.[15] It was undoubtedly due to his persistence that among the new extensions of the road was one from Blackhawk to Central City, a remarkable switchback which he first worked out himself. It was probably the only unprofitable project toward which he encouraged the road. He had obligated himself to do it, and paid most of the cost of the right of way out of his own pocket. On May 21, 1878, Central City celebrated the event.[16] In the meantime, the Union Pacific vetoed the extension of the main line to Julesburg, but enabled Loveland to connect with its main line a few miles from Cheyenne, and to extend the South Clear Creek line to Georgetown. In 1879, Gould secured complete control of the Kansas Pacific, Loveland had to retire, and the entire group of roads was consolidated the following year.

While Teller had been assuming a more important role in the economic affairs of the Territory, he had not shirked his duties as the leading citizen of the "Little Kingdom of Gilpin." From the very first he had borne a share of the burdens involved in membership on the city council and the school board. These positions were not always the kind that increased his popularity for he was often in the midst of hot

---

[14] Hall, *Colorado*, II, 94-98, 407-24 ; Smiley, *Denver*, pp. 598-600. See also clippings in the Dawson Scrapbook from the Denver *Daily Tribune*, Jan. 1, 1879, and the Denver *Post*, April 3, 1909.

[15] Loveland to Teller, Dec. 27, 1877, May 6, 17, 1878 ; Berthoud to Teller, Oct. 29, Dec. 27, 1877, Feb. 3, 18, 1878 ; Sidney Dillon to Teller, Dec. 21, 1877 ; John Truck to Teller, Jan. 6, March 1, 2, 3, 26, 1878 ; C. C. Welch to Teller, March 22, 1878, Teller Letters.

[16] Teller to Central City mayor and council (copy), Jan. 15, 1878 ; O. H. Henry to Teller, May 16, 1878, Teller Letters.

local contests, and sometimes stood out nearly alone against community sentiment. In 1871 he used court action to force the school board to admit the few Negro children in Central City to the public school. When a politically disappointed lawyer tried to organize a local labor party, Teller went to the organization meeting and took the floor to defend the record of the Republican Party, pointing out its legislative achievements, and calling the roll of laborers whom the Gilpin County Republicans had elected to public office.[17] When local improvements were needed, the community looked to him to supply the leadership and capital necessary to produce them.

The prospect of rail connections had caused a revival of optimism in Central City, and the local people began to demand more evidences of a city. There was no first-class hotel in the gulch, and local pride demanded one. Public meetings were called to discuss the matter, but at first without success. Teller finally offered to erect a $20,000 building if the community would furnish the site. Eventually this was secured through public subscription.

Enthusiasm ran high, boom times again seemed to be in the offing, and Teller was induced to expand his plans to include a $60,000 building. His brother, Willard, came in with him as a partner on the project, and by the time they had their four-story, brick "Teller House" erected, it was reported to have cost $87,000.

In June, 1872, the building was completed, furnished by the lessee, and ready for its dedication. It was a great day for the gulch and for Teller, when the "largest and finest hotel in Colorado," "Central's proudest enterprise," held its open house. Now Central City could hold up its civic head when a visitor of note arrived. And just a year later President Grant reached the city and walked from his carriage into the Teller House upon a sidewalk temporarily paved with thirteen hundred dollars' worth of silver bricks. Central was not to be outdone by Denver or any other upstart city.

The following year, when the fire that Bayard Taylor had foreseen destroyed most of Central's business district, the brick walls of the Teller House and a stone building opposite prevented its spread in that direction, and the Tellers' office and houses were among those saved. The Teller House

---

[17] *Miner's Register,* Aug. 17, 1871; Perrigo, *op. cit.,* pp. 180, 347-48.

Central City, Colorado, in the early seventies—Teller's $87,000 hotel in center of picture.

was to remain even in its later period of shabby decay as Gilpin County's proudest treasure.[18]

To the railroad and hotel building and attempts to develop new industries such as iron smelting at Golden, Teller added interests in a vast number of minor projects. Telephone and telegraph companies, irrigation projects, theaters, smelters, fruit farming, and, above all, mining projects gave him ample opportunity to use his energy and capital. Most of these projects were temporarily profitable, and only when the gulch played out as an important producer of minerals did they become liabilities.

But this decline was not yet evident in the early seventies, and except for his failure to gain the political recognition he desired, Teller had nearly everything for which he could wish. Had not his political ambition been so well developed and had he been content to practice law and give close attention to his investments, "he must," as an associate later wrote, "have made large accumulations."[19]

Teller's retirement from active politics after the election of 1868 did not mean that he had lost interest in a political career. Willard Teller continued to be moderately active in the Republican territorial organization, usually as the leader of the opposition to the dominant faction. When Chaffee was nominated for delegate in 1870, Willard was named chairman of the central committee by the state convention, an appearance of unity that the party press hailed as "the best day's work ever done by the Republican Party in Colorado."[20] But H. M. Teller remained in Central City keeping his own counsel, which worried Chaffee and his friends, who feared that the lack of Teller's active support in the campaign might easily mean the difference between victory and defeat. One of the Federal officeholders who owed his appointment to Chaffee, Irving W. Stanton, approached Teller a few days after the convention and secured a promise to deliver three speeches for the Republican ticket, in which Chaffee would not be mentioned by name. The speeches were made, and the appearance of unity gave Chaffee a majority in Gilpin, which had gone Democratic two years before, and he was elected.

---

[18] *Miner's Register*, June 25, 26, 1872; April 29, 1873; Denver *Daily Times*, June 26, 1872; Chase Withrow, *Reminiscences;* Perrigo, *op. cit.*, has a slightly different account, pp. 446-50.

[19] E. T. Wells, *op. cit.;* Hal Sayre, "Early Central City Theatricals and Other Reminiscences," *Colorado Magazine*, VI (March, 1929), 51.

[20] *Daily Colorado Tribune*, July 14, 15, 1870.

Stanton later recalled an incident that happened after the election, when he and Chaffce were on their way to Denver from Central City, which shows that the personal feeling between Chaffee and Teller was probably not as bitter as many contemporaries thought:

Arriving at the Guy House, half way to Golden, about dinner time we had our team cared for and Mr. Chaffee and I stood on the steps of the hotel waiting for dinner to be served. When the coach from Denver drove up, on the seat with the driver, Hank Hawk, was Mr. H. M. Teller, who got down and shook hands with me. He then offered his hand to Mr. Chaffee, who accepted it, and then and there these two men, who for years had been political enemies, talked with each other for some minutes. Teller told Chaffee of meeting in Denver, Miss Minnie Overton, a cousin of both of them, who had just come from Wisconsin to accept a position in the Denver public schools.... I confess I was anxious when I saw Mr. Teller on the coach....[21]

Teller never harbored personal grievances for long, and at no time in his career did they play a large part in determining his action for any length of time. Nevertheless, Teller and Chaffee made no truce at this time, and their political wounds were not yet healed.

Always sensitive to reform movements, Willard Teller evidenced great interest in the Liberal-Republican organization in the East as the election of 1872 approached. When a local branch of the rebel group was organized, the younger Teller joined it, resigning the chairmanship of the Republican central committee. In hopes of attracting H. M. Teller also, the Liberal-Republican convention in Colorado nominated him for delegate, but he "politely and firmly declined" by telegraph. A. C. Hunt was then named for the place. But Teller took no part in the Republican convention. Chaffee's group was in complete control and renominated its leader. The hit of the meeting was a speech by J. W. Hardin, local Negro leader, who, referring to Greeley and Grant, declared that "every colored man's sympathies were for the man who *whaled* and not the man who *bailed* Jeff Davis."[22]

Willard Teller opened Hunt's campaign in Central City, but his elder brother took no active part for either candidate. This was black treachery to those whose interests were hurt. Chaffee wrote to Frank Hall, editor of the Central City paper: "I know you and the Register will do your part. D——n these men who falter when clouds appear. I would

[21] *Ibid.*, Aug. 10, 1870 ; Stanton, *op. cit.*, pp. 147-54.
[22] Denver *Daily Times*, July 18, Aug. 1, 12, 1872.

stick to the Republican party for what it *has* done, such a record, it partakes of the Divine almost."[23]

An excellent indication of H. M. Teller's reputation is given by the way in which the pro-Chaffee papers treated him. Under the false impression that H. M. Teller had taken the stump for Hunt, the worst evil the Denver *Times* could impute to him was ambition:

> For a number of years the "Tellers" have enjoyed considerable popularity, and some notoriety, in this Territory. Henry M. Teller is a man of more than ordinary ability, and accounted—no doubt deservedly— one of the best lawyers in the West. He is a mild-mannered man, possessed of good personal presence, generally dignified, and is altogether a respectable and useful citizen. All this will be conceded by those who have a slight acquaintance with him, and have never had occasion to inquire critically into his secret motives and well-disguised ambitions. But he has inordinate ambition; and at all times and all seasons—early and late—he has labored zealously to impress the people of this Territory with his private and public consequence.[24]

Chaffee won with a rather large majority and returned to Washington for another two years. His close relations with Grant gave him control of the Colorado appointments, which he distributed among his circle of supporters, who were an outgrowth of the old Denver crowd, now called "the ring" by those outside the group. Beginning with the appointment to the governorship of S. H. Elbert, John Evans' son-in-law, the group came into complete control of the territorial government. Everything politically was going to Chaffee's liking until, as a local rumor had it, he quarreled with Grant over a poker game early in 1874. Without warning, the President began to remove the territorial officers who were Chaffee's friends and appoint others in their stead, Edward M. McCook being made governor in place of Elbert. Denver and Colorado were thrown into a fever of excitement by the news. Elbert's friends called a meeting in Denver to protest against the action. H. M. Teller was there on a law case and attended the meeting. After it was over he wrote to Harper Orahood, a young attorney in his office:

> McCook has been nominated for governor & Chaffee telegraphed that he will resign if he is confirmed. They called a meeting to protest & we went in & took a vote of twenty to one for McCook. Charles spoke for Elbert and I did for McCook. The meeting was composed of the best men in Denver & it was pretty lively for them. I think they

[23] Chaffee to Hall, Aug. 4, 1872, Frank Hall MSS.
[24] Aug. 12, 1872.

may try to get up a meeting at Central or B. H. to protest. I hope you
will put your foot in it. If McCook is confirmed we will have the Ring
broken up completely. Chaffee will telegraph commands and try to get
telegrams to show the people are against McCook. I do not know how
you feel but I hope you will go for McCook. You have nothing to
expect from Elbert and his party. If Chaffee resigns all the better.[25]

From the press account of the meeting it is evident that
Teller's letter did not overstate the case much, as he had to
urge the meeting to give the supporters of Elbert a hearing.
Part of the reporter's summary of Teller's argument reads:

He knew that the government was carried on by a rather close
corporation—emanating from one house or family.... President Grant
and also the people of Colorado have been dissatisfied with his
[Elbert's] administration... [He] had governed the territory for
the benefit of the few.[26]

Chaffee led a losing fight against McCook's nomination,
which the Senate confirmed in June. This situation brought
Teller back into politics as the temporary leader of the Republicans. The Chaffee men who controlled the central committee planned to demonstrate their control over the party
organization by holding no convention, but Teller forced
them to call a territorial convention to nominate candidates.
When it met "it prostrated itself before the administration
at the dictation of Teller and McCook," or so it seemed to a
Chaffee newspaper.

Party harmony was impossible. Teller tried to secure
the nomination of a strong candidate for delegate, but Judge
James B. Belford, the only one available, refused to run
because, it was said, of threats made by Chaffee. Finally the
nomination went to H. P. H. Bromwell, whose chief recommendation was that he had been a friend of Abraham
Lincoln. The larger part of the Republican machine and
press refused to support the ticket, and Chaffee went to
Europe to escape the necessity of support or opposition.

To make matters worse, the Democrats nominated a
candidate of unusual strength. Thomas M. Patterson, a
native of Ireland, an able speaker and Colorado's principal
criminal lawyer, was a force to be reckoned with in any political campaign. With the Republicans divided, and their
governor, McCook, unpopular, defeat was difficult to avoid.

[25] Charles S. Thomas, "The Pioneer Bar of Colorado," *Colorado Magazine*, I (July,
1924), 193-94; *Rocky Mountain News*, Jan. 28, 1874; H. M. Teller to Orahood, Jan. 28,
1874, Teller-Orahood MSS.
[26] *Rocky Mountain News*, Jan. 28, 1874.

Certain injudicious acts of Governor McCook, played up by an unfriendly press, helped to arouse passion and rancor against the ticket. One Republican newspaper even threatened the Governor with lynching in the historic phrase, "Cottonwoods might again bear fruit."[27]

Against such a background a successful campaign was well-nigh impossible, and Patterson won over Bromwell, carrying Gilpin County as well as the rest of the Territory. With a large share of the party organization sulking, and with an uninspiring candidate, any other result would have been unexpected. The newspapers favorable to "the ring" were not backward in laying the defeat to Teller's management of the campaign. The Pueblo *Chieftain* remarked, "As an engineer corps of a lively political campaign, Mr. Teller and his friends have proved a humiliating failure."[28]

Colorado had experienced a large growth between 1868 and 1875, and it was inevitable that the statehood question should become pressing again. With the growth of population most of the objections had been removed. Grant soon replaced McCook with one of his personal friends, John T. Routt, an able man and a good diplomat. The new governor succeeded in patching up the quarrel between Chaffee and Grant, and established a good personal reputation among Colorado people. Chaffee and Patterson both devoted themselves at Washington to the advocacy of statehood, and by the use of influence upon the leaders of both parties they succeeded in getting an enabling act passed in 1876. There was now almost no opposition in Colorado, so a local contest did not develop. The Tellers were ready to welcome the changed status and had been for the past four years.[29]

Outside his brief period of activity in 1874, H. M. Teller had been out of politics since 1868. He was not even active in Gilpin County, but his friends controlled the party organization there. The party machinery elsewhere was in the hands of local leaders who had been allied with Chaffee, until the national administration had turned against him in 1874. Now he was back in the good graces of Grant, and, if the Colorado Republicans had a "boss," Chaffee was that man. His prestige was not lessened by the successful achievement of the statehood bill.

---

[27] Denver *Republican*, Sept. 7, 1874; *Rocky Mountain News*, Aug. 9, 1874; Denver *Daily Times*, Aug. 6, 8, 12, Sept. 15, 1874.

[28] Quoted in the Denver *Weekly Times*, Sept. 16, 1874.

[29] Willard Teller to Harper Orahood, Jan. 24, 1872, Teller-Orahood MSS.

Teller had no organization, but he was not without substantial political prestige. He was the most powerful and
best-known public speaker in the Territory. He had made a
few speeches for the Republican ticket in almost every campaign, and these were admittedly extraordinarily effective.
Probably more important still was his reputation as a lawyer. Teller was as close to being the leader of the bar as
anyone in the Territory, and one of his closest competitors
was his brother Willard.

On nonpartisan occasions when Colorado wanted to put
herself forward in the best possible light, Teller was invariably called upon to present her case. When Denver entertained one of the first of the meetings of Western governors to consider the problems of public lands, Teller was
the one Coloradan not in office who addressed the meeting.
His business interests had bound him firmly to Colorado in
a way that removed any suspicion of the exceedingly temporary local interests of many politicians. Partisan attacks
upon him in the past had been few and relatively ineffective.
As the time for statehood approached, Teller loomed up on
the public horizon as one of her ablest citizens.[30]

Statehood carried easily; Colorado became the centennial state; and the Fourth of July in Colorado was a double
celebration. After that politics became the exciting interest.
It was conceded from the first that if the Republicans carried the legislature, Chaffee would go to the Senate. His
control of the organization ensured that. Who the other
member would be was a matter of speculation. Both H. M.
and Willard Teller were considered to be possible candidates. Both of them took an active part in the fall campaign,
Willard conducting an extensive speaking tour over the
state.[31]

That H. M. was a candidate was never doubted. At least
since 1864 it had been commonly assumed that he would be a
candidate when statehood was achieved. With a railroad's
usual facility for placing public officials under obligation,
over three years before one of the directors of the Union
Pacific had assured Teller of his support. "If I can do
anything to aid in securing to you a place in the U. S. Senate
I shall be very happy to do so."[32]

---

[30] Hall, *Colorado*, II, 177; Fred A. Conant to Orahood, March 11, 1875, Teller-
Orahood MSS.

[31] Denver *Daily Times*, July 10, Sept. 1, 23, 1876; Hall, *Colorado*, II, 333, 334.

[32] Oliver Ames to Teller, Jan. 8, 1873, Teller-Orahood MSS.

After the election, which the Republicans carried by a small majority, the speculation continued as to the Senate. The leaders in the southern half of the state were somewhat resentful over the regularity with which the political plums went to the other half. The Colorado member of the House was to be Judge Belford from Central City, and Chaffee, formerly of Gilpin County, now made his home at Denver. The claim was raised by the candidates from there that the other senator must come from south of the Divide. Chaffee and his group were only too willing to back up a claim that would defeat Teller, and had the Republican members of the legislature from this region been able to agree upon a man, they could have elected him.

There were three southern candidates, and when the Republican members of the legislature caucused, they, with H. M. Teller, divided the votes in about four equal parts, although Teller always led. It seemed that Teller was the second choice of the supporters of each of the southern candidates. When it became apparent that none of these could be nominated, the delegates went to Teller, who was nominated and elected.[33]

A bit of sheer luck was now in store for him. When Teller and Chaffee reached Washington in December, they found that the terms to which they had been elected extended in one case only until March 4 of the following year, and, in the other, to March 4, 1879. They drew lots in the usual manner, and Teller drew the short term of three months. This forced the sitting legislature to choose a senator for the six-year term ending March 4, 1883. As they had just chosen Teller, it was only natural that they re-elected him to the long term. To Chaffee this was anything but pleasing, and he disgustedly wrote to ex-Governor Evans that he had been wise to quit politics.[34]

Teller's election was well received by the Colorado press. The comment of the Denver *Times* can be given as typical:

The election of Mr. Teller should be taken as a high compliment under any circumstances, but particularly under those which have just transpired. Without having been actively engaged in politics for many years, so that his friends could not urge party claims, and without having made a fight for the position, yet he has proven the second choice of nearly all of the Republican members. His universally recognized ability has secured him this high office.

---

[33] Denver *Daily Times*, Oct. 31, Nov. 4, 12, 14, 1876; Hall, *Colorado*, II, 358; Stone, *Colorado*, I, 429; Thomas F. Dawson, *Senator Teller* (Washington, 1898), pp. 87-91.
[34] McMechen, *Evans*, p. 154.

Outside of the state, comments were equally pleasant. Commented the enthusiastic editor of the Laramie (Wyoming) *Sentinel:*

> For weeks past we have fairly held our breath for fear geography would triumph over brains and Mr. Teller would be sacrificed to that absurd whim. Both of Colorado's new Senators are good and able men, but we regard Henry M. Teller as the peer of any statesman the present generation has yet produced.

The *Rocky Mountain News,* edited by William N. Byers, who had written the bitter arraignment of Teller eight years before, was more discerning:

> His speeches in the canvass just closed were among the most powerful and convincing efforts ever made on the stump in Colorado, their main element of force consisting largely in the conviction that Henry M. Teller never says what he does not fully mean. . . . Through all the vicissitudes of politics and an immense law practice he has maintained a spotless integrity, and the breath of calumny has never tarnished his name. A warm hearted and generous friend, an open, undisguised enemy, there is not a man acquainted with him, however much he may differ with him in politics or with reference to law points, but respects his moral courage, integrity of character, his courteous and modest bearing, and unflinching adherence to what he believes to be right.[35]

---

[35] Denver *Daily Times*, Nov. 15, 18, 1876; Dawson, *Teller* (1898), pp. 85, 86.

CHAPTER VII

THE DEFENDER OF THE WEST
1876-81

BY VIRTUE of their elections Teller and Chaffee were entitled to seats in the short session of the Forty-fourth Congress. On its opening day, December 4, 1876, they presented themselves and were sworn in.

The session was chiefly concerned with determining whether Tilden or Hayes had been elected President the preceding November. In the debates Teller took no part. He voted for the electoral commission and with his party on all other questions of a partisan nature. He took no part in debate in this session nor in the first session of the Forty-fifth Congress. Chaffee, presuming upon his experience in the House, was more active on the floor than Teller. As long as Teller had an aggressive colleague with whom he could work on friendly terms, he was satisfied to allow him to make the speeches on the floor of the Senate and give interviews to the reporters. Only an unsatisfactory colleague or a fight of real importance could bring him out of his senatorial obscurity. This was an advantage in the beginning, at least, as the older senators frowned upon participation in debate by newer men. Senator Preston B. Plumb, of Kansas, who took his seat three months later than Teller, refused to heed this practice, only to be held up to ridicule in the Senate and the Washington *Post:*

> And yet—such is life—there are those who think Plumb
> Would have figured still better had he been born dumb.[1]

From the time Teller entered the Senate in 1876 until 1889, all the Western country now included in the states of the Dakotas, Montana, Wyoming, Idaho, Washington, Utah, New Mexico, and Arizona was under the territorial form of government. This gave each territory a delegate without voting privileges in the House of Representatives. But on the floor of the Senate they had no voice whatever, and the most pernicious legislation could be enacted without an opportunity for effective protests. In the center of this vast region was Colorado, surrounded on all sides but one by territories. Colorado was to be the youngest state for thirteen

---

[1] W. E. Connelley, *Life of Preston B. Plumb* (Chicago, 1913), p. 233.

years. Her experience with carpetbaggers and the Federal bureaucracy had not been happy; and it was easy for one who had lived through her territorial period to see the problems of people in a similar position. Consequently, it was but natural that Teller, whose law practice had frequently taken him into these territories, should feel a special responsibility for the entire region, and to act, at times, as though he were the senatorial representative of the entire West. When he retired from the Senate thirty-three years after he entered it, Senator Thomas H. Carter, of Montana, was to point to this phase of Teller's career as the most significant:

> In a very broad sense Mr. Teller has represented the whole country, but in a special manner his voice has spoken not alone for Colorado but for all the great West.... Henry M. Teller helped to rock the cradle of these infant States and has ever been a watchful guardian of their interests.[2]

Teller's first participation in general debate is typical of this phase of his activity. He had planned to make his first speech a technical constitutional argument favorable to the land-grant railroads, but another matter came up that forced him to make his maiden speech a defense of Western people living under a territorial form of government. A judge had been appointed for Wyoming Territory who was from the first exceedingly unpopular. In order to rid itself of him, the territorial legislature had followed Colorado's example and gerrymandered its judicial districts in such a way as to give this judge a jurisdiction containing few white inhabitants, and, consequently, one in which there would be little legal business. The Judiciary Committee of the Senate, intent on maintaining the supremacy of the Federal Government and the independence of the judiciary, brought a bill into the Senate to annul the Wyoming gerrymander. The members of the Judiciary Committee, particularly David Davis and Roscoe Conkling, supported their bill vigorously, calling the legislature's action nullification and open defiance of the Federal Government. Teller rose passionately to the defense of Wyoming. He appealed for a reasonable consideration of the problems of a territorial government, pointing out that this was the only way in which a territory could limit the evil of an incompetent or corrupt judge. He related Colorado's experience with its judiciary as an illustration.

---

[2] Quoted in T. F. Dawson, *Teller* (1923), p. 25.

I have seen not only in Colorado, but in other Territories, justice dealt out by the dollar. I have seen men sitting on the bench, with the whole people of the Territory protesting, selling their judgments as notoriously as indulgences were sold in the early days [sic] of the Roman Church.

The only remedy was some action such as the Wyoming legislature had taken. In spite of his arguments and those of the two Nebraska senators, who, it might be presumed, were also acquainted with these conditions, the committee's bill passed.[3]

This was typical of much of Teller's activity in the early part of his career. The West was misunderstood and abused by Eastern—particularly New England—statesmen, and he set himself to put them right. Frequently Senators Hoar or Dawes would chide him for his sectional orientation on legislation, and his answer was invariably to point out the underlying localism of their own attitudes.

It happened at this time that certain far-sighted individuals were becoming alarmed at the rapid exploitation of American forests, and began to demand that they be conserved for future use. Chief among these was Carl Schurz, Secretary of the Interior, who cultivated the field where Roosevelt and Pinchot were later to reap the harvest. One of his first steps in this direction was to prosecute Westerners who removed timber from the public lands. This caused vast unrest in the West, as there was hardly a miner, railroad, municipality, fraternal lodge, church, or indeed any private citizen who was not technically a violator of the law. One of the cases started was a suit for one hundred thousand dollars against N. P. Hill's smelter at Blackhawk, and he immediately appealed to Teller to have the suit stopped.[4]

Against such a policy were lined up practically all people in the West. There was no legal method of securing timber from the public lands, and no method of acquiring timber lands in Colorado and other mining states. Had the law been obeyed, neither mining nor farming would have been possible in all the Rocky Mountain region, as fuel and shelter could be secured only from the timber on government land. To Teller the attempt to enforce the law rigidly was evidence of the East's lack of understanding of conditions in the

---

[3] *Congressional Record*, 45 Cong., 2 Sess., pp. 1169 ff., 1201 ff. The Wyoming people were very grateful for Teller's defense. C. E. Wurtele, E. P. Johnson, and John McThayer to Teller, all Feb. 25, 1878, Teller Letters.

[4] Hill to Teller, Oct. 10, Nov. 14, 1877; Jan. 2, 1878, Teller Letters.

West, if not another instance of its jealous desire to prevent
the growth of the West. Eastern senators and newspapers
had not hesitated to call the taking of this timber robbery,
which fanned Teller's anger to a white heat:

> Since I have been a member of the Senate I have noticed on every
> occasion when any subject has been presented that directly bore upon
> the interest of the West that the Senators who live farthest from the
> interest to be served have always had the most to say, and that too
> about plunderers, thieves, robbers, and frequently stigmatized people
> of the extreme West in that way.

He pointed out that there was no way for a settler or
miner to secure wood except to go upon the public lands and
cut it; that no legal provision had been made for acquiring
timber lands by settlers; and that free timber from the
public lands had always been the frontier American method.
"Like begets like," he warned, "and Senators should remember that when they bring up sectional issues and charges
against a whole class of people it may return to them again."[5]

For immediate protection the Senator wrote to his friend
Moses Hallett, judge of the Federal District Court in Colorado, before whom such suits would probably come, and
presented him with a legal argument that such "depredations," or a large part of them, were within the law. To put
the question beyond doubt, he and Chaffee worked out a bill
to make lawful the removal of such timber as was necessary
for "domestic" purposes.[6] They were not satisfied with the
Timber and Stone Act which the Pacific Coast senators
were sponsoring in order to open the Government timber-
lands to sale. This act, they thought, would result in individual monopolies of timber in each mining region. Hence
they opposed the inclusion of Colorado and the territories
within its provisions. For the region not included within
the Timber and Stone Act they succeeded in securing the
passage of the Timber Cutting Act, which allowed anyone
except a railroad corporation to go upon the "mineral"
lands and take out timber for any purpose except export
from the state or territory. Nevada was included within
both acts, and the territory of Washington was under the
Timber and Stone Act. The Timber Cutting Act corrected
the old condition that had made every miner a lawbreaker,

---

[5] *Congressional Record,* 45 Cong., 2 Sess., pp. 1862, 1906, 1979.
[6] Hallett to Teller, Dec. 16, 1877, Teller Letters.

although it failed to prevent the many abuses that depleted the timber supply.[7]

On this and similar questions Teller's attitude was the product of his experience and that of Western people generally. It was taken not only because he was the advocate of Western interests in the Senate, but because he was a Westerner whose frontier experience had taught him to think that way. However poorly this "rugged individualism," as a subsequent President was to call it, fits the industrial civilization of today, it had been the method of the frontier, and for Westerners to deny it would be to go back on their origins, and to proclaim that their own work was not good.

Particularly was this true regarding the exploitation of natural resources. In a debate on a bill to establish titles to certain valuable springs at Hot Springs, Arkansas, Teller declared his position in words that might be considered the classic expression of the pioneer:

... the whole trouble in this case in my judgment arises from the United States Government attempting to set apart a piece of land and control it because it has a spring on it. The entire principle is wrong; and we should have saved a good deal of money and a great deal of time, and the people of that section would have been infinitely better off, if the Government had allowed the first man that got there to take it. That ought to be the rule in reference to valuable springs or valuable lands. The man who has the enterprise to go and put his claim on the land in accordance with law ought to take it.[8]

There had been demands at various times in the past that the public lands containing valuable minerals should be reserved for the Government rather than be exploited by individuals. This was in essence another form of conservation, about which those who wanted the West to develop rapidly were opposed to those who wanted its development postponed.

The issue came up on a proposal to reserve the mineral rights in confirming certain land grants in the Mexican cession. Teller used all his knowledge of mining law and of Western conditions in attempting to prove that it was contrary to our treaty agreements and to good policy. Owners of land, he insisted, should be allowed to develop any mines possible. Although he failed to secure an amendment to

[7] *Congressional Record*, 45 Cong., 2 Sess., pp. 2412, 2640; *Senate Reports*, No. 122, 45 Cong., 2 Sess.; Thomas Donaldson, *The Public Domain* (Washington, 1884), pp. 358-59; Benjamin Horace Hibbard, *A History of the Public Land Policies* (New York, 1924), pp. 463-65.

[8] *Congressional Record*, 46 Cong., 2 Sess., pp. 125, 1695, 3231, 3266-70; *ibid.*, 46 Cong., 3 Sess., pp. 712-14, 754-61.

make the title to the minerals go with the general land title in these cases, he secured the adoption of other amendments to protect the right of the landowner against damage by the owner of the mineral rights. He brought in a bill in the Forty-sixth Congress to amend the law governing the securing of a mining claim, which was passed and became a law. On nearly all legislation affecting mining and public lands he offered perfecting amendments which improved the character of the bills, although he was not at this time on either the Mines and Mining or the Public Lands committee.

At the convening of the Forty-sixth Congress the Democrats were in control of both houses. Among their efforts to make political thunder for the campaign of 1880 was an attack upon Postmaster General David M. Key, by means of the Western mail routes. This attack upon the star routes was largely sectional in its nature, and the suspicion of extensive corruption in the system—later found to be correct—made it peculiarly susceptible to attack.

The star routes were those where the distances were so great, transportation facilities so poor, and population so scattered, that the revenues did not pay the cost of maintaining the service. Eastern newspapers and senators criticized the system severely, maintaining that the postal service should be self-supporting, and all unprofitable routes should be discontinued. The attack on Postmaster General Key came because of his improvement of this system by increasing weekly to semiweekly and sometimes daily service. Teller declared:

> I know what every man ought to know who has given attention to the history of the country ... that these star route services are the great engines which open up the Western country to civilization. We first open with slow mail.... In a little while come heavier settlements, more people, and they demand ... increased facilities.... Is there any reason why the government should not support the postal services as it supports the Army? ... He [Key] has given us a service infinitely better than was ever given to the people west of the Mississippi River.

Teller threatened to vote against the deficiency appropriation for the postal service unless the strictures on Key in the preamble were struck out. An amendment to this effect carried, before the bill passed both the Senate and the House.[9]

---

[9] *Ibid.*, 46 Cong., 2 Sess., pp. 1589, 1631; New York *Tribune*, April 3, 1880.

When a bill came before the Senate to renounce formally the debt the states contracted during the distribution of the surplus in the Federal treasury in the year 1837, Teller opposed it. He had no illusions that this "debt" would ever be repaid, but an occasion to read the Eastern senators a homily upon the golden rule he could not overlook.

> My experience has taught me that twenty-eight interested States are pretty sure to find votes in the Senate and in the House sufficient to pass a bill like this.... But when there was a bill here that was in the special interest of a few of the Western States, and when we were asking for the mere letter of the law, as we thought, the payment of 5 per cent on the sales of public lands, pretty much every Senator who voted for it was charged by Senators representing the States that derive the greatest benefit from this bill with being moved entirely by a desire to appropriate a portion of the public Treasury that did not belong to us.[10]

The problem which attracted Teller's attention more than any other in this period was the Indian question, and it remained permanently as one of his principal interests. On few subjects was he better qualified to legislate. All his life he had been in direct contact with Indians. In western New York his home had been close to a reservation, and at one time he had taught a school on its very edge. In Colorado he had had experience with the aborigines in a different stage of culture, and not infrequently his contacts had been like those of 1864 when he helped to prepare Denver for an anticipated attack, or when during his frequent trips across the plains he had found it necessary to go heavily armed. To these personal contacts he added a considerable knowledge gained from the study of the history of the problem in the United States, Mexico, and Canada. Here, as in the case of the public lands, there had always been a difference in attitude between the Easterner and the Westerner, even as far back as the colonial period, when the British Government represented the East.

When Teller entered the Senate in 1876, the Indian danger was being removed by the rapid disappearance of the frontier. This same elimination of wild country made the problem of fitting the Indian to civilized life more acute than ever. Custer had been killed the same year Teller went to Washington, and the policy of "peace on the plains" was still little more than a pious wish. Like the issue of conservation of timber, this problem brought Teller in opposition to

---

[10] *Congressional Record*, 46 Cong., 3 Sess., p. 264.

the official policy of the Department of the Interior and its Secretary, Carl Schurz. It is peculiar that these two men whose policies were alike on many questions should have been at swords' points over matters which each, as Secretary of the Interior, had a large influence in solving. Teller's opposition does not need to be put down to the political antagonism which had led to the popular sport among Republican politicians of taking "a whack at Schurz."[11] It arose from essential difference in policy, and from the pressing needs of the West at the time.

Teller had no touch of the too common frontier attitude that the only good Indian was a dead Indian. The outbreak of the Nez Perces under the leadership of Chief Joseph roused his admiration. When an appropriation bill came before the Senate to pay for their removal to Indian Territory he opposed it as unjust to the Indians. He compared their military feat with that of the ten thousand Greeks. As to the justice of their war, he declared:

> I believe no set of men ever went to war in the history of wars who had a better cause for war than the Nez Perce Indians, and if we paid out a million dollars it was our fault and not theirs.

He offered an amendment to the bill to force their return to Idaho but that was defeated. Then he supported an amendment to make their removal to Indian Territory contingent upon their consent, which also lost.[12] It is necessary to keep this phase of Teller's activity on the Indian question well in mind for one can otherwise fall into the error of classifying him with the enemies of that race. He had his own ideas of what constituted a statesmanlike policy, and to carry it out he sometimes worked with the professional defenders of the Indians such as Dawes and Hoar, and at other times with the more typical Westerners such as Plumb.

In his first years in Washington, no other problem held Teller's interest like that of the Ute Indians in Colorado. These natives had ceded a large part of their occupied land to the National Government three years before in return for an annuity. This the Government had neglected to pay in any manner that was satisfactory to the Utes, and in retaliation the Indians had begun to commit various depredations upon white settlers, usually no more serious than killing cattle or burning farm buildings. As these attacks easily

---

[11] *The Nation*, Jan. 16, 1879.
[12] *Congressional Record*, 45 Cong., 2 Sess., pp. 3236-39, 3266.

alarmed the settlers, who naturally feared more dangerous ones, it was a problem that deserved immediate attention.

After trying to secure a better arrangement for paying the annuities, Teller made careful inquiry in Colorado regarding the situation. When he returned to Washington in the fall of 1877 he was regularly in receipt of reports from Governor Routt regarding the situation—reports that frequently included requests to exert pressure on the War Department for troops and munitions to be used for protection. The deluge of unsolicited letters that descended upon Teller regarding the problem included everything from petitions from frightened and illiterate settlers to propositions which offered to make him wealthy by cutting him in on rich mining land then on the reservation. The most spectacular of the latter was a suggestion that if he and Chaffee would arrange the purchase of the land from the Indians, they, together with Governor Routt and James A. Garfield, would be included in a company of eight for the exploitation of the mineral land.[13] For more accurate information, Teller made inquiries among those who knew the Ute Indians through personal contact. The story he got from these persons was usually the same—corruption and inefficiency in the Indian Service and consequent failure to pay promptly the promised annuities kept the Utes hostile. "They [the Utes] are deserving of a great deal of credit for their sensible and orderly actions in the matter," wrote Uriah N. Curtis, certainly one of the best informed and intentioned of the experts.[14] "I fully agree with you," wrote Governor Routt, "that if the Indians are properly treated & the *Govt*. will fulfill its part of the contract according to treaty stipulations, we will have no trouble with them."[15]

By March 12, 1878, the Governor was writing Teller, "You are to be congratulated upon your success in getting our Indian matters in as good condition as they are.... Keep up the fight for the Indian Annuities, as their payment is the

[13] Agnes E. Spiva, "The Utes in Colorado" (unpublished thesis, University of Colorado, 1929), pp. 66-70 ; John T. Routt to Teller, Nov. 12, Dec. 17, 20, 31, 1877, Teller Letters. The proposal was from O. L. Matthews, of Ouray, Nov. 25, 1877, Teller Letters. Matthews obviously did not know Teller, as he gave him Garfield's name as a reference. The Ohio Congressman had been Matthews' schoolmate. Of a different character but tending in the same direction was a note from C. S. Thomas, rising young Democratic lawyer. "That such a country [near Ouray], rich with such splendid resources should be kept apart for the use of a wandering band of dirty savages, when it could so greatly add to the material wealth and prosperity of the entire State, is a matter which will suggest itself to you without further words from me." Jan. 28, 1878, Teller Letters.

[14] Teller Letters. Undated, probably Dec., 1877.

[15] Dec. 17, 1877, Teller Letters.

only thing that will prevent trouble." What Teller had done
had been to insist upon the payment of annuities and the removal of the agent. For a successor he recommended Uriah
N. Curtis. "I know Mr. Curtis & think he is a valuable man.
He is well acquainted with the Utes & speaks their language."[16] But Curtis was a citizen of Wyoming, and N. C.
Meeker, of the Greeley *Tribune,* was appointed, perhaps with
Teller's subsequent endorsement. Meeker, formerly agricultural expert on the staff of the New York *Tribune,* was
an honest and able man, but his knowledge of the Utes was
distinctly limited. Soon after he reached the agency he wrote
Teller a long report detailing the corruption and mismanagement that had preceded his appointment. He appealed to
Teller to use his influence with the Indian Bureau to secure
approval of the removal of the agency to a location to which
supplies could be sent without such great cost, and where
agriculture was possible. Under the rules from Washington
he could not issue rations to any Indian who did not work—
at farming. Actually, no farming was possible near the
agency.[17]

The agency was finally moved, and that made more
trouble because of the work involved, and because the Utes
naturally objected to creating a situation where they would
be forced to do farm work. When Meeker tried to carry out
the Bureau's orders and force the Indians to do farm work,
trouble began which reached a bloody climax in the fall of
1879. One group of the Indians attacked the White River
Agency, killed Meeker and his helpers, took three white
women captive, and outraged them. When a body of troops
under Major T. T. Thornburgh moved toward the agency
it was attacked, Thornburgh killed, and the Utes driven off
with great difficulty. This violent culmination of the long
series of Ute scares in Colorado filled the local people with
firm determination that such an uprising should not occur
again. Secretary Schurz attempted to find a policy that
would protect the Indians and also quiet public excitement
in Colorado. An army on its way to attack the Indians who
had opposed Thornburgh was stopped and peace negotiations
instituted through Chief Ouray. The women captives were
released. Then Ouray, accompanied by some other leaders of

---

[16] Note added to a letter from Curtis, Jan. 11, 1878, Teller Letters.
[17] Meeker to Teller, May 2 and especially May 27, 1878, Teller Letters.

the Utes, went to Washington in order to make an agreement with the Indian Bureau.[18]

These negotiations went so steadily in favor of the Utes it soon became obvious that the Indians guilty of the attack would escape punishment. This was very distasteful to Teller, although it must be confessed that the principal demand in Colorado was that the reservation be opened to settlement. In the meantime, Teller had acquired a new colleague in the person of Nathaniel P. Hill, of Blackhawk. The means of his election had left many political and personal antagonisms that made it difficult for the two senators to work together. As Congress was assembling in December, Hill announced himself as a supporter of the Indian Bureau agreement. Teller, however, introduced a resolution asking for the documents and prepared to contest the "treaty" when it reached the Senate. Late in February the Committee on Indian Affairs brought in a bill to ratify the agreement, and Teller countered with a series of amendments. The Governor of Colorado wrote Senator Hill that "People here universally favor Teller's proposed amendments." The obvious practicability of some of them forced the committee to substitute for the original bill one which embodied some of Teller's proposals.

As it then stood, the principal features of the bill were that the Utes gave up a large part of their reservation, for which they were to receive land in severalty and certain annuities. The White River Utes—those primarily concerned in the recent outbreak—were to be sent to the Uintah Reservation in northern Utah. The most notable change in policy was the granting of Indian lands in severalty. It was hoped by many friends of the Indians that severalty would result in their becoming peaceful farmers. This idea had become a cure-all among Indian reformers, and they induced Schurz—unwisely, as it proved—to make it a part of the solution of the Ute problem. The bill was popular in Colorado. It would open almost the entire great Ute Reservation to white settlement. William N. Byers wrote to Teller:

We all admire and approve your position and pluck on the Schurz-Ute bill. But a large majority of reasoning and reasonable men with whom I talk think you had better consent to the bill which will open

---

[18] Spiva, *op. cit.*, pp. 85-113; *Senate Executive Document*, 46 Cong., 2 Sess., Nos. 29 and 31; *House Miscellaneous Documents*, 46 Cong., 2 Sess., No. 38; Carl Schurz, *Speeches, Correspondence, and Political Papers*, edited by F. Bancroft (New York, 1913), III, 503-06.

about eleven twelfths of the reservation and remove all question as to
the right of mineral and other claims thereon. Then we will inaugurate
a fight for the balance. ... I fear if the present is rejected and Ouray
continues his masterly tactics we will have to submit to an enlargement
of the present reservation.[19]

But Teller had decided that the bill should be opposed.
"I am not here to be dictated to by anybody on this question,"
he declared when it was shown that opinion in Colorado favored the revised bill. Characterizing the plan as "an easy
solution of the Indian problem in one lesson," Teller delivered what the New York *Tribune* called a "furious assault
upon the policy of the Secretary of Interior." The advocates
of the new policy of severalty were the objects of Teller's
sarcasm:

These men knowing nothing of the magnitude of the undertaking,
assumed the responsibility without a doubt as to their success. All
other men are fools! Now will the Indian be civilized and Christian-
ized in a twelvemonth! He is to become self-supporting, and the great
drain on the public Treasury for his support will cease at once.

Teller pointed out that communal landholdings had
always been the Indian practice and that individual holdings
were against his customs and religion.

... the great trouble in our dealing with the Indian is our ignorance
of his laws, customs, character, and religion. We insist on treating
him as if he were a civilized man, when he ought to be treated as a
savage, full of superstitions and weaknesses that belong to savage life.

He ridiculed the idea that the Indians who had signed the
agreement knew what holding land in severalty meant, and
his criticism of the method of dealing with the Utes was
extremely severe.

I am sick of the Department management of Indian affairs. I do
not refer to the present officials, but I am sick of the management of
the past twenty-five years. ... [There] is not 5 per cent of the men
who have been on the border as Indian agents for twenty years,
that want to civilize the Indians. ... They know that when they have
done that their occupation is gone; their opportunities for stealing
and plunder are gone. ...

Teller showed that the Indians had won every important
point in controversy in their negotiations with the Indian
Bureau, that no one under the bill would be punished for the

---

[19] Governor Pitkin to Hill, March 24, Governor Pitkin to Teller, March 24, 1880, F.
W. Pitkin Letterbook; William N. Byers to Teller, March 20, 1880, Byers Letterbook;
Congressional Record, 46 Cong., 2 Sess., pp. 1768, 1797, 2001, 2059-65; Spiva, *op. cit.*,
pp. 114-34.

murders at the White River Agency or the attack on Thornburgh, but rather that the Utes were being rewarded by
increasing their annuities for no other reason that they
would understand except their depredations. The guilty
Indians, Teller emphasized, should be punished severely or
there would be continuous trouble with the Utes and the
Colorado frontier would not be safe. He preached a harsh
doctrine, and his colleague, Hill, called it a "narrow and
selfish view." It is worth while to note that some thirty
years later James McLaughlin, an expert whose devotion
to the Indians is unquestioned, had this to say about the same
affair:

> I say it with no bitterness toward the people themselves, but I
> feel certain that if the Utes had been thoroughly chastised after the
> Meeker massacre of 1879, they would not be the irresponsible, shiftless,
> and defiant people they are today.... They escaped retributive justice
> at a period of their tribal existence when the sense of their ill-doings
> was strong upon them, and they are the worse for it.

The only material changes Teller was able to get into the
second bill were to increase the annuities to the widows of
the murdered men, and to add an appropriation to provide
irrigation for the lands which were to be taken in severalty.
That the lands were untillable without irrigation had escaped the Secretary and the members of the committee. It
then passed the Senate with only fifteen votes in addition to
Teller's against it.[20]

Teller's prediction of failure for the severalty policy
among the Utes was proved correct by subsequent developments. The place assigned to them was found unsuitable,
and no land had been allotted the following summer when
Teller visited those on the La Plata River. It confirmed him
in his opposition to severalty. When a bill was brought in
to extend that policy to certain other tribes, Teller suggested
it be entitled, "A bill to despoil the Indians of their land and
make them vagabonds upon the face of the earth." He
quoted protests against the plan from the most capable Indian farmers, the Five Civilized Tribes of Indian Territory.
Agriculture was the important thing, Teller maintained,
and not lands in severalty.

As the bill would make all Indians taking land in severalty subject to state law except that land could not be alien-

[20] New York *Tribune*, April 3, 7, 1880; *Congressional Record*, 46 Cong., 2 Sess.,
pp. 2059-65, 2787-88; James McLaughlin, *My Friend the Indian* (Boston and New
York, 1910), pp. 372-87.

ated for twenty-five years, Teller introduced an amendment
providing that no Indian should be punished for polygamy
who was practicing it at the time he received his allotment
of land. This was adopted. Teller repeatedly insisted that
all these restrictions were of no value, because as soon as the
tribal status was broken the Indian was subject completely
to state law.[21]

Teller's attitude on Indian affairs forecast his policy as
Secretary of the Interior. From the first he had not taken
kindly to Schurz's plan of educating Indians at special
Eastern schools. In the Forty-seventh Congress, Senator
Dawes proposed an amendment to the Indian appropriation
bill to add five hundred thousand dollars for education.
Teller supported this amendment but used the opportunity
to express himself upon that subject.

> When you take these children to Carlisle and send them back they
> will be skilled in some things ... but the danger is that if you do not
> have a mass for them to associate with who have notions like unto
> theirs they will go right back to the same condition that their ancestors
> were in and they themselves were in before they were taken to Carlisle.
> Is that to be the history of Indian education? ... I will admit that it
> is very difficult to educate them if you allow them to go home and
> stay at the lodges over night; and yet I believe that the education of
> the children will have some little influence upon the adults, and I be-
> lieve that if you could bring the school within a reasonable distance,
> where the parents could occasionally go and see that their children
> were taken care of, where they could see that they were not improperly
> treated, it would add very much to the system. The Indian is as much
> attached to his children as the white man is.[22]

Part of Teller's great interest in Indian affairs was
brought about by his belief in their importance to the West.
He spoke on the question frequently when his chief purpose
was to defend the Westerners against charges of cruelty
against the Indian. When Senator Dawes presented a resolution on the Indian question signed by a large number of
prominent men and women, which directly intimated that
the people of the West were responsible for the difficulties
of the Indian problem, Teller arose to the defense of his
chosen people:

> It is not so, Mr. President. If they [treaties] have been violated
> the responsibility is with this body and not with the people of the
> frontier, who have greater interests at stake, who are more concerned
> in maintaining peaceable relations with the Indians than any other

---

[21] *Congressional Record*, 46 Cong., 3 Sess., pp. 780-82, 934, 1028.
[22] *Ibid.*, 46 Cong., 3 Sess., pp. 783, 1028; *ibid.*, 47 Cong., 1 Sess., p. 2475.

people in the world. . . . By their side we live, by their side we expect to
live, and by their side, if they do not expire in the course of time,
must our children live; and is it to be supposed that we want to
despoil them or keep them degraded? . . . I have as much regard for the
people who suffered in Colorado as for the people in Massachusetts who
are sympathizing with the Indians. I can safely say that some of the
people who suffered by that raid . . . are the peers, intellectually and
morally of the petitioners, or at least most of them. They are not
ignorant barbarians. They are made poor in property and poor in
spirit by the outrages perpetrated, and the Senator [Dawes] has
never found time to say a kindly word for them.[23]

The standing illustration of the pioneer's cruelty to the
Indian was the Sand Creek Massacre, and when anyone
wanted an example of the unworthiness of Westerners he
usually fell back upon it. It was shortly before Teller entered
the Cabinet that Senator Hoar quoted a part of the Senate
report on the tragedy in connection with another matter.
Teller immediately attacked its validity and defended the
character of the troops engaged in that affair. He gave a
detailed account of the incident and its surrounding conditions. He denied that it was a massacre, although he did
not deny atrocities on the part of the white soldiers.[24]

Teller never denied that injustice had been done to the
Indian, but he did insist that the fault here did not lie with
the Western pioneer. Easterners, whose ancestors had killed
off their Indians, were blaming the present evil condition of
Indian affairs upon his section, and the senator from Colorado was not the one to let that pass.

How far Teller's attitude differed from some other
Westerners' with wide experience among the Indians can be
seen in the following remarks from a speech of Senator
Plumb's delivered on the Ute question.

There is no possible education that can ever be given to a full-
blooded Indian . . . which will ever enable him to compete in any considerable degree in an industrial occupation or employment. . . .

He is simply here to get out of the way at the proper time. . . . Within fifty years there will not be probably one single full-blooded Indian
on the American continent; and within a hundred years there will not
be a single person living who in his features or in his blood will bear
the impress of a single characteristic of the Indian character. He will
be entirely gone.[25]

<hr>

[23] *Ibid.*, 47 Cong., 1 Sess., p. 1329.

[24] *Ibid.*, 47 Cong., 1 Sess., pp. 2455-56. In spite of these lapses from a pro-Indian
policy Teller was already accepted as trustworthy by the friends of that race. Those
who were attempting to drive the notorious "Indian Ring" out of the service, especially,
accepted his judgment on appointments. J. B. Wolff to H. L. Dawes, April 17, 1881,
Dawes MSS.

[25] *Congressional Record*, 46 Cong., 2 Sess., p. 2257.

One could easily think of reservation-born Charles
Curtis, one of Plumb's successors as senator from Kansas,
and subsequently Vice-President of the United States, as
divine retribution.

CHAPTER VIII

NATIONAL POLICIES AND POLITICS
1877-82

NATIONAL and local politics conspired to end the old antagonism between Chaffee and Teller soon after they reached the Senate. Possibly Teller's willingness to let Chaffee lead, or appear to lead, paved the way for reconciliation.[1] Teller's own partisans complained that the Denver papers were giving Chaffee credit for all both men were doing in Washington; but Teller was not disturbed, as the question of his re-election seemed to be in the distant future, whereas Chaffee's would be decided in the legislature elected in 1878. The immediate problems of the new state had forced the two senators to co-operate in order to get results, and the associations which resulted soon brought them into mutually satisfactory personal relations. This was hailed with joy by Republican friends in Colorado who had been embarrassed by a desire to work with both of them.[2] The close agreement between them also included Governor John L. Routt and James B. Belford, the Republican candidate for Colorado's seat in Congress, whose claims had been disallowed in favor of the Democrat, Thomas M. Patterson. By the spring of 1878 the relations between the senators were so close that during Chaffee's illness Teller was handling the patronage correspondence of both, with full power to act.[3]

When Teller and Chaffee reached Washington in 1876, they entered the lame duck session of the last Congress of Grant's last term as president. The presidency was soon to pass to Rutherford B. Hayes, who represented a somewhat different Republican Party than did Grant. The elder statesmen, Conkling, Blaine, Sherman, Cameron, and Morton, representing the older control of the party, were not congenial.

[1] In 1888, a then very unfriendly critic wrote of Teller: "He is master of the Machiavelian diplomacy of indirection, and he cajoled Chaffee and flattered his vanity by allowing the latter to lead him (or even appear to drive him) if it happened to be in the direction he wanted to go." Fitz-Mac (James McCarty), *Political Portraits* (Colorado Springs, 1888), p. 67.

[2] Irving W. Stanton wrote Teller in response to a favorable comment on his colleague: "I am glad to hear you speak of him as you do, and have always told him that you and he did not know each other. I feel an especial interest in the matter from the fact that I have always labored to bring about an understanding between you, fully convinced that the result would be a due appreciation of each other. I know him well. He is a true friend, and nobleman at heart." June 7, 1878, Teller Letters.

[3] Chaffee to Teller, May 7, 1878, Teller Letters.

Personal animosities were to create two main factions headed by Conkling and Blaine, together with some smaller groups. Both large factions were united against the President's Southern policies to a degree that justified Rhodes's much-quoted phrase, "Within six weeks after his inauguration Hayes was without a party." In the Senate his personal support was limited to Senators Hoar, Dawes, and Matthews. More of the President's appointees were rejected by the Senate than those of any other executive in the fifty years previous. Only the Democratic attacks on the Federal election laws and Hayes's title to his office brought the Republican members of Congress to his support.

Teller found himself rushed into this situation without time to orient himself in national affairs. He had studied national politics all his adult life, and could not have been in serious doubt as to policies, but he must have felt some uneasiness as to where he should place himself in respect to factions. Although never an extreme partisan, his old and new political contacts all tended to unite him with the Conkling "Stalwarts." His friendship with the New York senator, beginning in the fight over statehood in 1868, was an important tendency in this direction. Governor Routt was a Stalwart and Grant's intimate friend. While in the House of Representatives, Chaffee had frequently worked with this group and was now a personal confident of Grant's. His daughter was soon to marry U. S. Grant, Jr., and thus unite the two families. Chaffee was particularly intimate with Logan, Stalwart Illinois senator, but, like the astute political manager he was, he also kept a firm foot planted in the "Half-Breed" ranks.[4] His close associations, however, were with the Stalwarts, and as he and Teller gradually forgot their old enmities they inclined strongly to work together in national politics. These tendencies brought Teller into a fairly close relationship with the Stalwart Republican machine. In the long contest between Hayes and Conkling over the New York patronage, Teller supported the New York senator consistently, even voting against the confirmation of Hayes's appointees after it became well known that resistance was useless.

This contest was Teller's first contact with the questions of the civil service and patronage. At no time did he call

---

[4] Chaffee had urged Logan on Hayes for Secretary of War. In doing so he added: "I am authorized to say that Senator Blaine concurs as well as many other republicans with whom I have talked upon this subject." Chaffee to Hayes, Feb. 16, 1877, Hayes MSS.

himself a reformer or an advocate of the merit system; but the fight between Conkling and the administration for control of the New York customs office, together with the removal of certain appointees from office in Colorado, gave Teller a principle upon which to act. This was that competent officers should not be removed without cause. It may be that the principle was an unconscious outgrowth of a desire to help Conkling and protect his own Colorado friends, but he followed it consistently, and at times to extremes that were politically dangerous.

At first he had a difficult time defending his own course to brother Willard, who felt that H. M. was far too much governed by partisan considerations. Willard wrote:

> Of course Civil Service run as you say is a fraud, but you are one of the men whose duty it is to see that it is not allowed to be so. What I say is this—if removal of good men is attempted without investigation *vote no*, if appoinment of unfit men is made *vote no* & let it be clearly understood that it is for the reason that they are good men and should be retained or are bad men and should not be appointed or at least that you think so. I don't think I care but little for place but I'll be blessed if I would not give $1,000 to have the chance to *smite* by vote & voice either the Pres. or any other man when he attempted to make appointments or removals of the kind you speak of. Judge Davis [an Independent] is the only man in the Senate whose position I *envy*, & if I was there today elected by R. votes I should at all times on all occasions & with reference to all appointments & removals vote exactly as I thought best as to men, party or no party, Pres., or no Pres.—& then let them howl.... That's what I mean by supporting the Pres. & that's how far I would oppose him.[5]

The President's undoubtedly sincere desire for civil-service reform was exploited by his advisers and subordinates to partisan advantage elsewhere than in New York. This made a particularly difficult problem for the Colorado senators. The state's long experience under territorial government had given the politicians and public an immense distaste for carpetbag officials who were appointed by the Federal Government from outside the state, or, if local men, were frequently those who would have been extremely unlikely to hold a public office which was responsive to public demand. Now that admission into the Union had been accomplished, the Colorado public and the state Republican organization expected its senators to secure the appointment of Federal officials in the state who would be locally popular. With the inauguration of Hayes, Teller and Chaffee faced

---

[5] Nov. 16, 1877, Teller Letters.

the same problem as the other Republican senators, except in their case it was magnified by the carpetbag complex at home. Not long after the inauguration, the Colorado senators called upon the President to discuss certain appointments in Colorado.[6] The result of this meeting was unsatisfactory to the senators, and it marked the beginning of the ill feeling that characterized the entire administration. The tendency to align himself with the opposition to Hayes was not easy, as many of Teller's friends defended the President and urged Teller to support him. Even Uncle Henry at Erie, Pennsylvania, wrote to defend Hayes's general policy, to damn Conkling and Blaine, and, the unkindest cut of all, perhaps, to defend Secretary Schurz as a "profound statesman."[7] But the lack of patronage for the organization in Colorado, added to the dissatisfaction with the land and Indian policies of the Interior Department, determined the issue as far as Teller was concerned.

Circumstances also conspired to align Teller with the regular party members who were to oppose President Hayes's Southern policy. Nine days after he was admitted to the Senate, Teller left Washington for Florida as a member of a subcommittee of the Senate Committee on Privileges and Elections to investigate the presidential election in that state. The subcommittee left Washington on December 13, 1876, and spent the next month in Tallahassee, Jacksonville, and Gainesville taking evidence regarding the disputed presidential returns. The House, controlled by the Democrats, dispatched committees to each of the disputed states, and the Senate, controlled by the Republicans, did likewise. These had little influence upon the result, but the trip to Florida and the picture of Reconstruction politics that came before the committee confirmed Teller's agreement with the Radical Republicans. It was his first experience in this region, and his impressions were not favorable. "I am not in love with Florida either the country or the people," he wrote a Central City friend.[8]

The action of the President in withdrawing support from those Republican governments that still existed in the South was another bitter pill for many Republicans. His attempt to create a more respectable Republican Party there

---

[6] New York *Tribune*, Nov. 19, 1877.

[7] Jan. 19, 1878. Also letters of Henry C. Leach, Jan. 16, and T. N. Haskell, Jan. 30, 1878, Teller Letters.

[8] *Senate Reports*, 44 Cong., 2 Sess., No. 611; Teller to Harper Orahood, Dec. 30, 1876, Teller-Orahood MSS.

Jerome B. Chaffee, wealthy Denver politician, territorial delegate to Congress, Colorado's first senator, and a frequent foe of Teller.

by using appointments to attract former Democrats to the Republican Party only excited disgust at its obvious ineffectiveness. The party in the North was no doubt opposed to it, and the President's own state of Ohio went Democratic in the fall of 1877. Teller's letters late in 1877 indicate the direction of his thinking:

The Ohio election has made the Democrats wild with joy & has made the Rep. all mad. Even Garfield is ready to fight Hayes. All say that the Civil Service reform is a humbug & that the President only requires its enforcement as to the applications of Members & Senators, that he when his friends *want* anything pays no attention to it & if there is no vacancy he makes one.

As for Civil Service it is a fraud on the people. The President talks Civil Service & violates its rules everyday. He is mighty thin— I think the smallest man that ever was President. He thinks he is a great man a 2nd George Washington only somewhat improved.... The fact is that Hayes is an exceedingly vain weak man & thinks he is making a record for goodness etc. He really believes that he can build up a party in the South that will help elect a Rep. President in 1880. What an *Idiot* he is.[9]

Teller's experience in investigating the Florida election paved the way for another which was to bring him into national prominence for the first time. When Congress assembled after the election of 1878, a Senate resolution was adopted to have a special committee investigate the congressional elections in certain states where there was suspicion of fraud. This was a Republican move to secure evidence of political corruption in the South for use in the campaign of 1880. When the older Republican senators could not agree upon one of their number for the chairmanship, it was offered to Teller, already agreed upon as a committee member. Commented the Republican New York *Tribune:*

The Committee is a strong one.... The chairman, Mr. Teller, though new to the Senate, is a very able lawyer, and a persistent pushing man. He is in the habit of going to the bottom of any subject he attacks.[10]

A subcommittee, with Teller in charge, left for New Orleans early in January. The chairman made a favorable impression there. Observed the New Orleans *Times:*

Altogether he is a pleasant sort of man to meet, and looks as if he has come to perform his duty and will perform it, although he is evidently not overly jubilant about it.[11]

---

[9] Teller to Orahood, Oct. 14, Dec. 18, 1877, Teller-Orahood MSS.
[10] *Congressional Record,* 45 Cong., 3 Sess., p. 304 ; New York *Tribune,* Dec. 18, 19, 20, 27, 1878.
[11] New Orleans *Times,* Jan. 7, 1879.

In this city they listened to tales of violence in elections
that were some of the worst in the history of American
politics. "We are at work," Teller wrote to a friend on
January 8, "& I guess we can find enough to keep us here
all the time we have to stay. It is damnable evidence &
proves these fellows are savages."[12]

After taking testimony here they went on to Charleston,
South Carolina, where they held similar hearings. When
they returned to Washington in February, some evidence
was also taken in regard to Mississippi. Teller, as chairman,
took the leading part in questioning the witnesses, worked
his committee hard, and probably wrote the majority report.
This was presented to Congress on March 1, and was ordered
printed. The hearings before the committee had been public
and attracted a great deal of attention. Special correspondents covered the hearings for the important daily papers,
and the opposition press admitted that "there was no un-
fairness in the action of the committee."[13]

The majority report was a fair summary of the testimony, although the Democratic members of the subcommittee refused to sign it. "In Louisiana both violence and
fraud was extensively used; in South Carolina, while violence was not rare, fraud was more largely relied upon."

The aim, the report pointed out, was to perpetuate regular Democratic control. Independent Democrats, even
though they were white and Confederate veterans, were
treated as badly as Negro Republicans when they opposed
the regular party nominees. National legislation to prevent
this, at least in regard to the election of congressmen, was
recommended.[14]

In the closing days of the Forty-fifth Congress a debate
which extended over into the next Congress served to unite
the Republicans behind the President. The Democratic
majority in the House had attached to certain appropriation
bills riders repealing the Federal election laws. The Republican Senate disagreed, and a partisan debate on the election
laws was the result. Teller participated only when Senator
Morgan charged Republican corruption in the election in
Colorado, an ideal counterattack against the report of the
Teller committee. Having just returned from the Southern
investigation, Teller was not only able to reply to the

---

12 Teller to Orahood, Jan. 8, 1879, Teller-Orahood MSS.

13 News and Courier (Charleston), Jan. 31, 1879.

14 Senate Reports, 45 Cong., 3 Sess., No. 855; Congressional Record, 45 Cong., 3 Sess.,
p. 2189.

charges against Colorado, but also to contrast electoral methods used there with those used in the Louisiana and South Carolina elections. "His speech in defense of his people and his arraignment of the Southern bulldozers made one of the most telling effects of the debate," wrote a delighted Republican editor.[15]

Because of the disagreement between the two houses, the appropriation bills failed of passage, and President Hayes called a special session of the Forty-sixth Congress to meet on March 18. In the new Congress, the Democrats had majorities in both houses for the first time since the Civil War, and the temptation to use the opportunity to force the President to accept the repeal of the election laws as the price of appropriations was too great to be resisted. To President Hayes this was "revolution," and his conciliatory attitude toward the South was found to have distinct limits. The special session was taken up with the partisan debate engendered by this situation. Commented *The Nation:*

> They are having a delightful time in Congress on both sides in the complete absence of all serious business. One side is giving loud utterance to the "rebel yell," while the other is rescuing Anthony Burns from the custody of the United States Marshall at Boston.[16]

The official issue for debate was the appropriation bills with the riders on the subject of the election laws.

Teller made one long, partisan speech during this debate. He defended the President's use of the veto power, and quoted from Democratic platforms and statements to show that they had approved of its free exercise in the past. He pointed out several well-known vetoes of Democratic presidents, not forgetting, Western-like, Buchanan's veto of the homestead law, and attempted to show an inconsistency between their present position and that of the party in the past. Always, in his somewhat deaconlike manner, he quoted chapter and verse. He defended the constitutionality of Federal control of elections in a legal argument quoting Supreme Court decisions and the practice of Democratic administrations before 1861. Then he went on to describe electoral conditions in the South, painting an unpleasant picture: "This sudden fear of the Army has grown out of the fear of protection of a people who are entitled to vote

---

[15] *Congressional Record*, 45 Cong., 3 Sess., pp. 1025-28; New York *Tribune*, Feb. 6 1879.

[16] C. R. Williams, *Life of Rutherford B. Hayes*, (Boston and New York, 1914), II. 170-207; *The Nation*, April 3, 1879.

[and who] must have national protection or they will have no protection at all."

This was sound Republicanism, and it could hardly be foreseen that its author would one day prevent the passage of the Force bill. However, even by this time Teller had broken with his party by opposing the use of the military as a part of a *posse comitatus* in enforcing election laws. The contest continued for some time. But Hayes's firm refusal to make concessions, and the vigorous defense of the Republicans in Congress, brought about victory for their party.[17]

Teller once more made use of the information gained by the committee in the Senate. This was just as the session before the election of 1880 was drawing to a close. The Senate was devoting itself "with patriotic singleness of purpose to the work of formulating issues for the campaign." Teller delivered the principal Republican speech, in which he gave a detailed description of the Democratic frauds in South Carolina. Although it was partisan and meant for campaign use, it was not extreme and contained no suggestion of waving the bloody shirt. In the words of an overenthusiastic Republican, "He assailed the Democracy as a party unmercifully. He wound up by declaring that the party had done nothing in the present Congress, and did not dare do anything—not even go into caucus upon any measure of public importance. They were a unit only in regard to the removal of such safeguards as still remained about the ballot box."[18]

Politics in Colorado had developed along lines that were not satisfactory to Teller. The main factor was that Chaffee retired, or tried to retire. His health was very bad in the spring of 1878, and the fight with President Hayes disgusted him with national politics. Moreover, he had issued a very conservative statement on the monetary question that had been badly received at home. The result of all this was that Chaffee abruptly announced that he would not be a candidate for re-election to the Senate. He wrote Teller:

I never felt better over any act of my life. I am perfectly willing anybody else shall occupy all the places in the Government. I want no more of them. There is no dignity practiced in the Senate, nothing but a scramble for the floor. I think you take the right course in ignoring men and working for the Party. There will doubtless be a great scramble for my place. Whoever gets it I hope will be better

---

[17] *Congressional Record*, 46 Cong., 1 Sess., pp. 511-17.
[18] *Ibid.*, 46 Cong., 2 Sess., pp. 3750 ff.; New York *Tribune*, undated clipping, 1880.

satisfied with it than I am and appreciate it more. I have not taken this step because I think any real necessity required it, but I am sick of the whole business—I'm sick of it, really disgusted with it and this gives me a good opportunity to get out. I don't think it will hurt the party. Every one will feel more necessity to work.[19]

With Chaffee out it was generally expected that his successor would come from southern Colorado, but in the Republican state convention a southern candidate, Frederick W. Pitkin, was named for the governorship. After his election that fall, the Republican-controlled legislature was not under the expected pressure to choose a senator from that region. Although not generally considered a possible successor at the time of Chaffee's resignation, Nathaniel P. Hill had long been actively preparing to contest for the senatorship, and Teller had been warned of it by friends.[20] Acting on the good advice of General W. A. Hamill and the Wolcott brothers, Hill contributed heavily to the Republican campaign fund, and quietly committed many of the party's candidates for the legislature to his cause.

With Chaffee's return to reasonably good health in the summer of 1878, he lost the disgust with politics that had induced him to announce a retirement. The prospect of Hill as his successor was far from pleasing to Chaffee, and from many Republican leaders in Colorado who noted the sharp contrast between Chaffee's easy management and Hill's imperious manner came pressure upon Chaffee to enter the race. Too late, as it proved, he became a candidate for re-election. Teller gave him his support,[21] but Hill's pledges from the members of the legislature were too numerous to be overcome. After a sharp, hot contest Hill received the caucus designation over Chaffee and was elected to the Senate. Hill had a large capacity for hate and he "never forgot or forgave Senator Chaffee" and his friends. His wealth, his strong Eastern connections, and his very accomplished wife enabled him to assume a prominent position in Washington society. He immediately allied himself with the Hayes administration—as, for instance, in his defense of Schurz's Indian policy—and began the distribution of the

[19] June 16, 1878, Teller Letters.

[20] John Truck to Teller, Jan. 3, 1878, Teller Letters.

[21] Willard Teller, to whom the politicians in Washington were "a precious lot of Rascals all around," was displeased when H. M. engaged actively in the struggle for Chaffee's re-election. Angered too by his neglect of some legal matters, the younger brother wrote to Orahood: "His head is so full of his political advancement that I fear he is forgetting everything honorable & praiseworthy in his pursuit of a 2nd term." Dec. 3, 1878, Teller Letters.

bulk of the patronage in Colorado. Teller was immediately put on the defensive to try to protect the Federal appointees in Colorado, most of whom he and Chaffee had recommended. The removal of these began almost immediately, and Teller had to warn even the best of them to watch their steps carefully and let no condition arise that would give a shadow of cause for complaint which could be used to justify a removal. Thus, from the opening of the Forty-sixth Congress in March, 1879, Teller had personal opposition in the Senate, in the Republican Party, and in Colorado which was politically uncomfortable.[22]

After his defeat for the Senate, Chaffee resumed his active control of Republican politics in Colorado. As the election of 1880 approached, Senator Hill came out for Blaine for president, and Chaffee with the assistance of Routt and Teller declared for the Stalwart candidate, Grant. Colorado's six delegates went to the national convention, and, with Chaffee and Teller there to help keep them in line, voted for Grant to the bitter end. After James A. Garfield was nominated, they supported Chester A. Arthur for the vice-presidential nomination.

With Garfield's election Teller's political position in Colorado continued insecure. Hill was the accepted leader of the Blaine Half-Breeds, and as this faction's influence in the administration grew, his control of the Colorado patronage increased. Chaffee and Teller were both on friendly personal terms with Garfield, and Chaffee was rendering him substantial aid in keeping General Grant from open opposition.[23] But Blaine's active fight on Conkling, by means of the Robertson appointment to the collectorship of the port of New York, was bound to place Teller at a greater distance from the President. His factional alliance and the declared principle of permanent tenure for competent officeholders on which he had based his entire defense of his own supporters in Colorado against Hill's attacks, would have to be repudiated if he voted for the confirmation of Robertson. Although the fight was hopeless he opposed this appointment to the end.

Teller had some influence in the administration through his friend S. J. Kirkwood, Secretary of the Interior. But

[22] N. P. Hill to Frank Hall, nine letters written in 1879, Frank Hall MSS.; W. N. Byers to Teller, Nov. 28, Dec. 9, 1879, Byers Letterbook; Charles S. Thomas, "Fifty Years of Political History," in James H. Baker and Leroy R. Hafen, *History of Colorado* (Denver, 1927), III, 909-10.

[23] Chaffee to Garfield, Jan. 10, June 30, 1881, Garfield MSS.

this was comparatively a small matter, and Hill's obvious control of the Federal patronage in Colorado drew to him all the pie-counter brigade. Coming up for re-election in 1883, with the national administration in the hands of his enemies for the most part, Teller's political future looked dark indeed in 1881 and the early months of 1882.[24]

Teller's time was not all occupied by practical politics and his role as defender of the West. He was ambitious to take a leading part in more national political questions, many of which affected his section only incidentally. In his position on these there was not much more in his background than the idealism of the antislavery fight that looked toward liberalism as it is interpreted today. True, there was in the rather mild political radicalism of Godkin little to which he was opposed, unless it conflicted with a definite sectional interest. He would and did say kind words for such unpopular proposals as votes for women. But this is about all that can be said for his liberalism at this period of his career. In general his reaction to national economic questions was what would naturally be expected from one of his background—a corporation lawyer, a mine owner, and the president of a small railroad.

In keeping with this was the first carefully prepared argument he gave in the Senate, which related to laws of 1862 and 1864 concerning the Union and Central Pacific Railroads. The proposal was to force the companies to provide sinking funds to pay the Government's loans. Teller objected to it on the constitutional ground that it impaired the obligation of contract. He argued that while there was no specific restriction in the Constitution forbidding the United States Government from impairing the obligation of contract, yet all constitutional principles and sound public policy were against it. "There never was a violation of constitutional law or individual rights by legislative action that did not find its excuse in the cry that the public good demanded it."[25]

Here, it would seem, was a rising politician well on his way to follow the path of the typical railroad senator of his generation. As the recipient of large fees from the Union Pacific in the past he found this was the natural road to take. "Jay Gould writes me complimenting you on your argument on the Funding Bill," Loveland informed Teller.

[24] Kirkwood to Teller, April 28, May 2, 9, 23, 1881, Kirkwood Letterbook, No. 1.
[25] Congressional Record, 45 Cong., 3 Sess., pp. 1932-34.

"He is well pleased. Says he heard your argument."[26] But this was to be the only time Teller fell into that rôle.

By 1881 he was sponsoring legislation to forfeit all land grants to railroads not already earned by the terms of legislation. Perhaps the key to this change was a shift in public sentiment in the West regarding such grants. Undoubtedly it was made easier by the action of the Union Pacific in 1880, when it secured complete control of the Kansas Pacific and consolidated it with the Colorado Central and Union Pacific, creating a complete monopoly of transportation in the northern half of Colorado.

Possibly Teller's most thoroughly creditable legislative activity during the period from 1876 to 1883 was his consistent and unselfish opposition to that very popular form of appropriation classified as pork. He attacked such a bill in the Forty-fifth Congress on two different occasions on the ground that many of the items were a useless waste of the taxpayers' money. Some of the proposals were worthy, and he proposed to separate the national projects from those local in character. In the next Congress he assumed the leadership in the hopeless and thankless task of opposing this vote-catching legislation.[27]

His years of service as a teacher had given Teller a broad interest in education. A bill frequently before Congress in this period proposed to establish an endowment fund with a portion of the proceeds from the sale of public lands, the interest of which was to aid education in states having a large number of illiterates. This was a practicable form of Federal aid to the South for Negro education. Teller's strong carry-over Abolitionism and his nationalism were apparent in his vigorous support of the bill, as well as his amendment to use the proceeds immediately instead of building up an endowment. This became the "most notable feature of the discussion" in the Senate. He also wished to confine its use

---

[26] April 1, 1878, Teller Letters. In his first years in the Senate, Teller was thought by his intimates to have considerable influence with Gould. Loveland, who believed Gould much more favorable to local Colorado Central interests than the other Union Pacific directors, had urged Teller to warn Gould to keep out of the fight between the Denver and Rio Grande and the Sante Fe or he would burn his fingers. (May 6, 1878, Teller Letters.) Chaffee had urged Teller to work on Gould to give Denver passenger and freight accommodations equal to those of Cheyenne. (Dec. 26, 1877, Teller Letters.) Teller had, of course, given up his income as legal representative of the Union Pacific on his election to the Senate, but he was still a director of the Colorado Central. Eventually Willard Teller and Orahood secured the Union Pacific account for their new law firm. When Teller's old partner, Hiram A. Johnson, asked the Central Pacific for a pass, Huntington sent the request to Teller for his endorsement. The pass was granted. C. P. Huntington to Teller, Oct. 20, 1877, Teller Letters.

[27] *Congressional Record*, 45 Cong., 2 Sess., p. 4584; *ibid.*, 45 Cong., 3 Sess., p. 2216; *ibid.*, 46 Cong., 3 Sess., pp. 2141-42; *ibid.*, 47 Cong., 1 Sess., p. 1914.

to elementary education. He argued that illiteracy was a pressing problem that would never be worse than it was at the present. An endowment could have no influence for years, and, in the meantime, children were growing up uneducated. College education was not so pressing a need, and would take care of itself as a demand for it grew out of common school education. His amendment was adopted in the Committee of the Whole, but lost on a tie vote in the Senate. The bill itself never became a law.

Later Teller introduced a bill to establish a Federal board of public education to aid in the support of the common schools, but his appointment to the Interior Department removed him from the Senate soon afterwards.[28]

One of the most bitterly fought issues in the Forty-seventh Congress was the proposal to exclude Chinese immigrants. It is safe to assume today that the American people are agreed upon the principle of immigration restriction, however much they may disagree as to the methods of carrying it out. In 1882 there was no such agreement. Americans liked to think of their country as the refuge for all the oppressed, as the Utopia of a better social, political, and economic order to which the ambitious of the world might come and prosper. It was chiefly on the Pacific Coast, where the evils of competition with coolie labor were apparent, that sentiment was bitterly opposed to the Chinese. Teller had seen just enough of that competition in Colorado and the Territories to understand its probable effect upon American labor. These Western members of Congress, who were Republicans for the most part, united with the Southern Democrats whose beliefs regarding "inferior" races made them natural allies, and with some Eastern members, to pass a Chinese exclusion bill.

Teller entered this debate with his usual aggressiveness, making what the Chicago *Tribune* called the "only speech of note" in that long debate. He carefully based his opposition on the ground that the restriction was necessary to protect American labor:

"I am anxious," he declared, "that the man who toils as a common laborer should have opportunities to educate his children, to make his children the equals of every other man's children in the land, and that cannot be done if you deny to him the protection of the law under circumstances

---

[28] *Congressional Record*, 45 Cong., 2 Sess., p. 3746; *ibid.*, 46 Cong., 2 Sess., pp. 179, 218, 288; *ibid.*, 47 Cong., 1 Sess., pp. 21, 2402; New York *Tribune*, Dec. 18, 1880.

like these." He drew analogies from the experience of Greece, Rome, and the American South with slave labor to show that when a type of labor is performed by a class of people who are considered to be definitely inferior, that it is considered degrading by the general population. The contrary argument, that America was an asylum for the oppressed, had great force with Teller. His position was that if the Chinese citizen were fleeing from oppression and "intended to better his condition by coming here with reference to his liberty," he would not exclude him no matter what his color. His statements regarding race superiority were somewhat surprising, considering his Abolitionist background, and laid him open to attack, for that was not a popular sentiment among Eastern Republicans. Senators Dawes and Hoar, in particular, presented long, carefully prepared rebuttal arguments against Teller's speech, attacking particularly his statements about racial superiority. They gave him some uncomfortable moments and forced him to state his belief in detail, which he did in these words:

> I do not deny that there are some men in China who are the equals of any other people morally and intellectually.... I say that the Caucasian race (as a race) is superior in mental force, intellectual vigor, and morals to any other branch of the human family. Then I say that there are grades in the Caucasian race.

He chided Hoar for his lack of consistency. The Massachusetts Senator had been chairman of the Republican National Convention in 1880 when a Chinese exclusion plank was adopted. Why, Teller asked Hoar, had he not risen up then and declared, "This is contrary to the principles of the Declaration of Independence; this is a violation of the rights of humanity, and it ought not to be done"?

He then went on to restate his belief in racial inequality, quoting Lincoln to show that it was good Republican doctrine. Equality was a well-sounding theory, a "sentiment that does more credit to a man's heart than it does to his head." But that whole question was incidental to the purpose of this bill, which was to protect labor. "I would rather be charged," Teller concluded, "with a betrayal of some of the sentimentality possessed by the Senators from Massachusetts than that the people should truly say I was forgetful of the great interests of the great mass of the men who labor and who are the strength, the support, the glory, and the hope of the American Republic." That oratorical flourish at the end was so unusual with Teller that it deserves recording. His speech, according to the then friendly Chicago *Tribune,* "completely shattered Mr. Hoar's argument."[29]

The proposal which was to concern Teller more than any other in his political career was bimetallism, specifically presented by the question of the coinage of silver. Silver mining had become an increasingly important industry in Colorado, and as the price of silver began to decline there was an immediate demand for its remonetization as a means of increasing its price. Chaffee, whose great wealth and growing Eastern interests had given him much of the point of view of the gold-standard advocates, was inclined to oppose any new silver coinage. What Teller's attitude was in 1878 is not clear in the record, for he never spoke upon the question, partly because he was still new in the Senate, and possibly because he knew very little about it. It was thought in Colorado that he was a much stronger supporter of silver coinage than Chaffee, and the Democratic press there did not raise the objections to his work that it did to Chaffee's.[30]

In the fight over the Bland bill in the Senate there were three general groups, of which the moderates or compromisers under Allison, of Iowa, was the largest. There was little difference between the free-coinage group and some of the compromisers, except that the latter wanted a bill they could pass over the President's veto. Although Teller probably would have voted with the free-coinage group, had it been able to carry its proposal, he followed Allison and voted for the amendments restricting the amount of silver coinage. His own amendment, providing for unlimited issues of paper backed by silver, received scant attention.[31] Four years later he came out emphatically for free coinage and explained his action on the Bland bill in this manner:

> I have not heretofore been very radical on this question. I voted for the Amendment that curtailed the coinage of silver.... I voted for it because the wise men of the Senate stood up here and predicted such disasters to the nation if we allowed the free coinage of silver. They made suggestions of that character so that to some extent they frightened me, and I said, "We will try this and see how it works and if it works well for a year or two we will enlarge it," and I propose as far as my vote is concerned to endeavor to enlarge it.

---

[29] *Congressional Record,* 47 Cong., 1 Sess., pp. 1645, 1671-1713; Chicago *Daily Tribune,* March 7, 9, 1882.

[30] *Rocky Mountain News,* Jan. 19, 27, Feb. 6, 9, 1878.

[31] In 1898, in an exchange with Allison, both senators agreed that the determining factor had been the desire to get a bill that could be passed over Hayes's veto. *Congressional Record,* 55 Cong., 2 Sess., p. 1157.

In the spring of 1882 he introduced a resolution into the Senate looking toward free coinage, but was prevented from urging it by his appointment as Secretary of the Interior. It was at this time that he made his first statement of political independence on that issue. It reads:

> Mr. President, I was educated in the Democratic party, and when it failed to represent my sentiments, I had the courage to get out of it; and I propose upon this question to represent myself, and not allow the Republican party to be put in the position of misrepresenting the wishes of the great people of the West and South.

This declaration of his independence of party control on the question of bimetallism makes it clear that Teller's break with the Republican Party fourteen years later was not made on the spur of the moment or without considering all that it involved. Significantly, Hill's friends in Colorado used the statement to discredit Teller with the local Republican Party.[32]

---

[32] *Ibid.,* 45 Cong., 2 Sess., pp. 1112, 1054, 1076; *ibid.,* 47 Cong., 1 Sess., pp. 447-49, 2100; New York *Tribune,* April 7, 1882.

CHAPTER IX

TELLER JOINS THE CABINET
1882

BY THE END of Teller's fifth year in the Senate, he occupied a place of respectable although not unusual importance. He had no superficial brilliance and made no vivid impressions. A reporter for the New Orleans *Times* described him in 1879 as "a man of some forty-five or six years of age, medium height and dark complexion. His hair, formerly coal black is now deeply tinged with gray, as is also his moustache and whiskers. His eyes are small and sparkling, his figure well knit, yet not over shapely, and his whole appearance that of a retired man of respectable agricultural pursuits. His address, while being dignified, has none of the free, aggressive and rush-of-business like air, so much affected by the modern senator. Altogether he is a pleasant sort of man to meet."[1] Probably what appeared to a Southerner as "a retired man of respectable agricultural pursuits" best indicates Teller's general appearance. He dressed, as did most of his colleagues, in a black frock coat that reached to his knees, a soft felt hat, and rather heavy boots. His slenderness, pompadour, and beard made him appear much taller than he measured. He usually wore a heavy beard with a shaved upper lip—a rustic style made popular by Lincoln—but on at least one occasion he allowed his mustache to grow and achieved a somewhat more modern facial appearance. When he appeared on the floor of the Senate, his graying, stiff dark hair, combed rather unsuccessfully straight back, was his most distinguishing characteristic.

Teller's election to the Senate had affected his finances adversely. Possessing a substantial income and much prospectively valuable property when he entered the Senate, both of these deteriorated afterward. His farm near Morrison was valuable, but produced little income that reached the senator. By this time he also had two Colorado farms, one near Boulder and the other near Grand Junction. Next to his own career, these three farms provided him with his greatest pleasure, and he spent a considerable share of his "vacations" looking after them and building them up. But

---

[1] Jan. 7, 1879.

they were never important income producers. Probably this hunger for fine farm property was in part compensation for the poor and ill-equipped farm of his boyhood, but more than that it was the typical expression of proper well-being by a pioneer rural American. His daughter, who had a deep understanding of her father, wrote that "he coveted every good farm. He kept buying land adjoining his several farms, giving as an excuse that he wanted to straighten a line or get more pasture, but we knew it was because he loved to buy farm property."[2] This love for farms was an expensive luxury.

All his investments in Gilpin were to prove of steadily decreasing value because of the failure of the local mines. It may well be doubted whether they added anything to Teller's wealth after he went to the Senate. His income from his law practice went down to a small fraction of its former total, as the new firm of Willard Teller and Orahood had taken over the more profitable business, and the elder Teller's practice was limited to what he could care for when Congress was not in session. He was dependent almost entirely upon his salary as a senator and these small earnings.

Living in Washington was not cheap. Writing to Orahood after he had been there over a year he observed, "It takes just about my salary to live here in fact quite the salary & perhaps a part of the mileage." His mining property was being worked most of the time, and there was always a chance for a lucky strike. A letter to Hal Sayre, his partner in several mining ventures, written ten years after he was elected to the Senate, is rather typical of a large correspondence extending over a period of thirty years:

I have your letter of some days since saying you had signs of pay in the Columbia. Well I hope you have but I have not changed my mode of living nor indulged in any unusual luxuries on account of the prospect of pay in this property. Still I can't help but feel that it is there or "thereabouts." . . . I wish we could sell for I am as you know pretty hard up & a sale would help me very much.[3]

At no time during Teller's life at Washington was he otherwise than "hard up" and a little feverishly anxious for a strike in one of his mines that might put him beyond the

[2] Emma Teller Tyler, "Reminiscences."

[3] Teller to Orahood, Feb. 2, 1878, Teller-Orahood MSS.; Teller to Sayre, Feb. 7, 1886, Hal Sayre MSS.; Emma Teller Tyler, "Reminiscences."

necessity of rather severe economy for a United States senator.

The rearing of the children was Mrs. Teller's care. There were now three, all born at Central City—Emma A., John Harrison, and Henry Bruce. They made a part of the Teller household at Washington, attending local schools until they were old enough to go to college, when Emma was sent to Wellesley and the boys to Yale. The boys graduated in law as well as arts, and then moved to Colorado, where Harrison took charge of the Grand Junction farm and Bruce practiced law. After graduation, Emma lived at home until her marriage in 1898 to George E. Tyler, a young physician, and then they, too, went to Denver to live.

The seasonal routine of living in Washington that was to last throughout the thirty-three years Teller was in public life, was now well established. Living in the capital city from fairly early fall—especially during the years when the children were in school—until late spring, they usually spent their summers in Colorado, but sometimes went to New Mexico, Arizona, Idaho, California, or western Canada for part of the season. The journeys to and from Washington almost invariably included a stopover at Morrison to visit with the Tellers there, especially the Senator's mother and sisters, who had lived first on his farm near the town, but, after the death of John Teller in 1879, had moved into Morrison. The Tellers did not spend much of their time in Central City after 1880, and after their house had been sold to make room for a new county courthouse they had no home there. Denver replaced Central City as their usual home, and while there they either made Willard Teller's large new house their headquarters or lived in one of the hotels.

Teller's daily routine was not greatly different from what it had been in Colorado, and was in many ways typical of a person with his rural background, strict Methodist home training, and studious habits. He arose early and worked among his plants until seven-thirty, when breakfast was ready. After breakfast he went to the Capitol to work at his office—unless committee meetings interfered—until time for the Senate to meet. Following adjournment, he went home for dinner and afterwards read the many Colorado, Washington, New York, and Chicago papers, which he did very rapidly, dropping each one on the floor of his study as he finished it. Then other reading, letter writing, or preparing speeches kept him busy until close to midnight. Statistical compilations fascinated him, and he would pore over a new *Statistical Abstract,* or *Report of the Treasury Department* for several evenings on end, reducing the tables into simpler comparative statements, sometimes for use later in a speech, but usually merely for his own information and amusement. His regular order was broken only by guests or unusually pressing public business.

House guests from Colorado or other parts of the West were frequent in Washington, although formal social affairs were rare. Teller had few recreations. He read regularly, and here his interests outside economics and politics ran to popular science and nature. The *Scientific American* was his favorite magazine, but he read the hunting and fishing periodicals also, as well as the standard monthly reviews. He seldom read imaginative literature, but shared an enthusiasm with his friend Hal Sayre for John Burrough's nature essays. His aesthetic interest was similarly limited. Cultivating flowers was its principal expression and had been a regular avocation since his first years in Central City. He took pleasure in shopping for fine china and porcelain, and when in New York or Chicago with time on his hands he would frequently spend it in that way, sending his purchases either home to Mrs. Teller or to his mother at Morrison.

During his summers Teller always found some time for fishing, and usually enough for camping and perhaps even hunting in the fall. In Washington he walked or drove every pleasant Sunday afternoon out into the open country and wooded sections about the city. His children remembered these trips partly because their father told them the names, common and scientific, of every tree and flower they saw, and by constant drilling taught them to recognize and name them. Music and the theater had little interest for him, and both dancing and card playing were taboo in the Teller home, at least after the children arrived.[4]

Mrs. Teller's life in Washington, outside the management of her home, centered about her church and its welfare work, as it had in Central City. Especially active in the Home Missionary Society, she found time for other charities, and even organizations such as the Indian Rights Association, which did not always approve of her husband. The entire family attended church with puritan regularity. Just

---

[4] Tyler, "Reminiscences."

what the Senator's religious beliefs were it is extremely hard to determine. He could not have lived a more circumspect life had he been a proclaimed member of the Methodist Church; nor could his support of that church have been greater. On the other hand, he occasionally took an opportunity to announce that he was not a church member, and frequently contrasted the sectarian unfavorably with the Christian. His unwillingness to identify himself publicly with a church was well known among his associates. When an old friend of his boyhood in New York wrote him, asking for help in securing better mail service for the village of Granger, he told of the religious revival then taking place at Short Tract, adding, "I hope as I may hear from you along to hear that this same influence has come into your heart & that you have consented to accept Christ."[5]

Undoubtedly Teller found his place in the Senate very much to his liking. All his background in politics and law, and all his unexpressed ambitions joined in making it a desirable office. Next only to the presidency it was the place where a statesman could best exercise his talents. Compared with a governorship or a cabinet position, it was far more desirable for a person of Teller's personality and background. He had shown no real desire to change and, although Mrs. Teller sometimes complained of the disruption of settled family life necessitated by it, she eventually came to prefer living in Washington to any other place.

At the opening of the Forty-seventh Congress, Teller's position within the Republican organization in the Senate was becoming much improved. He had now acquired one of the better seats on the floor—the front seat on the center aisle. His committee positions were also more to his liking. Taking advantage of openings in the bulwark of the Senate rules of committee membership, he gradually secured better assignments. During the Forty-seventh Congress he was chairman of the Pensions Committee, and a member of the committees on Railroads, on Claims, and on Privileges and Elections. After Conkling's resignation Teller secured the vacancy left on the very desirable Committee on Judiciary and resigned from the Privileges and Elections group.

At the same time, Teller was conforming more and more to senatorial tradition in his manner of speaking upon the floor. He had a fine contempt for the florid declamation

---

[5] G. H. White to Teller, Feb. 1, 1878, Teller Letters.

currently popular, and the most damning description he
could make of an argument was to call it "oratory." His own
speeches were oral lawyer's briefs without embellishments.
With possibly one exception he never wrote out a speech
before delivery, contenting himself with the careful arrangement of his evidence and depending upon his verbal ingenu-
ity for effective presentation. This accounts for their repe-
titious character and lack of readability. His delivery and
his bearing during debate were, all through his life, largely
influenced by his experience before the bar. In his first
controversies on the Senate floor his attitude was frequently
that of the attorney pleading his case before a Colorado
court, and at times he charged at those who opposed him in
a manner reminiscent of his famous legal contests in Colorado. The senatorial wit, Ingalls, and its privileged de-
nouncer, Edmunds, had more than one occasion to resent
Teller's blunt speech.[6] Bitter, sarcastic Edmunds was nothing new to the Coloradan; as Chaffee pointed out, he was
just such a character as Willard Teller.

There was only one cloud on the horizon of his political
future. Could he maintain his seat in the Senate? His term
would expire March 4, 1883. With Garfield as President,
Hill had the edge in the distribution of patronage in Colorado, and he directed it where it would undermine the
strength of Teller and Chaffee. Should Hill's friends control
the state Republican convention of 1882, Teller's senatorial
career would be ended—at least temporarily, and most likely
permanently.

Chance entered into this situation in the form of an
assassin's bullet which killed President Garfield and made
Chester A. Arthur President. This incident played havoc
with the well-laid schemes of various politicians. Garfield's
administration was dominated by the Blaine faction of the
Republican Party. Arthur was one of Conkling's Stalwarts
in New York, who had never seriously disagreed with his
leader except to become the Republican vice-presidential
candidate. The friends and political allies of Arthur and
Garfield were the opposite poles of the conservative Republicans. Teller's relations with Arthur were more intimate
than Hill's relations with Garfield. Arthur's first official
act as Vice-President—that of appointing a committee to inform the President that a quorum was present in the Senate

[6] *Congressional Record*, 46 Cong., 1 Sess., index; *ibid.*, 47 Cong., Special Sess., pp.
33-34, 525; *ibid.*, 47 Cong., 1 Sess., p. 146.

—was to single out Teller for one of the small honors it was his privilege to award. So with Arthur's succession to the presidency, Teller gained, not complete control of the Colorado patronage, but at least a preponderance of influence in its distribution. Naturally enough he proceeded to rebuild some of the breaches in his political fences. Yet the Hill strength in the Republican Party in Colorado, marshaled by Hamill and the Wolcott brothers, was large, and the eleventh-hour dominance in the distribution of the Federal patronage was not enough to ensure a Teller victory.

Other changes were pending. President Arthur was replacing the Garfield Cabinet by members of his own choosing. He began by selecting men who would be loyal to him personally and not antagonize seriously the important factions. He wanted no domination by Conkling or anyone else. So it developed that his appointees were almost entirely Stalwarts with whom he was personally friendly, and who had not been identified with extreme partisanship. His process of reconstruction was gradual, and it was not until the spring of 1882 that he made his last selections.

The newer states of the West had seldom had Cabinet members selected from among their politicians, and they were beginning to demand such recognition. After Garfield's election, the Colorado Republicans had urged the appointment of John L. Routt to a Cabinet position, preferably the Department of the Interior. Teller and Hill went to Mentor, Ohio, where Garfield was living until the time of his inauguration, and urged the appointment. For some reason Chaffee refused to join in the endorsement and possibly Hill's support was "only ostensible," as Schurz charged, but Teller backed his public endorsement with an emphatic private one. The Department of the Interior finally went to Senator Kirkwood, of Iowa, in a last-minute change, when his colleague Allison refused the Treasury Department. Kirkwood was not a complete success as head of this department, which had become the catchall of the Federal Government's administration. The pressure of office seekers and the administrative details that he was unable or unwilling to delegate to others buried him helplessly under their weight. After seeming to consider retaining him, which might have been a wise political move, Arthur took steps to select his successor, and the Far Western states again exerted pressure to have one of their leaders chosen.[7]

---

[7] Teller to Garfield, Feb. 18, 1881, and Chaffee to Garfield, Nov. 19, 1880, Garfield MSS., T. C. Smith, *Life and Letters of James Abram Garfield* (New Haven, 1921), II,

Senator Sargent, of California, at first the most prominently mentioned candidate, was "generally conceded" the
office in January. In the meantime, Teller was urging
Chaffee for the position if Kirkwood were to be replaced.
Public opposition developed to the appointment of Sargent,
and the Stalwarts Logan, Cameron, and former President
Grant urged Chaffee's appointment. Arthur was in a difficult situation. If he appointed Chaffee it would be said that
Grant and the Stalwarts were dominating the administration; and Arthur was insisting on being President. In this
case, as in so many others, he accepted none of the outstanding alternatives, but decided to make his own
appointment.

President Arthur asked Teller to call at the White House
on the evening of March 13. The Senator called as requested,
expecting to hear that Chaffee would be named. But the
President, in that gracious manner that was natural to him,
informed Teller that he wanted to appoint him instead. He
told Teller that he felt his interests in the department and
his legal experience would make him an ideal Secretary.
Teller had no alternative but to refuse. He was pledged to
Chaffee's candidacy to such a degree that he could not consider the appointment. Moreover, he liked his position in
the Senate, and had fair prospects of re-election to the
full six-year term the following year. Three days later
Arthur sent for Teller and again urged him to consider the
appointment. Then Teller informed his associates in urging
Chaffee's selection, Cameron and Logan, and his personal
friends in Colorado of the situation. They all urged acceptance. Senator Cameron telegraphed Chaffee, who was wintering in Florida, and he added his urgings to the others.
Then the news leaked out. The reception in Colorado and in
all the West was very favorable, but it was not until April
that Teller informed Arthur, "My State urges acceptance
and I can't decline."

He was appointed on April 6. In Colorado and the West
generally there was rejoicing. In that section, at least, the
Department of the Interior was the most important of all.
Westerners would be sure of reasonable rulings on questions
affecting public lands. Even Senator Hill's newspaper, the
Denver *Republican*, conceded the "preeminent fitness" of the

1058, 1081, 1094-95; Bancroft, *Speeches, Correspondence and Political Papers of Carl
Schurz*, IV, 83; Hall, *Colorado*, III, 28; Stone, *Colorado*, I, 432; Dan Elbert Clark,
Samuel Jordan Kirkwood (Iowa City, 1917), p. 363.

appointment. They were particularly pleased in Central City. "The Kingdom of Gilpin is again heard from."[8]

---

[8] New York *Tribune*, Jan. 11, 27, Feb. 11, March 22; Chicago *Daily Tribune*, March 22, 25, 28, 31; Denver *Republican*, March 21-27, April 7, particularly the dispatch signed "Moss Agate"—all 1882; Hall, *Colorado*, III, 30; S. H. Elbert to Chaffee, Nov. 24, 1881, Logan MSS. The different accounts of the appointment vary considerably in details. I have followed what seemed to be the most consistent with other factors in the situation.

CHAPTER X

TELLER'S appointment to the Cabinet was received with mild favor over the country, although the Half-Breed papers complained about the removal of Kirkwood and insisted that the factional alignment of the President could be the only reason for the change. Generally, it was remarked that there was no good political reason for the appointment. Chaffee with his political connections would have added party strength to the administration, but Teller would add little that would be of partisan advantage.

As the new Secretary stood before the public as an advocate of certain definite policies his appointment was usually seen in relation to his probable influence upon these. The New York *Tribune* was typical of the Republican press:

> The comment upon the proposition among Mr. Teller's associates is generally favorable. No one questions Mr. Teller's ability and there is no stain upon his record.... Mr. Teller is of very positive convictions and especially so with some of the important matters over which, as Secretary of Interior, he would have control.... He doubtless will begin a vigorous Indian policy, but there is no reason to think he would do the nation's wards injustice.... Mr. Teller is the chief promoter of the movement to recover from the railroads such portions of their land grants as have not been earned in accordance with the terms of the original grants.[1]

The personal commendations were numerous and gratifying. Conkling, although cool to the administration as a whole, wrote warmly to Teller:

> I rejoice for the commonweal that you have charge of the greatest as I think of the government's Departments.... That you will render eminent service I feel sure, and no one—no not one wishes you fame, happiness, success, with more heartfelt interest than your friend,
>
> ROSCOE CONKLING.

The Cabinet meant a changed social status, and the Tellers were forced into a society which was probably the gayest the city of Washington had ever experienced. President Arthur had a background different from that of his predecessors. He was accustomed to mingle with the New

---

[1] New York *Tribune*, April 7, 1882; *The Nation*, April 13, 1882; *Harper's Weekly*, April 15, 1882.

York "Four Hundred," and he now made social functions in the capital follow the example of those of the city. This was in striking contrast to the prohibition dinners of President Hayes and the relative simplicity of such commoners as Grant and even Garfield. Whether they wished to or not, the Tellers were to bear their share of these functions. President Arthur's first state dinner, which they attended, was the beginning:

Dinner was served in fourteen courses, with which there were served eight varieties of wines, each variety having its appropriate wine-glass. The guests were two hours at the table, and the menu was eulogized, especially the terrapin, which was highly commended by the epicures who enjoyed it.

Never very comfortable at formal affairs of any kind, one can scarcely imagine that the Good Templar was entirely at ease here. Probably he did not fit in too badly, although his friends continued to make fun of his dislike of social affairs. "I see by the papers," Walter Q. Gresham wrote him just before Arthur's administration ended, "that you are having a gay time in Washington. My only fear is that you will become a regular dude, as you are naturally inclined in that way anyhow."[2]

Although on friendly terms with his fellow Cabinet members, Teller represented a different attitude on many public questions. As the Chicago *Tribune* noted when he was appointed, it was the case of "a good silver man in a Gold-bug Cabinet."

After Teller had agreed to accept the appointment he voted to override the President's veto of the Chinese Exclusion bill. There are no adequate sources available for determining what went on in Cabinet meetings. Arthur's most important veto—that of the rivers and harbors bill—was in line with Teller's policy while in the Senate, and he admitted he had advised that action. He was clearly and unquestionably out of step with the policy of the Treasury Department and did not hide his objections, although in general harmony seems to have prevailed. Walter Q. Gresham, the liberal judge, and William E. Chandler, usually remembered as the acme of partisanship, were the two members with whom Teller was most intimate. On the few occasions when Teller represented the administration, as at the New Orleans

---

[2] Conkling to Teller, April 27, 1882; Gresham to Teller, Jan. 22, 1885; Tyler MSS.; Ben Perly Poore, *Reminiscences of Sixty Years in the National Metropolis* (Philadelphia, 1886), II, 462.

Exposition and the opening of the Northern Pacific Railroad, he did so with a dignity that reflected credit upon his chief. At the ceremony of uniting the rails in the latter instance, a critical observer who found William M. Evarts' speech very tiresome had only high praise for Teller's.[3]

Teller admired and respected Arthur, and after his experience in the Cabinet any unfriendly criticism of Arthur brought him instantly to his defense. Thirty years after his appointment to the Cabinet—years that had not seen Teller in agreement with occupants of the presidential office—the Coloradan told a reporter, "Chester A. Arthur was the best man and the most loyal friend that ever sat in the White House in my time. He was every inch a man."

The work in the department was hard and exacting. After Teller had been Secretary for a year, he wrote to his predecessor:

> I find the work never lets up in this department. Every day is alike, unless it is that it grows worse instead of better. I come to the office at half past eight, and go home at five, and still do not get the work done.

The chief burden was the responsibility that had to be delegated to subordinates who could not be adequately supervised. When Teller again became a member of the Senate he was a persistent influence there for adequate provision for salaries and clerical help. Five years after he left the Cabinet he was to tell the Senate:

> No poor man can afford to be a member of the Cabinet any more, and there is no man who is fit to be a member of the Cabinet but what can earn more money outside. . . .
>
> Why there are $1,800 clerks in the Interior Department, nay $1,600 clerks, who pass upon more values every year than the entire Supreme Court of Arkansas. . . . I speak advisedly when I say that the interests intrusted to the Secretary of Interior, upon which he passes judicially and from which there is no appeal and no revision, are greater than all the interests passed on by the Supreme Court, with its nine judges, and yet he gets less salary than any member of that court.[4]

[3] Chicago *Daily Tribune*, March 24, 1882; clippings in J. S. Randall Morgue; Gustave Koerner, *Memoirs*, Thomas J. McCormack, editor (Cedar Rapids, 1909), p. 679.

[4] Denver *Republican*, May 24, 1912; Teller to Kirkwood, June 16, 1883, Kirkwood MSS.; *Congressional Record*, 51 Cong., 1 Sess., p. 2525. In 1930 a former employee of the department remembered Teller as "an indefatigable worker, being at his desk at eight o'clock every morning and never leaving until after five. He wrote most of his decisions himself, rarely using a stenographer, but his writing was almost undecipherable and the typists and stenographers who had to copy it were often bunched together, trying to help one another out and sometimes they had to admit defeat and go to him for a solution, which always amused him very much, especially if he could not read it himself. He was one of the kindest, most sympathetic men to work under, always willing to help the unfortunate and the quickest to recognize and acknowledge conscientious service." Helen Herzog Greeley to the author, March 3, 1930.

H. M. Teller as Secretary of the Interior, 1882.

But Teller's interests in a Cabinet position were those that involved the assumption of responsibility. His experience in the Senate had turned his ideas upon many problems into definitely formulated policies, in the soundness of which he earnestly believed. Now it was his opportunity to carry them out. He had been a severe critic of the Department of the Interior when Schurz was at its head, and now the control was his own. It was a pleasant prospect, and the severe limitations of a department head's power were not as apparent then as they were later. He made the transfer without impairing his friendship with the incumbent, Kirkwood, and retained almost all of the latter's appointees in office. Teller was determined that the department should function efficiently, and he succeeded in impressing his subordinates with his ability. The letters of several of them to their former superior, Kirkwood, give ample evidence of this, although specific policies were sometimes criticized adversely.[5]

In a sense there were two phases of Teller's administration of the Interior Department: one, the more or less bureaucratic administration of its numerous functions in accordance with the Secretary's general policy, and the other, the assumption of leadership in securing new legislation which would assist in carrying out that policy.

The Indian Service took more of Teller's attention than any other phase of his work. Some apprehension was evident among the professional friends of the Indian that his policy might not be what they desired—a fear that grew out of Teller's local interests, it seems, as many of them had found him a helpful adviser in their problems. Confessed Superintendent H. R. Pratt of the Carlisle Indian School:

When he [Arthur] appointed as his secretary of the interior Mr. Teller of Colorado, a western man, I felt apprehensive, but this disappeared immediately when I learned to know Mr. Teller. Mr. Teller visited Carlisle early during his secretaryship and was several times a guest of the school. His kindly talks to the students and counsel to the superintendent were invaluable.[6]

Teller's former colleagues in the Senate knew him better. Dawes immediately appealed to him for a plan to solve the Indian problem, which if outlined in his annual report to Congress would have added weight. " . . . you are the only

[5] A. C. McFarland to Kirkwood, May 27, 1882; H. Price to Kirkwood, June 16, 1882, and J. H. McCannson to Kirkwood, Oct. 23, 1882, Kirkwood MSS.
[6] Richard Henry Pratt, *The Indian Industrial School* (Carlisle, [1908?]), p. 34.

one from position and power and knowledge of Indian character who can do it." Teller attempted to satisfy Dawes, and although his opinion of Teller's plan is not available, his colleague, Senator Hoar, was enthusiastic. He wrote Teller:

> I have read very carefully, and with great satisfaction, your report for the year just closed. I think that part relating to the Indians all that could possibly be desired. Last winter I went through all the reports of your predecessors for more than twenty years. Yours seems to me the best one I have ever read. It deals with the question practically, courageously and humanely. Its authority coming from a person of so long an experience in a frontier state, will be very great and if its recommendations are adopted, the Indian problem will, in a few years, disappear.[7]

Not all of Teller's actions pleased this group. It had been the practice to parcel out the Indian agents among the religious bodies engaged in missionary work among the tribes, a practice which, though backed by the best of intentions, had developed into a system of appointing broken-down clergymen, whose lack of vigor greatly handicapped the service. To refuse to continue this system would result in one of the types of difficulty it is good politics to avoid, and the Commissioner of Indian Affairs feared to do it. With Arthur's approval Teller began filling vacancies without respect for the wishes of the churches formerly concerned. Thus he antagonized some of the groups interested in Indian welfare, but at the same time, he always held, he increased the efficiency of the service and made his successor's way easier.

The only solution of the Indian problem, Teller insisted in his reports, was vocational education, an idea that has been seconded by many more recent authorities. Teller wrote in his last report:

> The greatest agency for the civilization of the Indian is the manual-labor school. Indeed, I do not think I shall be far out of the way if I say the only agency for that purpose is the manual-labor school.... [It is] only necessary to multiply their number, so as to include all Indian children of school age, to forever set at rest the question as to "what shall be done with the Indians."

During his administration, aided by enlarged appropriations for that purpose, there was a great increase in the number of Indian schools and pupils. The nonreservation schools were increased from two to six, and there was a

---

[7] W. H. Lincoln to H. L. Dawes, April 3, 1882; Dawes to Teller (copy), Sept. 19, 1882, Dawes MSS.; G. F. Hoar to Teller, Dec. 5, 1882, Tyler MSS.

general increase in the number and effectivenss of reservation schools.

His plans were greater than he could induce Congress to carry out. In his first report he detailed a plan for financing manual-labor schools, and made a strong plea for the creation of a permanent school fund by using part of the proceeds from the sale of public lands. The plan was worked out in such a way that for an expenditure of five or six million dollars each year about one half of the Indian children could be educated in these schools. But by the time he made his last report he was demanding provisions adequate to care for all Indian children. The plan of education included the Indian youth of both sexes, for Teller correctly foresaw that educating the males while leaving the females in the old state of tribal habit and custom would make little permanent improvement in the status of the race. Reservation schools should be improved and continued, but the emphasis, he contended, should be placed upon the manual-labor schools. He recommended that graduates of these schools be given equipped farms to prevent them from slipping back into the economic ways of their fathers.[8]

As an immediate means of preventing Indian outbreaks and encouraging farming, Teller urged that the natives should be immediately disarmed and dismounted. He continued to urge this at some length, proposing that the arms be purchased from the Indians at twice their value. He protested against paying cash annuities to the Indians, and wanted power to pay them in livestock and farm machinery.

The reservation system, he advised, should be continued until the Indians "are enabled to compete with their aggressive and avaricious white competitors." The reservations should be kept large enough to take care of the increase in their tribe, but any surplus of farm lands should be opened to white settlement, after purchase from the tribe, if it had a title. Then the Indians should get a legal title to the reservation lands that remained.

Teller had two reasons for decreasing the size of the reservations. One was to provide homes for white settlers, and this was important in his mind. The other was for the civilization of the Indian. As long as he was on a large reservation he could not be induced to adopt any civilized

[8] *House Executive Documents*, 47 Cong., 2 Sess., No. 1, Part 5, xiii-xvii; *ibid.*, 48 Cong., 2 Sess., No. 1, Part 5, iii-vii; Francis E. Leupp, *The Indian and His Problem* (New York, 1910), p. 121; Warren K. Moorehead, *The American Indian in the United States* (Andover, 1914), pp. 200-10.

mode of living. If he were restricted, so that hunting was no longer profitable, it would be easier to induce him to begin to raise stock, or even to cultivate land for a living. If this seems like severe treatment, it need only be recalled that the severalty policy forced a more complete and rapid change upon the Indian. To carry out his policy Teller began negotiations with certain tribes that had immense reservations to open parts of them to white settlement. In two cases where the Indians refused to accept any arrangement, President Arthur, on Teller's recommendation, opened parts of them to settlement by executive order, shortly before his term was over. To the sentimentalists among the friends of the Indians this was robbery. They held with simple faith that any kind of an agreement with an Indian tribe to occupy a certain territory gave them a full title to that land, morally if not legally. Particularly those who had been angered over the elimination of church control in the service were given a weapon, and they used it with a will to attack the administration of Teller and Arthur. They induced President Cleveland to revoke these orders, and temporarily checked the inevitable development.

As could have been expected, Teller made no recommendations for a general severalty policy, although his Commissioner of Indian Affairs, Hiram Price, did. Teller's policy was to give each tribe a legal title to the tribal lands, "leaving to the Indians to determine the question of allotment for themselves." This would make the transition from the tribal savage to a civilized citizen slower and less painful.

The Five Civilized Tribes in Indian Territory had an adequate title to their lands, which Teller defended against all attacks. They had a great surplus of land, however, which they regularly leased to near-by cattlemen for grazing purposes. The money received was far from the true rental value of the land used, and for this reason Teller urged Congress to give the department power to take charge of the leasing of these lands in order to protect the Indians' interest. His only power, as he saw it, was either to prohibit leasing altogether or to permit it. As it returned a substantial revenue to the Indians for the use of what otherwise would have been idle land he would not forbid it, but wanted authority to regulate it and secure a fair rental. No such authority being given while Teller was in the Interior Department, he followed what has been called the "absurd policy" laid out in his letter to one of the lessees, Edward

Fenlon. The department, it declared, would not recognize any agreements or enforce them. Furthermore, legislation or a change in departmental policy might cause it to break all leasing agreements. Pending this, however, agreements could be made if the Indians and lessees wished. The result was anarchy, as the competition for the leases led to intrigue, conflicting leases, and threats of violence. Seeing only this and the fact that the "cattle barons" were getting the leases at less than their real value, the Cleveland administration forbade the practice altogether, and ordered the cattle removed.[9]

Teller established an ingenious piece of legal machinery for settling disputes among the Indians, and at the same time giving them some practical training in the exercise of the citizenship they would eventually gain. This he called the Court of Indian Offenses. As worked out by the Indian Commissioner, it consisted of three Indians, usually the ranking members of the police force. They were to try cases and enforce penalties for breaches of a group of rules drawn up to prevent certain evil practices connected with tribal ceremonies and customs. "It is believed that such a tribunal, composed as it is of Indians, will not be objectionable to the Indians and will be a step in bringing the Indian under the civilizing influence of the law." The Indian agents reported the excellent operation of this system, and Teller urged that appropriations be made for the payment of the Indian judges, and that legal authority be given them to punish minor offenses. Although this system did not prove to be a cure-all for the ills of reservation life, it was a persistent influence for good. As late as 1928 a group of investigators of Indian administration recommended the continued use of the system.[10]

An interesting incident was Teller's appointment of Helen Hunt Jackson to investigate the conditions among the Mission Indians of California. Mrs. Jackson was a Colorado Springs woman, who was on friendly terms with the Teller family, and made her home with them when in Washington. Naturally, she counted upon the Secretary to help her in

---

[9] *House Executive Documents*, 47 Cong., 2 Sess., No. 1, Part 5, iv-viii; *ibid.*, 48 Cong., 1 Sess., No. 1, Part 5, xiii-xv; *ibid.*, 48 Cong., 2 Sess., No. 1, Part 5, ix-xi; *Senate Executive Documents*, 48 Cong., 1 Sess., No. 48, p. 199; Robert McElroy, *Grover Cleveland* (New York, 1923), I, Chapter IX; Herbert Welch to Dawes, March 25, 1885, Dawes MSS.; E. E. Dale, "History of the Ranch Cattle Industry in Oklahoma," *Annual Report of the American Historical Association*, 1920, pp. 314-15.

[10] *House Executive Documents*, 48 Cong., 1 Sess., No. 1, Part 5, xii; Lewis Merriam and associates, *The Problem of Indian Administration* (Baltimore, 1928), pp. 17, 769-75, 777-79.

what had become her chief purpose in life—aiding the Indians. Although she sometimes lost patience with the slowness of Teller's support of what she thought was necessary, he endorsed her report on the Mission Indians and urged Congress to carry out its recommendations. She gave him credit for his help, and shortly before he left the department she wrote to Mrs. Teller in high praise, mixed, perhaps, with hope:

> I wonder if you will think I am taking an unpardonable liberty in putting these papers into your hands, thus to make sure of their going *directly* into your husband's. I hope not; and I am sure you would not, if you knew how intense is my desire to be able to accomplish one more thing for these poor Mission Indians, before Mr. Teller leaves the Dept.
>
> I cannot tell you how my heart aches at the thought of his going. I do not dare to look forward to what may happen in the next four years. I have no hope whatever of men's being in the Ind. Bureau or the Int. Dept. who will carry out Mr. Teller's views.
>
> But there is one comfort. He will be in the Senate....

Teller's administration of Indian affairs was singularly free from trouble, and with considerable pride he was able to write in his last report:

> It affords me great satisfaction in my third and last report to be able to say that the past year has been one of peace among the Indians and that no outbreaks have occurred....
>
> At no time in the history of our intercourse with the Indians have they shown a greater desire to abandon their savage life than during the last year. They have welcomed (with few exceptions) all the agencies provided for their benefit, and have shown a commendable disposition to adapt themselves to the new order of things.

Teller's conduct of Indian affairs was well received in general. "Posterity will bless you for what you have been able to do in this direction," praised Frederick Douglass when he read Teller's last report. Even in the partisan press there was little criticism of his policies, except in Colorado, where Hill's paper made political capital out of recommendations that looked favorable to the Indian.[11]

If there were any other phase of his work in which Teller displayed the same interest that he did in Indian affairs it was upon the subject of public lands. The principal object of the land laws was to enable the actual settler to build a

---

[11] Helen Jackson to Mrs. Teller, Jan. 27, 1885; Frederick Douglass to Teller, Dec. 15, 1884, Tyler MSS.; *House Executive Documents*, 48 Cong., 1 Sess., No. 1, Part 5, xi-xii; C. C. Davis and W. A. Alderson, *The True Story of Ramona* (New York, 1914), pp. 11, 49-52, 82, 187, 223; *Harper's Weekly*, Dec. 20, 1884; clipping from Denver *Republican*, Dec., 1882, Dawson Scrapbook; Ruth Odell, *Helen Hunt Jackson* (New York, 1939), p. 193.

farmstead in the new country at a minimum of expense, and to prevent the land from falling into the hands of speculators who would hold it for a rise in value. But Teller found them far from perfect.

The homestead and pre-emption laws, designed to secure to the actual settler lands at a reasonable price, have become agencies by which the capitalist secures large and valuable areas of the public land at little expense.

Teller repeatedly urged the repeal of the timber culture and pre-emption laws, as they no longer served their original purpose, and were the means of alienating public lands to speculators. He also recommended a large number of changes in the homestead laws which would facilitate the bona fide settler and handicap the speculator in securing land.

Teller indicated his attitude clearly in rulings made on cases which came before the department. He had an intimate acquaintance with the conditions under which homesteads were taken and a solid sympathy with the actual settlers. An examination of the printed decisions of the department shows that he frequently overruled the land commissioner in cases where he suspected that the settler had not received justice.

A case that illustrates Teller's attitude is that of *Lunde* versus *Edwards*. Edwards, a rural preacher, had filed on land near Grand Forks, Dakota Territory, but had failed to begin a legal residence on his claim because severe weather prevented the completion of a house. He had, however, raised a small crop and laid the foundation for his house. Because of Edwards' failure to begin his residence Lunde brought action against his entry, which was sustained by the Commissioner of Public Lands on technical grounds. In reversing his decision Teller wrote:

This Department will not lend its power to the accomplishment of an effort to defeat an honest settler and deprive him of his labor and improvements on mere speculative and technical grounds. It is not asserted nor pretended that Lunde had a particle of interest in the land, or even desires it for his own settlement. He is a saloon-keeper, residing in a town, without a family, and not likely to have such urgent need of a home as to entitle him to the privilege of appropriating that of a settler whose good faith has been sufficiently manifested by his efforts, although not fully complying with the law.[12]

---

[12] *House Executive Documents*, 48 Cong., 1 Sess., No. 1, Part 5, xxi; *Decisions of the Department of Interior and General Land Office* (Washington, 1883), II, 164.

In large parts of the West, cattlemen were fencing public land and keeping the homesteaders out. In no place was this more general than in Colorado. When Teller took office he immediately ordered legal action against such ranchers, and urged Congress to enact laws that would enable him to order the removal of such fences without the red tape of court action. He publicly advised homesteaders to cut fences on Government land which barred them from soil on which they wished to file claims. Later when he was criticized by a member of the Senate for not removing more of them, he was able to point to his recommendations for legislation and lay the blame upon the shoulders of his critic for not securing Congressional action.[13]

The laws governing the cutting of timber on the public domain were interpreted liberally, as would be expected from Teller's pronounced stand on this question in Congress. The Timber Cutting Act, which he had helped to enact, after listing certain states and territories, added to its scope the ambiguous phrase, "all other mineral districts of the United States." Teller gave his opinion—later reversed by the courts—that this meant all mineral districts found outside of the states and territories named. The Right-of-Way Act, which gave the railroads free timber for construction purposes, presented a difficulty in the phrase "adjacent to the line of road." Teller ruled that it did not necessarily mean adjoining.

> The right is given to cut timber, and it is immaterial to the government whether it is within 1 mile of the road or 50 miles distant. The spirit of the act is, that from the country having the benefit of the railroad the timber must come.... The railroad company should be allowed to cut timber at any point within the neighborhood of the line of road so being constructed.

This ruling has come in for a great deal of criticism by conservationists, but there is no disputing the fact that it carried out the intent of the law. These criticisms usually overlook the severe restrictions upon the use to which such timber was to be put. It could legally be used for original construction only, not for repairs, improvements, fuel, or public sale. When the road opened for public use, the right ceased.[14]

---

[13] *Congressional Record,* 49 Cong., 1 Sess., pp. 48-49; *House Executive Documents,* 48 Cong., 1 Sess., No. 1, Part 5, xxxii; Louis Pelzer, *The Cattlemen's Frontier* (Glendale, Calif., 1936), pp. 171-91; Ora B. Peake, *The Colorado Range Cattle Industry* (Glendale, Calif., 1937), p. 73.

[14] *Decisions of the Department of Interior,* I, 610-11, 697-700, II, 811-14; John Ise, *United States Forest Policy* (New Haven, 1920), pp. 62-64.

Teller inherited a good situation in the department regarding appointments. Partisan politics in the clerical appointments had not been the practice there, and it was not introduced by Teller. Only in selecting employees of the department in Colorado did he go out of his way to secure partisan advantage. He saved the best of the clerks in the Pension Bureau, when they had completed their work on the census of 1880, for other divisions of the department. He had no objections to women clerks, as many had, and consequently gave employment to a large number of that sex. The Pendleton Act was passed and its rules put into operation during his term of office. After a brief experience with it, he observed in his final report:

The law has in a great measure relieved the Department of the importunities of applicants and their friends for positions, and will, I think, when it is fully understood save the heads of the Department much time heretofore lost in listening to appeals for positions when it was impossible to comply with such requests. I think the system a valuable one, and one that ought to have the hearty support of both executive and legislative departments of the Government.

In the main the administrative work was very pleasant in spite of its exacting nature. The feeling of achievement compensated for the hard work. But there was one great drawback. All through his three years he was pursued by his former colleague, Senator Hill, with covert charges and insinuations to which he could not reply. This attack upon every policy that could be twisted to appear in a bad light was carried on through the columns of Senator Hill's Denver *Republican*, in some of the Half-Breed newspapers elsewhere, and in Congress. Teller wrote a Denver friend in 1884:

I have been somewhat annoyed by Hill's talk, but it does not influence anyone here; still it is not pleasant to have the Senator from Colorado back biting and slandering me all of the time. He won't investigate anything, and if the Democratic House will, I shall be pleased to have it done; all the Democrats know that I am willing, and even anxious. . . .

Usually the attack from Congress was disguised as a resolution of inquiry—"sneaking behind a resolution," Teller described it. It taught Teller a lesson that he did not forget. When he returned to the Senate he lectured that body on its duty toward the heads of departments, delivering this ultimatum:

... I want to give notice here to everybody that although the administration has passed into the hands of the political party with which I
am not affiliated, yet as a Senator, having due respect to the dignity of
the Executive Departments of the Government, I never intend without
at least a protest, that that administration shall be treated by resolutions of this Senate as the late administration has been treated.[15]

In addition to threatening an investigation of the Interior Department, Hill's attack centered upon one policy—
the "Backbone" land grant. The practice of giving land
grants to railroads was no longer popular in the West, and
the practice of letting them retain old grants to which their
title was cloudy was still less acceptable. Teller, in line with
popular Western opinion, had been an opponent of both at
least since 1880. If his old association with the Union
Pacific had any influence upon his opinions, it was not apparent in his action. Teller complained in one of his reports:

Until patents issue to the companies or their assigns, the legal
title to the granted lands remains in the United States. Such lands are,
therefore, not subject to taxation by State, Territorial, or municipal
authority. The companies permit these large bodies of land to rest
in this situation, and grow valuable by the lapse of time and the
settlement of the country, thus obtaining all of the advantages of public protection and enhancement of values, without contributing to the
maintenance of the public authority or of the common institutions of
municipal organization by the aid of which such enhanced values
may be secured.

This refusal of the companies to select their land within
a reasonable time was unfair, and Congress should legislate,
Teller urged, so as to force their selection of all land to
which they had a legal claim.

In January, 1882, Teller had introduced a resolution into
the Senate which would declare that all lands, so far un-
earned by the railroads in accordance with their grants,
were forfeited. His opinion was not changed by his new
duties. A little over a year after he entered the Cabinet he
wrote to Kirkwood:

You know I have no sympathy with the land grant system, and
never did have. I introduced a bill to repeal all the acts giving
lands, where the roads had not complied with the terms of the grant,
and I recommended in my report last fall, the forfeiture of such grants,
but I will respect the laws as they exist, no matter what my private
opinion may be.

---

[15] *House Executive Documents*, 48 Cong., 2 Sess., No. 1, Part 5, xxix-xxxi; *Congressional Record*, 49 Cong., 1 Sess., pp. 7, 14; Teller to Dawson, Feb. 1, 1884, Teller MSS.

And the law as interpreted by the courts and the Attorney General always had been that a grant did not lapse legally because the railroads failed to fulfill their part of the contract on time, unless Congress annulled it by positive action. Teller repeatedly urged that Congress take some action to repeal these grants so that large amounts of land would not be lost. Without such legislation, if a railroad completed its building operations twenty years later than the time specified in the original grant, it could demand patents to the land in question, and the Secretary of the Interior, under the law, had no other course than to grant them. This attitude of Teller's, plainly stated in his official reports, was to lead to the one act of his official career which more than any other laid him open to Hill's criticism.[16]

In 1871, the usual grant of land to railroads had been made to the New Orleans, Baton Rouge, and Vicksburg Company, popularly known as the Backbone Railroad. This company never built its projected railroad, and in 1881 a group representing the defunct company assigned its grant to the New Orleans and Pacific, a line which would have competed with the Backbone had the latter been built. The New Orleans and Pacific was partly constructed in 1881, and quickly completed its road. Upon completion it presented the Interior Department with a claim for land in proportion to the amount of road it had constructed since securing the Backbone grant. Kirkwood, who was then at the head of the department, submitted the legal question to the Attorney General, who returned his opinion soon after Teller succeeded Kirkwood. That opinion upheld the legality of the transfer and the right of the New Orleans and Pacific to lands for the line built since acquiring the grant. This opinion was in line with that of all previous opinions and court decisions. Bills were then pending in both branches to forfeit the Backbone grant and transfer it to the New Orleans and Pacific. Obviously three courses were open, each of which had supporters. The Secretary of the Interior could recognize the claim and issue patents for the land; or Congress might annul the Backbone grant and transfer it to the New Orleans and Pacific; or Congress might annul the grant and refuse it to the New Orleans and Pacific. Eight

[16] *House Executive Documents*, 47 Cong., 1 Sess., No. 1, Part 5, xxxi; *ibid.*, 48 Cong., 2 Sess., No. 1, Part 5, xix-xx; Teller to Kirkwood, June 6, 1883, Kirkwood MSS. The agent appointed by the state of Kansas to protect its interests against the railroads with large grants found the Interior Department under Teller a striking exception to the generally pro-railroad national government of the seventies and eighties. See Samuel J. Crawford, *Kansas in the Sixties* (Chicago, 1911), pp. 354-58.

days before the Attorney General's report was made, the Senate Committee on Railroads reported and the Senate adopted the report, holding that the new company was entitled to the grant, and no forfeiture was necessary. Patents would have been issued then, but for the press of business in the department, and, when shortly afterwards members of the House Judiciary Committee requested that none be issued until they had investigated, nothing was done. Then on March 13, 1883, Teller recommended to the President that the patents should issue, and Arthur concurred on March 16. Senator Hill saw an opportunity here for creating an issue in Colorado which would be detrimental to Teller. Playing them up in the Denver *Republican,* he caused rumors of corruption in the grant to be circulated, and Teller cautiously held up the patents, probably hoping that the Forty-eighth Congress would take some action that would preclude his.

Teller's need of Republican journalistic support in Denver was supplied by Thomas F. Dawson, of the Denver *Times.* To him Teller confided his own case, and Dawson defended him against the attacks in the *Republican.* This intensified a friendship that was to last for the rest of their lives. Teller did not demand anything unreasonable of Dawson. "I do not want you to do anything," he wrote, "that will embarrass you either in your business or socially. I can stand Senator Hill's attacks without sacrificing my friends."

When Congress met in December, 1883, Senator Hill introduced and later called up a resolution directing the Secretary of the Interior to furnish the Senate with all papers on file relating to the grant and its transfer. Senator Ingalls, of Kansas, took this opportunity to point out Hill's peculiar relation to the proceedings:

> Without any observation as to the somewhat vulgar and homely but not entirely inadequate adage about the obscenity of the bird that defiles its own nest, I wish upon the threshold and in the vestibule of these proceedings to declare and announce that in my judgment, which I believe to be shared by the country, the Department of the Interior has never been administered with more fidelity, with more integrity, with more honesty in all of its branches than under its present efficient and honorable head.

The resolution was adopted without opposition. On May 7, 1884, Hill made a long argument on the question and introduced a bill to cancel the grant. The substance of his argument was the uselessness of making the grant, which

Teller would admit, and that the Secretary of the Interior was not bound to accept the Attorney General's opinion on the law. It was obvious that Hill had failed to make an issue in the Senate, and the speech was chiefly for home consumption in the approaching campaign. Later in the same month, Senator Van Wyck, of Nebraska, submitted a resolution for the investigation of a report that the New Orleans and Pacific had used bribery to gain favorable congressional action, but the resolution was rejected after some debate.

In the meantime the House had passed a bill to forfeit the grant and transfer it to the New Orleans and Pacific Railroad. Its Judiciary Committee, however, reported 13 to 2 in support of the Attorney General's opinion of the law that the company was now entitled to the land, and the Secretary of the Interior might issue patents. The result would be the same in either case. This remained the situation until after the election of 1884, when the controversy assumed much greater prominence.[17]

Teller was getting his taste of the relatively unprotected position a Cabinet member is in, and it was not pleasant. "Won't you be glad when you get out of the Interior Department and back into the Senate again?" asked Kirkwood, who knew the correct answer.[18]

---

[17] The important documents are conveniently printed in the *Congressional Record*, 49 Cong., 1 Sess., pp. 7-15, 41-49; *ibid.*, 48 Cong., 1 Sess., pp. 55-57, 3911-16, 4273, 6056-57; *Senate Executive Documents*, 48 Cong., 1 Sess., No. 31; Teller to Dawson, March 8, April 18, Nov. 1, Dec. 11, 1883, June 3, 1884, Teller MSS.

[18] Kirkwood to Teller, Jan. 23, 1885, Tyler MSS.

CHAPTER XI

THE CABINET AND COLORADO POLITICS
1883-85

TELLER'S membership in the Cabinet had important repercussions in Colorado. The Republican Party there was never a well-disciplined machine obedient to the voice of a leader; and with the rapid growth of the state it became a collection of local factions held together at times by a leader who could successfully compromise the self-interest of most of them. Chaffee had been such a leader in the past, but with his election to the Senate his interests had moved East and neither his knowledge of local conditions nor his intimate acquaintance with the local leaders was as important as it had been before 1876. Hill, who aspired to Chaffee's position, lacked the qualities necessary for a successful politician. Domineering, inclined to remember and punish fancied slights, he probably would not have gone as far as he did had it not been for W. A. Hamill, Henry and Edward Wolcott. Henry Wolcott was his assistant in the Boston and Colorado Smelter, and Edward was one of the most promising of the younger lawyers.

Teller's successor in the Senate would be chosen in January of 1883 by the legislature elected for the most part in 1882. Chaffee and Teller had been determined since the campaign of 1880 that the office should not go to a Hill candidate, but that Teller should be re-elected. Hill was commonly reported to have declared that he would bankrupt himself before he would let Teller be re-elected. Chaffee in 1881 had assured President Garfield that Teller would be returned, but that was partly a boast. The Cabinet appointment changed this situation. Teller wanted to serve out his term as Secretary of the Interior. On the other hand, he, no less than Chaffee, was determined that Hill should not name his successor. Then, too, Hill himself would be up for re-election in January of 1885, in a legislature largely chosen in the election of 1884. Whoever was elected governor in 1882, if he were a Republican, would have vast influence in the election of the Republican members of that legislature. As the Senate was the great political prize, the state election of 1882 was primarily a fight for Colorado's two seats in the Senate.

Early in August, after his appointment to the Depart-

ment of the Interior, Teller returned home. He was enthu-
siastically received in Denver. Senator Hill's paper made a
gesture of conciliation. "No man was ever more popular
among the people than he. Personal enemies he has none."
When he reached Blackhawk on the former Colorado Central
he was met by an escort in carriages and on horseback, and
taken to the Central City opera house, where a public welcome was held. It was sweet revenge for the statements Hill
had made in Washington that Teller was without strength
at home, and could not carry his own precinct.[1]

Teller remained there the rest of August, receiving delegations of politicians from other parts of Colorado. The Hill
forces had centered upon the popular Henry Wolcott as their
candidate for governor. Because of the key position he
would hold if elected, neither Teller nor Chaffee would consent to his nomination. When the primaries were held to
elect delegates to the county convention, the group designated by common consent "Teller delegates" carried Gilpin
County by a large majority, receiving a majority in Blackhawk, the former residence of both Hill and Henry Wolcott.
Anti-Hill groups were similarly successful in a majority of
the county primaries, and Teller returned to Washtington.

Henry Wolcott was far more popular than Hill, and his
strategy was to keep the latter in the background; but this
was impossible, and the candidate was sacrificed to his associate. In the Republican convention which opened at Denver
on September 14, 1882, factional lines were closely drawn.
William A. Hamill and Edward Wolcott marshaled the Hill
forces, and Chaffee and Willard Teller—"Prince Willard,"
the Hill press called him—those of the opposition. After
some preliminary skirmishes, E. L. Campbell, the candidate
of the Teller faction, was nominated for governor over
Henry Wolcott, and the Hill faction was decisively beaten.
After the convention a large part of that group bolted the
ticket and supported the Democratic nominee for governor.
Bolting the party nominee would not set well with the national organization, to say nothing of the administration,
and Hill hastened to assure Secretary of the Navy Chandler
that the split in the convention had not been into anti- and
pro-administration lines, or that Secretary Teller had taken
any part in the fight. The Wolcott men, he insisted, had
been Grant men in 1880.

---

[1] Chaffee to Garfield, June 30, 1881, Garfield MSS.; clippings from *Register Call*,
Dec. 13, 1882, and *Richmond Inquirer*, Jan. —, 1882, Dawson Scrapbook; Denver
Republican, Aug. 17, 1882.

Charges of fraud in the convention and election were made against both factions. Teller's statement of the result was confided to Kirkwood in a letter written shortly after the election, which had been a general Democratic victory that boded ill for the Arthur administration.

Kansas, Michigan, Massachusetts and Colorado, all with democratic Governors,—it beats the d--l. You ask if Hill was at the bottom of it in Colorado. He was the head and front of the bolt, although he had not the courage to openly support the democratic candidate, he furnished the money, or at least part of it. . . . Our candidate for Governor was a first-class man. About three years ago he made some temperance speeches, and that hurt him badly with the Germans. We elected the entire ticket except Governor. Belford [congressman] will have about 1,500 majority, and we shall have 53 members of the legislature out of 75, with two contestants who ought to be seated. So there is no danger of a democratic senate. Hill and his crew are now attempting to consolidate the democratic vote on Wolcott, hoping to secure enough republicans to elect him Senator; but it cannot be done.[2]

The failure of the faction to elect its candidate for governor was hailed by the Half-Breed papers as a rebuke to Teller's leadership. And in a sense it was, but the principal victory lay with his faction and with him personally.

When the legislature met in January, there was a widely split field of Republican candidates for the Senate. Every wealthy mineowner in Colorado seemed to want to go to the Senate, and those who had supported the Chaffee-Teller faction demanded it as their just reward. Most striking among these was Horace A. W. Tabor, an uneducated miner, who by an unbelievably lucky series of strikes had become rich beyond the dreams of even the most optimistic prospector. His favors to the organization had already made him lieutenant governor. Thomas F. Dawson recalled years later that when Tabor appealed to Teller for support, on the basis of his munificence to the campaign treasury, Teller replied, "You are mistaken in supposing that I could elect you if I wished. I could not do so if I wished, I would not if I could. . . . I know you are not fitted by education, temperament, or general personal equipment for that office."

The fight soon degenerated into an endurance contest between several candidates who had claims upon the sup-

---

[2] Thomas F. Dawson, *Life and Character of Edward Oliver Wolcott* (New York, 1911), I, 160-69, 180-81; Hall, *Colorado*, III, 33; N. P. Hill to Chandler, Sept. 25, Oct. 4, 1882, Chandler MSS.; Teller to Kirkwood, Dec. 5, 1882, Kirkwood MSS.; a series of clippings on the election of 1882, J. S. Randall Morgue; Denver *Republican*, Aug. 12 to Nov. 4, 1882.

port of Chaffee and Teller. After ninety-two ballots, Tabor was elected for the brief remainder of Teller's term, and Thomas M. Bowen, another wealthy miner—noted outside of Colorado as the "great poker-player of the Western plains"—was chosen for the full term. It was victory for the Teller-Chaffee Republicans, but neither senator was any great credit to the group, and Tabor was particularly unfitted for the Senate.

In his sudden accession to wealth and prestige, Tabor had lost what sense of proportion he once possessed, and became the center of a large number of grafters who bled him of his vast wealth and urged him on to unseemly extravagances. He divorced his wife, a thoroughly respectable influence, and began to live openly with a young woman known locally as "Baby Doe"—sometimes as "Baby Dough." It fitted in with his ideas of propriety to stage a flamboyant marriage ceremony in Washington with the President and other prominent public officials as guests. Shortly afterward it became public knowledge that a previous secret ceremony before he arrived in Washington had made this one unnecessary.

When his term was up on March 4, he left for home, and Teller expressed his relief to Dawson:

> Tabor has gone home. I thank God he was not elected for six years; thirty days nearly killed us. I humiliated myself to attend his wedding because he was Senator from Colorado,—but Mrs. Teller would not. I felt I could not afford to say that the State had sent a man to represent her in the Senate, that I would not recognize socially, but I could not have kept it up with all the exposure of a secret wedding in St. Louis etc. a great while. Tabor is an honest man in money matters, and I believe he is truthful, but he has made a great fool of himself with reference to that woman, and he ought now to retire and attend to his private affairs.[3]

Any pretense that peace could be maintained between Hill and the Teller-Chaffee faction in Colorado was now obviously foolish. The fight was on for the senatorship election of January, 1885, and this time there would be no going by default to second-raters. Hill would be re-elected, or Teller or Chaffee would replace him. The gage of battle being drawn, Hill in Washington and his paper in Denver, did what they could to make Teller's administration of the De-

---

[3] Dawson, *Teller* (1923), p. 27; Stone, *History of Colorado*, I, 432; New York *Tribune*, Dec. 2, 1884; Teller to Dawson, March 8, 1883, Teller MSS.; Hall, *Colorado*, III, 39; David Karsner, *Silver Dollar* (New York, 1932), pp. 93-282.

partment of the Interior a failure in the eyes of the Colorado public.

During the years 1882 to 1885 Teller was more active in Colorado politics than at any time since the fight over statehood in the middle sixties. His two immediate objectives were to secure delegates to the Republican National Convention of 1884 pledged to Arthur, and to have a dominant voice in selecting Hill's successor in 1885. To secure these objectives every department appointment within Colorado was given to those whom Teller considered friends and supporters. "If I do appoint any man who is not my personal or political friend in Colorado, it will be because I am not informed as to his status," he promised his supporters in 1883.[4]

The problem of securing the Republican nomination for President Arthur was no easy task; for in spite of an able administration, Arthur had no real appeal to voters or party workers. The Half-Breeds were as bitter as though Arthur had turned the administration over to Conkling, and the more important Stalwarts were not much more friendly. Some of the former, calling themselves "Garfield avengers," were especially persistent in discrediting the administration. Teller became active in trying to reconcile the New York Stalwarts to Arthur's candidacy, but Conkling was out of politics and Platt was angered at Arthur's failure to turn the New York patronage over to him. This anger grew in the mind of the now dominant New York Republican leader, and Arthur's eventual consultation on some Federal appointments did not appease him. He went over to the Half-Breeds in support of Blaine.

Others of the old Stalwart group were intensely opposed to Arthur, and for a time looked to the use of several different candidates, eventually centering upon General Grant as a means of preserving their identity. In spite of the efforts of Teller to keep him friendly to Arthur, Chaffee was in the midst of this movement, and at first got behind the candidacy of Senator Logan, attempting to bring both Grant and eventually Blaine—for Chaffee had always maintained fairly close relations with the Maine statesman—to the support of the Illinois Stalwart. The scandal of the Grant and Ward brokerage firm, in addition to certain other factors, eliminated Grant. Blaine himself became more active

---

[4] Teller to Dawson, April 18, 1883, Teller MSS.

Senator Nathaniel P. Hill. A former professor at Brown University, he began his Colorado career by introducing improved European methods of ore reduction in gold mining.

as a candidate, and Chaffee, knowing well the weakness of Logan's prospects, interested himself in uniting the forces of the two candidates to pursue a common course at the convention.[5]

The situation in Colorado was all favorable to Blaine, who was very popular there, as everywhere, with the active Republican politicians. The Sherman leaders at the Republican National Convention had hopes of help from Hill, but he had supported Blaine in 1880, and his actions then committed him at least against any vigorous opposition to the latter. Blaine had substantial support in Colorado that was not tied closely to Teller, Chaffee, or Hill, and the supporters of these leaders had no appetite for a drag-out fight against the Half-Breed leader. After the undercover union of the Logan and Blaine groups, Chaffee's problem was solved, for it meant the sponsoring of Blaine in Colorado and securing delegates who would take Logan as a second choice in case of a deadlock.

While Teller's part in all of this is not absolutely clear, it is evident that he stayed out of the campaign for delegates in Colorado, but continued to urge the support of Arthur publicly and privately upon his personal supporters, and professed to believe he would be nominated.

"I notice that the Tribune is again sneering at the President," he wrote Dawson, on February 21 of the election year. "I am quite confident that the President will be nominated at Chicago. I believe he is 20,000 votes stronger in New York than any other man who has been talked of." To another leader who had proposed a different political move, he wrote, "I am for the President and no one else. Of course, I shall do all I can for whoever is nominated. I think it will be President Arthur."

When the Colorado convention assembled, Blaine supporters dominated every faction but Teller's immediate friends. The body adopted resolutions praising President Arthur and his Secretary of the Interior highly, and then adopted another favoring Blaine as the Republican candidate for the Presidency.

Teller always insisted he could have secured the Colorado delegates for Arthur if the President had permitted him to make an active campaign for them—an active campaign

[5] A. O. Scott to Chandler, Dec. 18, 1883, T. C. Platt to Chandler, Dec. 3, 1883, Chandler MSS.; Chaffee to Logan, June 3, 1883, May 19, May 25, 1884, S. B. Elkins to Logan, May 24, 25, 1884, Logan MSS.; Matilda Gresham, *Life of Walter Quintin Gresham* (Chicago, 1918), II, 501, 577.

meaning the use of the appointing power to swing the state
machine into line. Arthur refused to let any Cabinet member
become active in this way and to exercise the full powers
of coercion at his command. It may well be doubted, too,
that, given support from the executive, Teller could have
swung Colorado away from Blaine. Neither his friends nor
enemies ever credited him with much of the manipulative
political ability that Chaffee had in abundance. "He is not
gifted with political shrewdness," Chaffee had confided to
Logan.[6]

There was a disposition among some of the administration supporters to make Gresham their second choice and to
try to give him a dark-horse status as someone for the
Arthur delegates to go to if the President's nomination
proved impossible. Whether or not Teller was a party to this
is not clear, although we do find him warning Gresham on
March 2 that Chaffee and Conkling seemed to have plans
for bringing out Grant at Chicago, plans which he did not
think Logan "was in on."[7]

Arthur's campaign was badly managed at the national
convention, and he came out a poor second, the Blaine-Logan
ticket Chaffee sponsored going before the voters in opposition to Cleveland and Hendricks, the Democratic nominees. Chaffee was rewarded with the chairmanship of the
executive committee of the Republican Party and played
an important part in the campaign. Had Blaine won,
it is likely that Chaffee would have been rewarded with a
place in the Cabinet. He had proved himself an able manager
in national as well as in Colorado politics.

After Blaine's defeat some of his supporters blamed it
upon the lukewarm support he received from the Arthur
administration. This was surely an unjustified complaint, if
Teller's work is any means of judging. In fact, the only
unquestionably reprehensible action or lack of action in
Teller's administration of his department was in the fur-
therance of the party ticket in the presidential campaign
of 1884. As his commissioner of pensions he had inherited
a spoilsman politician in the person of W. W. Dudley, appointed by Garfield. As a part of the attempt to carry debatable states for the ticket, Dudley left Washington after

[6] Teller to Dawson, Feb. 21, 1884, Teller to General R. A. Cameron, no date, Chaffee
to Dawson, March 15, 1884, Teller MSS.; C. C. Davis, *Olden Times in Colorado* (Los
Angeles, 1916), pp. 283-87; Sherman to Foraker, May 31, 1884, in Foraker, *Correspondence with Senator Sherman; Missouri Republican*, May 2, 1884; Chaffee to
Logan, June 3, 1883, Logan MSS.

[7] Teller to Gresham, March 2, 1884, Gresham MSS.

handing in his resignation, "to become effective November 1." He then devoted his time to the campaign in Ohio and Indiana, using a large force of pension appraisers in what cannot be dignified by any other term than trading pensions and prospects of pensions for votes for the Republican ticket. In spite of this, and although there is no doubt that Teller was aware of it, no effort was made by the Secretary of the Interior or by the President to restrict the activities of their subordinate.[8]

Teller assumed the lead in the campaign in Colorado. The combination of factions opposed to Senator Hill defeated the latter in the state convention and nominated the state ticket. Up to the eve of the election, Hill's group threatened to bolt, but both the state and national campaigns in Colorado were Republican victories.

During this campaign, E. O. Wolcott withdrew from Hill's group and publicly attached himself to Teller. In his speech at the Blaine ratification meeting in Denver on July 16, and before the state nominating convention, the younger Wolcott had decried the factional split in the state organization:

I suppose it is a necessity in Colorado, where we have one statesman to the square acre and only one office to the square mile; but the trouble is that blows are given and scars received which are never obliterated. But on this occasion, when we meet as friends and brothers, and under our common flag, and with one battle-cry, it is pleasant for us all to remember some things, and among them it is pleasant for us to remember that during the last three years of the present administration, the most important cabinet office in the gift of the Executive has been filled with dignity and ability by a Colorado gentleman. The success which he has achieved is our success, and we share in his honor; and I tell you, when the influence of the Teller family, either in politics or in morals, ceases to be felt in Colorado it will be the worse for us.

Wolcott was not an unwelcome ally, for Teller recognized that the Wolcotts had been the source of much of Hill's real political strength.[9]

As Republican factions opposed to Hill had controlled the state convention, they also had a large majority of the Republican members of the legislature, who would choose his successor to the Senate. Hill's own supporters were so numerous that if they all united with the Democrats they

[8] *The Nation*, Oct. 2, 1884; *House Reports*, 48 Cong., 1 Sess., III, No. 2683; John W. Oliver, *A History of Civil War Pensions* (Madison, 1917), pp. 108-17; William H. Glasson, *Federal Military Pensions in the United States* (New York, 1918), p. 197.

[9] Dawson, *Wolcott*, I, 172-76, II, 230.

could name the next senator. Colorado tradition has it that
Teller did not want to return to the Senate, and only the
fact that the opposition to Hill, some of it friendly to other
candidates such as Routt and Tabor, would not unite on
anyone but Teller, induced him to accept. However, Teller
had informed his friends long before how he stood. "I can't
say yet whether I shall be a candidate for the Senate or not.
If I am not Chaffee will be and I shall support him." If
nothing more, Chaffee's health forced him out. It is unlikely that he could have been chosen, for there were anti-
Hill factions bitterly opposed to him.

When the legislature opened, the older man took
charge of Teller's headquarters. The strategy of the Teller-
Chaffee Republicans was to draw Hill's legislators into a
caucus on the election of senator. The latter were wary, as
this would very likely prevent later co-operation with the
Democrats. Eventually they went into the caucus and were
defeated, Teller having a clear majority of all Republican
members. Hill's supporters then withdrew, and on January
20, when the first ballot on the senatorship was taken in the
legislature, they still voted for Hill, and divided the vote so
that no one had a majority, although Teller was close to it.
The next day Hill withdrew, and Teller was elected to the
regular term in the Senate.

There seems to be no question that Teller's desire to return to the Senate was great. Although his finances had
suffered by his membership in the Cabinet, his taste of public life and political power had been extremely pleasant.
Then the emotional satisfaction of replacing Hill must have
been great. Teller carried almost no personal animosities,
but by 1885 his dislike of Hill was probably more intense
than any other he ever felt.

Teller's election to the Senate marks the end of an epoch
in the development of the Republican Party in Colorado.
Hill's faction was obviously a sinking political ship, and his
former supporters began to make their peace with the
enemy. Hill retained control of his influential paper and,
largely through it, some power in Republican politics. But
as a contestant for important office he was killed by his
defeat for the senatorship in 1885. Thus ended what one
Colorado historian has called the "mightiest" political struggle in the state.[10]

    [10] Teller to General R. A. Cameron, no date, Teller MSS.; Davis, *op. cit.*; Hall,
Colorado, III, 39-44; Thomas, "Fifty Years," pp. 910-11; Stone, *Colorado*, I, 433; New
York *Tribune*, Jan. 20, 21, 1885; Gunnison *Daily Review Press*, Jan. 9-21, 1885.

Within a little more than a year Chaffee was dead. No one in Teller's day had proved so able at managing the state party organization. But E. O. Wolcott soon rose to a position of leadership in the party circles that in a measure filled the place left by Chaffee. For ten years after 1885 Teller was to take a much smaller part in the details of Colorado politics. He was much happier when he could leave the organization work in charge of a Chaffee or a Wolcott, and devote himself to other things. It is not improbable that the party profited by such an arrangement. Teller made an ideal front; his integrity was unquestioned, and his claims to distinguished statesmanship had some basis in commonly recognized fact. But when it came to the difficult task of keeping the competing factions that made up the Republican Party in Colorado all working together, his talents were inadequate.

Teller's election to the Senate enabled him to reward a faithful supporter. Thomas F. Dawson, who through the Denver *Times* had so ably defended Teller against the Hill-controlled press, went to Washington as Teller's private secretary, a position he held as long as Teller remained in the Senate.

Hill's defeat for re-election did not silence him immediately, and he still had a few shots of the artillery class left for the Secretary of the Interior. Consistency, if not personal animosity, demanded that he continue his fight on Teller to the end. Back in Washington to finish his senatorial term, he chafed impatiently at the lack of action on the Backbone grant which was his only weapon. Four days before the session closed and his term ended, he introduced a resolution declaring that, in the opinion of the Senate, no patents should issue until that body acted on its pending— but now dead—bill relating to the transfer of the grant. His resolution was not passed.

Just before Teller left the Cabinet he caused patents to be issued for the same land which was included in the bill before the Senate—and which the Attorney General had ruled that the Secretary of the Interior was obliged under the law to patent.

As Teller stepped, so to speak, from the Department of the Interior to Hill's seat in the Senate, he was met in the special session called by President Cleveland with a resolution introduced by Senator Van Wyck, of Nebraska, a persistent enemy of corporations and Hill's only supporter, requesting the new head of that department to inform the Senate as to the facts relative to the issuance of the patents, charging by indirection that the transaction was very irregular and surrounded with suspicious circumstances. A few days later, Van Wyck delivered a speech upon his resolution, in which he declared that the grant was "at the dictation and in the interest of corporate wealth whose power had grown to be as omnipotent and whose aggressions as deadly" as those of the historic slave power. After reciting the history of the grant, he claimed that the matter was in controversy in Congress, and hence the Secretary had no right to issue the patents.

Teller replied immediately, and not very courteously.

> I suppose, Mr. President, it [Van Wyck's resolution] has accomplished the purpose for which it was introduced. It has enabled the mover of this resolution to appear before the public, not for the first time, but as he has on various occasions, as the special champion of the laboring classes, the down-trodden people of the country, and as the special opponent of corporations and corporation influences.

He went on to show that it had always been the practice to issue patents on similar grants in this manner, and that Van Wyck had never found fault with it before. The Secretary had no option in the matter, Teller insisted; he was bound "by common courtesy, by common decency, if not by the very terms of the law" to follow the Attorney General's opinion. The idea that an administrative department should suspend action except temporarily because legislation is pending "is abhorrent to every idea of justice and right." The executive must act according to law. That he had done so, he submitted detailed proofs.

The question of the grant hung fire for some time, and, finally, at the request of the new Secretary of the Interior, L. Q. C. Lamar, Congress passed a law granting to the railroad company the land already patented. Teller held that this was unnecessary, but supported it. As a matter of fact, what Congress did was to approve Teller's action, and in Lamar's second report he specifically stated his approval of it. This and the action of Congress, which served to reaffirm the grant, were victories for Teller, and, following the charges of Hill and Van Wyck, they were not unpleasant experiences.[11]

Of Teller's work in the Department of the Interior it is

---

[11] *Congressional Record*, 48 Cong., 2 Sess., p. 2261; *The Nation*, March 12, 1885; Washington *Post*, March 10, 17, 1885.

difficult, even at this late date, to make an authoritative evaluation. Three things only were subject to substantial contemporary criticism: Dudley's campaign activities, the Backbone grant, and the opening of certain Indian reservations. Regarding the first, the complaint was entirely justified. Criticism regarding the others has usually been from biographers of Cleveland who need a dark background against which to paint a shining picture. The best of these, in referring to the public-land policy, concludes: "Arthur's Secretary, Henry M. Teller, was personally honest but had leaned in a deplorable way to the Western demand for rapid exploitation of our national wealth."[12]

Knute Nelson, low-tariff Republican, expressed the Westerner's experience with Secretary Teller when he wrote, in 1909: "I found him one of the ablest, best, and most efficient Secretaries of the Interior we have ever had since I became acquainted with the administration of our Government."[13] Few Cabinet members are able to influence the work of their departments permanently, because their terms are so short. Teller's greatest influence on the affairs of the Department of the Interior was exercised in the Senate after he had ceased to be its head.

On March 4, 1885, Grover Cleveland was inaugurated President, and Teller moved back to the Capitol. As the Senate gathered for the ceremony, observers noticed that Teller sat with Senators Garland, Bayard, and Lamar, all to be members of Cleveland's Cabinet—Lamar being his own successor. Teller did most of the talking in the group, and Garland, especially, listened to him "with great amusement."[14]

[12] Allan Nevins, *Grover Cleveland* (New York, 1932), p. 225.
[13] Dawson, *Teller*, 1923, p. 32.
[14] New York *Tribune*, March 5, 1885; *Harper's Weekly*, March 14, 1885.

CHAPTER XII

SECTIONALISM AND NATIONAL POLITICS
1885-92

THE MOVE from the Cabinet to the Senate was, in several ways, a relief for Teller. The Senate was a place where things were done in a more leisurely manner than in the departments. It was more suited to the ability of a lawyer, although it may be doubted that Teller enjoyed it as much as he did the sense of power that went with his Cabinet position. The political situation was considerably changed in 1885 from what it had been when he first entered the Senate in 1876. Not only were the Democrats in control of the House and the presidency, but the situation within the Republican Party itself was greatly changed. The older leaders had either died, or retired, or were about to do so. The economic issues pushing to the front would make impossible in the future such personal cliques as the Stalwarts and Half-Breeds. Inflation, the regulation of trusts, taxation, and banking were of such evident interest to classes and sections that new factional alignments were necessary, alignments that were destined to cut across party as well as factional lines.

In one respect conditions had not changed. The West was still under a territorial form of government and unrepresented on the floor of the Senate. For five years more Teller was to be as he had been in the past, the unofficial representative of the territories in the Senate. The Department of the Interior had, in a sense, been a continuation of Teller's connections here, and his return to the Senate marked no break. His correspondence with the territories and his senatorial activity on their special problems was as great as it had been from 1876 to 1882. This entailed a large amount of work for Teller, and it was with a feeling of relief that he looked forward to the day when they would have representatives of their own in the Senate. Toward this end he worked persistently, introducing bills for the admission of particular states, and supporting all such proposals before committees and on the floor of the Senate.

Teller's committee selections—necessarily a compromise with the senate rules and his colleagues—further indicate his interest in the West. His personal choice—to which, because of his former membership, he had strong claims—

was the Judiciary Committee, but he did not ask for that now. Instead, he became a member of the committees on Public Lands, Mines and Mining (of which he was chairman), Privileges and Elections, and Patents. These continued to be his committee assignments for the next six years, with such additions as the Special Committee on the Five Civilized Tribes, and, for two congresses, that on the Revision of the Laws of the United States. In the Fiftieth Congress he transferred his chairmanship to the Committee on Patents to allow W. M. Stewart, of Nevada, newly returned to the Senate after an absence of several years, to take over that on Mines. Committee work is unspectacular and attracts little interest, but it is there that the important work in Congress is done. Teller's abilities were execptional in this kind of work. "One of the best Senators for committee service with whom I was ever associated," Senator Shelby M. Cullom was to write many years later.[1]

These years are the most important in Teller's public career from the standpoint of constructive legislation; although with a divided political control in Washington much of this legislation did not get into law until after the election of 1888. The earlier period was a time of planning.

Throughout American history the laws relating to public lands have created a sectional issue whenever Congress proposed to change them. "Free lands to settlers" was a fundamental principle to every Westerner, Teller included. Back of it was a philosophy of government, Jeffersonian in character, which Teller had been exposed to all his life and which he never saw a reason to doubt. Teller declaimed in 1888:

The man who lives upon a farm is never an anarchist; he is never a communist, he is never a revolutionist. It is the men who live upon the farms who are the safety-valve of the nation and the world. The great cities are a source of danger to the body-politic. The more men you can put on the land to till it with their own hands, the better it is for the country.

He tried to educate his colleagues on the need and value of larger areas as farms than they were accustomed to see in the East. Especially, he wanted to refute the common charge running through the magazines that the independent American farmer was passing away and being replaced by a system of European tenantry and large landholders. The decrease in farms of less than fifty acres was, he in-

[1] Shelby M. Cullom, *Fifty Years of Public Service* (Chicago, 1911), p. 231.

sisted, a sign of prosperity. The great increase in the number of five-hundred to one-thousand-acre farms was a cause
for congratulation. "This is the class of farms upon which
... live the intelligent American farmers. This is the class
of farms from which the boys go out to fill all the American
colleges, to fill nearly all the learned professions in this
country, and to control and dominate commerce, politics and
religion." Most of the farms above one thousand acres in
size were also a healthy sign, he thought, and their existence
was no justifiable text for "magazines and newspaper articles and of rostrum speeches *ad nauseam*," deploring the
passing of the farmer.[2]

The legislation of greatest importance that Teller helped
to shape during the late eighties and early nineties was that
governing public lands. In 1886, 1887, 1888, and 1889 laws
of importance on this subject were passed and were followed
in 1891 by a substantial revision of the entire system. This
legislation grew largely out of the work of the Senate Committee on Public Lands under the chairmanship of Preston
B. Plumb. The committee was controlled by Westerners,
and in this period brought out more significant legislation
than any that had been enacted since the passage of the
Homestead Act. It was in line with the recommendations
Teller had made as Secretary of the Interior. The right of
a railroad to withhold its lands from surveys in order to
prevent taxation was carefully regulated. The pre-emption
and timber-culture acts were repealed so as to prevent the
fraudulent entries that permitted corporation control of
large areas. The privilege of commutating homestead entries by purchase was restricted for the same purpose. The
security of a land title acquired by a bona fide settler was
further protected. The President was empowered to establish forest reserves, the first step toward a policy of forest
conservation, and one which the Westerners were later to
regret. It was a large achievement, although far from ideal,
and its main features are still the law of the United States.
Referring to the revision of 1891, Teller later told the
Senate, " ... there has been no single act since I have been
in public life that has brought so much comfort to the people
of the West, and especially to the section in which I live, as
that act." An examination of the *Congressional Record*
shows that Teller had introduced bills embodying most of

---

[2] *Congressional Record*, 50 Cong., 1 Sess., 7027; *ibid.*, 52 Cong., 1 Sess., p. 2266;
ibid., 49 Cong., 1 Sess., pp. 5956-58.

these features, but naturally those passed usually came from the House or Senate committees, and are typical products of the committee system of legislation.[3]

One feature particularly Teller's marked the beginning of the reclamation work of the Government. In the Fiftieth Congress he introduced a joint resolution directing the Secretary of the Interior to investigate the practicability of constructing reservoirs for the storage of waters on the public lands. This was carried through successfully in the spring of 1888, and to give it value the Colorado and Nevada senators prepared an amendment to the general appropriation bill, appropriating money to carry on the resolution, and providing that such reservoir sites would be withdrawn from entry. In the spring of 1888, Teller and Stewart, of Nevada, carried this through the Senate against the wishes of the appropriations committee, and it became the law. Some features were added in conference, however, that resulted in such large withdrawals of land that the Westerners protested vigorously against it. But the law was of great future importance in that it came at the proper time to prevent the monopolizing of reservoir sites.[4] When the final and most important of the laws revising the land system was passed in 1891, Teller retired permanently from the committee dealing with the public lands.

Unlike the Committee on Public Lands, the Committee on Mines and Mining was too well satisfied with existing laws governing that occupation, especially in the territories, to want to make extensive changes. The one attempt the Westerners made to revise these laws taught them that any modifications would probably be highly undesirable to the West when Congress had finished with them. For that reason the Westerners on the committee used their influence successfully in maintaining the *status quo,* and that is the significance of their work.[5]

While it is obvious that Teller picked his committee assignments because of specific legislation, one exception was that he did not get on the Committee on Indian Affairs—

---

[3] *Congressional Record,* 52 Cong., 2 Sess., 1926; *ibid.,* 58 Cong., 1 Sess., p. 5679; Benjamin H. Hibbard, *A History of the Public Land Policies* (New York, 1924), pp. 388, 420-21, 431; Connelley, *Life of Preston B. Plumb,* pp. 360-62, 439-48.

[4] *Congressional Record,* 50 Cong., 1 Sess., pp. 2337, 7012-32; *ibid.,* 51 Cong., 1 Sess., pp. 7070-73, 7282-83, 7413-14; William M. Stewart, *Reminiscences* (New York, 1908), pp. 349-52; Hibbard, *op. cit.,* 430-31; R. J. Hinton, "Irrigation and Legislation," *Belford's Magazine,* Oct., 1890.

[5] *Congressional Record,* 51 Cong., 1 Sess., p. 614; Effie Mona Mack, "William M. Stewart" (unpublished thesis, University of California Library, 1930), pp. 126-31.

although he could not, of course, be on all the committees in whose work he had an interest. In relation to the Indians, the legislation that was in immediate prospect, the Dawes Act, was so well-matured by 1885 that membership on the committee that reported it would have had little significance. Then, too, Teller was opposed to individual allotments of land and the granting of citizenship to Indians; he advocated tribal allotments and continued tribal organization. He made no extended opposition to the bill as it now came from the Committee on Indian Affairs.

This bill provided that individual Indians might select land to be held in severalty and be granted citizenship. The Government was made the trustee of his land for twenty-five years in order that he might not sell or trade it away. This limitation was incorporated because of the objection that had been urged that severalty would make the Indian landless. After restating his argument against severalty, Teller contented himself with attempting to amend the Senate bill in two respects. First, he succeeded in eliminating the Osage Indians, along with the Five Nations, from its provisions. They held an absolute title to their reservation already, and he did not want to force them to divide it up. Then he tried unsuccessfully to amend the bill in such a way as to give the President the power to settle white people on alternate quarter sections of the land selected by the Indians. If they were going to be forced into the white man's ways as rapidly as the bill contemplated, Teller declared this would speed and ease the process of racial amalgamation which was clearly in prospect.

> Give our people under such discretion as the President may exercise, the right to go upon the Indian lands and make, side by side of the Indian farm, a farm tilled by an aggressive and enterprising Anglo-Saxon, and in a little while contact alone will compel these people to accept the civilization that surrounds them on every side.

Dawes agreed to accept the amendment if Teller would limit it to reservations made by executive order. This Teller refused to do, as it would then only apply to a few Indians. He was willing that compensation be provided to the Indian for the lands taken, but his proposal was voted down.[6]

Teller's interest in Indian affairs is shown in numerous arguments, amendments, and bills introduced to carry out

---

[6] *Congressional Record*, 49 Cong., 1 Sess., pp. 811-13, 941, 969, 1558, 1688, 1762-63; Esther Fager Cooper, "The Genesis and Application of the Dawes Act" (unpublished thesis, University of Iowa Library, 1924), pp. 78-87.

his own ideas. He held to the protection of the Indian's property wherever he had a legal title, as in the case of the Five Civilized Tribes, and against any compensation where, as in most cases, the Indian had only a right of occupancy. He favored generosity upon all Indian relief bills.

The Civilized Tribes in Indian Territory were a hobby with Teller. For several years he served on the select committee of the Senate that dealt with their problems, once as chairman, and probably did not exaggerate when he said that for every quarter of an hour's study any other senator had spent upon these Indians' problems, he had spent a full hour. He repeatedly insisted that they had a title to their lands which Congress could not alienate without compensation.

He made two personal investigations of conditions in the Indian Territory during his career, and was always found defending the tribes' rights to their land, insisting that the tribal status should continue as long as possible, in order to protect them against some of the evils that would accompany citizenship. "Senator Teller has always been a true friend of the Cherokee people....We know if anyone should question it, 23,000 Cherokee people would rise up and say 'nay,'" commented the official newspaper of that nation in 1894, when it was criticizing Teller's proposal to establish a Federal court in Indian Territory to try certain types of disputes.[7]

Upon the question of Indian education, Teller maintained the interest he had demonstrated in the Department of the Interior. In following through the Indian appropriation bills as he invariably did, he was a persistent influence for larger appropriations for schools. Shortly after he returned to the Senate, he made a fight for his project for compulsory education for Indian children. The bill was a moderate one, giving the President power to apply the law where he saw fit, and to make increased appropriations for schools. He drove it through the Senate in 1888 but never succeeded in getting it by the House. This rather simple step, which would have aided greatly in bridging the gap between civilization and savagery for the Indian, was destined to be postponed many years. In the meantime, school superintend-

---

[7] *Congressional Record*, 50 Cong., 1 Sess., pp. 2186, 2251; *ibid.*, 50 Cong., 1 Sess., 2186, 2251; *ibid.*, 50 Cong., 2 Sess., pp. 2602-04; *ibid.*, 51 Cong., 1 Sess., pp. 1196-98; *ibid.*, 52 Cong., 1 Sess., pp. 3739, 3741, 3749, 4092; Meredith H. Kidd to Dawes, May 11, 22, 1894, Dawes MSS.; *Cherokee Advocate*, April 18, May 23, 1894.

ents were forced to resort to bribery to get children into
their schools.[8]

The most bitter controversy regarding Indian education
in the nineties was the quarrel among religious bodies to
which the Government gave financial aid. This was an old
system in the Indian Service for which no one in particular
was responsible. Teller's plans for Indian education had
contemplated replacing the church schools with Government
vocational schools. He had no faith in sectarian education.
"They will have religious and moral instruction," he said,
speaking of Government vocational schools. "...They will
not ... have the tenets of the Calvinist taught them, but they
will know the great fundamental truths of Christianity and
morality, and that is all they need to know."

But for immediate purposes it was a question of church
schools or restricting Indian education. The schools belonging to many church bodies had not been successful, and they
were gradually discontinued until the bulk of the institutions
remaining were under the control of the Roman Catholic
Church. As a phase of the nativistic movement, which swept
the country in the nineties under the leadership of the
American Protective Association, the demand was made
that Government aid to these schools be discontinued. So
strong was this demand that Cabinet members were made
and unmade by their stand on the question. It was as bitter
in Colorado as elsewhere, and Teller returned home from
one session of Congress to have three different committees
wait upon him, urging that he support the abolition of Government aid to religious schools. Government, rather than
church, schools had long been Teller's policy, but he was not
willing to abolish the latter immediately. He told the Senate
in 1890:

> I have observed that the Catholics have been the most successful
> educators of the Indians of any people in this country. They have done
> it with less money, and they have done more of it on their own account
> than any other denomination.

He was ready to turn all Indian education over to Government schools as fast as they were provided. But he would
"never vote to turn the Indian children out of a denomina-
tional school until the Government had opened an opportunity for them to go into another school." There should be

---

[8] Leupp, *The Indian and His Problem*, pp. 32-33; *Congressional Record*, 50 Cong.,
1 Sess., pp. 1184-86.

no favorites, either, and when the House eliminated all grants for Catholic schools from an appropriation bill, he questioned the right of Hampton and of Lincoln University, two other nongovernmental schools, to be included. Teller voted to continue all appropriations to such contract schools as had been receiving them heretofore. Throughout his career in the Senate, he continued to support such sectarian schools as could not be replaced by Government schools, always supporting increased appropriations for education, and urging a compulsory-attendance law.[9]

The Indian Service was not benefited by the changes in administration when the Democrats came into power. The demands of the spoilsmen were met to a sufficient degree to load the service with a large number of inefficient and uninterested political appointees. When R. H. Pratt found the new administration forcing untrained teachers on him for the school at Carlisle, he appealed to Teller and Dawes for help. A similar change occurred when the Republicans came back into power in 1889, and again with the return of Cleveland in 1893. Some change in policy was necessary. By 1892 there was a large section of congressional opinion favorable, as it had been in the seventies, toward manning the Indian Service with army officers. Teller opposed this now as he had before.

> I have no criticism to make of any officer in connection with the Indians ... except to say ... I have never yet known a single officer, if I may except Capt. Pratt, who has not regarded it as his whole duty and his entire duty to maintain peace. ... I do not know where they have taken hold to lift up the Indian and make him a civilized being. Their training is not in that direction and they do not do it.

Later, Teller developed a plan of his own to remove the Indian Service from politics and give it a permanent staff. His plan was to substitute for the Commissioner of Indian Affairs a nonpartisan board of three members, one Republican, one Democrat, and one army officer. This bill, although it once passed the House, failed of enactment.[10]

Next to Senator Dawes, Teller was more influential in determining Government policy toward the Indian than any-

[9] T. Bentley Mott, *Myron T. Herrick* (Garden City, 1929), p. 58; A. W. Dunn, *From Harrison to Harding* (New York, 1922), I, 82-84; *The Nation*, Jan. 12, 1893; *Congressional Record*, 51 Cong., 1 Sess., p. 7651; *ibid.*, 53 Cong., 2 Sess., pp. 2502-03; *ibid.*, 54 Cong., 2 Sess., pp. 2040-45; *ibid.*, 56 Cong., 1 Sess., pp. 3831-48, 3898, 5937; *ibid.*, 56 Cong., 2 Sess., pp. 1372-73.

[10] Pratt to Dawes, Aug. 3, 1886, Dawes MSS.; *Fifteenth Annual Report of the Executive Committee of the Indian Rights Association* (Philadelphia, 1898), p. 32; Cooper, *op. cit.*, 153-58; *Congressional Record*, 52 Cong., 1 Sess., p. 2393; *ibid.*, 54 Cong., 1 Sess., p. 485.

one else connected with the Government. From the professional friends of the race he received little or no credit for what he did, and only his colleagues in the Senate realized its importance. He had antagonized many of the former when, as Secretary of the Interior, he took the control of the Indian Service out of the hands of the religious organizations, and when he had opened certain reservations to white settlement. He had little patience with many of these people and often ridiculed their proposals. His opposition to the severalty policy and the destruction of the tribal organizations further antagonized them. It was fruitless to question these policies during Teller's lifetime, but today, when one finds these same groups trying to undo the work Teller opposed, it may well be doubted that the status of the native American would be less desirable had the Coloradan's advice been followed. Except in his opposition to these policies, Teller was regularly found working with the acknowledged champions of the Indian.

Utah was a special Western problem growing out of the Mormon practice of polygamy. Probably no subject since slavery had stirred up so much unreasoning hatred and discussion among nonpolitical groups. The attitude toward the Mormons was more antagonistic in regions surrounding Utah than it was in other parts of the country, except possibly in those parts of Missouri and Illinois where the group had once lived. The Edmunds Act of 1882 had taken away all political rights from those guilty of cohabitation with plural wives, and the control of elections had been placed in the hands of a Federal board. Teller voted for this law. Its enforcement was accompanied by a period of prosecution in which many of the sect's leaders fled the country, and about three hundred were convicted of unlawful cohabitation. Public opinion was still not satisfied, and new legislation came up in Congress in 1886 proposing to limit the right of suffrage by a test oath and to seize the property of the church. It had large majorities behind it, including the strength of almost all churches and newspapers. Colorado politicians thought it wise to denounce the group with special vehemence.

Teller's acquaintance with Mormons was old. The sect had originated not far from his birthplace. He had been in Utah on numerous occasions on legal work, knew many Mormons, and admired many of their characteristics. Teller's well-known views on the sect led to the most emphatic denunciation he received as Secretary of the Interior. It came from the bitterly anti-Mormon Salt Lake City *Tribune*.

We believe that in the place where his heart ought to be Secretary Teller is as good a Mormon and no better man than George Q. Cannon. We believe that polygamy has no horror for him; we believe that in his coarse and sensual, animal nature, he secretly grieves that it is not, under our laws, the legitimate thing for a man to swap off or ignore a woman as soon as her fresher charms leave her. . . . We refer to the man in this way from his known bearing on the Mormon question for years past. . . . We believe he is an enemy of the Republic, and that it is the duty of every free man in the West to despise, if not to hate him.

The proposal in 1886 to subject Utah to further Federal control did not receive Teller's support as had the Edmunds Act of 1882. He offered about the only vocal opposition in the Senate. He gave as his opinion that if it had not been for the persecutions carried on by carpetbag officials sent to that territory, polygamy would have been ended long ago by reformers among the Mormons. Describing the bill as one that "bristles everywhere with vengeance and blood," he defended the Mormons with his customary energy.

They are honest, painstaking, hard-working, industrious people. I went to their capital city when there were 15,000 people there and to their credit it must be said that there was not a place in it where whiskey could be sold, not a grogshop in the length and breadth of the land, not a house of prostitution, not a gambling place in the whole Territory with 80,000 people. . . .

You cannot expect that these men will bastardize their children without a struggle; you cannot expect that the president of that church who married his wives more than a generation ago will put them from him and declare that they are prostitutes. You ought to have some respect for the prejudices, for the feelings, and the religious bigotry of these people.

Only a few Southern Democrats and New Englanders joined with Teller to vote against the bill, but a silly rumor started that Mormons had entered into a political trade with him and had helped elect him to the Senate.[11]

Along with the other unrepresented parts of the United States was that great no man's land known as Alaska. As Secretary of the Interior, Teller had insistently urged Con-

---

[11] *Congressional Record*, 49 Cong., 1 Sess., pp. 461-62, 511-13, 565; *ibid.*, 51 Cong., 1 Sess., p. 6330; O. J. Averell to Chandler, Dec. 16, 1882, and enclosed clipping, Chandler MSS.; Frank J. Cannon and Harvey J. O'Higgins, *Under the Prophet in Utah* (Boston, 1911), p. 86. Teller was paired against the bill. Mrs. E. N. Chapin, *American Court Gossip* (Marshalltown, 1887), p. 152.

gress to provide it with a government and a school system. He followed this up in the Senate by introducing and securing the passage of several bills dealing with fisheries, Indian schools, and geological surveys. Of greater interest was the introduction of reindeer into that region. Dr. Sheldon Jackson, a Presbyterian missionary in charge of education in Alaska—sometimes called "Shellgame" Jackson by the white residents for his work in promoting missions and protecting the natives—became convinced that the prosperity of the natives of Siberia could be communicated to those of Alaska if the domesticated reindeer of the former region were introduced among the Americans. The raising of these animals would provide the natives with a livelihood to replace the already disappearing wild game upon which they had formerly lived. He secured private donations to bring over a few of the animals for a trial, and, as it seemed feasible, he went to Washington to secure Government aid. As Jackson had been in Central City in its early days, it was only natural that he should go to Teller for help. The plan was not unlike Teller's early hope of making the Indian a rancher, as an easy step from his native state to general farming, and Teller became Jackson's champion. He succeeded in getting modest appropriations to carry out the experiment for several years. It was a small matter in which other senators were willing to humor the Coloradan, as one senator phrased it, by stocking "Teller's reindeer farm." Reindeer were brought across from Siberia every year until the Russian government prohibited their export. In gratitude for Teller's work, Jackson and the others interested named the receiving point Teller Reindeer Station, which in time became the modern town of Teller, Alaska. By 1921 some three hundred thousand head of these animals were established in America, being cared for by the natives, who thus made a living from the sale of the meat. It was a small thing, but as Major General A. W. Greely wrote in 1925, it "promises in its results to be the most important benefit ever accorded the natives by the United States."[12]

One of the greatest problems Congress attempted to solve in the eighties was the regulation of interstate commerce.

[12] Lena Mae Lunsford, "The History of Domesticated Reindeer in Alaska" (unpublished thesis, University of Missouri Library, 1933), pp. 8-12; *Twenty-Ninth Annual Report, Lake Mohonk Conference of Friends of Indians and Other Dependent Peoples,* 1911, pp. 72, 73; *Congressional Record,* 51 Cong., 2 Sess., p. 1019; *ibid.,* 52 Cong., 1 Sess., pp. 228, 1314, 1847, 4546-47; *ibid.,* 54 Cong., 1 Sess., pp. 1552, 2474, 3602, 6375; *ibid.,* 48 Cong., 2 Sess., pp. 3914-17; A. W. Greely, *Handbook of Alaska* (New York, 1925), Chapter 19.

When Walter Q. Gresham, whom Arthur had placed on the Federal bench shortly before he left office, announced his decision in the Wabash case, it put the burden directly upon Congress. Teller did not take a very active part in the discussion of the proposal. He offered an amendment to prohibit the giving of passes by railroads to other than employees of the road and argued unsuccessfully for it as ending a political and commercial evil. Naturally he objected to the lack of legal prohibition against charging less for a long than a short haul. What representative of a Rocky Mountain state could do otherwise? Although not willing to hold up a bill to secure this, he gave the following notice to the railroad companies:

> I will join with a number of others who I know are of the same mind to declare that either the railroads voluntarily must discontinue these outrageous proceedings or the strong hand of the law shall compel them under fear of their officials going within the door of the penitentiary.... [13]

Bold, vain words!

Teller's record in the Senate the first years after his experience in the Cabinet was of the same general character as before. Partisan on most issues, he was independent and individualistic on many others. He voted with a small minority against the Beck resolution, which declared that senators should not do legal work for railroads, on the grounds that where such work had no relation to the Government, it was not reprehensible. A senator could be left to his own judgment in each case, "if he is fit to stand in his place." "It [the resolution] contains a principle by which I am governed, not to engage as the attorney of anybody or any interest that will come to this body for legislation in any shape or manner." But senators found it necessary to earn incomes beyond their salaries, he argued, and lawyers need not be precluded from practicing their profession. The popular demand for the resolution was temporary and unthinking, and a dignified Senate should stand out against it.[14]

Much to the disgust of Senator Sherman and the Ohio Republican organization, Teller, Evarts, and Logan joined with the Democrats in the Committee on Privileges and

---

[13] *Congressional Record*, 49 Cong., 1 Sess., p. 4357; *ibid.*, 50 Cong., 1 Sess., pp. 6001-04.

[14] *Congressional Record*, 49 Cong., 1 Sess., pp. 6039-44; *ibid.*, 49 Cong., 2 Sess., pp. 1128-29, 1358-60; *Public Opinion*, July 3, 1886.

Elections, to recommend the seating of Henry B. Payne, Democrat, as senator from the Buckeye state. His election had taken place under questionable circumstances that included the suspicion that the Standard Oil Company had paid for the result. Teller insisted that the Senate, in dealing with the question, was in the position of a court. He told his colleagues:

> I realize as well as anybody can the danger of filling this great body with men who only represent a bank account.... I am for discouraging rich men who have no claim upon the public, who have no fitness for official station, from occupying a place here simply because they are wealthy; but if we proceed to condemn these things we must condemn them within the law; we must follow the usual procedure or else we shall be worse than they.[15]

In any question that came before Congress dealing with the army, pensions, or anything remotely connected with the Civil War, a senator who had not seen service in the Union Army was apt to have his patriotism impugned, especially if he opposed the military group. This happened only once to Teller. Senator Logan sponsored a bill to increase the army from twenty-five to thirty thousand men, insisting that this was necessary to meet the danger presented by organized labor, communism, and anarchism—a general fear raised by recent labor troubles. Teller opposed it on the ground that it was unnecessary and might tend toward the suppression of citizens' rights. Senator Logan, in replying to Teller's argument, insinuated that the opposition was none too patriotic. Teller replied briefly:

> The main answer the Senator made to my objection to the bill yesterday was that on some great occasion, when a large number of soldiers were parading, showing the signs of their service, at which of course the honorable Senator was present, he did not observe my face. Mr. President, I was not there. I have never made any boast of having been in the Army. I have never made this Chamber ring with the statements of the service I had rendered to the country, either in the Army or anywhere else. We all know the Senator from Illinois was in the Army. We are not likely to forget it, for if the Senator should fail to remind us of it on every occasion, the very change in his methods of treating us in the Senate would call our attention sharply to the fact.[16]

The education bill that Teller had urged before he went into the Cabinet was again back in Congress, now known

---

[15] *Congressional Record*, 49 Cong., 1 Sess., pp. 7269-70, 7311-12; *Public Opinion*, July 31, 1886; *The Nation*, July 22, 29, Sept. 16, 1886; *Harper's Weekly*, July 31, 1886.

[16] *Congressional Record*, 49 Cong., 1 Sess., pp. 2878, 2906; *The Nation*, April 22, 1886.

as the Blair bill. It was, in general, a proposal for Federal aid to the common schools in states with a large amount of illiteracy, chiefly for Negro education in the South. Teller gave steady support to the unsuccessful bill. In 1887 he voted with fifteen other senators for a woman-suffrage amendment to the Constitution. The year before, in urging the admission of Washington into the Union, with a constitution which provided for woman suffrage, he had said,

I am in favor of letting Washington settle that for herself, as she has done, and all honor to the new State ... that she is to be the first to take this great step in the march of improvement, and that which is eventually to come to all the States in all the land.

In 1889 he voted with thirteen other senators for a prohibition amendment to the Constitution. Four years before he seems to have been against this idea; on a proposal to exclude liquor from the Senate chamber, he objected to an amendment to add a penalty of expulsion for breach of the rule. That, he thought, would be punishing a state.

I am in favor of temperance, but I believe after all it is a question that must be persuasively addressed to the public mind. I doubt whether you can make people temperate by law, and I speak after much thought upon the subject, Mr. President, and I speak as a person who has never tasted in any manner or at any time either spirituous or vinous drinks.

He voted against the Presidential Succession Act because of its failure to provide for the calling of a new election in case of the death of both the President and Vice-President.

Teller urged closer diplomatic and commercial relations with the nations of southern South America; he proposed to have each Cabinet member assume responsibility for the advice given the President, by making it a matter of public record; he opposed secret sessions of the Senate, except in matters relating to foreign affairs. He favored repealing the prohibition against pensions to veterans of the Mexican War who had been in the Confederate Army. He opposed purchases of convict-made goods by the Government in competition with free labor. Teller's whole attitude toward labor at this time was frontier *laissez faire*, if we except the legal prohibitions of Chinese, convict, and contract labor. Like his colleagues, he was not "class minded," and did not conceive of a permanent labor class.

When the laborer shall decline to be considered or treated as a class having different wants and interests, needing different legislation,

with different aspirations and ambitions from that of the balance of
the citizens of the Republic, and shall with confidence in their strength
... demand that which is clearly their due—the right to self-control,
an open unobstructed highway out of the ranks of mere labor into
any and all other occupations, employments, professions, and places
that they are qualified to fill—then will there be an end of the supposed conflict between capital and labor.[17]

Many of these attitudes show an individualism that was
sufficiently marked to cause Senator George G. Vest to remark: "I knew that while the Senator did vote the Republican ticket he had some of the habits of the Democratic
Party."[18] But Teller's work was only partially of this
nature. He was a leader of the Republican Party, and stood
with it on all partisan issues, taking an active part in debate.
As the election of 1888 approached he was its chief defender
upon the floor of the Senate, being particularly well situated
to defend the Arthur administration in comparison with
Cleveland's. To this work he devoted himself with a whole
heart and effective results.

His attack upon the Democratic Party was upon the
issues of tariff, Chinese immigration, civil service, coinage
of silver, and the fisheries treaty. On the latter subject
Teller made the longest speech he had delivered in the
Senate. There was something incongruous in a senator from
the Rocky Mountains discussing the question of fishing off
Newfoundland. Possibly Teller's activity on this question
and on certain tariff rates far removed from Western interests was an unconscious compensation for his usual con-
centration on work in the interest of the Far West. But
chiefly they were partisan questions upon which he was
acting as a party-conscious Republican.[19]

Upon the question of civil service, his activity was not
so much an attack on the Democrats as it was a defense of
Arthur's administration. Teller was in an ideal position to
defend it on this count, as his own department had been
notable for the lack of politics in its appointments. This was
not altogether Teller's work, for since Schurz's incumbency
politics had not been influential in the routine appointments—a policy Teller had generally followed. This was
readily admitted by the Democrats in the Senate as far as

---

[17] *Congressional Record*, 49 Cong., 1 Sess., pp. 129, 192, 252, 3317; *ibid.*, 49 Cong.,
2 Sess., pp. 1002, 1073, 2376; *ibid.*, 50 Cong., 1 Sess., pp. 9550-51; *ibid.*, 50 Cong.,
2 Sess., p. 2166.

[18] *Ibid.*, 49 Cong., 1 Sess., p. 6848.

[19] W. Stull Holt, *Treaties Defeated by the United States Senate* (Baltimore, 1933),
pp. 143-49.

that department was concerned. Teller himself attacked the appointments that had been made in the Pension Bureau by the Democrats. Although these were under the civil service law, none but Democrats had been appointed—a situation, Teller insisted, that could not have come about "without a plain violation of the law." When he blandly suggested that possibly that condition was accidental, Senator Francis M. Cockrell, who was leading the Democratic defense, observed, "The innocence of the Senator from Colorado is truly commendable and refreshing."

Upon the specifically Western issues, Teller's speeches in the Senate were Republican documents for the campaign in that section. His speech on silver, although admitting that the Arthur administration had been as bad, was effective in proving that the Democrats had no claim to the support of those who favored free coinage of that metal.

On the Pacific Coast, Chinese immigration was the issue which had determined national elections in the past. In order to revive this issue for the coming campaign, a bill providing some further restrictions was brought into the House by a Pennsylvania Democrat, William L. Scott, a personal friend of President Cleveland. It was all a political trick, Teller declared, to pass this bill through a Democratic House and then have it die in a committee of the Republican Senate. Then the Democrats would go to the country as the friend of labor. But the Republicans, Teller told the other side of the Senate, were ready. They refused to move a reference of the bill and would not oppose its passage. Now the Democrats would have to make it a law or admit they were opposed to it. Then, so far as the record is concerned, Teller quoted the only verse of any kind he ever used in a speech. As for Scott, said Teller,

> He digged a pit
> He digged it deep
> He digged it for his brother;
> But for his sin
> He did fall in
> The pit he digged for another.

He made a long historical argument to prove that in the Western states it had always been the Democratic organization that had favored immigration, and the Republican that had opposed it. It was effective propaganda and was used extensively in the West.

Most of these were, in a sense, local issues. The great issue that was emphasized everywhere in the campaign was the tariff. Cleveland's famous message on the question had assured that. The Democratic House and Republican Senate both enacted bills. Shortly after Cleveland's message was made public, Teller delivered a speech on the question in the Senate that was intended and used for campaign purposes. Referring to the President's message, he declared, "At home and 'abroad, everywhere, it had been received, not as an attack upon a defective tariff . . . but for the purpose of destroying the protective system." In proof of this he offered quotation after quotation from the British press, jubilant in tone over the prospect of an American revenue tariff. Tariff for revenue only was a new policy, Teller attempted to prove, and not historic Democracy. By quoting from Jefferson, Jackson, and Benton, he attempted to show that, except for Calhoun, Cleveland was not in the line of Democratic tradition.[20]

Teller also played an active part in the Republican National Convention of 1888. In the state campaign two years before he had taken little part beyond acting as temporary chairman of the state convention and eulogizing Jerome B. Chaffee. Some Republican dissatisfaction enabled the Democrats to elect popular Alva Adams governor, although the bulk of the Republican ticket won. As the campaign of 1888 approached Teller became more active, as he was particularly interested in securing delegates to the national convention who would support a Western presidential candidate, preferably his colleague of the Cabinet days, Walter Q. Gresham.

Gresham was the candidate of the reform element in the Republican Party, including some of the Mugwumps who had bolted Blaine in 1884. These were not powerful in the Republican convention, however, and here Gresham's support came from those states, like Illinois, where railroad regulation was popular. The greatest weakness of his candidacy lay in his failure to carry his home state, Indiana, which, after a warm contest, had gone to Benjamin Harrison. Teller brought Gresham the support of most of the Colorado delegation and aided him in other states and territories. The same thing that made Gresham a strong candidate in the West—his views on railroad regulation—made

---

[20] *Congressional Record*, 50 Cong., 1 Sess., pp. 2094-2101, 6610-27, 7213-21, 8216-56, 8501-02, 9563-65.

him a weak one in the large Eastern states, and his cause was hopeless unless he could gain the support of some delegation such as Pennsylvania's or New York's.

Teller worked on the New York delegation. When Tom Platt came to Washington early in June, Teller urged him to support Gresham, but all he got was Platt's promise to call on Gresham when he arrived at the convention in Chicago. "Platt wants it understood that he is a power," Teller warned Gresham. Teller went to the convention and continued his activity, but had no success with the New York group, for even though some of them expressed a desire to vote for Gresham they were not willing to break away from their leaders. Teller blamed his failure on Depew's antagonism to Gresham's well-known views on railroad regulation. Teller denounced Depew as a railroad lobbyist to every Westerner he met.

Congressman Jehu Baker was more expressive on this point: "They are not afraid of Judge Gresham's attitude on the protection question," he told a reporter. "But the New Yorkers are like the links of a sausage, made of the same gut. The first link is Jay Gould; the second is Vanderbilt; the third is Depew; and the fourth is—Blaine."

The Colorado delegation voted first for Gresham, then for Allison, of Iowa, and finally went to the only other Western candidate, Harrison, who was nominated.

Mrs. Gresham relates that when Platt demanded the appointment as Secretary of the Treasury as his reward for bringing the New York delegation to Harrison, Teller served notice on the president-elect that he would defeat Platt's confirmation in the Senate if he were designated by the President. While this may be true, Teller had more substantial reasons for opposition than his anger at Platt's work in the convention. He and the other Westerners wanted someone in that place who had a different background on monetary issues. They got such a man in William Windom, but before long had cause to be as disappointed as though they had failed to influence the President's choice.[12]

During the campaign, Teller led the fight from the platform in Colorado. Silver was the important issue there rather than protection, and Teller had no difficulty in con-

[21] Teller to Gresham, May 19, June 5, 27, 29, 1888, Gresham MSS.; Charles Edward Russell, *These Shifting Scenes* (New York, 1914), pp. 111-31; Gresham, *W. Q. Gresham*, pp. 576-610; St. Louis *Republic*, June 23-26, 1888; *Official Proceedings of the Republican National Convention, 1888*, pp. 159, 163, 199; New York *Tribune*, June 22-24, 1888; Irving Howbert, *Memories of a Life Time in the Pike's Peak Region* (New York, 1925), pp. 267-68.

victing the Democratic administrations of opposition to
free coinage. The Republican plank seemed favorable, and
the local group carried the state for the Republican ticket,
giving Harrison the largest majority it had ever given a
presidential candidate.

Following the election, the legislature had to choose a
successor to Senator Bowen. E. O. Wolcott, the most active
Republican leader in the state, had approached Teller for
his support for the Republican nomination to Congress in
1886. Teller, who was friendly to the incumbent, had urged
Wolcott to wait two years and try for the Senate. Wolcott
had followed that advice and now won an easy victory over
Bowen in the Republican caucus and later over the Democratic candidate in the legislature.

Wolcott's election was welcome to Teller. He was an
extremely likable individual, and Teller became very fond
of him. Although incapable of sustained mental effort, his
abilities as a popular orator were extraordinary even for
the Senate. Few, indeed, of his contemporaries were his
peers in this respect. His relations with Teller were very
friendly, and for the next seven years they worked in close
harmony. Teller sponsored Wolcott in the Republican organization, secured good committee assignments for him and
then advised him not to hold back, but to engage in debate
immediately—advice which the younger man followed with
success. Teller depended upon him to carry a large share
of the burden of debate. They were a strong pair, each contributing what the other lacked. Wolcott, with New England and Yale background, was soon a social favorite in
Washington and able to exercise an influence that Teller did
not have. Probably no state in the Union had more effective
representation in the Senate during the next twelve years
than Colorado. It needed it, for issues were rapidly coming
to the front which required extraordinary ability in order
to protect local and sectional interests.[22]

To aid in meeting these, the Westerners were successful
in bringing into the Union six new states in 1889 and 1890.
To Teller this was a great victory and a great personal relief.
Now he was free to leave the committees which were especially concerned with the West and become a member of the
more important groups which usually are composed of senators of long experience. As the new Westerners took their

    [22] Dawson, *Wolcott*, I, 179-92; R. F. Pettigrew, *Imperial Washington* (Chicago,
1922), pp. 203-04; Thomas, "Fifty Years," pp. 913-14; Stone, *Colorado*, I, 433.

Edward O. Wolcott, Teller's colleague from 1889 to 1901.

places on committees, Teller shifted his assignments to the Judiciary, Appropriations, and Rules committees. Among the senators from the new states he was the recognized leader for their section. The West's strength in the Senate was increased severalfold.

CHAPTER XIII

TELLER AND THE CAUSE OF FREE SILVER
1888-91

THE DEBATE on the Bland-Allison bill in 1878 had found Teller unprepared. He had, of course, a lawyer's and a businessman's knowledge of finance, but his education did not extend beyond that. He became painfully aware of this during the debate and saw immediately that it was a subject upon which he must be informed. As early as 1874 the value of the silver produced in Colorado had exceeded that of gold, and the year after the Bland-Allison Act was passed it was four times as valuable.[1] Here, certainly, was an issue upon which a Colorado senator would need to be an expert.

No statesman ever prepared himself upon a public question with more care and industry than Teller did in becoming familiar with the question of money. All his legal training and experience and his natural aptitude for study helped to make that preparation adequate. He purchased the standard works upon finance and began his study. Not to be too much tied to theory, he subscribed to the leading American financial papers and read them regularly. Later, he added the English *Economist* and *Statist*, and finally the French *L'Economiste*. Like a professor keeping abreast of his specialty, Teller followed every new development in all phases of finance, corresponding with American and European economists, digging into histories formerly unknown to him for the light they shed upon the immediate problem, and burdening the representatives of foreign nations in Washington with requests for information regarding particular phases of their national monetary systems. It need not be emphasized that he approached the problem from a prejudiced point of view because silver mining was a local interest. He was conservative by nature, and a businessman with the business point of view. He respected the opinions of bankers, men of great wealth, and the editors of the financial papers. But his study coming in connection with the growing silver interest at home made him an intense advocate of bimetallism, and left him with a poor opinion of the financial knowledge of bankers when they got away from the immediate problems of discount and exchange.

---

[1] Charles W. Henderson, *Mining in Colorado*, p. 69.

Nevertheless, the fact that he was advocating before the public what was, in part at least, a selfish local interest, irritated his conscience, and he returned repeatedly to the charge that the silver cause was more than that. He said in 1888:

> I admit that if I had not lived in a silver-producing State I might never have had my attention directed to this subject. I might have been willing ... to accept the statements of doctrinaires and ill-informed people as to facts; but if my attention had been directed to it and I had studied it as I have studied it, I would have the same views if I lived in Connecticut that I have living in Colorado.[2]

The problem that Teller saw was this: Through almost all the historic period mankind had used two metals, gold and silver, as money. The supply of these had increased as man's needs increased, and they together had supplied a satisfactory medium of exchange that kept values fairly well stabilized. The use of two metals had the advantage that in case of a difference in the established values, the one with the lower value became the temporary standard and brought it into greater demand and the values back to something like the ratio originally set.

This, itself, helped to prevent any great changes in the system of values to the detriment of either creditor or debtor. One metal checked the other in such a way as to stabilize their comparative value. This almost ideal system had been interferred with in recent times. In 1867 an international conference had suggested that the double standard be abolished and replaced with an international unit of one metal, much as it might have recommended the adoption of the metric system by all countries. This idea was seized upon by the public and private creditor class in all countries in an effort to go to the gold standard. England was already there, and Germany went soon after the conference, bidding for gold wherever she could get it and throwing her vast amount of silver coin upon the bullion market. The United States followed in 1873 with an act that passed unnoticed at the time, for few silver dollars were in use, as the coinage ratio in the United States undervalued silver in comparison with the market price and the ratios in use elsewhere. Many of the smaller European nations followed, and soon gold was in great demand. Silver, being in far less demand, was declining in value in relation to gold.

---

[2] *Congressional Record*, 50 Cong., 1 Sess., p. 2440.

Two other factors came in to emphasize these tendencies. The world's production of gold lessened greatly, while that of silver increased, which meant that the cost of mining gold had become greater and that of silver less. But the problem did not end with the changing value of the two metals. All other kinds of property also fell in value relative to gold, and a great change in relationships followed. Debts increased in value, and the burden of the debtor became a continually increasing one. This was the main problem as Teller chose to see it. The gold standard meant, under conditions which then existed, a continual appreciation of the standard of exchange and a steady increase in the debts of all debtors. There never was a clearer case of a debtor-creditor struggle, with the creditor having the advantage of a government-made appreciation—government-made because it had changed the legal standard in 1873. Nowhere in the world was this condition so evil as in the United States, for here the gold standard appreciation came as a supplement to an appreciation of the paper (greenback) standard of the Civil War. The resumption of specie payment, however great its necessity, had the effect of making the debtor redeem his borrowings in dollars worth far more than those he had originally received. Before this contraction was over the appreciation of the gold standard began, and the same condition of enriching the lender at the expense of the debtor continued.

It was not so much the evils of the past that Teller emphasized as the promise of continued deflation. He saw no prospect of the production of gold increasing in such a degree as to check the steady fall of prices and the steady increase of debts. This great cause of human misery could be ended in only one way that seemed just to Teller, and that was to re-establish the free coinage of silver. Free coinage of silver by the United States would encourage other nations to take similar action, and a bimetallic system would be re-established in the world. It would cause immediate inflation; we might go to the silver standard alone—Teller admitted that—but this was a small evil compared to the constant grinding of the monetary system upon the farmer and debtor.

Teller was as careful as usual in his position on this question. A few times in the heat of debate he fell into oracular statements, such as that silver had been made standard money "by the fiat of the Almighty, when He created the two metals," but these were exceedingly few.[3] Extremists among the silver men might shout about the "crime of '73," but Teller never did; they might lump their opponents together as "goldbugs," but he would not; they might flatter with repetition such arguments as W. H. Harvey popularized in *Coin's Financial School,* but Teller never would. He addressed himself to the economist and informed public opinion, and in that lay his great strength. The opponents of free silver listened to him, and his own partisans depended upon him to keep their campaign directed at attainable goals. It was said that the English and French bimetallists read his speeches with great interest.

The Bland-Allison Act remained for a long time a popular compromise over the silver issue. It was not satisfactory to Teller or any other convinced bimetallist, but political conditions were such that any change looking toward bimetallism was not possible. Nevertheless it was urged. Teller had urged free coinage in 1882, and denounced John Sherman's conduct of the Treasury Department in purchasing only the minimum required by law. The same year he introduced a resolution declaring that the purpose of the Government was to establish free coinage, but his entrance into the Cabinet had prevented further agitation in the Senate until he returned in 1885. Soon after that, he urged free coinage in a long speech, and criticized the administration for its manner of carrying out the Bland-Allison Act. His objection here was that every administration, including Arthur's, had used every means in its power to discredit silver as money. It had administered the law in such a way as to make the smallest amount of coinage possible, and warned against the danger of the use of silver money. In the subsequent Congress he again urged free coinage, and pointed out the continued rise in the value of gold standard money, comparing it unfavorably with the silver standard in Mexico, where values were remaining fairly well balanced, and with bimetallic France, where he thought they were much more stable.[4] But these attempts were unsuccessful, and it was anticipated that they would be. A majority of the Senate was not for free silver, though these members were bimetallists

---

[3] *Ibid.,* 51 Cong., 1 Sess., p. 4646. Although Teller did not emphasize it, he always insisted that any international agreement for silver coinage should be at the ratio of the Latin Monetary Union, 15½ to 1. See his statement in the *Arena,* Jan., 1896.

[4] *Congressional Record,* 47 Cong., 1 Sess., pp. 446-49, 681-82, 2100; *ibid.,* 49 Cong., 1 Sess., pp. 747-55; *ibid.,* 50 Cong., 1 Sess., pp. 2434-40.

in theory almost without exception, if we can accept their declarations.

The change that raised hopes for silver legislation was the admission of new Western states, which made it possible to overcome the anti-free-silver majority in the Senate, and the election of 1888, which had given the silver men a presumptive majority in both houses of Congress, with a President who, they believed, was friendly toward silver legislation.

At the Republican convention of 1888, the silver men had demanded a platform that was favorable and a candidate who would not veto a free coinage bill. Referring to the Westerners, Teller wrote his own candidate, Gresham, "I have assured them that you are not hostile to Silver money & that you will not be controlled by Wall St. if elected." The resolutions committee framed a straddle plank on silver that many of the silver advocates believed pledged the party to positive action in the direction of free coinage:

The Republican party is in favor of the use of both gold and silver as money, and condemns the policy of the Democratic Administration in its efforts to demonetize silver.

Senator William M. Stewart, of Nevada, asked for and received what he believed were assurances that Harrison, if nominated and elected, would not veto a free-coinage bill, and most of the silver men went to him after Gresham and Allison proved improbable nominees. With a favorable-sounding plank, and the known opposition of Cleveland to silver, the Republicans had little difficulty in piling up a larger than normal majority in Colorado. Harrison's cordiality immediately after the election led Teller to believe the remonetization of silver was possible.[5]

When Teller returned to Washington in the fall of 1889 for the opening of the memorable Fifty-first Congress, he began the greatest fight of his career—that for free coinage. The Republicans at last had control of both houses of Congress and the Presidency. The senators from the new states were apparently as strong for silver as Teller himself. Then, too, Teller had a colleague in Wolcott, who, although about to take his seat for the first time, would soon assume first rank as an orator and debater. For help in organizing the

---

[5] Mack, "Stewart," pp. 204-12; Teller to Gresham, May 19, 1888, Gresham MSS.; Benjamin Harrison to Teller, Nov. 14, 1888, Teller MSS.; Teller to Hal Sayre, Dec. 30, 1888, Sayre MSS.; *Congressional Record*, 51 Cong., 1 Sess., p. 6173.

Western silver men there were the two senators from Nevada. John P. Jones, older in the Senate than Teller, was a man of unusual ability and striking personality, but ordinarily inclined to be inactive. His colleague Stewart, although badly handicapped by his record of having voted for the "crime of '73," was, for all his Santa Claus appearance, a vigorous and an able fighter. In some respects Plumb, of Kansas, was a more effective supporter, as no suspicion of personal silver-mining interests hung about him. These with the senators from the new states and the rural Democrats of the South and West represented the real strength of silver and inflation.

But first of all there was party strength to be maintained, and if the Republicans as an organization were to enact legislation they would have to maintain party lines. There were demands from several party factions for legislation, each representing definite economic interests. Silver, tariff, trust regulation, were to compete within the party with the more purely partisan issues such as the Elections bill. Pledges had been made regarding most of them during the recent campaign, and, with complete Republican control, there would be no excuse for the party if it failed. A compromise program all around was desirable, at least from the standpoint of the party.

Such seems to have been the wish of the administration and the Republican leaders in Congress—Teller alone excepted. There is little direct evidence upon the exact nature of disagreement between Teller and the other leaders, but that it was there is clearly evident. In keeping with the compromise idea the new Secretary of the Treasury, William Windom, submitted a plan for silver legislation that was aimed at raising the price of silver, and did not, in any direct way, aim at the general price level or eventual free coinage. President Harrison in his message to Congress likewise put himself on record in words that could only be interpreted as opposing free coinage, but left the way open for some such legislation as his Secretary of the Treasury proposed.

On January 20, Teller called on President Harrison to oppose the Windom plan and urge free silver in its place. Harrison held no brief for the Windom plan, but wanted a "Republican bill." He also informed Teller that he would veto any bill "going so far as to be unsound."[6] After this Teller knew that free coinage was impossible in that Con-

---

[6] James A. Barnes, *John G. Carlisle* (New York, 1931), pp. 219-20.

gress. It was clearly evident that the President might be able to stop such a bill in the House, and if not checked there, he would surely veto it. Not even the Senate would pass such a bill over his veto.

But the silver men were not entirely helpless; they could hold up the tariff, if necessary, to secure some favorable action on silver. It is not likely that the Republican silver senators were willing to go so far in this as to prevent a tariff bill, for there was a strong tendency, especially among the patronage-hungry senators from the new states, to stay in the good graces of the administration.

Nevertheless, Teller determined to make a fight for free coinage. He introduced a free coinage amendment to the purchase bill under consideration by the Senate Committee on Finance, and gave notice that the Senate would have to go on record regarding it. After that the consideration of the monetary legislation was transferred to several informal party caucuses, the object of which was an agreement on legislation that would keep the Republican organization intact. A subcommittee of both House and Senate Republicans, considering the question in April, came to an agreement on a silver-purchase bill of four and one-half million ounces of silver each month, to be paid for by "silver bullion treasury notes." Senator Aldrich reported to Harrison on April 23 that all were agreed on the compromise except Teller, who proposed to fight for free coinage but would take what he could get. Teller informed a reporter that he was determined to work first for free coinage, and if that failed, to fight for making the proposed treasury notes legal tender. He would oppose any bill that gave the Treasury the power to redeem silver certificates in bullion. The other silver men were apparently unwilling to back him to the limit in opposition to the new purchase act.[7]

On the floor of the Senate he characterized such plans as the "Trojan horse" of the gold monometallists. "It is no answer to me," he declared, "to say 'It will put the price of silver up to 129,' or that 'it is a silver bill.' If it should put up the price of silver to 150 it would never receive my support." It was, he held, merely a proposal to redeem paper money in the commodity of silver, and would not affect the problem of an appreciating standard. It might give us a better supply of currency, but that was all. "We must be squarely upon a

---

[7] St. Louis *Republic*, April 24, 1890; Dawson *Wolcott*, I, 210.

gold basis or we must recognize silver as money. There can be no half-way about it.... "[8]

The House passed a close approximation to the caucus bill, plus the legal tender provision Teller had demanded, and the Senate committee reported that as a substitute for its own bill. Plumb moved a free coinage amendment which was adopted, and the bill passed. There was no expectation that free coinage would result, but Teller was determined to make the Senate and House both go on record, and, if possible, force Harrison to veto the bill. The administration and partisan Republicans generally were very anxious to prevent the latter because of the influence it might have in the campaign of 1890. The pressure they were able to exert upon the Republican members of the House was intense. This, together with certain adroit legislative maneuvers of Speaker Reed, brought out a safe majority against the bill.

Teller informed the Senate that this was a clear repudiation of the public will as expressed in the last election.

The firmness of Harrison against free coinage, in contrast to his apparent friendliness before election, embittered Teller, and he spared neither the administration nor his party in his denunciation. The other silver men followed, and Wolcott, especially, delivered an extreme attack upon the administration—evidence of the split the party leaders had tried to avoid. This split extended to patronage matters, and from this time on there was little co-operation between the White House and the Colorado senators.[9]

After the defeat of the Senate free-coinage amendment the bill went to a conference committee. Any hope of free coinage, or of forcing Harrison to take the responsibility of a veto, had been lost through the administration victory in the House. The silver men might still have brought more pressure by holding up the tariff or attaching to it a free-coinage amendment, but they were as a whole more inclined to maintain party harmony by compromise. Teller seems clearly to have been willing to go much further in this direction than the others, but he could not secure sufficient support. The senators from the new states, upon whom he had

[8] *Congressional Record*, 51 Cong., 1 Sess., pp. 4645-50, 4900-01.

[9] *Ibid.*, p. 7021; Francis E. Leupp, "Personal Recollections of Thomas B. Reed," *The Outlook*, Sept. 3, 1910; William A. Robinson, *Thomas B. Reed*, pp. 243-46. James F. Wilson in a letter to Allison (June 28) put the Republican problem pointedly: "I am sorry that the Senate put free coinage in the silver bill. If the House should concur and the President veto the bill, we will have a bad job on our hands; for, of course, the bill could not be passed over the veto, and we should all be at sea again on that question." Allison MSS.

counted, proved to be too susceptible to party discipline and administration pressure for any drawn-out fight. Nevertheless, the silver men refused to take up the tariff bill in the Senate until the compromise on silver was agreed upon. The Republican members of the conference committee worked this out, and the silver men staked out their last trench on monthly purchases of four and one-half million ounces of silver, and legal tender quality for the resulting currency. This they got in the final draft, which was to bear Sherman's name. It will be noted that the legal-tender provision had not been included in the earlier caucus measure, and it was partly, at least, as a result of Teller's persistence that the silver men insisted on it now. The report was strictly a Republican Party measure. Teller declared that he voted for it "reluctantly" because it might raise the price of silver and be a step in the direction of free coinage. If there had been any remote opportunity for free-coinage legislation in this Congress, he would not have supported the bill. It was a Republican measure designed to maintain party harmony and to make the passage of a Republican tariff possible. Later, when the bill became discredited, Sherman and other Eastern Republicans declared it did not have their approval, but at the time it passed, it received the praise and approval of the Republican leaders and the financial press. It was, as Teller afterwards said, a "sop to the West" to keep it Republican. Beyond question some of the silver advocates thought more highly of the purchase law than Teller did, and a few Western Republican newspapers praised it as the solution of the silver problem.[10]

The feeling within the Republican ranks in the debilitating July heat in Washington became very hostile. When the silver Republicans broke away from the caucus decision and voted for free silver, the dean of the party, Senator Edmunds, read them a lecture on party loyalty, which did not improve the situation. Senator R. F. Pettigrew, of South Dakota, was also a native of Vermont, and Edmunds took occasion to reprimand the younger man personally for his failure to follow the caucus decision. Pettigrew illustrated the party morale by answering:

---

[10] *Congressional Record*, 51 Cong., 1 Sess., pp. 7020-22, 7107-09; St. Louis *Republic*, July 10, 11, 1890; Fred Wellborn, "The Influence of the Silver Republican Senators, 1889-1891," *Mississippi Valley Historical Review*, XIV (Mar., 1928), 462-72; Newlands to Harrison, June 5, 1890, in Stephenson, *Aldrich*, pp. 437-38; *Public Opinion*, July 19, 1890; Barnes, *Carlisle*, p. 186; Gresham, II, 638; Robert F. Hoxie, "The Silver Debate of 1890," *Journal of Political Economy*, I (Sept., 1893), 535-87; Mack, "Stewart," pp. 222-23.

I will tend to my own affairs. Further than that, if there is any more of this bossing, enough Senators from the new states will go over to the Democrats and will organize the Senate, and you'll have to pack up your whiskey jug and get out of that Judiciary Committee room.

The party lacked unity, and Harrison failed to give it much. There is no doubt that the Republican willingness to pass the Sherman Act was due primarily to a realization that they could not maintain party unity without it, and without party unity a tariff could not be enacted.[11]

Toward the Sherman Anti-Trust law enacted during the session, Teller manifested a lack of interest. He introduced a bill of his own to prohibit combinations from controlling the rights to patented articles, but never pushed it with any vigor. He voted for Reagan's amendment to the Sherman bill to add criminal penalties for breaking the law, but protested that as then phrased the bill would not touch the Standard Oil Company and could be used against farm organizations and labor unions. He urged that this last be corrected beyond a shadow of a doubt. "My real objection to this bill is that it is delusive." It might do some good, but he doubted it very much.

With the Silver Purchase Act passed, the legislation pressing for attention in the Senate was the McKinley tariff and the Elections bill, both of which had passed the House. The silver senators had obligated themselves to support the tariff by party support of the Purchase Act. Teller seems to have played little direct part in these trades because of his dissatisfaction with the silver legislation. As Sherman said, he was an "off ox" on all these questions.

Certainly he was on the Elections bill, better known as the Force bill. This was an attempt to give the Federal government greater control of national elections in the South, in order to protect the Negro in his right to vote. Harrison was favorable to such a bill and actively urged it. As a preliminary to the struggle, the issues of the Civil War had been warmly debated in the spring of 1890 on the Blair bill for Federal aid to Negro education. Teller took the Southerners to task for their opposition, telling them that everyone else was trying to let the dead past bury its dead. He was for Negro suffrage as he always had been, but admitted great difficulties existed in the race problem. The main difficulty, he found, was in the failure of the white South to attempt to solve the problem. Teller explained:

---

[11] Dunn, *From Harrison to Harding*, I, 64, 89; *The Nation*, June 19, 1890.

I do not want for myself drastic laws to compel you to treat them properly. I want you to do it without. I want you to do it because it is right that it should be done, and I am willing . . . to trust the people of that section, if they will but show a disposition on their part to take hold and try to solve this great question.

That was on March 14, and it meant that Teller might not support a Force bill.

On April 24, Hoar introduced the expected bill for the regulation of elections. When he did, Pugh, of Alabama, speaking for the Democrats on the Committee on Elections, declared:

If this bill becomes a law, its execution will insure the shedding of blood and the destruction of the peace and good order of this country. Its passage will be resisted by every parliamentary method . . . allowed by the Constitution of the United States.

Teller also made a brief statement.

As a member of the committee that reported this bill, I assented to its being reported, but I have desired to reserve the right on an examination of the bill (which I have had no fair opportunity yet to examine thoroughly), the right to vote for it in whole or in part or to participate in making amendments to it if I should think amendments ought to be made.[12]

The Republicans were far from agreed upon the question, although the dominant politicians were insistent that it be carried out. The Lodge bill in the House was more extreme than Hoar's plan, and in the Republican caucus of that body it carried by only one vote, but such are the mores of the faithful party member that a majority of one in the caucus of the majority party meant a majority in the House of Representatives. Under Speaker Reed's dominating control, it was put through without extensive debate and by almost unanimous party support. In the Senate there was considerable Republican opposition to the bill. Evarts of the committee did not like it any better than Teller, but he would go with the majority, easing his way by telling a story on Chancellor Kent. Evarts had once visited the venerable jurist with a group of lawyers, and as it was Sunday, the group attended church in a body. One of the lawyers irri-

---

[12] *Congressional Record*, 51 Cong., 1 Sess., pp. 2232-34, 2471-72, 2560-61, 2571-72, 2611, 3760 ; *ibid.*, 51 Cong., 2 Sess., p. 1233. After Teller's speech of March 14 on the Blair bill, Senator George, of Mississippi, made this comment: "If all of us on both sides of the chamber in dealing with this question . . . would bring to its solution, if solution is possible, the temper, the charity, the kindness, and the good feeling, and the statesmanship exhibited by the Senator from Colorado, I think a great deal of the trouble would be removed."

tated Kent by being several words behind the congregation in reading the responses, and the old lawyer broke out afterwards with "Davis, why can't you descend into hell with the rest of the congregation?"

Evarts was not Davis, he informed the committee, and he would go with the rest of the congregation. But Teller would not, unless the congregation saw fit to follow the path he wanted to use. He had voted to report the bill with numerous amendments and without any promise of final support or opposition.[13]

The Elections bill created an immediate problem for those who were insistent upon passing the tariff bill. The Southern Democrats would unquestionably filibuster the former to the limit of their ability. If it were brought before the Senate before the tariff was passed, there would be little chance of enacting either without closure. It was already July, congressmen wanted to recess in order to take part in the fall campaign, and the short session beginning after the election was an ideal opportunity for a successful filibuster. To ensure success with both bills the Republican organization would have to introduce closure, and the recent success of Speaker Reed in modifying the House rules made many of them willing to do so. But not all, and unless closure were voted, the tariff people would have to postpone the Elections bill or lose out themselves.

The Republican caucus had begun consideration of the tariff and of the Elections bill before the silver act was passed. In spite of rumors of serious opposition, the press reported that the caucus of July 10 had agreed that a change in the rules of the Senate was necessary, and voted 28 to 5 to appoint a committee to study methods of closure. The five votes against were Teller, Plumb, Wolcott, Blair, and Edmunds. At least the last was against closure on principle and not necessarily against the Elections bill.

Four days later the caucus found among its own members more opposition that would not be removed by a majority caucus decision. For a time, the group seems to have moved along the line of modifying the Elections bill in order to make it acceptable to a large enough group of Republicans to secure a majority for closure. This too failed. August 1

[13] Wellborn, *loc. cit.*; *The Nation*, Aug. 7, 1890 ; George F. Hoar, *Autobiography of Seventy Years* (New York, 1913), II, 150-65 ; George F. Hoar, "The Fate of the Election Bill," *Forum*, April, 1891 ; McCall, *Reed*, p. 175.

arrived, and there was no evidence that either piece of legislation was nearer enactment.[14]

On August 4, Teller addressed the Senate, stating his purpose of voting "as a general rule" for the tariff bill, as it came from the Senate committee. However, "hasty legislation was bad legislation," and, notwithstanding the numerous protests against debate on the bill, he "did not propose to be frightened into any haste or expedition." He would oppose any changes in the Senate rules. "The speech of Senator Teller," exulted *The Nation*, "settles in the negative the question of whether 'Tom' Reed can make the Senate change its rules in order to rush through the McKinley Bill and the Force Bill."[15]

It was already apparent to the tariff people that the consideration of the Elections bill would only handicap them; besides that, the threat of a Southern boycott of Northern products caused them to pause. Even the New York *Tribune's* suggestion that the Elections bill "carries within itself the assurance of future tariff bills by the hundred" did not appear as desirable as one definite raise in rates before the approaching election disturbed conditions. Senator Quay, of Pennsylvania, apparently acting on a suggestion that came directly from a manufacturer in his home state, and, it was rumored, indirectly from James G. Blaine, proposed a resolution to set a date for a vote on the tariff and then adjourn. This proved so popular with the Republican senators that they began to work toward that end without formal action on the resolution. The Democrats were pleased, and willingly let the tariff come to a vote. That they had some understanding with Quay has frequently been charged. Before giving up entirely, Hoar secured an agreement from the Republican caucus to take his bill up as soon as the short session opened in December, and fight for it to the end. He insisted that this was agreed to in writing by a majority of the Senate, including closure if the caucus voted for it.[16]

The silver Republican senators supported the McKinley tariff and secured high rates on the two products in which they were principally interested—wool and lead. Their support of the tariff, Teller later insisted, was an obligation

---

[14] St. Louis *Republic*, July 12, 15, 20, 29, 1890; Stephenson, *Aldrich*, 438, note 18.

[15] *Congressional Record*, 51 Cong., 1 Sess., p. 8105; *The Nation*, Aug. 7, 1890; St. Louis *Republic*, Aug. 5, 1890.

[16] Wellborn, *loc. cit.*; St. Louis *Republic*, Aug. 8, 10, 14, 15, 20, 21, 25; Atlanta *Constitution*, Aug. 15, 16, 17, 22; *Public Opinion*, Aug. 16; *The Nation*, Aug. 21; *Harper's Weekly*, Aug. 23, 30; Edmunds to Morrill, Sept. 9, 16, 1890, Morrill MSS.

assumed as part of the party compromise regarding silver and tariff. "Upon my judgment I would never have voted for the McKinley Bill."[17]

The Congressional elections of 1890, which followed the enactment of the McKinley tariff, were an overwhelming defeat for the Republicans. Low-tariff Democrats replaced Republicans in the East, and free-coinage and low-tariff Democrats replaced them in the West and South. Seldom has a party suffered such an overwhelming reversal at the polls. However, the Republicans would control Congress until March 4 through their majorities elected in 1888.

In some partisan minds, the defeat revived the demand for the Elections bill. They thought they saw in it a means of preventing such disasters as they had just experienced. Outside of purely partisan groups, however, Northern opinion against the bill was stronger than it had been in the summer. There was no longer any general desire there to protect the Negro's voting rights.

Immediately after the session opened, Teller delivered an attack on the bill. He favored its general purpose, he insisted, of protecting the Negro in his voting rights, and was ready to vote for a proper bill. The original Lodge bill had been vicious. The Senate committee's amendments, he admitted, removed some of the bad features; but not all, and those in charge must remove the rest. "If they do not, I shall exercise the right I have always exercised at such times, to vote according to my judgment and my conscience." A few days later he repeated that he was willing to vote for the bill if certain amendments were adopted. Senator Stewart then attacked the bill, and Wolcott followed, both taking ground in more direct opposition than Teller had. Both had opposed it in the Republican caucus before, but now their opposition was being placed on record.[18]

Just what was going on during December in the informal Republican caucuses is still unknown. Yet they began to consider more action in the direction of silver coinage, although the Sherman Act had just gone into effect. It may well be that an attempt was being made to secure silver support for the Force bill and closure, in return for increasing the amount of silver coinage. At least, rumors to that effect were current, and charges were made in the House and in

---

[17] *Congressional Record*, 54 Cong., 1 Sess., pp. 4561-62.

[18] *Ibid.*, 51 Cong., 2 Sess., pp. 169, 867, 881-85; *The Nation*, Dec. 11; St. Louis *Republic*, Dec. 6, 7, 1890.

the press that its only purpose was a private speculation in silver on the part of a group of senators. An agreement seems to have been considered to increase the amount of silver purchases for 1891 above those provided for in the Sherman Act, and a bill for this purpose was introduced. Possibly it was felt that the Republican House leaders who wanted the Elections bill badly could be forced to support this silver legislation. Two factors destroyed any hope of such a bargain. Teller had no great desire for more silver legislation of the purchase type; he clearly saw, as he had seen the year before, that it did not materially help the free-coinage cause. Many Eastern Republicans were decidedly against it also, and were not inclined to support another Sherman Act even for an Elections bill.

The silver senators' repudiation of the new purchase bill came when Teller called it "Wall Street's Bill," and Stewart introduced an amendment to it providing for free coinage. There was just a chance that a free-coinage bill passing the Senate in the lame duck session might also pass the House. The evident popularity of free coinage in the South and West in the recent election might induce some congressmen from these regions to change their votes, and the declining fortunes of the administration, with its patronage largely used up, may have led the Silverites to believe it possible. It would be something for the silver cause to force Harrison to veto a free-coinage bill. Then Teller charged that the Republicans were dilatory regarding the Elections bill and were using it to prevent consideration of silver. Plumb introduced a silver bill and announced that if the Elections bill were not out of the way soon he would move to displace it with his bill.[19]

Senator Hoar moved on, confident that closure and his bill would be adopted. Early in January the Republican organization sent out word to all absent members urging them to return so as to be present when the question came to a vote. Senator Jones received the notice and returned to Washington, being met at the train by Teller, Stewart, and Wolcott. The next day, January 5, McConnell, of Idaho, was seated, and he with his colleague Shoup gave the Republicans a still larger majority. Clearly unconscious that anything of importance was impending, Vice-President Morton went to lunch, leaving a Democrat, Harris, presiding. Another

---

[19] St. Louis *Republic*, Dec. 11, 12, 14, 17, 24, 27, 30, 1890.

Democrat held the floor, speaking against the Elections bill. Teller, Jones, Stewart, and Wolcott were seen to gather in a small group in the rear of the room. Stewart asked the Senator having the floor to yield and moved that the Senate take up the silver bill, to which he had introduced his free-coinage amendment. The temporary presiding officer declared the motion in order, and confusion reigned on the Republican side.

Vice-President Morton rushed back to his post with a piece of quail between his teeth, and his napkin still in his hand. But it was too late; the roll was being called. There were two Republican votes, in addition to the Colorado and Nevada conspirators, sure for displacing the Elections bill—Washburn, of Minnesota, and Stanford, of California. These were not enough with the Democrats to be sure of winning, but when McConnell, who had been added to the roll a few hours before, voted yea, it was evident where the extra Republican votes were to come from. Both senators from Idaho voted yea, and Stewart's motion carried 34 to 29, including a paired Democrat, who should not have voted. Not counting this, the motion had a majority of 4 and the Elections bill was displaced.

The very partisan Republican press denounced the Republican bolters in extreme terms. "These names," threatened the New York *Tribune*, "are not likely to be forgotten," and another reverted to prewar terminology to describe them as "doughfaced northern allies." A substantial section of the Republican press, however, instead of criticizing, suggested that the bill was properly killed, and a good riddance.[20]

The administration was not without weapons to strike back. Four days after the silver bill displaced the Elections bill, President Harrison sent his nominations for members of an international commission on coinage to the Senate, and they included the name of N. P. Hill, of Denver. Newspapers speculated over whether or not Teller would oppose his confirmation. The Governor and other Colorado Republicans urged him and Wolcott to let the appointment be confirmed, as a rejection might mean the appointment of an antisilver member. As soon as the silver bill with the free-coinage amendment was out of the way, the Colorado senators made public a reply:

---

[20] Wellborn, *loc. cit.; Congressional Record,* 51 Cong., 2 Sess., p. 912; St. Louis *Globe-Democrat,* Jan. 6; *Public Opinion,* Jan. 10; *Harper's Weekly,* Jan. 17; St. Louis *Republic,* Jan. 6; Atlanta *Constitution,* Jan. 6, all 1891.

Mr. Hill's nomination was intended and is everywhere recognized here as an affront to the Colorado senators for their course. . . . His conduct in the past . . . justify us in procuring rejection . . . but . . . we concluded to request his confirmation.[21]

The silver bill was quickly passed by the Senate in a form providing for free coinage. With this out of the way, the administration made its last desperate attempt to get the Force bill through the Senate. When Hoar moved that it be taken up, the Idaho senators, their duty to silver done, went with the organization, and the vote stood 33 to 33. Vice-President Morton cast the deciding vote to make a majority for taking up the bill. About six weeks remained of the session, and the bill would be lost unless closure could be applied. Aldrich introduced a closure motion, and a majority voted to consider it, the Colorado and Nevada senators voting with the Democrats on such motions.

On January 19, Teller told a reporter that at least ten Republicans would be against closure on a direct vote. At the same time, a reporter heard the rumor that Teller would move to take up some appropriation bill and again displace Hoar's bill, believing that at least eight Republicans would vote with him. After some consultation with Democratic senators, it was decided to make the motion on the bill for reapportionment of representation instead. Probably the fact that this had special constitutional justification determined the choice. Without notice to the Republican organization senators, Wolcott made the motion in the midst of the closure debate. Hoar moved to table it and was defeated 34 to 35. Then Wolcott's motion carried by the same majority of one. Cameron, of Pennsylvania, voted with Teller, Wolcott, Stewart, Jones, and Washburn. Senator Ingalls, of Kansas, up for re-election in the Kansas legislature, paired for the motion. The Elections bill was dead.[22]

As Teller had predicted, the first time the consideration of the bill had been displaced, charges were freely made that the silver men had made a trade with the Democrats for support of free coinage, a charge that James Ford Rhodes repeated in 1919. Teller vigorously denied any such arrangement. Unless we assume that they got nothing in exchange, it is impossible to find a basis for this charge. The Sherman Act was out of the way before the Force bill came up in the

---

[21] Washington *Evening Star*, Jan. 10; Omaha *World-Herald*, Jan. 19; St. Louis *Republic*, Jan. 16, 1891; *Congressional Record*, 51 Cong., 2 Sess., pp. 1079, 1767.

[22] *Congressional Record*, 51 Cong., 2 Sess., pp. 1324, 1667, 1740; Atlanta *Constitution*, Jan. 26, 27; St. Louis *Republic*, Jan. 27, 28, 1891.

Senate. No other silver legislation that had any chance of enactment was in prospect. The second free-coinage bill that had passed the Senate was entirely dependent in the House on Republican votes, and the best the Silverites could expect would be to force Harrison to veto it. Democratic votes in the House were useless for this purpose, as it would take Republican votes that had been against free coinage the summer before.[23]

Exactly why the silver senators opposed the Elections bill so strenuously is not easy to determine. Washburn, Cameron, Ingalls, and Stanford were no doubt evidence of the opposition of conservative Republican opinion, and as far as the Kansas senator was concerned, of the Farmers' Alliance. Possibly Jones belongs here also. Stewart probably did not favor Negro suffrage. But Teller did. Undoubtedly there were constitutional objections to certain parts of the bill that Hoar refused to change, and to which Teller had objected years before. Teller insisted all through the debate that he would vote for the bill if these were removed. These facts, together with a burning resentment toward the administration and Eastern party leaders for their refusal to enact a more favorable silver bill, seem to be the most reasonable explanation.[24]

The public reaction to the work of the Republican silver senators varied. Cameron was burned in effigy in Pennsylvania. Partisan Republican papers used terms like traitor and Judas, the latter in reference to the asserted silver trade. Democratic and independent, as well as some Republican papers, approved their course. "The Bancroft of the future will be forced to give these three Republican senators [Teller, Stewart, Wolcott] an honorable place in history," offered the Democratic St. Louis *Republic*. "Their names should be immortalized."[25]

---

[23] *Congressional Record*, 51 Cong., 2 Sess., p. 941; James Ford Rhodes, *The History of the United States from the Compromise of 1850* (New York, 1919), VIII, 363. On this point Wellborn concludes, " . . . the only thing they [Democrats] could have given . . . was support of Stewart's free coinage bill. This they were quite willing to do, consequently there was no occasion for a bargain."

[24] *Congressional Record*, 52 Cong., 1 Sess., p. 3445.

[25] St. Louis *Republic*, Jan. 27, 30, 1891.

CHAPTER XIV

SILVER BECOMES THE PARAMOUNT ISSUE
1891-92

TELLER'S part in the campaign of 1890 in Colorado had been small. Congress had remained in session throughout September in the press of work on the tariff bill. This made little difference, as far as his candidacy for re-election to the Senate was concerned, since there was no public opposition to him among the Republicans. A Republican legislature was all that was essential.

When he returned to Colorado after the passage of the McKinley Act, he met a difficult situation within the state. There was a wide split in the Republican organization in Denver, now beginning to experience some of the usual evils of corrupt city politics. Worse than this was the record of the Republican state administration, which was being charged with corruption by some of the Republican leaders themselves. The state convention had made partial amends by nominating John L. Routt for governor, and the campaign was well under way.

Trying as always to keep himself as separate as possible from the local factions and issues, Teller took the stump for the state ticket in opposition to Thomas M. Patterson, who was leading the Democratic campaign. Patterson had recently purchased the *Rocky Mountain News* and was making it a potent political force in the state. Teller's speeches were largely concerned with his own course in national politics, but they defended, rather lamely, the state organization as well. The general trend to the Democrats was evident in Colorado, and near the end of the campaign it seemed to Teller like anyone's victory. He wrote Dawson on the first of November: "If the state goes democratic we will have until March 4th to pack up our things & get out and I am confident that I will be happier out than in." But contrary to the trend over the country, the Republicans in general won in Colorado. Several Republican candidates for minor offices, who were opposed by Hill's newspaper, were defeated in close races, but Routt was elected governor, and the legislature was safely Republican. There was no good reason to suspect that there would be any opposition to Teller's re-election to the Senate. The Republicans had made their campaign for the legislature on the necessity of returning Teller to the Senate, and even many of the independent and Democratic papers during the campaign had been repeating the chorus, "The state needs Teller."[1]

When the legislature met, the Republicans split into two factions that refused to meet together for any purpose. Teller, who had thought his return safely secured, had this problem to ponder over during January, 1891, when he was in the midst of the fight over the Elections bill. The members of both Republican factions were pledged to Teller's election, but the bitter feeling carried with it the danger of manipulation, and there were constant rumors and charges of undercover plots to elect some other Republican. To prevent any last minute chicanery, a pledge was circulated among the Republican members of the legislature of both factions, pledging them to vote for Teller.

> Whatever differences may exist on other subjects in the minds of the members of the Republican party in Colorado, there is but one sentiment throughout the state respecting the senatorship. Your splendid services to the country and to Colorado are recognized and appreciated by every good citizen within the limits of this commonwealth.... We therefore take pleasure in assuring you that we shall each of us consider it our privilege ... to cast our ballots for you for the Senate.... "

This was signed by forty-seven Republican members of the legislature, a majority, and the fact telegraphed to Teller. Late in the month, and just before the final displacement of the Force bill, Teller's friends succeeded in bringing the legislative factions together long enough to re-elect him to the Senate for six more years.[2] He had made no personal effort to secure his re-election; his patronage was severely limited; and his relations with the national administration were very unfriendly. Had there not been a great public issue in which Colorado was intensely interested, and had not Teller been recognized in the state as its most able

---

[1] Teller to Dawson, Nov. 1, 1890, Teller MSS.; *Rocky Mountain News*, Nov. 1-4; Denver *Republican*, Oct. 30-Nov. 5, 1890; Dawson, *Wolcott*, I, 197-99. Teller's final campaign speech in Denver brought out this poem published in Patterson's paper:

> Sophistry, cant and greed;
> Answers long gone to seed;
> A solemn face
> His words to grace;
> *His* part—a glorious deed.
> November, drear and chill—
> The frost upon the hill;
> The beech-nut gapes, and Teller quakes
> At the impending public will.

[2] E. M. Ammons to T. F. Dawson, Jan. 21, 1891, Teller MSS.; Denver *Republican*, Jan. 7, 9, 10, 20, 21, 22; St. Louis *Globe-Democrat*, Jan. 7, 1891.

advocate, he might easily have failed of election. Locally he was in an enviable political position.

After the passage of the Sherman Purchase Act, the eyes of the silver leaders had been focused on the price of the metal. Many of them and their journalistic supporters had expected that the law would cause a solid improvement in its price. The immediate result was a substantial rise, partly the result of speculation and partly of the increased market made for silver by that bill. Its price in relation to gold reached a point higher than it had been since 1878. It began to decline immediately thereafter, however, and early in 1892 was back at its old level, and continued to decline. Unfortunately for its sponsors, the act was in operation at the time of great business uncertainty. The failure of Baring Brothers in England in 1890 had created a small panic there, which tended to be communicated to the United States. It started a tendency toward the marketing of American securities held in Britain in order to liquidate the resources of hard-pressed banks. Gold exports from the United States, however, were prevented for a time by extraordinary exports of farm products, which caused a large balance of trade in favor of the United States. Nevertheless, the entire financial structure was in need of improvement. The banking and commercial classes, seeing a danger that the United States might be forced to a silver basis by exports of gold, began a concerted move to repeal the Sherman Act. Aided by the press, they began to demand that the parties pledge themselves to its repeal, and force such a bill through Congress. The unpopularity of the legislation in the East led the regular Republicans to try to shift the responsibility for its enactment, and now the myth, "It saved us from free silver," began to be cultivated.

With a hope of checking this movement against the use of silver as money, Teller delivered a long speech in the Senate on the question early in January of 1892. First, he absolutely refused to accept any responsibility for the Sherman Purchase Act for himself or the silver Republicans. It was not their bill, but the party's measure, from which he had expected little.

> If disaster comes, as it will, I have no doubt, if this policy is persisted in, let it be laid at the door of the men who for fifteen years steadily resisted what I believe to be a very general public demand for the use of silver on equal terms with gold.

Next, he attacked the fiscal policies of the administration, and waxed sarcastic over President Harrison's suggestion that the way to secure international bimetallism was to accumulate gold and force Europe to use silver. A debtor nation accumulate gold! We cannot keep our gold if Europe wants it, as long as she holds our securities and the balance of trade is not in our favor. A serious problem was admitted—seventeen years of world-wide depression due to an appreciating standard of value. Bimetallism was the only safe remedy.

> I believe that free coinage in the United States would bring the whole world to the use of silver, as it was prior to 1871. On that point I may be mistaken. I do not claim any infallibility.[3]

Part of his program included the defeat of Harrison's nomination, if in any way possible. To do this, Teller and a number of other silver Republicans joined forces with certain state leaders in the East, especially T. C. Platt and Quay, who were opposed to Harrison. They centered upon James G. Blaine as the only leader popular enough to win over Harrison. His record on silver was satisfactory. Teller's attitude is clearly stated in a letter to R. W. Steele at Denver, written shortly before the New Year.

> I do not think *we* can afford to send a delegation to the National Convention that is for Harrison. It would be a declaration that all our zeal for silver was a pretence. If however Mr. Harrison is nominated we can give him our support and still insist that we disagree with him on the silver question. I think Blaine will be the nominee and I believe he is the only man we can elect and that appears to be the general opinion here.... I was greatly shocked at the death of Plumb and as you say the West has lost a good friend and so have I. I fear his place will be poorly filled from Kansas.

Teller never had much love for Blaine, but was making the best of a bad situation. Four years before he had confided to Gresham, "The Pacific Coast people have been for Blaine because of his silver record.... I do *not* trust him on that question at all."[4]

Hill, with his newspaper, the Denver *Republican,* and the support of the Federal officeholders, was trying to have the Colorado delegation to the national convention pledged to Harrison. To counteract this, Teller and Wolcott gave in-

---

[3] *Congressional Record,* 52 Cong., 1 Sess., pp. 147-51.
[4] Teller to R. W. Steele, Dec. 29, 1891, Teller MSS.; Teller to Gresham, May 19, 1888, Gresham MSS.

terviews in the *Rocky Mountain News* of February 14, 1892, advising against sending Harrison delegates to Minneapolis as detrimental to the cause of free coinage. Wolcott predicted that if Harrison were nominated, and the Democrats also named a gold standard candidate, "silver will fall to fifty or sixty cents an ounce within the next eighteen months." Secretary Blaine's public announcement that he was not a candidate hurt the chances of those opposed to Harrison, as they could not unite upon anyone else, and a campaign against a candidate and not for one is always difficult.

But the silver men moved forward resolutely. The Democratic victory in the congressional election of 1890 had brought to the House what was thought to be a free-coinage majority. Although the chief issue in the campaign had been tariff, it seems highly probable that a majority had also committed itself to free silver, and there was no question about the silver majority in the Senate. The proper move on the part of the silver men, then, was to pass a free-coinage bill, and force Harrison to take a public stand on the direct issue before the convention met at Minneapolis. Under the Democratic leadership of "Silver Dick" Bland the move began in the House. But the forces of the administration were busy, and pressure of all kinds was brought to bear upon those Republicans who were not very firm in the faith. Similarly, Eastern Democrats exerted pressure upon their Congressmen. On March 24, 1892, "the night free silver was killed," the bill came to a vote in the House. A motion to table it resulted in a tie vote, to the immense surprise of the silver men. The number of those who dodged voting was large, and many of them had colleagues announce in their absence that they were for free coinage, but, as they were not paired, it helped Bland not at all. Political jujitsu, the influence of the press, of the financial interests, and of the administration had defeated a fairly clear expression of a popular demand. Everyone admitted it was a severe defeat and unexpected.

Undeterred by this, the silver Republicans went on with their program. On April 20, a few days before the Colorado Republican convention met, Teller delivered their challenge in the Senate. Referring to the action of the House, he declared that it had contained "a great majority" for free coinage when it assembled, and, untouched by political pressure, it would have acted in that direction. He challenged anyone to deny his analysis of the case. Its defeat was due to the power of patronage, added to the organized activity of every New York bank. They were opposed to a gesture of friendliness toward silver, for fear it would aid bimetallism in Europe, and in the world.

Does anyone suppose that the men who hold the credits of the world ... and who take by reason of the present condition of affairs financially ... nearly 40 per cent more from the people who owe these debts than they would under a proper system of currency, will tamely and quietly surrender the advantage which they have secured by so much effort and so much labor? ... [5]

When the Senate passed a free-coinage bill in 1890, he related, it was defeated in the House "by undue and improper executive interference." The silver men had been told to take the Sherman bill or nothing. Now, the same forces that put that upon the Republican Party were trying to force its repeal, and would attempt to place the Republican Party at Minneapolis "in antagonism to silver."

I want to say now to the Senate, and I am saying it here that it may reach the American public, that it may reach the leaders of the Republican party ... if the Republican party stands for the gold standard, the four silver producing states will not, in my judgment, hereafter be able to act in cooperation with the Eastern Republicans. ... Why should we do so? ... But like our party, the Democratic party is in the toils of a power it dare not offend, and the danger is that these two great political parties in their anxiety to secure the State of New York, controlled as it is by a little circle in and about Manhattan Island, will neglect and repudiate the interest of the great masses of the country and act exactly alike on this silver question.... When you have given to the dollar a purchasing power, as you have now, 30 per cent more than normal, when you have added to it by the destruction of the silver of the world as you propose, so that a dollar will buy what it took two dollars to buy when bimetallism existed, you have doubled the debt; you have put upon the struggling debtor a burden that he cannot stand under.... This is the great debtor period of the world. ... Can you view the prospect with equanimity? ... I may be a fanatic. I may be an enthusiast. Every word I have uttered upon this subject lies close to my heart. I believe it ... and I warn my party ... it cannot afford to put itself on the side of contraction to the extent of one-half of the volume of money of the world, either by deliberate action in that direction or by a refusal to affirmatively act in opposition to that attempt.

---

[5] Dawson, *Wolcott*, I, 201; *Congressional Record*, 52 Cong., 1 Sess., p. 2543; *Harper's Weekly*, April 9, 1892; W. D. Orcutt, *Burroughs of Michigan and the Republican Party* (New York, 1927), I, 329-35; *Public Opinion*, April 2, 1892; A. M. Arnett, *The Populist Movement in Georgia* (New York, 1922), p. 134.

"The Republican National Convention will make its own
response, and undoubtedly a sufficient one, to the bulldozing
spirit of Senator Teller's remarks," wrote the New York
Tribune. "His repeated votes with the Democrats . . . on the
bill to secure honest elections, and on some other measures,
do not entitle him to higher consideration at the hands of
the convention than would be accorded a Senator from any
other small State." "There have been few abler speeches
made in the Senate since the days of Benton upon questions
of finance," praised Patterson's *Rocky Mountain News.*
Hill's Denver *Republican* regretted "that any Republican
Senator . . . should do or say anything designed to disorga-
nize or disrupt the Republican party on the eve of a Presidential election." A new Democratic congressman from
Nebraska, W. J. Bryan, wrote Teller the day after the
speech was given: "I will be greatly obliged if you will send
me as many copies of your speech as possible for distribution
in Nebraska."[6]

When the Republican convention met in Colorado to
select delegates to the national convention, it hissed Hill's
statement that Harrison was friendly toward silver, and
chose an unpledged delegation to go to Minneapolis. Among
the delegates were Teller and Wolcott. E. M. Ammons wrote
to Dawson that the sentiment at the convention was "that we
should make the strongest fight possible for what we wanted
at the Minneapolis convention and—take what we can get,
on the theory that whatever we shall be able to get must be
through the Republican party."[7]

Shortly before the Republican convention met, Senator
Sherman delivered an address in opposition to free coinage
that was the declaration of the East for the benefit of the
convention. Teller replied to it. One of the factors that had
always troubled the silver men and was to continue to do
so was that their opponents all proclaimed themselves convinced bimetallists. "Bye and bye metallists," Wolcott had
called them. Teller forced Sherman to define his bimetallism,
and it proved to be the gold standard with subsidiary silver
coins. Teller truthfully observed, "He might as well have
said that he was a trimetallist, and was in favor of gold
as a standard, and silver for 10-cent pieces and copper for
cents."

But what roused Teller's wrath was something else. The

   [6] *Congressional Record,* 52 Cong., 1 Sess., pp. 3438-46; *Public Opinion,* April 30,
1892; New York *Tribune,* April 21, 1892; Bryan to Teller, April 21, 1892, Teller MSS.
   [7] Ammons to Dawson, April 28, 1892, Teller MSS.

administration was carrying on negotiations to secure an international agreement for the use of silver as money, and was having the usual difficulty of overcoming the general European belief that the United States had inexhaustible supplies of silver that it was trying to foist upon other countries. Yet with these negotiations pending, Sherman had stated that if silver should go to par we would produce five times the present bullion production, and gave an unknown silver senator as his authority. This statement, said Teller, showed on the face of it the "grossest ignorance" and yet, backed by the authority of Sherman, it would be accepted as true in Europe. "Did he think it his duty to put in the way of the proposed conference that obstacle?" Were the Eastern Republicans sincere in regard to an international agreement, or were they trying to kill it by indirection? The feeling between the Republican factions was not made more pleasant by the debate.[8]

When the Republican convention met at Minneapolis early in June, Blaine had raised the hopes of the silver men by resigning from the Cabinet, and placing himself in the way of the nomination. Teller told a reporter that "while Blaine, perhaps, was not his personal choice," he was for him because he could win and Harrison could not. It was the first national convention at which Teller played a prominent role. As a nonsmoker, he must have enjoyed a quiet smile over the advertisements for the "Teller Cigar" brought out by an enterprising Minneapolis dealer.

The Colorado delegation took the lead of the delegations from the Western states and had printed on their badges, "Blaine and Free Coinage." On the afternoon of June 6, a caucus was called of all prosilver delegates. About one hundred and fifty presented themselves and organized by electing Teller chairman.

The first question raised was whether to discuss the platform or the candidates, and the chairman immediately answered, "the candidate." The plank made no difference, he informed the group, if Harrison was nominated. This excited the Harrison delegates from California and other Western states, but Teller, aided by John P. Jones, of Nevada, kept the meeting driving toward an agreement on Blaine as the silver candidate. Harrison delegates from

---

[8] *Congressional Record*, 52 Cong., 1 Sess., pp. 4707-12, 4751, 4752. Bryan thought forcing Sherman to define bimetallism was a victory for silver, and wrote Teller congratulating him. "You are doing valiant service for the cause." Bryan to Teller, no date, Teller MSS.

states ordinarily for silver refused to leave their candidate. The meeting was tumultuous and came to an end without a formal agreement. It probably accomplished its purpose in drawing a fairly clear line between Harrison and those silver delegates not already pledged.

Teller represented Colorado on the resolutions committee and served on the subcommittee on coinage. With him were Jones and three anti-free-silver men led by Representative Cannon. It was announced that Teller and Jones would try to secure a plank that would obligate the candidate to sign a free-coinage bill if it were passed. After dividing two to three against a free-coinage plank, Teller drew the compromise that was finally adopted. In the meantime, the tariff committee reported a plank on lead and wool that was expected to be the silver delegates' share of the platform. After it was adopted, Teller and Jones made a fight for the adoption of their plank, and for placing it in the platform next after the tariff. They won. The plank read:

> The American people, from tradition and interest, favor bi-metallism, and the Republican party demands the use of both gold and silver as standard money, with such restrictions and under such provisions, to be determined by legislation, as will secure the maintenance of the parity of values of the two metals so that the purchasing and debt-paying power of the dollar, whether of silver, gold, or paper, shall be at all times equal. The interests of the producers of this country, its farmers and its workingmen, demand that every dollar, paper or coin, issued by the government, shall be as good as any other.
>
> We commend the wise and patriotic steps already taken by our government to secure an international conference, to adopt such measures as will insure a parity of value between gold and silver for use as money throughout the world.

This was their last victory in the convention, if indeed the compromise can be called a victory; Harrison had an absolute majority, and only a miracle could defeat him. The officeholders everywhere were pledged to him. Wolcott told the convention that he had a list of over one hundred and thirty Federal officeholders who were delegates to the convention, and that two or three thousand more swarmed about Minneapolis on political business. The first trial of strength resulted in a small but safe victory for the President, and then, as H. T. Peck writes, the "timeservers" went to him in a body. Wolcott, selected by Mrs. Blaine to make her husband's nominating speech, stimulated a great demonstration. But the votes were for Harrison, who was nominated on the first ballot. The Colorado, Idaho, and Nevada delegates voted solidly for Blaine, as did half of the California delegation. That fight was over and lost.[9]

The Democrats nominated Cleveland, and adopted a plank condemning the Sherman Purchase Act in terms that were adapted to either silver or anti-silver constituencies. The Democratic candidate's utterance and record on the question left no question that he was an enemy of free coinage. Now both major parties had candidates opposed to free coinage, and each had a compromise or a meaningless plank on the question in their platforms.

Teller returned to Washington after the convention and helped push a free-silver bill through the Senate, apparently for the purpose of making a record. The silver majority in the Senate was now only four, as the tendency to stay with the party had brought some former silver men into line. The same was true in the House, where a majority of eighteen killed a bill that had a majority in its favor when Congress had assembled. The campaign was driving both Democrats and Republicans into line with their presidential candidates. Out in Colorado, Hill's faithful newspaper told an unbelieving state that had the bill passed, Harrison would have signed it.[10] The election was to be fought with both great parties opposed to free coinage.

In Colorado many of the young Republicans were organizing "Silver Leagues," and joining the new Populist Party, which had come out for free coinage. The Democrats, led by Patterson, were bolting Cleveland and supporting the Populists. With this support, the new party was in a strong position. The Republican Party, too, was in grave danger of losing its supporters. The local leaders were telegraphing Teller that it was necessary for him to come home before the convention of the silver clubs to prevent their stampeding to the Populist candidate, Weaver. Teller wrote to Dawson from Morrison, where he was visiting his mother and nursing a bad attack of asthma: "I don't intend to do so. I am not going to antagonize the men who did so much to aid us in securing a decent plank in the National platform. I will wrestle with that when I am obliged to do so."[11]

---

[9] New York *Tribune*, June 6, 7, 8, 1892; Minneapolis *Journal*, May 31-June 11, 1892; Dawson, *Wolcott*, I, 204; *Proceedings of the Tenth Republican National Convention* (Minneapolis, 1892), pp. 54, 81, 86, 117-19, 141; H. T. Peck, *Twenty Years of the Republic*, p. 287; Charles Edward Russell, *These Shifting Scenes* (New York, 1914), pp. 216-43.

[10] *Congressional Record*, 52 Cong., 1 Sess., pp. 5714-19, 6133; *Public Opinion*, July 9, 23, 1892.

[11] Teller to Dawson July 24, 1892, Teller MSS.

The Republicans put up a vigorous campaign in Colorado. Teller addressed the state convention, emphasizing the superiority of their platform over that of the Democrats. Wolcott and several old friends assured him it was the best speech that they had ever heard him make. Later in the month, Teller opened the campaign with a speech in Denver that was well received, but he wrote Dawson afterward that Weaver would carry the state if a vote were taken then. The Republicans were having trouble raising money for the campaign, and Hill's overenthusiastic support of Harrison was hurting the ticket. The enthusiasm the Populists were arousing resulted in near violence at some of the Republican rallies, and Teller heard more hissing and catcalling than he had ever before experienced in Colorado. Nevertheless, he stumped the state thoroughly. On October 10, he thought they would win with their state ticket, but was only hopeful of the electors. On October 16, he wrote Dawson: "Sherman's speeches at Cincinnati & Philadelphia hurt us badly but I don't suppose he cares.... [The] chances on the electoral ticket are in our favor."

But in the end, Weaver carried Colorado, Nevada, Idaho, and Kansas. The Populists elected the governor of Colorado and the two congressmen. It was a bad defeat and did not help Teller's reputation as a leader. In commenting on the senatorial aspects of the election in a letter to Dawson, he concluded: "Yet I got a good deal of satisfaction out of some of the *results*. Perkins who went back on Silver is left. Felton who ought to have been with us & was against us also will return to private life & in both cases we will get I think Silver men. Sanders of Montana is also another whose loss I will not greatly deplore."[12]

---

[12] Teller to Dawson, Sept. 12, 18, Oct. 10, 16, Nov. 13, Dec. 1, 1892, Teller MSS.; clipping from Denver *Republican*, Sept. 18, 1892, Dawson Scrapbook. Perkins and Felton were senators from Kansas and California, respectively.

CHAPTER XV

IMMEDIATELY after Cleveland's election, a demand arose from banking and other creditor groups that the Sherman Purchase Act be repealed. This had not been an issue in the campaign. The Democratic platform, although it condemned the purchase law as a "cowardly makeshift," declared for both gold and silver as standard money. Except in the West, where both parties gave their platform and records as pro-silver a slant as possible, the tariff was the issue of the campaign. Nevertheless, the fact that Cleveland with his intense personal conviction against silver money was to be President, that he would follow the advice of bankers on monetary questions, and that his party, which contained the great majority of pro-silver members in Congress, could be subjected to executive and party pressure, all made a favorable background for repealing the Purchase Act and strengthening the gold standard.

Individual members of the creditor group began to put pressure on Cleveland toward this end soon after his election. They were joined by Eastern newspapers, and Cleveland began to drift toward their plans.[1] He had a simple, almost childlike faith that the people who knew most about monetary problems were the large bankers, and that their advice was not only expert but disinterested. With all possible credit to his courage and independence, it must be admitted that he was to follow a monetary policy that would not have been different had it been made entirely in the office of one of the large banking houses.

This move for repeal was aided immensely by the unsettled economic condition over the United States. A vast number of factors, some world-wide and some local, had combined to put the financial world in a position of uncertainty. Writes the financial historian, Davis R. Dewey:

> A cloud of apprehension seemed to settle over the country, not that a revision of the tariff or a new monetary system was in itself feared, but blind uncertainty as to the future paralyzed action.

The continued export of gold, in a large measure the result of conditions in Europe, which prevented the usual sale

---

[1]Nevins, *Cleveland*, pp. 523, 524; Barnes, *Carlisle*, pp. 250-54.

of American securities to cover the adverse balance of trade, drew that metal steadily from the United States. As the exporters of gold had only to present United States money to the Treasury to secure gold, this movement tended to deplete the reserve the Government had built up for the redemption of greenbacks. This danger of depleting the Treasury's supply of gold was increased by the failure of the Government to maintain an adequate surplus, by the decreased revenues under the McKinley Tariff Act, and by the purchases of silver bullion necessary under the Sherman Act. If the reserve should become exhausted, the Government would be compelled to issue silver.[2] If, the Eastern press kept insisting, it fell below one hundred million dollars, panic would threaten.

The bankers and the Eastern press laid the difficulty to the Sherman Act, and that alone. Teller sensed the coming attack on silver purchases soon after the election and prepared to meet and anticipate it wherever possible. Senator John R. McPherson introduced a bill for the virtual repeal of the act, and Teller addressed himself to the question shortly after Congress reassembled for the short session of the Fifty-second Congress.

> I charge now that the men who are howling about this matter are not alarmed. They do not fear that we are going to a silver basis. . . . They think that the export of gold . . . can be used . . . as a means of repealing the so-called Sherman Act of 1890. I wish to say to them that they may butt their heads against the wall if they choose; but they have not the votes . . . to repeal the law, and it will not be repealed in this Congress.

On February 3 he called attention to the "indecent methods" being planned by those demanding repeal. He read into the record an article from the New York *Herald* of the day before.

> He [Cleveland] has resolved to make the stopping of the Treasury purchase of silver his policy and fidelity to that policy a test of fidelity to him and his Administration. . . . those who resist the unconditional repeal of the Sherman law will . . . be expected to stand aside and yield in the distribution of the patronage to those Democrats who advocate repeal. Every Democratic member of Congress has a rival in his own party for the caucus nomination. There are few Congressional districts in which the President cannot, by his influence widely and wisely exerted, make a majority candidate out of one who is now . . . a minority candidate in a Democratic caucus.

---

[2] Economists seem agreed upon the complicated factors involved in the situation. For an exception see W. Jett Lauck, *The Causes of the Panic of 1893* (Boston, 1907).

Then Teller pointed out the work being carried on by certain large banking interests in lining up the organizations of businessmen to urge repeal upon Congress. He read a circular which had been sent around to banks urging them to bring pressure to bear upon Congress for repeal, and he charged that certain of the banks were making loans dependent upon opinion regarding repeal. He had no difficulty in showing that the export of gold was not caused merely by a lack of faith in the ability of the Treasury to maintain gold payments, using English and French financial papers to support his arguments. Two weeks later he spoke on another move to strengthen the legal position of the gold standard, a proposal to make silver dollars and certificates redeemable in gold. He related an attempt of New York banking houses to discredit the silver certificate by refusing to honor it in clearing-house transactions, although it was legal money and honored at the Treasury and in every bank in the United States outside of New York.

A few days before the session closed, he informed the Senate that he had received confidential information from New York that a concerted effort was being made at that place to deplete the Government's gold reserve. He put his finger then on the weakest spot in the Government's financial structure, and that was the power of financiers who controlled the money market to force almost any condition they wished by co-operation among themselves. They could break down the reserve and force the Government to sell them bonds, or they could keep it adequate. The stability of the Treasury's reserve was dependent upon their wishes. The day before Congress adjourned, Teller presented an offer from the Denver Clearing House Association of one million dollars of gold coin in exchange for legal tender notes. The next day Cleveland was inaugurated, and Congress adjourned.[3]

Teller had gone to California after the inauguration of the new President in order to get some rest undisturbed by too close contact with Colorado politics. While there, he watched financial conditions grow steadily worse, and the press clamor for repeal increase. The price of silver was declining steadily, and word from Colorado indicated some of the larger mines would have to close. Then, on May 4, the

---

[3] *Congressional Record*, 52 Cong., 2 Sess., pp. 429-30, 1132-37, 1729-33, 1786-90, 2338. The correctness of the account in the New York *Herald* is borne out by a letter from Cleveland to Carlisle, Jan. 22, 1893, in Allan Nevins, *Letters of Grover Cleveland* (New York, 1933), pp. 314-15.

highly speculative National Cordage Company failed, and in a few days a nation-wide panic was on, the fault, the bankers assured the country, of the Sherman Purchase Act.

Late in June, the British government announced that the mints of India were closed to silver coinage, and Cleveland, who had advance information of this move, followed with a call for a special session of Congress in August to repeal the Sherman Purchase Act. The price of silver dropped sickeningly; nearly all Colorado mines closed, and the smelters began to close soon afterward. Silver was the principal Colorado mining industry, and its ending had disastrous effects upon other types of mining closely associated with it. Teller was in Denver in July when runs began on its banks. By October the relatively small state of Colorado ranked third in its total of closed bank liabilities, and the percentage of business failures was over twice that of the country at large, in spite of the fact that nearly all the Colorado banks were sound and eventually reopened.

There was danger of starvation in Colorado. Relief committees were organized in the large mining towns, and a large camp with tents and a breadline was established in Denver for the destitute. The footloose left the state in vast numbers. They caused so much trouble in attempting to get away that one railway took several trainloads East at no cost to the passengers. Even with this relief, there promised, by the end of the summer, to be from thirty to fifty thousand unemployed out of a population of half a million. If conditions did not improve the number would probably increase during the fall and early winter.[4]

Public opinion in Colorado, excited by these real troubles, was fanned to greater heat by the ill-concealed rejoicing of some Eastern newspapers and bankers over her plight. Now, so went the suggestion, maybe the West will listen to reason on the silver question. Referring to the bank failures in Denver, the Chicago *Record* noted, among other causes, that "the wild talk of its politicians of late has alienated other business communities and thus denied it the succor and sympathy which are due that splendid city." For over two months, at least, the New York banks had been refusing to rediscount the notes of Western banks, possibly because

---

[4] Forest Lowell White, "The Panic of 1893 in Colorado" (unpublished thesis 1932, University of Colorado Library) ; Leon Webber Fuller, "The Populist Regime in Colorado" (unpublished thesis, University of Wisconsin Library, 1933), pp. 124-25; *Harper's Weekly*, July 29, 1893.

of sheer inability, but with the open suggestion that all such
accommodations depended on repeal. Reprisal was in the
air. Threats of repudiation of debts owed in the state to
Easterners, actual secession of the mining states, and state
silver coinage, were all urged by individuals and mass meetings. The more conservative groups repudiated these
schemes, but they indicate something of the temper and
problem that faced Colorado.

A state-wide mass meeting was opened in Denver on July
11. The Populist Governor, Davis H. Waite, a patriarchal
old gentleman with a passion for hell-fire oratory, addressed
the group in words that were to be quoted in part over the
entire country.

> Our weapons are arguments and the ballot—a free ballot and a
> fair count. And if the money power shall attempt to sustain its
> usurpations by the strong hand, we shall meet that issue when it is
> forced upon us, for it is better, infinitely better, that blood should flow
> to the horses' bridles than that our national liberties should be
> destroyed.

Headlined in the large cities of the country as "An Appeal
to Arms," the press had little difficulty in making the Colorado cause appear to be one allied with revolution and
anarchy. The day following, the convention adopted an address to the people of the United States that was so much
more moderate than the Governor's oratory that it received
the endorsement of the Denver Board of Trade:

> The people of Colorado, standing in the gloom of impending
> disaster and representing in condition and sentiment the people of
> Montana, Idaho, Wyoming, Nevada, South Dakota, Utah, Arizona,
> and New Mexico, with reverence for the Constitution and unswerving
> loyalty to the general government, ask for your calm and candid
> consideration of the following facts before you give your approval to
> the destruction of silver as money, and to the final establishment of
> the single gold standard of values, and thus at one stroke change all
> debts to gold debts and inaugurate a never-ending rise of gold and
> continued corresponding fall in the price of every commodity....
> Unconditional repeal! That means striking from the laws the last
> remnant of legislation that secures coinage of silver. It fixes the
> United States firmly in the ranks of the single standard countries.

It reminded the East of the support protective tariffs
on manufactures had received from the West; it reminded
the South of Teller's and Wolcott's work against the Force

bill. Finally it charged the entire movement for a gold standard to a world-wide plot of the creditor classes.[5]

Teller had taken no part in this meeting, for he was not in complete accord with many of its leaders. Neither did he attend the National Silver Convention that met in Chicago, just before Congress opened. Instead, he returned to Washington early to prepare for the opening of the special session. By the time Congress assembled business had picked up slightly, and the price of silver had improved somewhat over its recent low.

The pressure for repeal that bore down upon the members of Congress as they assembled in Washington in August of 1893 has probably never been equaled for any other legislation. The entire press of the East and most business organizations outside of the mining states were demanding immediate repeal. There was no question about it—so the bankers declared—the act was the cause of the panic. "The only absolute cure," proclaimed the *Commercial and Financial Chronicle*, "is the repeal of the Silver Purchase Law," and the daily press added loud amens.[6] Wrote John Hay to Henry Adams:

> All men of virtue and intelligence know that all the ills of life— scarcity of money, baldness, the comma bacillus, Home Rule, J——, and the Potato Bug—are due to the Sherman bill. If it is repealed, sin and death will vanish from the world ... the skies will fall, and we shall all catch larks.[7]

The ground upon which Teller was to lead this fight against deflation was not one he would have selected had he been in a position to choose. He had no love for the Purchase Act, and had held out against it until he was sure he could get nothing better. The practice of purchases of a monetary metal was contrary to all the principles of money he followed. But he had no choice. With the closing of the India mint and the consequent decline in silver in terms of gold, free coinage would be more difficult than ever to establish. Coming at this time, repeal would force the price of silver down still further and make that change more remote. Moreover, the sheer needs of Colorado had at last forced Teller to consider frankly the price of silver and the

---

[5] White, "The Panic of 1893"; Leon W. Fuller, "Governor Waite and His Silver Panacea," *Colorado Magazine*, X (March, 1933), 41-47; New York *Tribune*, July 11, 12, 13, 1893; *Address of the People of Colorado to the People of the United States*, printed leaflet.

[6] July 22, 1893; *Public Opinion*, Aug. 5, 1893.

[7] John Hay, *Letters and Diaries* (Washington, 1908), II, 264.

immediate future of his own state. Purchase did to some
extent keep up the price of the metal, and under the depressed conditions in the state that was a great aid.

President Cleveland took the lead in demanding repeal.
In his message to Congress he laid the blame for the panic
and depression on the Purchase Act. "The simple assertion
of the President," Teller told a reporter, "that the present
financial condition is due to the Sherman law does not make
it so. His premises are wrong and his conclusions naturally
fall to the ground."[8] The President, using the very potent
weapon of his appointing power, and taking no heed of the
destruction of his own party, moved remorselessly toward
his object. Senators, he is reported to have said, were "a
lot of damned old patronage brokers," and he could take
care of them as well as the House members. Champ Clark
states that when Congress assembled, the silver men in the
House were in a clear majority, but by the time the question
of repeal came to a vote, it was defeated by a vote of over
two to one. "Patronage did it, and there is no use blinking
the facts." Patronage plus the pressure of business and the
press, perhaps. The fight in the House was brief. The
official leadership on both sides fought for repeal, although
Bland succeeded in keeping half of the Democrats loyal to
silver. The two new Colorado representatives, John C. Bell
and Lafe Pence, both gave a good account of themselves in
the debate and silenced some of the critics of Populism at
home. The high honors on both sides, however, went to
young William Jennings Bryan, who combined close reasoning with unusual oratory in a masterly plea against repeal.
The administration singled out Bryan for punishment because of his firmness for silver coinage. Teller presented to
the Senate documentary evidence that in Nebraska, Democratic postmasters' appointments were postponed, and applicants were forced to attend the State convention and work
against Bryan and for repeal, before the actual appointments were made.[9]

In both houses the debate was a notable one—"the greatest debate," writes Oscar Underwood, "since the days when
the political division began on the slavery question."[10] After

---

[8] St. Louis *Globe-Democrat*, Aug. 8, 1893.

[9] Arthur Dunn, *From Harrison to Harding*, I, 118-20; Champ Clark, *My Quarter Century of American Politics* (New York, 1920), I, 321-22; *Congressional Record*, 53 Cong., 1 Sess., Appendix, p. 355.

[10] Oscar W. Underwood, *Drifting Sands of Party Politics* (New York, 1928), p. 269. The best description is Jeannette P. Nichols, "The Politics and Personalities of Silver Repeal in the United States Senate," *American Historical Review*, XLI (Oct., 1935), 26-53.

the bill had passed the House by a large majority, newspaper polls regularly showed a majority for it in the Senate. Senator Voorhees, of Indiana, the chairman of the committee on finance, and always a free-coinage man, had been brought over to the side of repeal by what Rhodes well calls "a discreet bestowal of offices" to his relatives and friends, as well as by a reasonable desire to work with the President and to give the Democratic Party a chance of holding itself together until it redeemed some of its campaign pledges.[11] Even former silver Republicans, such as Senator W. C. Squire, of Washington, had been high-pressured into voting against their convictions. They had a ready excuse at hand. Numerous self-proclaimed bimetallists in Congress had been frightened by the newspapers and bankers until they were now advocating repeal as a means of bringing about bimetallism. Repeal the Sherman Act, ran their argument, and silver will go so low in price that it will force the European states to adopt bimetallism. Teller, with a better understanding of the situation, protested against this comfortable theory:

> I believe that you have reached the crucial point; that if you turn this corner and demonetize silver ... there will be slavery as objectionable as that which formerly existed in this country, except they will have the right to move from one quarter section of land to another. ...

Teller realized that if the United States repealed the Purchase Act, silver would be discredited as money metal far more than ever; it would decline in value still further compared with gold, and bimetallism would then be an almost impossible goal. The appreciating gold standard would be fastened upon the world for all time. That was the important question.

> It outweighs the tariff. It is beyond doubt the greatest question which has been presented to the American people at any time; equal in my judgment in importance to the question whether the country should remain united or be divided.

"Words that he will be compelled to eat, but he expressed the the unpatriotic spirit of his followers," commented the New York *Herald*.[12]

When it became obvious that there was a Senate ma-

---

[11] Nevins, *Cleveland*, pp. 541-42.
[12] *Congressional Record*, 53 Cong., 1 Sess., pp. 217, 1350, 1419, 2467.

jority for repeal, the silver men frankly proclaimed that they would talk the bill to death. They would, Teller proclaimed, debate the question in detail, and after they had exhausted the subject, they would resort to such constitutional means as were available to prevent its passage. Closure, Teller had declared early in the session, could not be adopted, as too many in the Senate were committed against it, particularly the Democrats, who had so boldly upheld the right to filibuster on the Force bill. Their right to obstruct action, Teller held, arose out of the fact that neither Congress nor the administration had a mandate of any kind for repeal. It was legislative action being forced upon the country by powerful special interests without any chance for ascertaining the popular will.

> Go to the people with this question. Take the public sentiment on it, and if they elect a House of Representatives and the third of the Senate . . . then we will surrender.[13]

The hammering of the press upon the silver senators was terrific. "I have never," wrote Professor Edward W. Bemis, of the University of Chicago, "since slavery days seen our American press so unfair as it is on this silver question." The New York *World* addressed an open letter to Teller, telling him that he represented only the equivalent of a New York county, and that he had better "be still and listen." *Harper's Weekly* labeled the silver senators "Enemies of the Public Welfare" in a long editorial and a page of sketches; and newspapers experimented with such epithets as "mining camp and sagebrush Senators," "fanatics," "cossacks," "border ruffians," "bandits," disloyalists," "traitors," and "lunatics."[14]

Once, during the long debate, these epithets irritated Teller until he lost control of himself. The break came at the end of an exhausting speech that had run over parts of three days, and during which Teller had been having a bad time with asthma. Nervous and worn out after several sharp exchanges with opposition senators, he began to describe the probable effect of repeal on the mining states. An observer wrote:

> As he proceeded he became more and more wrought up to a pitch of intensity unlike anything ever seen on the floor. He paced up and

---

[13] *Ibid.*, pp. 2639-44.

[14] Edward W. Bemis, "The Silver Situation in Colorado," *Review of Reviews*, Sept., 1893; *Congressional Record*, 53 Cong., 1 Sess., p. 1349; St. Louis *Globe-Democrat*, Oct. 16, 21; New York *Tribune*, Sept. 4, 1893.

down the narrow space behind his desk earnestly gesticulating, while, with a voice tremulous with emotion and his eyes wet with tears, he pictured the misery he saw in the future for the people whom he loved. The spectacle was so striking and unusual that it riveted the attention of every Senator. The words poured forth from Mr. Teller's lips in a passionate torrent so carried away was he with his theme, and when with clinched fist, he denounced the "damnable bill," the galleries burst forth with applause.... When he concluded he sank to his seat buried his face in his hands, and presented a living picture of the misery he had so touchingly described.[15]

The Republicans in the Senate, as in the House, were far more unanimous for repeal than were the Democrats, whose President had made it an administration measure. They encouraged the Democrats to take the lead, but joined with them, and in so doing, repudiated any responsibility for the law. Senator Sherman repeated his tale that the Purchase Act had "saved us from free coinage." Teller, of course, would not let that go by unchallenged, and he clearly showed the nature of the party compromise back of the measure, the impossibility of free coinage in 1890, and insisted that the Republican Party and Sherman personally could not dodge responsibility for the act.

Teller took general charge of the fight against repeal. The Democrats who were standing out against the President were numerous and willing to co-operate, but did not want to appear too prominent in the filibuster. Under Senator Isham G. Harris, of Tennessee, the silver Democrats such as Morgan, Vance, Pugh, Vest, Cockrell, and Jones, of Arkansas, engaged actively in the debate against repeal, but did not regularly engage in obstructive tactics. These were left principally to Teller's group of Republicans and to the Populist senators who were co-operating closely with them.

In his own part of the debate, Teller devoted the bulk of his attention to demonstrating that the Purchase Act was not the cause of the panic. The causes were world-wide, but one of them that the press was overlooking was the part the bankers had played in trying to bring pressure for repeal. To show this he read into the record an account of a meeting between Secretary of the Treasury Carlisle and a group of New York bankers before the panic began. The account was from the New York *Sun* of April 28, a source certainly not unfriendly to bankers:

[15] *Congressional Record*, 53 Cong., 1 Sess., p. 1422; Washington *Post*, Sept. 13, 1893.

As Mr. Carlisle outlined the policy of the Government, it was shown that nothing would be done that would in any way retard or check the determination of Cleveland's Administration concerning the repeal of the Sherman law. There is a determination also to show the miners of silver the evils of the Sherman law upon their own fortune. ... This work ... has been started by a number of bankers in the solid communities of the East. They are daily refusing credits to the South, Southwest, and West, fearing the effects of the Sherman law. ... The bank presidents, replying to Secretary Carlisle, cordially informed him that they would be ready at all times to cooperate with him.

A few days later, the same paper thus interpreted the meaning of the conference:

The statement of Mr. Carlisle to the New York bankers makes it clear that, while Mr. Cleveland works in Congress, the bankers will be expected to work ... doing their utmost to pinch business everywhere in expectation of causing a money crisis that will affect Congress powerfully from every quarter.

The bankers, Teller informed the Senate, had not tried to bring on the panic; they had merely attempted to create enough of a disturbance to give an argument for repeal.

When the future historian tells the world of the great financial panic of 1893 he will say: "In the winter and spring months of that year the New York bankers and financiers sowed the wind, and during the summer months reaped the whirlwind."

Teller followed this with evidence to show that after the panic had begun, and especially since Congress had assembled, similar measures had been taken by the bankers and other creditor groups for the same purpose. His evidence was usually from the financial pages of the daily papers. Typical was the following from the Philadelphia *Press* of September 22:

There are ominous rumors in the street that New York will again put the screws on the Senate. Whether this is street talk or not remains to be seen, but the hardening of the rate of sterling exchange at the time of large merchandise exports and in the middle of our exporting season, looks as if gold exports would be made to influence the silver lunatics ... the banks of New York are still witholding money from merchants ... because of a tacit arrangement not to unloose it until the Senate votes for repeal. Now, if the gold exporting movement began, that would be another striking occurrence on which to impinge public thought, and on which a popular argument could be based.[16]

---

[16] New York *Sun*, April 28, May 1, 1893; *Congressional Record*, 53 Cong., 1 Sess., pp. 1018-25, 1062-68. There is a letter quoted in Paxton Hibben, *The Peerless Leader* (New York, 1929), p. 151, purporting to be from the "National Bankers' Association," sent out to its members March 12, 1893, that directs the retirement of one third of their

As the debate continued in the Senate with no sign of a chance for a vote, Voorhees rather foolishly tried to force one by holding the Senate in continuous session. Teller and Dubois warned him that it was useless, but the contest began. Teller, Wolcott, Stewart, Jones, Dubois, and the Populists by turns held the floor. Senator Allen, the new Populist senator from Nebraska, spoke, without leaving his feet, for over fourteen hours, "a good speech too," and others filled in lesser periods. When some thirty-seven hours of continuous session had passed, Stewart was on the floor boasting that he could talk forever, and Voorhees capitulated. The silver men had won this skirmish.

Now, the Senate Democrats began to consider a compromise that would save the party from disruption. The basis of the agreement was a law repealing the Purchase Act, but postponing its action to a future date. The press denunciations of the silver men redoubled. Even before this demonstration of strength *The Nation* had darkly hinted:

The truth is that the Senate is in a state of revolution. It may need a counter-revolution to put the country once more in the path of progress.

The demand for a reapportionment of the Senate was made, as it always is when a sectional question goes against the East, and the usual articles began to appear upon the "Decline of the Senate." Repeal was now a secondary issue, argued the embattled editors, the primary one being "between revolution and constitutional democracy . . . the people on one side and a lot of political robber barons on the other." The Vice-President was urged to take the control in his own hands and put the question. *The Commercial and Financial Chronicle,* as the organ of the banking groups, added its threats:

Possibly a favorable Senatorial decision can only be reached after a greater sacrifice has been made than the people have yet suffered, ending probably in general insolvency and liquidation. That situation can be forced if the Senate so wills it, and will be forced unless the unconditional repeal is accomplished before long.[17]

---

circulation and one half of their loans in order to put pressure on Congress to repeal the Sherman law by means of a "money stringency." The citation, however, is incorrect. Matthew Josephson, *The Politicos* (New York, 1938), has similar evidence. See especially Chapt. 15.

[17] *Public Opinion,* Oct. 19; *Harper's Weekly,* Aug. 12, 26, Sept. 2, 16, 23, Oct. 28; *The Nation,* Sept. 28; *Commercial and Financial Chronicle,* Aug. 5, 19, Sept. 2, 23; all 1893. It is interesting to observe that Teller, although he was the accepted leader

Keppler's caricature is typical of the press during the fight against repeal. Teller and Wolcott are at the windows; Peffer, Jones, Stewart, and Vest are already outside.

A majority of the Senate were reported to have signed the agreement. But when presented to Cleveland, he let it be known that no compromise was wanted, and the administration and party pressure applied to those Democrats who were even moderate silver men became unbearable. The pounding of the press, the patronage of the President, and the activities of the business groups in their own states —stimulated by the well-organized campaign sponsored by the metropolitan banks—were too strong. The cry that repeal would end the depression was having its effect on the general public. All that was needed, Senator Sherman had declaimed, was to "give the Senate force and power to pass this bill, and in ten days the skies will brighten, business will resume its ordinary course, 'and all the clouds which lower on our house shall be in the deep bosom of the ocean buried.' "

With the end of the possibility of a compromise, the Democrats had to surrender. Senator Isham G. Harris, according to Arthur Dunn, went over to Fred Dubois, who was the floor leader of the silver Republicans, and said, "Dubois, I told you that we would stand by you until hell froze over. We have had another look at our hand and must lay down."[18] That was the end. There was no use of further obstructive tactics. A free-coinage amendment was voted down 28 to 39. The silver men began their valedictories. Allen, Peffer, and Stewart were agressively threatening. Cameron, the one Easterner who stood true to his belief in bimetallism, made no apologies for his stand. Jones and Wolcott delivered polished orations and received ovations from the galleries.

Teller arose on October 27 in a chamber as "silent as death," and, in words which "will long be remembered for their solemnity, the thrill of sympathy which they aroused . . . and for the sincerity and earnestness which emphasized each word," addressed not the Senate so much as the country at large. As for Colorado he declared:

We are neither cast down nor dejected. . . . We do not disguise the fact that we are to go through the valley and the shadow of death.

of the silver forces in the Senate, generally was treated better than the others. "Mr. Teller is a fine example of the old-time Senator, courteous always, though terribly in earnest, and he is rarely guilty of a serious breach of decorum. . . . Quite different, however, is it with his silver colleagues." New York *Tribune*, Oct. 18, 1893; also, editorials Sept. 11 and 15. An unsigned article in the November, 1893, *Forum*, "The Decline of the Senate," classifies the silver men, excepting Teller, either among those who hold their seats chiefly on account of their wealth or "political accidents."

[18] Nevins, *Cleveland*, 545-46; New York *Tribune*, Oct. 20, 22, 25, 1893; Dunn, *op. cit.*, I, 121.

We know what it means to turn out our 200,000 silver miners in the
fall of the year . . . we are ready and willing to meet the occasion. . . .
But, Mr. President, the iron will enter into our souls. We shall not
forget that in this contest . . . the men with whom we have stood
shoulder to shoulder in the economic battles heretofore, have almost
to a man forsaken us. We in the States of Nevada and Colorado have
held those States in the Republican column for many a year. We have
maintained a Republican majority in this chamber by our votes. We
have stood by our Eastern brethren who believed in the protective
system . . . even when it would have been to our local interest to vote
against certain measures. . . . But how much aid . . . have we had from
them? How much sympathy? . . . We shall not abandon the faith that
is in us. But when we shall be asked to yield our judgment to their
judgment upon economic questions in the future, if we do not respond
as promptly as we have in the past, I trust they will not be surprised.

Although the industries of Colorado were to be destroyed
by this legislation, the East need have no fear, for Colorado
would pay its debts to the last cent. So much for Colorado.
As for the larger consideration of the monetary standard,
the contemplated action,

. . . is the most terrible moment of my legislative life. . . . I fear that
we are entering upon a financial system from which there is absolutely
no escape. . . . I know, as I stand here, there will be no favorable
legislation for silver until the American people are heard from at the
ballot box. . . . I do not underrate the great agencies with which the
people will have to contend. I know that it is the combined capital
of the world. . . . I know that they have the power to control the great
agencies of thought. . . . [The] stake is too great to be lightly given up.
It is not for a day; it is not for a year; it is for the great future they
are contending. The men who own the money of the world, the bonds,
the interest-bearing securities, know that if they can put this country
upon a gold standard . . . prices will go as they have been going,
gradually lower and lower; individual opportunities will be less and
less. . . . I am an optimist. . . . But I cannot contemplate the condition
of the people now threatened without great apprehension; nay more
without absolute terror. It strikes me to my very soul. . . . I warn the
American people that if they do not now resist they will speedily
enter upon a system of industrial slavery which will be the worst
known to the human race.[19]

The repeal bill passed.
This was complete defeat for the silver group, beyond all
question. In spite of the claims of Democratic organs and
leaders favorable to silver that it cleared the decks for a
straight-out fight for free coinage, the historian cannot
overlook the fact that Teller spoke with prophetic insight

---

[19] Washington *Post*, Oct. 28, 1893 ; *Congressional Record*, 53 Cong., 1 Sess., pp. 2890-
91. The reporter of the New York *Tribune* wrote that Teller spoke with "great bitterness," but was listened to "with deepest respect and sympathy." Oct. 28, 1893.

when he said it was a crucial moment in American monetary history, second in importance only to the demonetization of silver in 1873.

Could better leadership have brought a more desirable result? The Populist senators had urged Teller to continue the filibuster to the bitter end, without the help of the Democrats, but Teller had rejected the plan. A filibuster is usually possible only near the end of a Congress, such as the short sessions were before the adoption of the Twentieth Amendment. But repeal was being fought in a special session that preceded both of the regular sessions. Congress could easily have been kept in session steadily until such time as the filibuster failed, as fail it would; for soon enough administration Democrats would unite with the Republican senators to vote closure. The filibuster had gone about as far as it was possible to carry it. It had failed to defeat or modify repeal, but it had drawn a line on the silver question that all the compromises in both parties could not obliterate. The filibuster, added to Cleveland's refusal to compromise, had made the issue and it would have to be met. Nowhere among the silver men was there criticism of Teller's leadership. Elsewhere, the bitterness of the fight had left unhealed wounds, although several of the organs supporting repeal gave generous tributes. Thus wrote a Washington reporter for the anti-silver St. Louis *Post Dispatch*:

On the Republican side the honors were universally accorded to Mr. Teller. The Colorado Senator has always been regarded as a strong man in the Senate. But as a leader of the minority in this fight his spirit has served to rouse his followers to their best exertions, and first and last the Colorado Senator has been the heart and brains of the whole silver contingent. He planned the battle, looked after the details of execution, threw himself into the breach whenever an occasion presented itself and fought hard and gamely throughout.... As he proceeded to develop daily some new quality of leadership, even the men who were opposing him felt obliged to extend to him the meed of their admiration.[20]

The defeat seemed to increase Colorado's respect for her senior senator. The hopeless struggle in the Senate and the bitter denunciations in the Eastern press had roused among the people of that state an emotional surge of gratitude toward her defenders, especially toward Teller. Congress adjourned immediately after voting repeal, and when the senator reached Denver he was welcomed with an immense

---

[20] Nov. 3, 1893. See also the editorial in the St. Louis *Republic*, Nov. 1, 1893.

public reception. Never before had Colorado honored one of her sons like this. There was band music, which Teller hated, laudatory speeches, and exhausting handshaking. But all who counted in Colorado were there to do him honor, and after three months of constant press vituperation and nerve-racking antagonisms in the Senate, it was highly satisfactory. Colorado would, he told them,

...suffer somewhat by the repeal of the Silver Purchase Act, yet, Colorado... is not destroyed, nor, even in any way permanently injured.... If we cannot mine silver at a profit... we can mine iron, coal, and gold, and we will have prosperity and riches....

It would have made your heart throb with pride and joy and pleasure and everything else—wrote a Denver attorney to Dawson—to have witnessed the reception given to Mr. Teller at the Browne Palace the other night. Marcus Daly has to cry about it when he tells how they threw flowers on Mr. Teller.

Another observer added:

I could only compare the feeling here to... the feeling the country had for Lincoln.... [If it had been in the East] nothing could save Mr. Teller from the White House.[21]

The morning after the reception, Teller left for Mexico, partly to escape the lionizing of his friends, but chiefly to observe at close range the operation of a monetary system on the single silver standard. Former Senator Reagan of Texas wrote him from Austin:

If Congress shall fail to repair the evil done by the unconditional repeal of the Sherman law, I predict the next fall will produce the largest political graveyard that has ever been seen in this country.

"The silver campaign," observed a Western editor who was more optimistic than Teller, "is not nearly over. The Bull's Run Campaign only has been fought. The Gettysburg victory comes next year, and in 1896 the gold-bug's Appomattox."[22]

---

[21] R. W. Steele to Dawson, Nov. 24, 1893; R. J. F. to Dawson, Nov. 22; Teller to Dawson, Nov. 10, 1893, Teller MSS.; *The Nation*, Nov. 23, 1893.

[22] L. M. Keasby, "The New Sectionalism—A Western Warning," *The Forum*, Jan., 1894; Reagan to Teller, Nov. 21, 1893, Teller MSS. Teller had been making a special study of Mexican finance for some time. M. Romero to Teller, Sept. 22, 1893, Teller MSS.

CHAPTER XVI
CREATING A NATIONAL CAMPAIGN ISSUE
1894-95

THE DEFEAT of the silver men by the repeal of the Silver Purchase Act had definitely placed upon them the necessity of assuming the aggressive if they were to try to bring into being a bimetallic monetary system by means of free coinage. Unless positive action were soon taken by some of the great commercial nations, the trend toward the gold standard would continue, appreciation would increase, and the difficulty of establishing bimetallism would be greatly enhanced. Great Britain, as the great creditor nation, had no interest in stopping appreciation, and this made an international agreement very unlikely. The hope of the bimetallists lay chiefly in the United States. Free coinage there would stimulate other nations to establish free coinage. Then gold might decrease in actual value and silver would increase in relation to gold, until the old ratios were re-established. It may have been a forlorn hope, but if it failed, at least the steady appreciation of the gold standard would be checked. The cause was great, and to it Teller bent all his energy.

In the meantime, there was one other possibility: the Treasury might be forced to pay out silver because of a lack of gold. While this would be legal, the administration was bitterly opposed to it and would prevent it, if at all possible. The bankers, too, had their eyes on the reserve and were in a position to see that it was maintained. If silver redemption began, most economists and bankers of the day professed to believe, a great inflation would at once result. Teller was not so sure but thought it possible. In the light of the experience of devaluating the gold dollar in 1933, it would seem that this danger was overrated.

Repeal might well have been the end of any attempt to secure free coinage if it had succeeded in doing what its advocates had so confidently predicted for it in 1893. But it did not bring back prosperity; it made no noticeable dent in the prevailing depression; it did not even relieve the Treasury of fear for its gold reserves. If anything, conditions grew worse as commodity prices continued to decline.

As a practical problem, the silver cause was in a bad way. The drop in silver prices made the differences in value of the silver and gold dollars—assuming that free coinage at 16 to 1 would mean a silver standard with no increase in silver values as the gold men claimed—so great that moderate bimetallists and inflationists might well hesitate. Politically, the case was no better. Cleveland was effectively destroying the Democratic Party as a possible victor in a national election, and the control of the Republican organization left little hope of free coinage there.

The element in the situation that made the cause at all possible was the continuance of the severe agricultural depression into 1894 and 1895. The prices of farm products had declined to unheard-of lows; farms were being lost by foreclosures all over the West, and drouth was driving back the farming frontier in the Great Plains states. These rural catastrophes and the resentment that grew out of them had benefited the Populist Party, which, largely because of its clear stand for free coinage, had carried Nevada, Colorado, Idaho, and Kansas in the election of 1892.[1] Everywhere old-time politicians were inclined to ridicule its platform, members, and candidates. It had a sufficient number of leaders with personal idiosyncrasies such as Senator Peffer, or inclined toward intemperate speech, such as Governor Waite, so that judicious publicity soon made the group the laughingstock of the metropolitan press. Wolcott, because of his Eastern training and experience, and because of his resentment against being classified occasionally with them on the silver question by the press, built up a violent antagonism toward the small party and went out of his way to express it. Teller, on the other hand, respected the group and co-operated with its members in Congress. On various occasions he called the Senate's attention to the uniquely American character of the movement and praised the political independence of its members.[2]

Teller stayed in Mexico until after the regular session of Congress was well under way. He came back convinced that the experience of Mexico had borne out his own calculations that the single silver standard had maintained a more stable price level than had the gold standard. Bimetallism was still his ideal of a monetary system, but if there was no choice but a single standard, and either a rising or a falling price level, he would choose the silver standard and a rising price level. The financial issue would not down in Washington as long

---

[1] John D. Hicks, *The Populist Party* (Minneapolis, 1931), Chapter 11.

[2] *Congressional Record*, 52 Cong., 2 Sess., p. 1733; *National Watchman*, Oct. 6, 1893.

as depression reigned over the country. The Treasury could not maintain its gold reserve, not only because of withdrawals of gold, but because revenues were running behind expenditures. After vainly appealing to Congress for provision for an issue of bonds—a proposal that had been in the offing since the latter days of the Harrison regime—the administration announced that it was offering an issue of bonds under the old act providing for the reserve.

From the beginning of the discussion of issuing bonds to protect the gold reserve, Teller had opposed the policy. But in the case of this particular issue of bonds, Teller generally agreed with the gold men, at least upon its legal aspects. The more extreme silver men criticized the action of the administration considerably, and in some cases even asserted that the bonds would be found illegal and would not be redeemed. Senator Stewart introduced a resolution declaring that it was the opinion of the Senate that the Secretary of the Treasury lacked authority to issue the bonds. Teller repudiated these suggestions. "If the bonds are issued we shall be, in my judgment, under both legal and moral obligations to redeem them without reference to the disposition that is made of the money." The Treasury, he agreed with Sherman, had a legal right to sell bonds to protect the reserve, but not, as was supposed, to meet deficiencies in revenue too—although if the latter were done it would not decrease the obligation of the Government. Teller's position here was probably legally correct, and his stand went a long way in keeping the opposition to the issue from unreasonable extremes.

He criticized the administration for not correcting the deficiency in revenue, arguing that the proposed tariff bill would not correct it and that it seemed to have no other plans. He proposed the use of the silver in the Treasury as a means of meeting this deficiency, basing his plea on the fact that the policy of the Treasury did not contemplate its use as reserves, and therefore it might as well be coined and paid out to meet bills. As for the gold reserves, he did not think a bond issue necessary, although no one could deny the right of the Secretary of the Treasury to issue bonds for that purpose if he wished.[3]

Teller took compensation during the session for many of the blows that had fallen on him during the repeal fight, by calling attention to the conditions of the country and the

[3] *Congressional Record*, 53 Cong., 2 Sess., pp. 1629-31; Barnes, *Carlisle*, p. 312.

Treasury since repeal, and contrasting it with the predictions made by its advocates during the debate the previous autumn. He found satisfaction, one can be sure, in reading Sherman's prediction quoted in the previous chapter, and in recalling the predictions of the claimed bimetallist that repeal would cause the gold standard countries to welcome international bimetallism.[4]

The depresson brought on other issues, only indirectly related to the monetary system, that could not be ignored. The widespread unemployment and inadequate relief system resulted in large groups of unemployed men in various parts of the country, starting "marches" on the Capitol. As the press reported the advance of these so-called "armies," a panic of fear was evident in Washington and other metropolitan centers. The principal group to arrive was the "Army of the Commonweal," headed by Jacob S. Coxey. It bore a petition for Government road-building to make work for the unemployed, the cost to be borne by an issue of non-interest-bearing bonds. The Washington police paid scant heed to the legal rights of the marchers and treated them with panic brutality. Eventually the leaders were arrested for walking on the Capitol lawn.

Senator Allen, Populist of Nebraska, introduced a resolution for an investigation of the affair. When Senator Sherman complained about wasting the Senate's time with such matters, Teller arose to advocate the adoption of the resolution. "I sympathize with these people," Teller admitted to the Senate. "I suppose it is unstatesmanlike." He agreed with Sherman that their proposals were impracticable, but suggested that he had heard many in the Senate, some from the Senator from Ohio, that were less defensible. They had a right to come to Washington, the leaders should not have been arrested for the technical violation of a statute, and the action of the police was indefensible. "If the police had behaved with as much decency as the commonweal army there would have been no trouble here at all." He appealed to the Senate to adopt the resolution, but wanted to be left off the investigating committee. "I know I should not be an impartial Judge."[5] It is indicative of fundamental differences between Teller and Wolcott that the younger senator had made an oratorical attack upon these armies a few days before Teller spoke.

[4] *Congressional Record*, 53 Cong., 2 Sess., pp. 2622-25, 2931-35.
[5] *Ibid.*, 53 Cong., 2 Sess., pp. 4566-67.

In the meantime, the House had been trying to redeem the party's tariff pledge in the campaign of 1892, and the Wilson bill had arrived in the Senate, with substantial tariff reductions together with a greatly enlarged free list and a small income tax. Immediately the Senate Democrats began to revise the bill in order to make it acceptable to them. The balance of their power was so small that the Louisiana and Eastern members had to be placated before it would pass. There were also rumors of agreements that seemed to include some of the Republicans who wanted to protect particular rates.[6] Teller took considerable delight in comparing the Senate amendments with the promises which the Democratic Party had made in the last election. He warned them that, although he liked the Senate amendments better than the House bill, he would not let Aldrich bind his vote on the bill in any way.[7]

The real issue—one that assumed a sectional slant beyond all question of tariff rates—was the income tax provision, included because of the need of revenue, and to satisfy the Western and Southern Democrats. It also brought clearly to the front the fact that there was no section where lines were drawn more tightly on economic issues than in the Northeastern group. To the New York press and that state's senators, the proposal of a 2 per cent tax on incomes over $4,000 meant "raiding the Empire State and the City of New York." The Eastern press, Democrat and Republican, with a few exceptions like the New York *World* and Springfield *Republican,* opposed the proposal almost as unanimously as they had opposed free coinage. "Communism" and "socialism" were coming into use as terms of reproach, and they were applied generously now. "Argument by epithet," Teller replied.

The debate gave Teller a wealth of opportunities to show up the inconsistencies in the reasoning behind the opposition. He took pleasure in contrasting the present speeches of Republican senators with those that had been used in defending the Civil War tax, and showed how Sherman, for one, had defended and justified the principle of the income tax in the sixties, and was now opposing the concrete proposal. What had been good Republican doctrine then was communism now. Teller argued that the law was constitutional, predicting that the tax would become a permanent

[6] Stephenson, *Aldrich,* pp. 112-21.
[7] *Congressional Record,* 53 Cong., 2 Sess., pp. 4161-65.

feature of the revenue system, and expressed a hope that it
would extend to all the world. He opposed its application to
income from securities issued by states.

The Populist senator from Kansas, Peffer, who was then
the principal butt of the wits on the Senate floor and in the
press gallery, introduced amendments that would have carried out his party's principle of a graduated tax, increasing
in proportion with the size of the income, and setting the
highest rate at 6 per cent on incomes above $100,000. "While
Senators smile at the idea," its sponsor said, noting the attitude of the senators about him, "it is based upon exact justice." His amendment received five votes, including Teller's.
The opposition, like that to silver coinage, was in the name
of justice and morality.[8]

On the tariff proper Teller usually voted with his party,
defending protection in general, and voting on particular
schedules in line with the interests of Colorado. His appeal
for protection for wool, both for the grower and manufacturer, brought him the public thanks of Senator Hoar.
Through a hot summer that was marked by the great Pullman strike in Chicago, and its suppression by United States
troops and courts, the tariff fight dragged on. The contest
had lost interest and meaning to Teller. "I cannot say when
I can get away but I mean to do so as soon as we dispose of
the appropriation bills—tariff or no tariff," Teller wrote to
Hal Sayre. "The thermometer stands at 95° to 96° and the
nights are as hot as the days. I want to get out to Colorado
and go to Boulder Park or somewhere where it is cool."[9]

With the Wilson-Gorman tariff passed and Congress adjourned, Teller returned to Colorado and, after a short rest,
turned his attention to the state campaign. Wolcott would be
up for re-election in the legislature that met the following
winter, and that, together with a strong attempt to regain
control of the state government, promised an exceedingly
interesting race. Interest was added also by the circumstance that the last legislature, under Populist pressure, had
adopted a law providing for woman suffrage, and this cause
which the Tellers had supported since territorial days was at
last to have a trial in Colorado.

Wolcott had been in Europe most of the summer attending an unofficial bimetallic conference, and that threw more

---

[8] *Ibid.*, pp. 6633-39, 6690-94; *Public Opinion*, June 28; New York *Tribune*, June
23, 1894.
[9] Teller to Sayre, June 25, 1894, Sayre MSS.

of the work on Teller than was usual. Since Teller's re-election in 1891, the senior senator had co-operated in attempting to build Wolcott up for re-election. Nearly every local bill for Colorado had been sponsored by the latter in the Senate, and he had been given every other reasonable advantage. Wolcott does not seem to have been excessively popular in the state at this time, and bitter complaints had been made against him after the 1892 campaign by some of the defeated Republican candidates.[10] But by the fall of 1894 these were smoothed over, and when Wolcott returned for the fall campaign, the conditions were favorable for a victory.

The issue as far as the state was concerned was Governor Waite, again the nominee of the Populists and Democrats, although Patterson had been opposed to his renomination. Undoubtedly Waite weakened the opposition to the Republicans, because of the numerous antagonisms he had built up during his term of office. The national reaction against the Democrats came to the help of the Colorado Republicans also. The latter nominated a hitherto inconspicuous Republican, Albert W. McIntire, and made Waite's record the issue.

One of the first problems the two senators had to meet was the energetic circulation in Colorado of a story that in the 1890 fight in Congress, after the House had passed the tariff and election bills, Harrison, McKinley, and Reed had conferred with Teller, Wolcott, Jones, and Stewart, and had informed them that if they would help pass the tariff and elections bills the administration would help put through a free-coinage law, but that the Colorado senators had refused. Teller and Wolcott found it advisable to get letters from McKinley and Reed denying any knowledge of such an offer and made them public.

The result of the election was very satisfactory to Teller. In accordance with the Republican trend over the country, they replaced Waite with McIntire, and elected John F. Shafroth, Republican, over one of the Populist congressmen. The Republicans also had a small majority in the legislature pledged to Wolcott. Toward the end of the campaign, Wolcott, unnecessarily it seems, had gone out of his way to declare his independence of parties on the silver question. "Whenever I believe that free coinage can be accomplished

---

[10] Wolcott to Teller, May 11, Aug. 8, 1894; Earl B. Coe to Dawson, no date, 1892, Teller MSS.

through some other party than the Republican Party I will leave that party."[11] These words were to return to plague him a year later.

Teller was not particularly active in the short session of the Fifty-third Congress. He defended the Republican policy toward Hawaii as he had the year before. Because of the attacks in the press and before the courts on the income tax, he delivered a speech in the Senate defending its justice and constitutionality. The question of the sale of bonds to maintain the gold reserve was frequently debated. Teller invariably opposed any legislation of that type that would, as he said, serve to strengthen the hold of the gold standard on the country. When Cleveland made his famous "private" sale to J. P. Morgan, Teller attacked it with his usual vigor, placing his opposition on the ground that the principle of competitive bidding had not been observed.[12]

The growing sectional and class antagonism that went in many cases far deeper than the monetary question was evident in a series of court decisions during 1895. The Sherman Anti-Trust Act was temporarily emasculated by the decison of the Supreme Court in the Knight case in January, caused largely by the halfhearted attempts of the Government in presenting its defense.[13] Late in May, the Court made public its decision in the Debs case, upholding the use of the injunction in suppressing the Pullman strike. A few days before that decision was made public, a ruling that well indicates the conflicting forces at work in American society was given out. It was a decision agreed to by only five of the nine members of the Court, and stood as the decision of the Court, and hence the law, only because one justice had recently changed his mind regarding the question. This decision declared the income-tax feature of the Wilson-Gorman tariff unconstitutional. Both the majority and minority reports were praised and damned by political leaders and newspapers with vehemence that had been heretofore reserved for free coinage. The reaction, as in the latter case, was largely sectional in character. Exceptions like the New York *World* called it the "triumph of selfishness over patriotism," but to the Eastern press generally it was the triumph of American institutions over communism. "Western

[11] Fuller, "Populist Regime," pp. 287-312 ; Wolcott to T. B. Reed, March 15, 1894 ; W. B. McKinley to Teller, March 17, 1894, Teller MSS. ; Teller to Sayre, Oct. 29, Nov. 6, 9, 1894, Sayre MSS. ; Dawson, *Wolcott*, I, 213-24.

[12] *Congressional Record*, 53 Cong., 3 Sess., pp. 2284-88.

[13] Nevins, *Cleveland*, p. 671.

repudiators and Southern ex-rebels struck hands to punish through the income tax law, those who had brought them to naught," declared the Brooklyn *Eagle,* somewhat more pugnacious than most perhaps:

> Whether that decision be the end or but the beginning of the war between civilization and loot in this country, welcome is the decision and ready are the friends of civilization to meet whatever is yet to come.[14]

This piling up of issues as the election of 1896 approached is somewhat confusing, but the lines appear fairly clear for the most part. It bid fair to be the most definite and undisguised class conflict in American political history.

As far as the cause of free coinage was concerned, the continued depression and the complete bankruptcy of the argument that repeal of the Sherman Act would cure it were reacting in silver's favor, especially in the South and West. Two large propaganda organizations for free coinage—the American Bimetallic League and the National Bimetallic Union—became active after repeal, and in 1894 and 1895 carried on their campaign of education by meetings and literature. Most of their expenses were met by the silver miners of Colorado, Montana, Idaho, and Nevada, who also contributed substantially to the support of certain weekly periodicals. But it was becoming increasingly difficult to raise money for the cause. The fall in the price of silver had bankrupted many silver miners and destroyed the main resources of others. Many others doubted the possibility of success, and some began to question whether free coinage would benefit extensively the silver producer. For, if the bankers were correct, and free coinage drove the United States to a silver standard at the current market rate, silver miners could profit from the resulting inflation only insofar as they were debtors.

The decline of financial support by the silver miners was partly made up for by the pamphlet war that began over free coinage after the election of 1894. Centering about Chicago, and stimulated by the vast popularity of W. H. Harvey's *Coin's Financial School,* the tracts poured from the printers in a veritable cloudburst. Economists, journalists, bankers, college presidents, and lawyers rushed into print to support Coin or to disprove him. James H. Teller, the youngest of the Senator's brothers and now a Chicago lawyer, joined the

---

[14] May 23, 1895.

rush with *The Battle of the Standards.*[15] The press of the
Middle West took up the contest, and it was a rare newspaper that did not have arguments on the silver question
for its regular editorial fare, to say nothing of the activities
of voluntary correspondents.

With control of the Democratic Party in the hands of the
gold-standard advocates, and the dominant Republicans in a
not substantially different position, there were demands for
an independent political movement for free coinage that
would unite into one group all its supporters now in the
traditional parties and in the People's Party. These demands
were discussed and agitated freely in Washington during the
early months of 1895.

Teller may still have had some hope that the Republican
Party would take a position on bimetallism in substantial
contrast to Cleveland's. There had been, even during the
fight over repeal, attempts to unite the causes of protection
and silver, partly to maintain Republican unity, but some
of them were broader in scope.[16] Back of them was the fact
that there was not a complete unity of interest between the
manufacturers and the bankers, rapidly as the latter were
gaining the ascendancy in the business world. In a broad
sense the financial group had backed Cleveland, and the
manufacturers the Republicans in 1892, and this divergence
was evident in the strategy of both the Republicans and the
free-coinage groups. It did not promise much after repeal, although optimistic Republican silver men kept nursing
the hope that it would.

There were repeated rumors during 1895 that the free-
coinage Republicans were preparing to bolt their party if
it declared for the gold standard, rumors that were not believed in the East, at least. *The Nation* expressed the general
view when it announced: "Of the Colorado and Montana
members [of the Senate] it may be said that their bark is
worse than their bite. They will threaten and bluster up to
a certain point and then they will surrender. Such Senators
as Teller and Wolcott have no idea of disrupting their
party."[17] An attempt was made by Dubois and Carter to
secure approval for a satisfactory proposal from the Na-

---

[15] Willard Fisher, "Coin and His Critics," *Quarterly Journal of Economics,* X
(Jan., 1896), 185-208; James H. Teller, *The Battle of the Standards,* with an introduction by Henry M. Teller (Chicago, 1896).

[16] Teller to R. P. Porter, Aug. 15, 1893, Teller MSS. The Wharton Barker MSS.
contain a large amount of correspondence with Teller and others regarding these
plans from 1893 to 1896.

[17] March 14, 1895.

tional League of Republican Clubs in the summer, but to no avail.[18]

The unanimity of the controlling factions in the party from all sections east of the Missouri River should have been evidence to the Westerners that they would get no help from them. Possibly it was. At least two weeks later a Washington dispatch to the Chicago *Daily News* related the information that a "Western Republican of national prominence" had predicted that the free-coinage Republicans would bolt the next convention. A plan, he had related, was agreed upon by Western senators and other leaders claiming to be able to control the delegations from all states west of Kansas, and South Dakota and possibly North Dakota and Nebraska. They would choose delegates to the Republican convention in regular form and support Senator Cameron, or some other silver Republican, for the presidential nomination. If no free-coinage candidate were nominated, the delegates from the Western states would walk out and wait on the Democratic convention, asking it to nominate a free-coinage man, preferably Senator Morgan. If the Democrats refused, the Westerners would make an independent nomination, with the hope of throwing the election into the House and then bargaining among the candidates.[19]

There was probably little more than talk in the proposed agreement the Westerner had seemed so certain about, but it was indicative of the trend of Western ideas as it became more and more evident that the East would stand out for the gold standard. Two days after the report appeared, Senator Kyle, Populist, of South Dakota, wrote to Senator Allen, of Nebraska:

> Why would it not be a good stroke for several of us to meet at a convenient point this summer—you and I, and Senators Teller, Shoup, Morgan and Turpie. We could find out what they would like as a basis of a combination in case both old parties declare against silver.[20]

As far as the East was concerned, it became more unanimous in its attitude toward free coinage during 1895. Writing from the atmosphere of Washington, John Hay, in the fall of 1895, indicated to Henry Adams what the trend was:

---

[18] O'Brien Moore in the St. Louis *Republic*, June 18-22, 1895.

[19] Quoted in the St. Louis *Republic*, July 7, 1895.

[20] July 8, 1895. Quoted in Marian Silveus, "The Antecedents of the Campaign of 1896" (unpublished thesis, University of Wisconsin Library, 1933), p. 47.

If you don't hurry back, there won't be a silver man in America
except you and Peffer, and even Peffer said in an interview the other
day that the jig was up. I think Reid and McKinley and Allison and
Harrison and Morton are all good gold-bugs now. A large majority
of Democrats have thought they were not, but the post-masters and
"deppity marshalls" have convinced them that they are,—at least,
such of them as go to convention.[21]

But the grain-farming West and the agricultural South
had been driven to a similar unanimity by the depression.
The Democratic repudiation of Cleveland was soon to show
that they were nearly as united as the East. If the cause was
lost in the East, it was still supreme in the Far West and
South. Only the Middle West, with its great farming interests, as well as its growing industrial and commercial
centers, remained questionable ground. Whether gold or
silver won the next fight would be determined in that section between Pennsylvania and the Missouri River.

In preparing for the struggle, the contestants were pointing their entire case toward the election of 1896. The Eastern press began to insist that the major parties take an
emphatic stand against free coinage in their platforms.
Politicians, especially prospective candidates for the presidency, wanted to avoid any commitments that would kill
their chances in any region. Two questions remained: What
would the parties do? What would the sections do?

---

[21] W. R. Thayer, *John Hay*, II, 125-26. Probably "Reid" should be "Reed."

CHAPTER XVII

REVOLT
1895-96

WHEN the Fifty-fourth Congress assembled in December of 1895, its various factions began the campaign of 1896. A very substantial number of the Democrats, now in a minority in both houses, were alienated almost completely from the Cleveland administration, but they were not agreed among themselves. The Republicans, with a large majority in the House and a plurality in the Senate, were only less disorganized. A breakup of parties was imminent. Among the Republicans, the Nevada group had already seceded. Senator Stewart had set up a Silver Party in that state in 1892, and Senator Jones went over to this organization also.[1] Nationally, it allied itself loosely with the Populists, and the two Nevada senators acted with the four senators elected by that party. Together, they held the balance of power between Democrats and Republicans in the Senate. Likewise, the position of the free-coinage Republicans was in question. Would they do as the Nevada group had done and join the Populists, at least for purposes of national politics, or would they work with the majority of the party?

As the time for the presidential election of 1896 approached, there developed two very distinct tendencies looking toward a realignment of parties. One was the feeling of many silver men that the day of compromise was over. Platforms such as the Republican of 1892 did not prevent Eastern members of that party from voting against all measures looking toward bimetallism, or from taking positive action against it, as in the repeal fight of 1893. The business interests in the East, on the other hand, were just as determined that the parties should end their straddle on the question and come out for the gold standard. The trend all over the East had long been definitely away from anything looking like silver coinage. Neither of the major parties had ever committed itself to free coinage, and with a Democratic President who was completely on the other side, it seemed unlikely that either would now. To one gaining his

---

[1] Some Republicans still insisted on calling Jones a Republican because he had been elected as one, and his vote was important on partisan measures. He seems to have been satisfied to classify himself with the Populists.

knowledge of politics from the Eastern press it must have
seemed improbable that either major party would declare for
free coinage in 1896, and hence possible that both might
even come out for the gold standard.

There can be little doubt that as far as Teller personally
was concerned, he returned to Washington for the opening
of the Fifty-fourth Congress determined to make the Republican Party declare for free coinage or leave that organization for one that would. More than that, he planned to take
as many Republicans as possible with him when he left. It
is quite evident that he looked forward at that time to the
probability that both major parties would either adopt gold-
standard or straddle platforms, and in that eventuality he
would unite such Republicans as he could command with
such silver Democrats as would bolt their party, and go in
with the Populist Party on a separate ticket committed to
free coinage.[2] That was only the extreme, however, and for
the present he would try to swing the Republicans and protectionists as far toward free coinage as possible.

Changes other than party shifts had come over the com-
position of the Senate since the election of 1894. Utah was
admitted in January, 1896, and late that month it presented
two Republican senators, Frank J. Cannon and Arthur
Brown, both presumably silver men. Cannon was well known
to Teller, as his Mormon father, George Q. Cannon, had been
before him. Thomas H. Carter, chairman of the Republican
National Committee, had been advanced by his state of
Montana from the House to the Senate, where he sat with
Lee Mantle, giving that state an unusually strong pair of
senators. North Carolina had in the new Senate a Populist
in the person of Marion Butler, and a Republican, Jeter C.
Pritchard, who were as definitely committed to free coinage
as any Westerner.

In his efforts to weld together a large group of free-
coinage Republicans who would defy the party, Teller had to
work against forces that were more potent than traditional loyalty to the party. The greatest was the very well-
founded expectation that pending some unforseen political
accident, the next administration would be Republican, and
for at least four years the patronage in the Western states
would be available to those politicians who were loyal now.

Less important, perhaps, was the declining relative sig-

---

2 E. B. Light to Barker, Aug. 12; B. R. Tillman to Barker, Dec. 3, 1895, Barker
MSS.; Marion Butler to Bryan, Jan. 8, 1896, Bryan MSS.; Mack, "Stewart," pp. 261-66.

nificance of silver mining in the Rocky Mountain states, due partly to the low price of silver, and partly to the great increase in other types of mining, especially gold mining. Certainly it would be impossible to keep the free-coinage Republicans a unit in opposition to the party that would soon be able to offer protective tariffs on wool, hides, and lead to their constituents. How large a group could be organized and maintained was the problem.

The tempo of the campaign for the Republican nomination for President was increased by the expectation that the nomination was equivalent to election. Speaker Reed, Senator Allison, and Governor McKinley, of Ohio, were all conducting energetic campaigns, but as time went on it became clearly evident that Mark Hanna, McKinley's campaign manager, was gathering the great majority of the delegates. All the candidates were being noncommittal on the monetary question, and such statements as they did make were aimed at not antagonizing Western delegates who would have votes in the convention. "They are all your metaphysicians' tabula rasa on which the majority of the convention can write whatever it pleases—16 to 1, or 60 to 1, gold, silver or lead. If their views do not suit they can be altered," declared *The Nation* in disgust.[3] But this apparent indecision did not extend to the controlling forces behind the dominant politicians. A gold-standard platform would be adopted. What were the bimetallists going to do?

The Republican politicians in Washington laid their plans for the campaign in 1896 so as to make the tariff the dominant issue. On that they could hold the party together; on that the candidates for the party nomination would not, during the early months of 1896, create any opposition that would lose them delegates at the convention. The strategy then was to pass a new tariff bill through the House and Senate, force Cleveland to veto it, and in the accompanying clamor create the issue to carry to the public in the campaign. More than that, the tariff would be concrete proof to the industrialists and to the woolgrowers and lead miners of the West that Republican victory was a worthy cause. If the Western Republicans wanted free coinage more than party success, it was obvious strategy to defeat these plans.

The large Republican majority in the House passed the Dingley tariff bill soon after Congress assembled, but the size of the group of Western Republican members who voted

_____
[3] March 12, 1896.

against it was a warning that party unity might not prevail upon the question in the Senate, where the Republicans
were dependent upon Populist votes for a majority. Jones
and Stewart were, of course, protectionists, and with these
additions the Republicans might make a majority. Yet the
fact that the House bill embodied very unsatisfactory rates
on Western products lessened the chances that they would
have such a majority.

On January 8, the Republican caucus voted unanimously
to instruct the Republican members of the finance committee
to report the Dingley bill without amendment. There was no
opposition to this caucus action, but when the proposal was
made to pledge all members not to attempt to amend the bill
on the floor of the Senate—an attempt to pledge them not
to add a free-coinage amendment—the Western senators
refused. Teller announced to the caucus that he would never
vote for another tariff bill unless it contained a free-coinage
provision. When asked if that were an ultimatum, he replied
that it was. Other Western senators supported Teller's
demand, although only Dubois was as emphatic in his declaration. The caucus broke up without an agreement.[4]

Wharton Barker, of Philadelphia, who had been editing
a weekly paper devoted to the two causes of free coinage and
protection, became active later in the month, and drew up
a declaration of principles which provided for free coinage
and a protective tariff equal to differences in the cost of production here and abroad. This was, in a sense, the public
declaration by the silver Republicans of the stand they had
taken in the caucus. The statement implied that the responsibility rested with the manufacturers to force the Republican Party to support the two proposals, and declared directly
that without silver no protective tariff legislation was possible. It was signed by sixteen Republican senators, including practically all those who would vote for free coinage
under any circumstances.[5]

Before the tariff debate reached the floor of the Senate
in any form, the President's request for legislation to provide
for issuing bonds came up. Teller used the occasion to denounce the private sale to Morgan of the year before as a
"lasting disgrace," and appealed for the public sale of any
new issues. But he put his chief efforts into a demand for
some solution of the Government's monetary problem. He

---

[4] St. Louis *Republic*, Jan. 9, 1896.
[5] *Congressional Record*, 54 Cong., 1 Sess., Appendix, p. 85; Wharton Barker MSS.

chided his Republican gold-standard colleagues with having
no plan to meet the situation, except continually issuing
more bonds. The administration's plan to retire all paper
currency by a large bond issue was, at least, a plan, but
would cause a disastrous contraction of currency. The gold
standard could not be maintained without one or the other,
Teller insisted. The only other solution was to abandon the
gold standard by the free coinage of silver and redemption
of legal tenders in gold or silver at the election of the
Treasury. Then the exporters of gold would have to depend
upon the banks for their supplies. No longer would financial
cliques in New York City drain the gold reserve at their
pleasure, as they were now doing, and force the Government
to give them profitable bond issues.

The silver senators of all parties substituted a free-coinage bill for the bond proposal and passed it. On the direct
vote, the free-coinage bill received the support of nearly
every Western Republican.[6] The silver senators controlled
the finance committee, and Jones refused to allow the Dingley bill to be reported to the Senate, possibly waiting to see
what action the House would take on the free-coinage bill
which the Senate had just passed.

In order to force the insurgents to support the Dingley
bill or assume open opposition to protection and thus decrease their standing with the rank and file of the party,
Senator Morrill moved to take up the Dingley bill. The motion lost, with Democrats, Populists, and four Republicans
voting against it. The Republicans were Teller, Dubois,
Carter, and Mantle.[7] Immediately afterward, the House
defeated by an enormous majority the free-coinage bill the
Senate had passed.

Teller had been unwell during most of the session, and
pessimism for the cause of free coinage colored his every
thought. Possibly, too, he was disappointed in the small
number of Republicans who voted with him against taking
up the tariff. If the sixteen or eighteen Republican senators
who favored silver in some form had united in this opposition, it would have been a much more effective protest and
threat. Just after the House defeated the free-coinage bill,
he confided his thoughts to his associate, Hal Sayre:

---

[6] *Congressional Record*, 54 Cong., 1 Sess., pp. 337, 471, 864-72.
[7] *Ibid.*, p. 1691.

I was pretty sick for a time and I confess I was somewhat scared afterwards when I talked with the doctor and it satisfied me that I ought to quit politics as *soon* as I can and take care of myself. If I can raise copper and fruit enough to make a living I will be content. We can do nothing for silver for a time. The House of Representatives is a gold standard body and the Republicans will put up and elect a Wall St. Candidate. The leading republican newspapers have teemed with abuse of those Rep who voted for free coinage and have read us out of the party. It will be impossible for any self-respecting man to continue in that party if he believes in Bimetallism. The demand is that we shall repudiate our financial views or go out. I will not abandon my views on finance and so I must go out not because I want to go out but because I am to be driven out. I am receiving a good many letters from our so called leaders in Colorado saying that I must stay in the party, that we must support the candidate no matter who he is or what his views may be on the financial question. And it is quite apparent that a great effort is going to be made to keep our party in line with the National party ticket. I don't believe we can carry Colorado on this platform and if we can I don't want to be on the platform. I prefer to go into private life. So you see I am compelled to find something to do. I can practice law of course if I can get any law business to do. I have been in hopes that the Crandall property in Arizona might turn out to offer some inducements to us and if that don't we may find something else.[8]

With the free-coinage bill killed by the House, Senator Morrill again moved to take up the Dingley bill on February 25, and once more had the motion voted down. This time a fifth Republican, Cannon, of Utah, who had been absent when the motion was made earlier in the month, joined Teller's group. It is to be noticed that had all five voted for the motion, it would still have failed unless a Populist had supported it. The other silver Republicans voted with the majority of their party. After this second defeat of the tariff the Senate witnessed a more bitter debate among the Republican senators than had taken place since the repeal of the Sherman Act. Morrill complained vigorously of the lack of a Republican majority. Teller replied by assuming responsibility for the defeat of the motion and defended those who had helped him. The bill, he said, was a very poor one, introduced solely for partisan purposes, with no expectation that it would become a law. "As this is a political play, we will play politics on our side." Since the free-coinage bill had passed the Senate, Teller pointed out, the metropolitan Republican press had been reading out of the party those eighteen Republican senators who had favored it.

---

[8] February 16, 1896, Sayre MSS.

We have been notified that unless we change our views upon the financial question and submit to the Cleveland Democracy and Morrill Republicanism of this country ... we must get out of the party. Mr. President, we can get along without the party as well as the party can get along without us.

"There was something almost savage in the way Mr. Teller hurled out the words 'Cleveland Democracy and Morrill Republicanism,' " noted a reporter.[9]

The next day the intraparty quarrel continued with a speech by Carter, who started a controversy over the meaning of the 1892 party plank on money. The Eastern Republicans seemed for the most part to agree that it committed the party to bimetallism at some future time, presumably to be effected by an international agreement. But Teller brought in Sherman's definition of bimetallism as the gold standard and subsidiary silver coins, and before the debate was over the Ohio senator had claimed that the platform of 1892 meant "bimetallism as we have it." This tricky use of the word bimetallism, which Teller could foresee being used in the coming campaign, aroused his anger to an unusual degree, and he denounced it as a deception and a fraud. The "bunco game" on the monetary question was over, and the West would no longer accept such straddles as the 1892 platform so that the Eastern Republicans could disown them afterwards by mendaciously claiming that bimetallism meant the gold standard. Forensically, it was one of Teller's best days, possibly because it was unpremeditated on his part, and, consequently, he was less careful than usual of his language. But the break in the ranks of the party was clearer than it had been before, and the efforts increased to pull the younger men, such as Carter and Dubois, away from Teller.[10]

While this debate was in progress, Washington had been the scene of an important political gathering. Attempts to unite all the pro-silver forces behind an independent movement had been numerous in the past two years, and another was taking definite form. On January 22, a conference called by the American Bimetallic Union met to organize a united silver party. Composed of a number of prominent silver advocates, including the leaders of the Nevada "Silver Party," and blessed by the attendance of a committee from

[9] *Congressional Record*, 54 Cong., 1 Sess., pp. 2100-01; Washington *Post*, Feb. 26, 1896.

[10] *Congressional Record*, 54 Cong., 1 Sess., pp. 2151-62; Washington *Post*, Feb. 27; St. Louis *Republic*, Feb. 27, 1896.

the People's Party, who looked on but did not accept responsibility for the meeting, the conference organized the National Silver Party. It was arranged that its national nominating convention should be held at the same time and place as the People's Party. The new National Silver Party was definitely associated in the public mind with the Populists.

The free-coinage Republicans realized that it would not add to their strength at home to appear to be drifting over to the People's Party, an organization most of them had been roundly denouncing the past four years. To prevent this impression from arising out of the coincidence of the conference at the very time the insurgent Republicans were demonstrating their freedom from party control, Senator Dubois informed the Senate and the country that the silver Republicans were not willing to follow Populist leadership in any organization. They differed from the People's Party, he declared, upon all questions except free coinage. They were protectionists above all other issues except free silver. Some days later, Congressman Charles S. Hartman, of Montana, made a speech in the House that was highly critical of almost all that the Populists stood for, in this way making clear that the break from the Republican Party was not a case of deserting to an enemy.[11]

The only drive the free-coinage Republicans made to capture their party organization was the attempt to join forces with the protected manufacturers in a common program. These efforts, of which Wharton Barker's declaration was a part, fitted in with a theory Teller had that it might be possible to line up a substantial group of producers—manufacturers, farmers, miners—against the bankers. Tentatively they had planned to get behind Senator J. D. Cameron, of Pennsylvania, as their candidate for the Republican presidential nomination; for, as an Easterner from a protectionist state, as well as an unselfish defender of free coinage, he covered both issues well.[12]

After Teller's group had defeated the move to take up the tariff bill for a second time, as though that were a demonstration of their determination and strength, they attempted to come to some sort of an agreement with the industrialists. After some preliminary negotiations, a Pennsylvania manufacturer, William Wilhelem, invited the free-

[11] St. Louis *Republic*, Jan. 22, Feb. 14; Washington *Post*, Jan. 23, 24, Feb. 14, 1896.
[12] Teller to Barker, Dec. 11; Mantle to Barker, Dec. 14, 1895, Barker MSS.

coinage congressmen to a conference in Washington with some twenty manufacturers—most of whom were interested in woolens. They also carried letters of approval from several more who could not be present. Teller, Dubois, and Carter all addressed the meeting, and it was made clear that they would oppose any protective tariff in the next Congress as well as the present one, unless free coinage were a part of it. Senator Cameron's name was brought in as a suitable candidate for the presidency upon whom all could unite. Most of the industrialists present seemed to agree to work along these lines.

The support, however, was only a small part of the Republican industrialists, who as a group were, of course, closely tied up with banking interests. The Manufacturers' Club of Philadelphia quickly repudiated the Washington meeting and free coinage.[13] It may be that Teller did not expect anything out of this, anyway, but carried it through because an appearance of industrial support would strengthen the insurgent Republicans working with him in their own states. Cameron's candidacy struck no fire anywhere in the East, and the free-coinage Republicans found it useless to push it in the West. In fact, Teller, at least, seems to have come to the conclusion that it was better to make the contest over the platform and not confuse the issue by supporting any particular candidate.

The Republican regulars were in no temper to allow Teller to lead the mining West out of the party without a struggle. They built fires behind the insurgents in their own states, and induced other politicians from that region to repudiate insurgency. They distributed widely the speech of Senator Hoar on February 26, in which he had appealed for party harmony on a basis of bimetallism through an international agreement.[14] By pointing to President Cleveland's advocacy of the gold standard as the only alternative to Republican policy, and emphasizing the tariff rates of local importance, they could make a strong appeal to an electorate traditionally Republican. Although the insurgents had popular and press support in the West in great abundance, it is easy to overemphasize the sentiment for repudiating the party that existed among Western Republicans.

It had become evident before this that Wolcott probably

---

[13] St. Louis *Globe-Democrat*, March 20, April 1; Washington *Post*, March 20, 31, 1896.

[14] T. G. Clayton to W. E. Chandler, March 18; W. F. Sanders to Chandler, March 13, 1896, Chandler MSS.

would not follow Teller in his plan of independent action, but
would stay in the Republican Party no matter what became
of the silver issue. He was in a different position, in some
ways, from that of most of the other silver men. His connections in Cleveland, where he had lived before moving to
Colorado, were inclining him strongly toward support of
McKinley, or, at least, of Hanna, who was an old friend.
With his large circle of Eastern friends, Wolcott had found
it very unpleasant to be on the unpopular side in the bitter
silver contests of the early nineties. He had been black-
balled at the exclusive Metropolitan Club of New York City
a few years before because, so went the story, of his silver
record in the Senate. To be classified repeatedly by the great
papers of the country as a silver lunatic along with Peffer
and Waite was not pleasant to a fastidious senator. Then
his very closeness to great political distinction made it all
the more difficult, because Wolcott was, by common consent,
one of the great orators in the senatorial tradition. Certainly
not until Beveridge reached the Senate was he to have a
rival in that body. Coloradans continued, however, to think
first of Teller when they ranked their political leaders, and
although Wolcott would have denied it even to himself, it
must have been difficult for the brilliant orator, lionized by
society in Washington, to play second fiddle to such an unspectacular figure as his colleague. Mr. Dooley probably expressed general opinion in his characterization:

> Wolcott's th' boy for me, Hinnissey. A quick, agile man with strong
> convictions, but not stubborn about thim. I wouldn't call him two-
> faced. That would be an injustice. Like his own beloved Pike's Peak,
> he catches th' sun on iv'ry side, and on iv'ry side he's beautiful.

On April 28, Wolcott gave to the press a letter addressed
to the chairman of the Colorado Republican Committee, in
which he declared that the Colorado delegates to the national
convention should, after a fight for a free-coinage plank,
"accept the will of the majority," but carefully phrased it
to imply that if the Democratic Party declared later for free
coinage some less loyal Republican policy might be adopted.
Governor McConnell, of Idaho, had publicly criticized the
free-coinage Republicans who had held up the passage of the
Dingley tariff, and left no doubt that he, with Senator Shoup,
would not let the silver issue drive them out of the Republican organization. "It is nothing less than an offer to sur-

render from the heart of the silver camp," commented *The Nation* on Wolcott's letter.[15]

These were direct challenges to Teller's leadership, and he had to reply to them. The issue should be made definitely and finally, party or no party. The day after Wolcott's letter was made public, Teller replied in the Senate by stating definitely that he would not support the Republican Party without a free-coinage platform.

> Holding, as I do, that the interest of the whole race is wrapped up in this question ... I should despise myself, as you ought to despise me, if I did not lift my voice against a system threatening such danger; and if I should lift my voice for one course and vote for another, you would have the right to accuse me of hypocrisy and deceit.

He defended the action of the Westerners who had held up the Dingley bill in order to make the monetary question the issue of the campaign. Then Sherman replied by defending the Dingley bill, and went back into the legislation of 1890 to repeat the statement of his opposition to the Purchase Act, and his support of it in order to prevent the passage of a free-coinage measure. But this time it drew from Teller a more direct rebuttal "in the interests of history and truth and exactness." In words which a Democratic organ described as "clear and sharp as the cracks of a cold chisel on a safe in the night time," Teller recounted the compromise that included the Purchase Act. "On the day the Sherman bill passed there was no more show of a free coinage bill becoming a law than there was of the heavens falling." Although the free-coinage senators knew Harrison would veto the McKinley bill with a free-coinage amendment, they determined to add it as a threat against the tariff. Then the Republican majority brought in the Sherman Act and passed it, in order that the silver senators would let the McKinley bill through without a free-coinage amendment. That was the "unvarnished history of the case." Teller explained:

> It was a sort of a compromise, and when they obtained the advantage of the compromise they proposed to leave us. I have never forgotten the alacrity, the haste and the zeal with which the Senator from Ohio and his associates in this chamber ... came to the rescue of the Democratic Administration when it asked for the repeal of that law.... We got no more sympathy and no more support than if we had been aliens in an alien land.[16]

---

[15] Dawson, *Wolcott*, I, 235-37; O'Brien Moore, "Free Silver Losing Ground in West," St. Louis *Republic*, April 30; *The Nation*, May 7, 1896.

[16] *Congressional Record*, 54 Cong., 1 Sess., pp. 4558-62; St. Louis *Republic*, April 30, 1896.

The interest in Teller's definite announcement that he
would bolt was somewhat obscured by the interest of the
press in his recital of the trade by which the Purchase Act
and McKinley tariff had been enacted.

There seems to have been a fairly definite understanding
looking toward action in the Republican convention among
Teller and those who were following his lead: Senators Dubois, Cannon, Mantle, and Carter, and Representatives Hartman, Wilson, Shafroth, Allen, and Charles A. Towne. This
included the bolting of the party if a free-coinage plank
were not adopted, and joining with such other groups as the
silver Democrats, Populists, and National Silverites, in a
fight for a definite free-coinage platform and candidate.

The plan meant first of all the bringing to the Republican
convention of delegations which were pledged to silver un-
compromisingly, and to a bolt if they could not prevent a gold-standard plank. Most of them would not go as
far as Teller. His own task was to keep the contests real,
and, at the same time, carry as many with him as possible.

On such a program only those men who were willing to
forego immediate rewards could be included. It was obviously "yellow dog" year for the Republicans, and, barring
a miracle, anyone they nominated for president would win.
The choice was easier for Teller than for his colleagues.
He was sixty-six years old, tired of politics, and in ill-health.
If he cared to return to the Senate, his position in Colorado
was such that he could bolt the party and still be re-elected
more easily than any colleague could, except the senators
from Nevada, who had already bolted. He had mentally a
free hand to make his own policy. It was not so with the
others, who as a group, were very young for the positions
they held, and in every case would have serious opposition
when they came up for re-election. Teller felt an immense
amount of gratitude toward them individually, and many
of his actions in the next six months can only be understood
by having clearly in mind his desire to give them the protection they had earned from him.

To carry out his part of the plan, Teller instituted an
extensive correspondence with the political leaders in Colorado. He wanted a delegation to the national convention
that was committed to silver above all considerations of
party. The majority of the politicians were opposed to this
procedure, as were the supporters of all the candidates for
the presidency. Early in May the Arapahoe County conven-

tion [Denver] defeated by a vote of over two to one a motion
to censure Wolcott for his stand against bolting. But public
opinion in Colorado was behind Teller. It was a foregone
conclusion that he would be chairman of the delegation, but
the opposition endeavored to secure the choice of Wolcott
and others as delegates who were sure not to bolt. To prevent this, Teller addressed a telegram to the chairman of the
state central committee, saying:

> I wish to say to the State Convention, through you, that I do not
> desire to go to the national convention, and cannot go unless the State
> delegation is in accordance with my ideas in declaring that in the
> coming campaign the silver question is the paramount issue.
> The State convention should act with the full knowledge that I
> do not intend to support a candidate on a gold-standard platform or a
> platform of doubtful construction.[17]

The fight was bitter, and it was only by a careful struggle that his friends won. Although the victory was absolute
on the surface, it was marred by the many antagonisms
created. When it was over, Ammons, one of the delegates,
wrote to Dawson describing the undercurrents at the
convention.

> There was a very strong sentiment among Mr. Teller's friends in
> opposition to bolting the national ticket, and I know that many of
> them intend to support the national ticket in any event. It was this
> element that made it hard for us ... and gave Mr. Teller's enemies
> their support in several of the closest contests.... It was hard to
> tell where anyone stood, and there was much bitterness expressed
> because of the difference of opinion on the proposition of bolting.[18]

The resolution with the implied permission to bolt was
carried in the resolutions committee by a vote of 24 to 18,
and Ammons thought it would have been still closer had the
issue been drawn directly. This part of the platform was
one of the most unusual ever adopted by a convention choosing delegates to a national convention:

> ... we declare to the Republican party of the nation and to the world
> that our Senior Senator in Congress, the Honorable Henry M. Teller,
> has our unqualified approval and support in the position he has so
> ably maintained in Congress for the cause of the free coinage of silver
> in its relation to the tariff.... We recognize in Senator Teller the
> ablest living exponent of the true principles of American finance and
> the most fearless and intelligent advocate in public life of the
> financial system which will best promote the comfort and prosperity

---

[17] *Rocky Mountain News*, May 8, 12, 1896.
[18] May 15, 1896, Teller MSS.

of the whole people and the whole world, and the delegates selected
by this convention are instructed to act in harmony with the views
of the Honorable Henry M. Teller as to the course to be pursued by the
Colorado delegation in the national convention, and that Senator Teller
is hereby selected as a delegate and appointed to lead the delegation
in the St. Louis convention.[19]

A friend wrote Teller after the convention, warning
him that "there is strong party feeling in the state," and one
of the delegates to the national convention thought it worth
while to write that he expected to stand by Teller no matter
what the others did. Shortly before the national convention was to meet, former Senator Stephen W. Dorsey wrote
Teller from Denver:

> I write this to say that from repeated conversations with some of
> the delegates to St. Louis I don't believe that the majority of them
> have the slightest intention of leaving the convention no matter who is
> nominated or what the platform may be.[20]

The Eastern press looked angrily at the challenge Teller
was forcing into the contest. The Philadelphia *Inquirer*
observed, "Senator Teller is in full command of Colorado.
... He is a member of the band of highwaymen who refused
to permit the tariff revenue bill to pass without a free silver
proviso." Not all of them were sure that the convention's
action meant a bolt, and many were inclined to believe it
indicated that Teller would try to make terms. In Montana
and Idaho the Republican state conventions endorsed the
action of Teller and his associates on coinage and tariff,
but, as in Utah, they refused to recommend that their delegates to the national convention bolt if the coinage plank
were unsatisfactory.[21]

The contest was now transferred to the Republican convention at St. Louis. In preparation for it Teller delivered a
long speech in the Senate in which he discussed free coinage
and its relation to the approaching election. The cause of
free coinage he based directly on the question of price
levels, declaring that there had been no depreciation of the
silver dollar anywhere as compared with commodity prices.
On the other hand, the present gold standard meant constan-
ly falling prices. "It means 21 per cent more of farm products than it did when you repealed the Sherman law." No

[19] Dawson, *Teller* (1898), p. 10.
[20] Will B. Coe to Teller, May 18; J. M. Dowling to Teller, May 18, Dorsey to Teller June 4, 1896, Teller MSS.; *Rocky Mountain News*, May 16, 17, 1896.
[21] *Public Opinion*, May 21; St. Louis *Republic*, May 16, 1896.

Bolters from the Republican National Convention.

Above, left to right: Congressman Charles A. Towne, Minnesota; Senator Fred T. Dubois, Idaho. *Below, left to right:* Senator R. F. Pettigrew, South Dakota; Senator Frank J. Cannon, Utah.

international agreement for bimetallism that had to include Great Britain was possible, and the United States was strong enough "to have a financial system of our own."

What the Republican party will do at St. Louis I do not know, but I believe I know enough of the public sentiment of the plain people, the honest people, to know that the party which inscribes on its banner, "The Gold standard" inscribes on its banner "Defeat."[22]

The lack of specific instructions created considerable doubt among the insurgents as to the proper course to pursue at the national convention. Some did not want to bolt until instructed to do so, and up to the hour that the small group walked out of the convention hall, no one knew how many would follow Teller. Apparently many did not make their final decision until the crisis came. As late as June 15, former Senator John J. Ingalls wrote regarding Teller's announced purpose to bolt. "To me it is hardly credible, but he has much of the Cromwell spirit and may be implacable."[23]

While the free-coinage Republicans were making preparations for a losing fight in their convention, the free-coinage Democrats were taking control of their party away from the administration forces with a speed and completeness that was as unusual as it was unexpected. All over the South and West, and in a substantial portion of the Middle West, the Democratic state conventions were selecting delegates to the national convention pledged to free coinage and repudiating the Cleveland administration in unmistakable terms. Among the candidates for their presidential nomination no one stood out as McKinley did in the Republican, but the leading one was Bland, of Missouri, and most of the others with substantial support were also committed to free coinage. Would the Democrats adopt a free-coinage platform and nominate a silver candidate in spite of President Cleveland?

The growing prospect of this during April and May raised a problem of great importance to the insurgent Republicans. It was all very well to plan to bolt from the Republican organization and to function for a time as an independent group if the Democrats were also pledged to a gold-standard or a straddle platform; but it was much more serious to bolt the old party in order to take a position in line

---

[22] *Congressional Record*, 54 Cong., 1 Sess., pp. 5997-6000.
[23] New York *Journal*, June 15, 1896.

with its chief opposition. In the latter case the bolters would
be between the devil of going over to the hereditary enemy,
and the deep blue sea of obstructing the success of the policy
that had caused their revolt. Teller was ready to accept the
first alternative, as his correspondence shows, but his younger colleagues were not, and the policy which they followed
was a compromise that protected the interests of their state
organizations. In this unsatisfactory position, they enjoyed
what comfort company could give them, for the Populists
were in a similar position. If the Democrats declared for
free coinage, they too would have the delectable choice of
committing suicide as a political organization or impeding
the success of their most important policy. Nor did the
silver Democrats, even with their remarkable successes in
state conventions, have an inviting prospect. Repudiating
their own party's record as they would do, and splitting
their organization, they could at best have but little chance
of success in the election. The only hope they could have of
winning lay in a complete union of all the disaffected Republicans and the Populists behind the Democratic ticket.
This made them open to suggestions of compromise.

Conferences of the factional leaders in Washington resulted in a tentative understanding among certain Southern
Democratic leaders, the insurgent Republicans, the leaders
of the National Silver Party, and a group of Populists. The
insurgent Republicans would bolt the St. Louis convention
and organize a political party. At the Democratic convention at Chicago an attempt would be made to secure the
presidential nomination for Senator Teller. If the attempt
were successful, the Silver Republicans, Populists, and National Silver Party would also nominate him, and a union
of free-coinage forces would be effected without destroying
any of the political organizations involved. If a Democrat
were named at Chicago or an unsatisfactory platform adopted, the Silver Republican, Populist, and National Silver
parties would unite upon a common candidate, or, at least, so
the Silver Republicans and Populists assured themselves.[24]

The Republican convention opened on June 16, and to it
came Silver Republicans who were delegates, and others like

---

[24] At a private dinner in April, Congressman Francis G. Newlands urged this plan
upon Senators Cockrell, Bacon, Jones, of Arkansas, and Blackburn, and upon Congressmen Bailey and Dinsmore. St. Louis *Republic*, April 28. Statements of A. J.
Warner, St. Louis *Globe-Democrat*, June 4; of J. H. McDowell, *ibid.*, July 2; of William
M. Stewart, *Rocky Mountain News*, June 11, all 1896. "I see that Teller has carried
out the programme, so far, all right." Marion Butler to William M. Stewart, June 24,
1896, Stewart MSS.

Congressman Towne, of Minnesota, who had not been so honored. Teller announced for the silver men that there would be no bolt unless the convention adopted an unsatisfactory monetary plank. In that event, however, they would quietly withdraw.

Before the convention assembled, the evidence seems clear that J. P. Morgan and other interested bankers had convinced Hanna and McKinley of the advisability of a gold-standard platform. To ensure its adoption and to prevent a disastrous bolt that might prove weakening to the party, representatives of the banking group swarmed about St. Louis as the convention opened. Indeed, they were so active that Hanna finally warned them, "You damned bankers will upset this whole thing, if you keep on." But, assured of the platform, they expended their efforts on keeping the Western delegates from bolting. McKinley would do what he could for silver, Hanna assured the Westerners, and would send another commission to Europe to try to secure an international agreement for bimetallism. Far more potent than this promise was the expectation that the Republicans would have the presidency after March 4. "Whatever we do, let's avoid a split," was the theme of their argument.[25]

Gold sentiment was well entrenched among the delegates. Someone had revived an old song made popular by Tony Pastor, and before long it was being sung, hummed, and whistled about the headquarters hotel.

> Gold, gold, gold—
> I love to hear it jingle.
> Gold, gold, gold—
> Its power is untold,
> For the women they adore it,
> While the men try hard to store it.
> There is not a better thing in life than
> Gold, gold, gold.

The only important question was how many of the delegates would walk out, and how many of the voters could be influenced by that action. It took Teller three days to reach St. Louis from Washington, as he was having such a severe attack of asthma that he could not stand continuous traveling. When he arrived he went into conferences with various groups of silver delegates and outlined the strategy for the convention. He told the Colorado delegates that the action

[25] T. Bentley Mott, *Myron T. Herrick* (Garden City, 1929), pp. 67-70 ; Thomas Beer, *Hanna* (New York, 1929), pp. 142-46.

of their state convention did not bind them to act as he did. He was Colorado's member of the committee on resolutions, and the only free-coinage representative on the subcommittee to frame the financial plank.

The real fight over the plank occurred in committee. Of the states and territories represented on the committee, ten only were for free coinage—California, Colorado, Idaho, Montana, Nevada, North Carolina, Utah, Wyoming, and the territories of Arizona and New Mexico. As in the vote on the question in the whole convention, North Carolina, the one Southern state where the delegates represented a real political party, was the only silver state outside the Rocky Mountain region. It is not likely that the effectiveness with which the delegations from the states of Kansas, Nebraska, and the Dakotas had been made to deny their former free-coinage commitments, or the unanimity with which the delegates from the South were going against public opinion in that section, made Teller feel any more friendly toward the national party organization.

In the committee the fight was protracted. When free coinage was defeated, compromise proposals were suggested and voted down. The gold-standard plank that eventually went into the platform contained a conciliatory pledge to attempt an international agreement to secure bimetallism, a position that Senator Hoar and the majority of the Eastern Republicans had taken in the Senate during the recent session of Congress. The control of the committee, as of the convention, was secure in the hands of the gold-standard men, although they were making it as easy as possible for free-coinage Republicans to stay with the party that upheld the gold standard.

When the issue was thus definitely decided, Teller addressed the committee:

Mr. President, I am going out. I am going to fight for the principle, and I have the belief in my heart that some day this great party that has done so much for the human race, and of whose future so much was hoped and expected, will come to a right view upon this question, and that we shall not take our declaration from Wall street or from Lombard street, but from the honest sentiment of the great heart of the American people; and if you will consult that heart and let Wall street alone, you will abandon that platform that declares for the gold standard.

Senator Lodge replied for the majority:

I wish to say for myself, what I believe I say for everybody else, that we accept and understand his position; that we honor him as a man of courage and conviction, that he takes with him, not only the profound regret of all Republicans that he should feel it his duty to act as he does, but also their sincere and entire respect.[26]

The next day the fight was made on the floor of the convention. The real battle was already lost, but the withdrawal had to be based upon the action of the convention to make it effective. The regulars were inclined to give the bolters ample time and opportunity for their demonstration, as they had the bulk of the Western delegates well in hand, and wanted to avoid anything that looked like dictation. Then, too, Teller had announced that there would be no dramatics. After the committee chairman, Foraker, had presented the majority report on the platform, including the plank that meant the gold standard, Teller was recognized to move an amendment. The Associated Press report reads:

> The name of Teller set the Westerners wild. In little scattering squads the handfuls of delegations who had been sitting under the banners of Colorado, of Idaho, of Utah, of Nevada, California, and Montana, and some of those from Tennessee and other Western and Southern States, were on their feet waving hats, flags, umbrellas, fans, and handkerchiefs and shrieking like mad. The fire spread to the galleries and swept across them until they seemed to be almost unanimously carrying on the cheer.

It was noticed that the newspapermen were particularly vociferous in their cheering. The clerk read the substitute plank for free coinage at the ratio of 16 to 1. Teller began to speak in support of the substitute. It was, in spite of his intentions, the most dramatic moment of his life; and although he realized that it was, he had little histrionic sense, and the impression he made came largely from the situation itself and from his own personality. Wrote a reporter for the St. Louis *Republic:*

> The magnificent old man bore a look of sorrow, but not of regret, at the step he was about to take. His voice was weak, and it was with difficulty that he could make himself heard when he first began his address. He steadied himself by resting his right hand on the table, and then when the cheering began again he ... advanced to the edge of the platform. There was no attempt at oratorical effect by the Colorado Senator. He was too weak physically for the effort which it was necessary to make. His deep earnestness was apparent to all. The respect he commanded was unbounded.... The political significance of the situation was lost sight of in the profound sympathy for the venerable Senator from the Mountain State.

---

[26] *Official Proceedings of the Eleventh National Republican Convention;* Dawson, *Teller* (1898), pp. 12-14; St. Louis *Post-Dispatch,* June 13, 19, 1896.

Teller reviewed briefly and temperately the monetary question, and called attention to the past platforms of the party. The plank declaring for bimetallism by international agreement was impossible for achievement as long as Great Britain was the great creditor nation. The only possible avenue toward bimetallism was for the United States to adopt free coinage:

I contend for it because I believe there can be no proper financial system in any country in the world that does not recognize this principle of bimetallism. . . .

I contend for it because I believe the civilization of the world is to be determined by its rightful or wrongful solution.

I am tolerant of those who differ with me. I act from my judgment, enlightened as best I have been able to enlighten it by years of thought and study. . . . It is a solemn declaration that the Republican party intends to maintain low prices and stagnated business for all time to come.

These statements were spoken in a monotone so low that it was difficult to hear him. Continues the *Republic* reporter:

Not a gesture was made for the first five minutes. When the Senator had concluded his plea for bimetallism he raised himself on tiptoe, and his right hand gave the same old gesture which he always employs to emphasize his earnestness. His strength was temporarily restored to him by a mighty effort, and, sweeping the space in front of him with a long reach of his arm, he shouted at the convention: "This is the first great gathering of Republicans since the party was organized that has declared the inability of the American people to control their own affairs. . . . As a bimetallist, I must," and his hands were raised in defiance, "renounce my allegiance to my party."

There were tears in Teller's eyes as he sat down, and tears in the eyes of many who heard him. There were also cheers from the gallery and hisses from the floor.

Foraker's motion to lay the substitute on the table prevailed by 818½ votes to 105½. Only the states that had supported it in the committee gave majorities against the gold standard, and only Colorado, Idaho, Montana, Nevada, Wyoming, and Arizona were unanimous. When the vote was announced the gold men had their opportunity, and they staged an enormous demonstration. The gold-standard plank was then adopted by about the same majority. The expected eventuality had arrived. The gold standard was in the platform.

Teller asked that Senator Cannon be allowed to read a statement. The young Utah senator, a small man physi-

AN ABSCONDING TELLER.

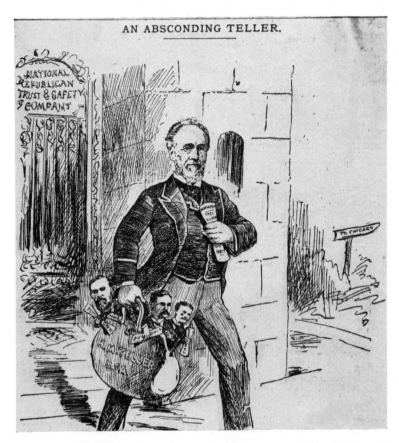

"An Absconding Teller"—H. M. Teller robbing the Republicans of
Pettigrew, Dubois, and Cannon at the June, 1896, national convention.

cally and rather foppish in his dress, proceeded to read. It
was a truculent statement of the causes that were forcing
the silver men to bolt the convention. He had to read against
constant interruptions which became an uproar at his last
words. Teller and Cannon started down the aisle toward the
entrance. Dubois and the Idaho delegation fell in behind,
as did those from Nevada and Colorado. A few other delegates joined, making twenty-three in all, but looking much
larger because of the inclusion of the alternates and newspapermen. The convention was on its feet yelling and catcalling at the departing delegates: "Go to Chicago!" "Take
the Democratic train!" Henry Cabot Lodge and Mark Hanna
yelled with the rest.[27]

Although more spectacular and dramatic than Teller
had anticipated, the number who withdrew was disappointingly small. Only one delegate from Montana, Congressman
Hartman, walked out. Senator Carter, who had worked
with the insurgents up to this point, remained in his seat.
Senator Mantle did likewise, but a short time afterwards he
too announced his withdrawal from the Republican Party
and adherence to the bolters. R. F. Pettigrew, of South
Dakota, a silver senator who, it seems, had not been working
with the insurgents up to this point, walked out with them
and helped to make up for the loss of Carter. Teller had
hoped to create such a public reaction in the mining states
by the withdrawal as to force those who had held out for
regularity to join the bolters. But he was disappointed. In
every state where the bolters left the party, the local organization was turned over to those who remained loyal,
and the national committee saw to it that they were bounti-
fully supplied with funds and effective promises of patronage. Yet others joined the bolters. Congressman Towne,
of Minnesota, who had made a reputation as an orator with
a silver speech the past winter, had marched out with the
bolters, although he was not a delegate. John Lind, of the
same state, and a former Republican Congressman, announced his agreement with them. All over the mining states
a large number of lesser Republican politicians announced
their opposition to the St. Louis platform and ticket.

What the bolters lacked in numbers they made up in
those spiritual compensations that go with defiance of the

[27] Dawson, *Teller* (1898), pp. 14-22; St. Louis *Post-Dispatch*, June 18; St. Louis
Republic, June 19; St. Louis *Globe-Democrat*, June 19; Chicago *Tribune*, June 19, 1896;
William Allen White, *Masks in a Pageant* (New York, 1928), pp. 211-13.

powers that be. As they walked out, Towne reminded a
reporter that it was the anniversary of Waterloo, an
ominous date for the Napoleon who was about to be nominated by the Republican convention. While the feeling of
exultation was upon them they met and organized the Silver
Republican Party. They issued an address to the public in
which they restated the argument for silver coinage, and
their reasons for bolting. It invoked the union of all parties
still to hold conventions in order to re-establish bimetallism.
To these conventions they offered the name of Henry M.
Teller as a candidate for President, upon whom all of them,
Silver Republicans, Democrats, Populists, and the members
of the National Silver Party, could unite.

> It is not merely as the exponent of monetary reform that we
> present this man to the people. It is true that he had waged a mighty
> war for the restoration of the money of the Constitution, and his name
> has been identified as that of no other living man with this great cause.
> But had his services been less demanded and less noticed in this direc-
> tion, the people would still have recognized in him for other labors
> a statesman of the purest type.

It was signed by the bolters, with the exception of Teller.
Spurred on by Dubois, Cannon, and Pettigrew, they were
offering the Democrats a candidate that the Silver Republicans could support. Then a group of Populists, led by H. E.
Taubeneck, chairman of that party's national committee,
who had been in St. Louis by prearrangement, issued an address calling upon the Populists and Democrats to make
Teller their candidate for the presidency.[28] With the bolting
Republicans, and the Populist Party, which had carried
four states in the last election, behind him, Teller was a
political factor to be reckoned with.

The spectacle of the bolting delegates had given the
nation the only thrill that came out of the convention. The
popular mind sometimes admires a minority if it is small
enough and bold enough, and Teller became better known
than he had ever been before. At the Colorado headquarters
reporters saw great stacks of telegrams to Teller, over six
hundred having arrived the morning following his bolt.
Later, letters praising him for his stand began to pour in
upon him in great numbers. "Five hundred Marion County
Republicans commend your course and are with you," is a
typical example of these messages. They came from every

[28] St. Louis *Republic*, June 19-21, 1896.

section—McKinley's home town, Boston, and New York, but especially they came from the West.[29]

When Teller left St. Louis he went to Morrison to visit his mother before leaving for Colorado. Just as the delegates for the Democratic convention began to assemble at Chicago, he left Morrison for Colorado.

Colorado had been stirred by the drama of the St. Louis convention. Local papers were filled with poor poetry celebrating the senior senator. Denver had planned a reception for him when he returned home that would make the one of 1893 seem small. Although he had postponed that return until July 1, and the enthusiasm that followed his action at St. Louis had had time to cool, there was no apparent decrease in it. He only escaped a "demonstration of welcome" at Omaha by arriving there off schedule. To ensure that everyone would be able to witness the reception at Denver, Teller was stopped at Greeley for a preliminary demonstration during the day of July 1, and reached Denver on a special train in the evening, along with a reception committee composed of city and state officials, old friends, and political opponents. The arrival of the train was announced by the explosion of a bomb, which set the crowd that packed the streets about the station cheering. Teller was escorted from the train to the open carriage drawn by six white horses, in which he, Governor McIntire, and Mayor McMurry were to ride in the parade.

The parade began with all the organizations in Denver, from the Societe Italiana Unione and Fratellone to the Beer Drivers' Union, taking part. Seven bands and two drum corps competed for the ear of the populace. Slowly the parade proceeded over the route of march, a route lined with bunting-decorated buildings and excited, shouting people.

The parade was barely under way when a feature not on the program interrupted the plans of the marshalls. A group of young men with a long rope seized the carriage of the guest of honor, unhitched the horses, attached their rope to the carriage, and proceeded to draw it at its appointed place in the parade. Through the city's streets it went, passing sidewalks crowded with cheering people. When the reviewing stand was reached, mounted police were necessary to make way for the man-drawn carriage. Here the Senator and his guides, together with Mrs. Teller, were conducted to

<hr>

[29] St. Louis *Post-Dispatch*, June 19, 1896; Teller MSS.

the reviewing stand, already occupied by the other delegates to the St. Louis convention, brother Willard, and other notables. From here they reviewed the remainder of the procession. When the marching crowd of citizens from the Little Kingdom of Gilpin reached the front of the stand, they halted and yelled until their honored citizen waved back his greetings. "It was the biggest and most spontaneous outpouring ever witnessed in the West," wrote the reporter on a local paper.

When the parade had all passed, speeches of welcome were made. "They see in you one who holds patriotism to be above partisanship," declared the Governor, and the mayor compared him to Horatius. The crowd was too large and too excited to be addressed like an ordinary gathering, and Teller, moved more deeply than he could express, contented himself with such few words as he could make audible between the applause of the cultivated, and the yells of "You bet" on the part of the more normal Westerners.

I realize that the cause we are all interested in has much to do with this great outpouring of the people of Colorado; that it is not only intended to signify your approval of my conduct, and the conduct of my associates at St. Louis, but to signify your determination to work in this cause until we shall triumphantly achieve that which is so dear to us and to all the people of this country, and that is a proper monetary system.... Fortunately for me, the people of this State have been in accord with me on great public questions.... I have endeavored to serve you—every hour that I have sacrificed and labored—is fully compensated by this magnificent demonstration of your generous approval.... I believe that all the friends of silver have to do in this country is to get together.[30]

---

[30] *Rocky Mountain News*, July 1, 2; Denver *Republican*, July 2; Chicago *Daily Tribune*, July 1, 2, 1896.

CHAPTER XVIII

JOHN THE BAPTIST FOR W. J. BRYAN
1896

WHILE Teller was being feted in Colorado the prelimi-
naries to the Democratic convention were in progress,
and he was a candidate for the presidential nomination of
that party. It seems fantastic that a Republican of Teller's
standing could receive serious consideration as the nominee
of the Democratic Party, but such was the case. What made
this possible was the militant free-silver majority in the convention, and the probability of Democratic defeat. The only
hope for a Democratic victory lay in a platform and candidate that would unite all the disaffected elements, particularly the Populists and Silver Republicans, under its banner. This was obvious political strategy.

It is clear that the Silver Republicans and Populists
were agreed to try to induce the Democratic Party to
nominate Teller—and, failing that, to nominate him anyway
through the Silver Republican and Populist parties. If the
Cleveland administration controlled the Democratic convention, the new party could, it was reasonably sure, carry
the bulk of the states west of the Missouri, and might even
displace the Democrats as a major party. At least a clear-cut
fight on the silver question would follow. It is not likely that
there was any impetus given to this movement simply by the
hope of making Teller president. It was done to unite the
silver forces in such a way as to save the faces of the bolting
Republicans and the Populists. Senators such as Dubois,
Cannon, and Pettigrew had been fighting Democratic political machines at home too long to think that they could expect any mercy from them if they bolted the Republican organization and supported the Democratic nominee for
president. The Populists were in a similar predicament.
If they united with the Democrats in support of a Democratic
candidate, their party was forever dead. This was especially
true of the Southern members of the party. The nomination
of a bolting Republican was a different matter, and they
were anxious to avoid the necessity of choosing between
supporting a regular Democratic candidate pledged to free
coinage, and opposition to such a candidate. Teller, although
a Republican, was the best-known advocate of free coinage
on July 1, 1896, and had endeared himself to the Populist

senators by his friendly treatment of them and by many lapses from regularity and support of such causes as the income tax. Patterson, in the *Rocky Mountain News*, emphasized these, and stressed Teller's record on railroad legislation as reason for Populist support.

How far Democratic leaders were involved does not appear, but it is clear that many of the senators of that political group were favorably disposed.[1] Most of them were either personal friends of Teller, or primarily interested in finding a candidate who had a bare chance to defeat McKinley. There was a newspaper story early in June that a group of Democratic senators had canvassed five hundred party leaders in the South and West by letter, asking if they were willing to support Teller if he were nominated. Out of 423 replies all but eight expressed a willingness to help make him president.[2] It was repeatedly charged both before and at the Chicago convention that a senatorial clique was trying to bring about Teller's nomination, and this manipulation claim was used by other candidates as an argument against Teller. When Senator Vest, of Missouri, was accused of being ostensibly for Bland and actually for Teller, he replied that he would not vote for anyone for the nomination "in the convention" who favored woman suffrage, and that included Teller. Josephus Daniels, probably W. J. Bryan's principal supporter for the nomination, made this explanation of the convention situation:

> The coterie of Democratic silver Senators who are on the ground, recognize Teller's great individual strength and his towering figure as a great champion of silver and privately most of them would like to see him nominated, but there is a general fear that the rank and file of the Democratic party would rebel against the selection of a man who so recently walked out of the Republican Convention.

This was the one great obstacle in the way of Teller's nomination by the Democrats. The obvious fact that a free-coinage plank would mean a bolt of the Easterners from the party, larger even than the bolt from the Republican, meant also that should a Republican such as Teller be the nominee, these bolters would have a weapon that would be effective in splitting the party. Senator Morgan wrote Teller on July 4, stating his own view of such a nomination:

---

[1] Additional evidence of this is implied in an attempt by Wharton Barker to turn their support from Teller to himself, largely by the argument that he could also command the support of the Irish-Americans. Barker to J. T. Morgan, June 11; to I. G. Harris, June 15; to Clark Howell, June 15, 1896 (all copies), Barker MSS.

[2] *Rocky Mountain News*, June 5, 1896.

If you are nominated at Chicago, I will give you the most earnest and cordial support of which I am capable. Yet I have some doubt if I, or anyone, could avoid a serious difficulty in answering the objection which the gold democrats would urge in this form, viz.: "You are invited to leave your party and its honest money creed, and vote for a republican in order to get an opportunity of paying your debts with inflated, unsound, and dishonest dollars, worth in fact, only 50 cents." That tirade is answered, if we hold to the organization of which we have control, and put the gold men in the category of bolters.[3]

A different reason was given to Arthur Dunn by Senator Cockrell.

Young man, when we win a Democratic victory we want a Democrat. I have served long in the Senate with Mr. Teller and I respect him, but the next Democratic President will be a Democrat and fill the offices with Democrats.[4]

The fact that the administration now expected a free-coinage platform and candidate on the Democratic ticket, and was preparing to assist the Republican ticket, both directly and through a separate gold Democratic Party, is an indication that Teller's nomination would have placed this group in a strong position to harm the free-coinage campaign.

To Dubois, Pettigrew, Cannon, Hartman, and Mantle it was a choice between nominating Teller at Chicago, or bringing him out as the candidate of the Populists and Silver Republicans. In no other way, they insisted, could the silver forces keep such states as California, Oregon, and the Dakotas from going Republican. A free-coinage Democrat as a nominee would mean a serious problem for the Republican bolters. Teller's nomination by the Democrats would strengthen the bolters immensely at home. It would unite the Republican organizations in the Western states behind the bolters from the St. Louis convention. Even at the time of the bolt it had been freely stated by those Westerners who refused to leave the party, that if Teller were nominated by one of the other parties, there would be no opposition to him in their states.[5] To carry out their plans, Dubois had gone from St. Louis to Springfield, Illinois, to interview Governor Altgeld, who would dominate the Illinois delegates to the convention. He was optimistic after the interview. Petti-

---

[3] Teller MSS.

[4] Dunn, *From Harrison to Harding*, I, 183.

[5] Statements of Senator Shoup and Governor Richards of Montana. St. Louis *Republic*, June 10, 19, 1896.

grew went to Arkansas to see Senator James K. Jones, a leader among the silver Democrats, and returned to Chicago with him. From here he wrote Teller that Jones was working to secure his nomination.

> It all depends upon Illinois and Ohio. If they will say that you can carry those states you will be nominated. . . . If the Democrats do not nominate you then the silver and populist conventions must do it. And we will defeat McKinley any way and unite the electors on you after election.[6]

At Chicago, the Silver Republicans established headquarters from which to make their fight for Teller. As the convention was assembling here were gathered the important Silver Republicans, a number of prominent Populists including Taubeneck, Patterson, and Weaver, the leaders of the National Silver Party, as well as several free-coinage Democrats who had declared openly for Teller. They tried to accomplish their purpose by two arguments. Without Teller as the presidential nominee, they urged, neither the Silver Republicans nor Populists could be induced to support the Democratic ticket. Furthermore, Teller was the candidate most likely to carry certain necessary states, such as California, Michigan, Illinois, and Ohio.

The attitude of the Democratic leaders toward Teller's nomination was frankly utilitarian. The Southerners were generally for him, as his candidacy, even though it did not strengthen the national ticket enough to secure a victory, would at least make sure that their present dangerous rival in local politics, the Peoples' Party, would be placed in a very weak position. Many of them also had grateful memories of the death of the Force bill. On the other hand, the Western delegates did not want Teller, even though they admitted that it would strengthen the ticket in their region. They could see no profit in naming a candidate who might help turn their state organizations over to the bolting Republicans and Populists.

A substantial number of Silver Democrats issued statements for Teller. Congressman Joseph Sibley, Pennsylvania Democrat, not only replied to Bryan's appeal for help by writing that he was for Teller, but issued a public letter in which he urged that the only hope of Democratic victory lay in nominating Teller; for with him as a candidate the party could carry Illinois, Indiana, Michigan, and possibly

---

[6] Dubois to Teller, June 26; Pettigrew to Teller, June 28, 1896, Teller MSS.

Ohio. He was positive, he wrote Bryan, that Teller would win.[7]

As the delegates began to assemble, only Bland and Governor Boise, the two candidates with the largest number of pledged delegates, were as prominently mentioned as Teller. The press reported that his supporters were receiving unexpected aid through letters and telegrams to delegates from local leaders who had become convinced that it would be a strong nomination.[8]

Teller did not make the task of the managers at his headquarters easy. He seems never to have taken his own candidacy very seriously, or, if he did, his lack of ability to "dissemble" hurt enormously his chances for the nomination He made statements repeatedly which ruined the strategy of his managers. When asked by a reporter if he thought the Silver Republicans would support either Bland or Boise, he replied, "Yes, I think our people would support either of those gentlemen or any other man of good character and ability, who is recognized by those favoring the free coinage of silver."[9] Immediately after his Denver reception, while starting for Central City, Teller told a reporter that he expected that Bland would be nominated. Repeatedly he was quoted as saying that he thought his nomination by the Democrats would be "injudicious." To prevent further such statements, Dubois addressed Teller a long note shortly before the convention opened:

In my judgment you will be the nominee of this convention, and will be endorsed by the conventions at St. Louis. Judge McConnell of Illinois is openly outspoken for you, and it is a reasonable probability that Gov. Altgeld will declare himself in your favor soon. Senators Blackburn, Daniel, and Jones are for you, and also ex-Senator Walsh, and Mr. Howell of Georgia.

The contest is between you and Bland. . . . McLean of Ohio is also for you.

The serious obstacle which confronts me is the statement, repeatedly made, that you will not accept a nomination at the hands of this convention, and that you will support the nominee of this convention.

Pettigrew and Towne and other loyal friends insist that if we undertake to support a Democratic candidate it will destroy them and the cause of Silver. I myself will not support a Democratic candidate of this convention.

In case they should nominate a Democratic candidate here it will be necessary for us in the interests of silver to join forces with the

[7] St. Louis *Globe-Democrat*, June 28, 1896; Sibley to Teller, June 25, Sibley to Bryan (copy), June 25, 1896, Teller MSS.
[8] St. Louis *Post-Dispatch*, July 5, 1896.
[9] Chicago *Daily Tribune*, July 1, 1896.

Populists, and nominate you at Saint Louis. In this way we can hold our Western states away from McKinley on the gold standard, and in this way only.

The Populists have been a tower of strength to us, and we have assured them that we will not desert them, but that in the event of a Democratic nomination here that we silver republicans would unite with them in your support.[10]

He added that he wanted Teller to telegraph and write to him that he would co-operate with the group at Chicago and work with them. Other members wrote in a similar vein.

On July 5, a letter from Teller was made public, which could hardly have been to his managers' liking, although it did admit the right to use his name as a candidate:

I have not changed my attitude from what it was at St. Louis in the least. There at the earnest solicitation of many gentlemen ... I consented that my name might be used in connection with the Presidency at Chicago. I told them frankly that I had no claims upon the Democratic party; beyond that I did not consider my nomination by the convention as possible; nevertheless, if, as my more partial friends thought, the Democratic delegates might believe that my candidacy would more likely bring to the ticket the necessary electoral votes than would that of one of the life members of the party, I would leave the matter in their hands and trust wholly to their discretion and patriotism.[11]

Teller's prospects of the nomination ebbed and flowed during the opening days of the convention. The coolness of many Democratic delegates from silver-mining states was in evidence, and a Colorado delegate was accused of "acting badly in a quiet way."[12] When H. E. Taubeneck declared that the Populist Party was opposed to Bland and would entertain no proposition for a compromise which did not "include Senator Teller as the head of the ticket," Teller's prospects brightened. Later, to supplement individual statements, the Populists united on an ultimatum:

To nominate a straight Democrat in a divided party, when millions of honest citizens stand ready to support a nonpartisan candidate is mere reckless experiment.... We feel confident that the People's party is willing to open the path of union upon Henry M. Teller.... We cannot be induced to indorse any candidate for President who has not severed his affiliations with the old political parties.

There was talk of various compromises such as a Teller-Bland ticket and later of a Teller-McLean ticket, to strength-

10 July 2, 1896, Teller MSS.
11 Chicago Daily Tribune, July 5, 1896.
12 A. M. Stevenson to Teller, July 5, 1896, Teller MSS.

en the Ohio campaign. A Washington delegate declared
Teller would make the strongest campaign of any candidate
in his state. Others made similar claims for Ohio, where
Teller had strong support among the delegates, and where
the favorite-son candidate, John R. McLean, was openly
urging the nomination of the Coloradan. On July 7, it was
reported that most of the Southern delegations would cast
their votes for him—after complimentary votes for Democrats on the first ballot.[13]

On the other hand, it played against Teller that the managers of his canvass began their campaign early, and created
opposition from most of the other candidates. The campaign managers for both Bland and Boise turned their
weapons on the outsider. The senatorial cabal story was
used as a background for an appeal to let none but tried
Democrats be considered. This plea was reinforced by
appeals to party history, and the ghost of Horace Greeley
was brought into the convention strategy to frighten the
delegates away from the temptation Dubois was holding out
to them. Misfortune hampered the Silver Republicans in
cases like the Illinois delegation, where antagonism between
Altgeld and some other delegates forced them to declare for
Bland before they were ready to make a record. The impression persisted until long after the convention was over that
Altgeld intended to start a stampede to Teller, but his statement of July 7, that he did not think Teller could carry
Illinois, was a severe blow to the hopes of the Silver Republicans. It seems, too, that Altgeld thought it more important
to secure for the Democratic Party the unity that a regular
party nominee would give it, than to conciliate other
parties.[14]

Another important factor was the dark-horse candidate, William Jennings Bryan—a dark horse only to the
press and public, it happens, as his papers reveal an astonish-
ing number of pledges of support from individual delegates,
the result of two years of active campaigning. He was on
excellent terms with the Populists, the Silver Republicans,
and the National Silverites.

Patterson's *Rocky Mountain News* favored Bryan next
to Teller as the silver candidate. Shortly after the conven-

---

[13] St. Louis *Globe-Democrat*, July 2, 6; Chicago *Daily Tribune*, July 4-8; Atlanta
Constitution, July 4, 8; Raleigh *News and Observer*, July 1, 4, 9; *Rocky Mountain
News*, July 7, 8, 1896.

[14] Altgeld to Dr. William Carroll, no date, Barker MSS.; *Review of Reviews*, Aug.,
1896.

tion opened, Josephus Daniels succeeded in swinging the North Carolina delegation, which had been suspected of Teller sympathies, over to Bryan. This gave the Nebraskan's candidacy possibilities, and the delegates and observers became interested.[15]

Now the question of supporting Bryan as the Democratic nominee was put to the Populists and Silver Republicans. The Republican bolters announced their refusal, but they did not sound as threatening as they had the day before. The Populist leaders at Chicago were in a serious quandary. They realized that they were gambling wildly on Teller, and if Bland were nominated they would be in a difficult position. Bryan as a candidate was much better. He had advocated bolting the Democratic ticket if the convention failed to declare for free coinage, and in that way had classified himself with those who put the issue above partisan advantage. Furthermore, they had not publicly declared they would not support him. Reluctantly, some of the Populists had to admit, on July 8, that they could not oppose Bryan.

Here, then, was the logical candidate—the one lifelong Democrat who could unite the silver forces behind him. The strategy and labor the Silver Republicans had put into the Teller boom were now deflected to Bryan. The definite declarations of the Populists that they would not support Bland or Boise had gone a long way toward preventing the nomination of either, and to the Democratic leaders, Bryan —provided that he could develop substantial strength among the delegates—was an escape from the apparent logic of nominating Teller. As Teller's chances declined, Bryan's increased. Some of the Southern delegations prepared to support Teller shifted to Bryan. The morning of July 9 found Bryan with Bland and Boise among the probable nominees.[16]

Teller's only chance now lay in a deadlock which might, by good strategy, be turned to his advantage. But before the day of July 9 was over, Bryan had upheld the cause of silver before the convention with his masterly "Cross of Gold and

[15] The pledges to support Bryan were numerous from the West and South. Some Populists, such as James Baird Weaver, had already told friends that they would support Bryan on the Democratic ticket. L. W. Rissler to Bryan, May 16, 1896. Josephus Daniels was for Bryan as early as June 1, 1895, and on April 30, 1896, he promised Bryan the support of the North Carolina delegation. Daniels to Bryan, June 1, 1895, April 30, 1896, Bryan MSS. *Rocky Mountain News*, June 13, 1896.

[16] "The Populists, despairing at last of winning with Teller, who has gone lame, have given notice that they will back Bryan." Chicago *Daily Tribune*, July 9, 1896. On July 8, Congressman Francis G. Newlands had written Teller that the possibility of Sibley's nomination was worrying Teller's supporters. Sibley, as a Democrat who could unite the silverites, had an appeal similar to that of Bryan's. Teller MSS.

TELLER'S LITTLE FLIRTATION.—From the *Journal* (N. Y.).

Homer Davenport's representation of Teller's candidacy at Chicago.

Crown of Thorns" oration. The silver delegates were wildly
enthusiastic, and confident that here was the Moses who
could lead them out of the wilderness of defeat. Everywhere
among them it reinforced Bryan's persistent solicitation of
support for the nomination. This, added to the evident fact
that he would in all probability unite the other silver parties
behind him, prevented any deadlock by making Bryan's
nomination a practical certainty.[17]

As far as the Silver Republicans were concerned, the
contest was over after Bryan's oratorical triumph. Teller's
supporters did not even place him in nomination, although
Colorado cast its votes for him on the first two ballots. The
other votes that had once seemed so certain for Teller went
to Bryan and made the bulk of his total on the first ballot.
The Silver Republicans had made Teller a John the Baptist
for another savior of the people.

If Teller was not disappointed at the result, it was because he had never allowed himself to believe that his own
nomination was possible. Bryan and a free-coinage platform
were enough of a victory to give him immense satisfaction.
The Senator had left Central City and had gone to Pueblo,
where the news of Bryan's nomination reached him. When
it arrived, Teller prepared willingly to give his support
to the ticket. The plank in the platform declaring for free
coinage at 16 to 1 by the United States alone was the bold
declaration that he had always wanted. Now a campaign
could be fought where it was not necessary to explain and
qualify and excuse the platform. As to Bryan, Teller told a
reporter the day of the nomination, "I consider the nomination an exceptionally strong one. Bryan is an able man of
high character, a strong friend of silver, and close to the
people. He will make an excellent President."[18]

---

[17] It would be easy, if one considered Bryan as a prophetically visional plotter, to
build up a case from the evidence that his activities leading up to July 10 were all
carefully planned to win him the nomination. His association with the Populists; his
activity at St. Louis, where he had been on intimate terms with the Republican bolters;
his wide solicitation of support among the delegates to the Democratic convention, as
well as his effective speech on the silver plank—all are good material for an indictment,
but it would be an unfair one. Bryan probably told the truth about it in 1925 when
he wrote to Mark Sullivan: "I regarded it [the nomination] only as a possibility and
counted on the logic of the situation rather than my speech. I had no thought of my
speech having the effect it did. I was fighting for a principle and found, as Jefferson
once expressed it that 'firm adherence to principle is the best handmaiden to ambition.'" Feb. 27, 1925 (copy), Bryan MSS. This is not to say that he was not
actively and intelligently conducting his own campaign for the nomination, aided
principally by "the logic of the situation," and making use of a chance to address the
convention as another opportunity to impress the delegates with his own availability.
Without the oration he might have been nominated, but it would only have been a bare
possibility. By far the best study of Bryan's compaign for the nomination is by Miss
Marian Silveus, who concludes that the oration was "a crucial factor." "Antecedents
of the Campaign of 1896," pp. 184-219. See also Charles M. Rosser, *The Crusading
Commoner* (Dallas, 1937), p. 38.

[18] New York *Tribune*, July 12, 1896.

Apparently Teller had informed the Silver Republicans at Chicago that any strong silver Democrat should receive their united support, for on July 7, Dubois, Hartman, Pettigrew, and Towne had addressed him a telegram:

We have a right and do insist that you shall make no declaration of any kind after the final action of this convention until you consult with your truest & best friends and with the men who in your judgment are the most earnestly devoted to the cause of silver. We are on the ground, know the situation better than you possibly can and have taken steps in the interest of the cause absolutely inconsistent with your letter. We again ask you not to take any position without consultation.[19]

When the news of Bryan's nomination reached Teller, he telegraphed Dubois at Chicago, "I think we should endorse Bryan at once. What do you think. Answer." Dubois replied, "We must say nothing. Many of your best friends are involved. . . . " To this Teller answered immediately, "It is a great mistake not to endorse Bryan at once. We will be compelled to do so. I will not be a party to a divided silver vote."[20]

The Silver Republicans at Chicago were in a serious quandary, and finally they decided to go to Colorado and confer with Teller as to their part in the coming campaign.

As Pettigrew could not go to Colorado with the others he wrote Teller, expressing his opinion and that of the others:

I feel sure that in the interest of the cause for which we are contending we cannot indorse Bryan and must name you at St. Louis on the 22nd. Bryan is a free trader and the platform indorses the Wilson bill with no duty on wool and but little duty on other farm products and in order to save Kansas, California, Washington, Oregon, Montana, North and South Dakota we must join the populists in another ticket, and after McKinley is beaten unite our electors on some man for President. If we should endorse Bryan, McKinley is sure to be elected and the "cause" is dead for years to come. You must run to save the Senate.

Only the Populist senator from South Dakota, J. H. Kyle, wrote Teller urging support of Bryan.[21]

Just how far the Silver Republicans had committed themselves to the Populist leaders in a program of common action to nominate Teller at St. Louis is not known, but at

[19] Teller MSS.
[20] Teller to Dubois, no date; Dubois to Teller, July 10, 1896, Teller MSS.
[21] Pettigrew to Teller, July 9, 10; Kyle to Teller, July 11, 1896, Teller MSS.

least there was some such understanding.[22] H. E. Taubeneck
had carried on the negotiations with them, and after the
Chicago convention he went to St. Louis to lay the grounds
for Teller's nomination. Dubois and Hartman went to
Colorado to meet with Teller. The other Silver Republicans
could not go, but they were in constant telegraphic communi-
cation with those who gathered at Manitou Springs, in order
to be out of the way of reporters and bothersome politicians.

From the first, Teller had made it clear to them that he
would not be a candidate in opposition to Bryan, and they
finally agreed that Bryan should be supported. After conferring with them Teller wrote Taubeneck, arguing that
the Populists must endorse Bryan:

> This is the time when partisanship should give way to patriotism
> & when sacrifice of party affiliation of personal preference must be
> made in the interests of the people. I have made my sacrifice and I
> will now support Bryan not because he is a democrat but because he
> is a statesman & a patriot & because I believe his election will inaugu-
> rate a new era in American politics that will give the plain people of
> the country what they have not had for some time a man in the office
> of the Government.

Dubois wrote also, urging that Bryan be nominated by
the Populists, but not closing the door to some other action.
He wrote Teller, who had gone to Denver:

> The truth is, Hartman and I cannot be positive until Cannon and
> Pettigrew are satisfied and we have made an honest effort to satisfy
> Taubeneck.[23]

Cannon, Pettigrew, Towne, and Mantle, who were
farther away, and had not been convinced by Teller as
Dubois and Hartman had, still favored the separate nomination. In order to get an agreement Dubois tried to bring
them all to Manitou Springs, and succeeded in bringing Pettigrew and Mantle there. The rapid drift of sentiment in
the West toward supporting Bryan reinforced the arguments
of Teller, and brought the reluctant Silver Republicans

---

[22] Hicks, *The Populist Revolt*, pp. 351-54. On July 6, Senator Marion Butler had
written to Senator Stewart: "I am extremely annoyed and concerned at these frequent
interviews purporting to come from Senator Teller, to the effect that he would support
Bland or any Democrat of that kind who might be nominated by the Chicago convention.... I cannot believe that our Western friends would betray us in this manner;
for it would be nothing short of betrayal.... If they will not take Teller ... it is the
duty of every true friend of silver to fight the Democratic party to the bitter death.
Please see Dubois ... or write yourself, urging him [Teller] to stand solidly by the
programme as agreed upon in Washington.... There is not a single Populist in the
South who will vote for any Democrat who is nominated at Chicago." Stewart MSS.
[23] Teller to Taubeneck (copy) ; Dubois to Teller; Dubois to Taubeneck (copy), all
July 13, 1896, Teller MSS.

around to support the Democratic nominees. "We are discouraged over the outlook," Dubois wrote Teller, "but will follow you." He wrote to Taubeneck: " ... under the conditions which we are powerless to change, the cause of the people and Mr. Teller's personality seem to demand that he is not a candidate before the St. Louis convention." Teller wrote to Senator Marion Butler, to Taubeneck, and other Populists, urging the nomination of Bryan, and declaring that he would not allow his name to go before the Populist convention. To Patterson he stated:

I will not be a party to any movement to divide the friends of silver in this campaign, and if we fail to concentrate on Mr. Bryan ... the fault will not be with the friends of silver who heretofore acted with the republican party. You are at liberty to show this letter to any member of the convention if you choose to do so.[24]

Those of the Silver Republicans who were able to reach Manitou Springs issued an address on July 20 in time to influence the Populist and National Silver Party conventions beginning the next day in St. Louis. Teller had drafted it so as to make the free-coinage Republicans feel that they were not joining the Democratic Party. It was a declaration of the bolters' loyalty to the old ideals of the Republican Party, and a protestation of their devotion to bimetallism. It concluded:

We urge all friends of gold and silver as standard money ... to give to Mr. Bryan and Mr. Sewall their hearty support. In advising this course we do not consider it necessary that they shall abandon or surrender their political views on other questions.

It was signed by Senators Teller and Dubois, Congressmen Hartman, Towne, Shafroth, and Wilson, and by A. M. Stevenson.[25]

Before this was issued Teller had sent a letter to Bryan by Patterson, promising him the support of the Silver Republicans:

I will not offer any suggestions to you save to advise you that as you were nominated without pledges of favor or privilege to anyone that you maintain that position and make no pledges or promises, so that you may go into the great office of President of the United States without the embarrassment that follows pledges and promises even if they are such as may be properly carried out.[26]

24 Cannon to Teller, July 14; Dubois to Teller, July 15; Dubois to Taubeneck (copy), July 15; Teller to Patterson (copy), July 16, 1896, Teller MSS.

25 Original of Manitou address, Teller MSS.

26 Teller to Bryan, July 15, 1896, Bryan MSS. The day before Teller wrote this letter, Charles S. Thomas, leader of the Colorado delegation at Chicago, had written him from

To Dunham Wright, his companion at Estes Camp in 1862, he wrote, "I am in hopes we have found our Lincoln in Bryan."[27]

The Populist and National Silver conventions nominated Bryan at St. Louis; but in the former the contest was bitter, and the compromise of a separate candidate for vice-president was necessary to secure Bryan's nomination. Teller took no part in these conventions, beyond the issuance of the Manitou address, and his personal letters to the Populist leaders. The result seemed on the surface very satisfactory; a straight-out fight for free coinage could now be made with all the bimetallists in one camp.

Teller set himself to do two things. First, he would bring all the support he could to the Democratic ticket, and second, he would protect his fellow bolters in every way possible. He sent Hartman to see Bryan and wrote the presidential candidate:

It appears to me very necessary that those of our friends who went out of the St. Louis convention should not become the subject of the combined attack of the Democrats Populists and McKinley Republicans.[28]

Dubois was up for re-election and to win he would have to get the local Democratic or Populist organizations to support him. Teller urged repeatedly and with great emphasis that the Silver Republicans deserved one place on the Democratic National Committee, and they were agreed that it should go to Dubois. As early as July 13, he telegraphed Senator James K. Jones, chairman of the national committee, urging that Dubois be placed on the executive committee. A week later he renewed his demand. Teller wrote:

It seems to me that an alliance between the Democrats and silver Republicans is a natural and proper alliance, and one much more likely to be permanent than one between the Democrats and Populists. It ... appears to me the Democratic party in the future will greatly need the aid and assistance of the silver Republicans to take the place

a liner on Lake Michigan. "Mr. Bryan I know most intimately. His one great weakness is loquacity and that I have begged him to be on his guard against. I have talked with him however about some things since his nomination and his reticence has been commendable. Nevertheless I have something to say to you which I will communicate to no other human being, and I feel sure if we shall win in November our State will have no cause for repining." Teller MSS. In 1930 Thomas could not recall what this last referred to.

[27] (Copy, no date), Teller MSS.
[28] Teller to Bryan (copy), July 20, 1896, Teller MSS.

of the gold standard Democrats you will lose. Dubois, like others, may
not be ready to step into the Democratic party at this time and he, as
is the case with some others, may have the hope that the Republican
party will abandon the gold standard idea in time. . . . I am not one of
those. I believe the Republican party will continue the party of the
gold standard idea, and instead of abandoning it will grow more
determined in its purpose to force that monetary system on the country
and will draw to itself all the Democrats who now advocate the gold
standard. If this is so the silver Republicans, so called, must either
join the Democratic party or the Populists. You can readily see where
the great mass of such voters are likely to go after the campaign,
whether we are successful or not. If your party is wise it can put
into its ranks a great number of the very best people of the country and
secure for its support a number of States heretofore controlled by the
Republican party.

Senator Jones, seemingly willing himself, was unable
to secure the committee's approval for this—none but Democrats should be on the committee. This appointment, Teller
felt, would give Dubois such prestige with the Idaho Democrats that they could not refuse to support him. Finally,
Teller induced Chairman Jones to send a representative to
Idaho, to try to pledge the local Democratic candidates for
the legislature to Dubois. He also induced Colorado Democrats to put pressure on their Idaho friends, but little success
attended these efforts in the end. On August 24, Jones wrote
Teller in self-defense, "I think when you know some of the
facts and things I have to deal with you will be surprised,
and will not so strongly disapprove of what I have done."
The Populists and Democrats in that state both voted against
fusion with the Silver Republicans, and that left Dubois to
lead a Silver Republican ticket against the fusionists on the
one hand and the regular Republicans, marshaled by Senator
Shoup and Governor McConnell, on the other. In spite of
the help of Congressman Wilson and the Silver Republican
nominee for Congress, William E. Borah, it was a hopeless
contest.[29]
The union of all free-coinage parties upon Bryan was
the kind of contest that Teller had visualized as desirable.
He had hoped that the relatively sharp issue drawn on the
monetary question would force all free-coinage Republicans
to support the Democratic nominees, as it probably would,
had that nominee been Teller, but with Bryan the nominee
he was to be disappointed. As late as July 27 he still had

---

[29] Teller to Jones (copies), July 14, 21, 24, Sept. 2, 3; Teller to Dubois (copy),
July 27; Dubois to Teller, Aug. 19, 1896, Teller MSS.

some hopes that Wolcott would finally declare for Bryan.[30]

But there were no more important secessions of Republicans. With the promises of an international agreement to establish bimetallism and higher tariffs on wool and lead as their principal arguments, and the prospects of Federal patronage, the Republican organization was far from dead in the silver-mining states. Colorado was no exception. The Republican State Central Committee, elected by the same convention that sent Teller to St. Louis, met on July 29 and voted to support the McKinley ticket. On August 1, Wolcott followed with an address to the voters that was a powerful argument to stand by the party. Declaring that bimetallism would only be "accomplished through the action and efforts of the Republican party" he praised protection and attacked the radicalism of the Democratic and Populist platforms. He chose for special denunciation the planks of the Democratic platform which criticized the decision of the Supreme Court in the income-tax case, and the action of Cleveland in suppressing the Pullman strike with Federal troops. It was well phrased to convince the conservatives generally and business interests in particular that the other features of Bryan's campaign more than offset the advantages of the free-coinage plank.[31]

Other Western states, both silver mining and agricultural, had similar experiences. Good crops and higher prices for grain soothed the farmers somewhat, and a trend toward the traditional party began. In September, Senator Carter, who had remained noncommittal up to that time, announced that he would support McKinley.[32]

From the standpoint of the Republican bolters the situation was very unsatisfactory. Their first necessity was to fill out the skeleton political party they had created in order to hold those supporters to whom the name Republican had an attractive appeal, and also to keep an organization under their own control in order to have some means of bargaining with the Democratic and Populist parties. For this purpose they organized a party in most of the Rocky Mountain states and in several others where silver sentiment was strong among Republicans. Little difficulty was experienced in fusion with the Democrats and Populists on a common slate of presidential electors pledged to Bryan, but in many states

[30] Teller to Jones (copy), July 27, 1896, Teller MSS.

[31] Dawson, *Wolcott*, I, 240-48.

[32] *Correspondence of Roosevelt and Lodge*, I, 233.

no satisfactory arrangements were found possible on the state ticket. After an attempt to unite all silver parties in Colorado upon a single state ticket failed, Teller had to content himself with joining his Silver Republicans to the Democrats, and in this condition went into the contest for state and local offices against two other groups—a fusion party of Populists and National Silverites, and the regular Republicans. In Montana and Nebraska legal obstacles kept the Silver Republicans off the ballot. In Utah and Montana close relations were maintained with the regular Republicans on the state ticket. The attention of the Silver Republicans for the remainder of the campaign was thus largely confined to local politics and directed in some states primarily toward maintaining a local organization against the forays of Democrats, Populists, National Silverites, and regular Republicans.

Before he left Colorado to start his speaking tour, Teller tried his hand at raising campaign funds. In past congressional campaigns the silver-mine owners and Colorado businessmen generally had been liberal contributors to the war chests of prominent congressmen committed to free coinage. They were not so liberal now, even with a presidential candidate pledged to their cause. The prospects of defeat were obvious. The declaration of Senators Wolcott, Shoup, Carter, and others that they would support McKinley, as the best hope for bimetallism, stimulated these prospects. On August 6, Teller wrote to Jones:

I could not do much in response to your telegram, but we sent ten thousand dollars at once. I am looking after money matters somewhat and I am in hopes our people will do fairly well. The most of the money we raise here will be from men who have been republicans.

On August 28, he wrote again:

Times are worse here than I have ever known, and it is difficult to get our people to do what in ordinary times they would do without persuasion. I am giving special attention to the collection of money and I feel that if I leave it now there will be little done.[33]

The Republican press was filled with exaggerated statements regarding the silver miners' "boodle fund," and it would be interesting to be able to state the exact amount raised, but unfortunately it is not possible to do it. It was commonly charged that an English syndicate which owned

[33] Copies, Teller MSS.

Australian silver mines had contributed $250,000 to the Bryan campaign fund. Another campaign story was that Colorado Springs alone had raised $500,000 for Bryan. The New York *World* for October 11 contained an estimate of the fund raised in Colorado, placing it at $306,592. That account adds:

The Mephistopheles of Colorado Silver Populistic politics, Senator Henry M. Teller, cuts no figure in the boodle-raising except to secretly encourage it. The wily old man is really a rich man, but keeps his property out of sight and pleads poverty. He has large real estate interests, which are in his brother's and other's names.

It seems probable that the Democrats received about $100,000 from Colorado. The realization of the hopelessness of the contest kept back large and numerous contributions. Teller secured a special donation of $2,500 that was sent to Dubois in Idaho, and the remainder went into the Democratic national campaign fund.[34] But the mining states were the only important source of funds, and the Democratic organization was seriously hampered in every activity by its poverty. In contrast, the Republican organization did not need to refrain from any activity likely to produce votes because of a lack of resources. They assessed the banks one fourth of 1 per cent of their capital—a small price to pay for continual appreciation or to prevent inflation; secured large donations from industrialists, including $250,000 from the Standard Oil group; and sent out an average of twenty campaign documents to every voter in the Middle West. Neither the eloquence of Bryan nor the class consciousness of farmers and laborers could win against that.[35]

Unquestionably Teller was deeply grieved at the national Democratic organization for not doing more for Dubois. This did not extend to Bryan, however, and Teller watched his speeches and public statements after the nomination with unconcealed pleasure. "I am pleased with Bryan's speeches," he wrote Senator W. V. Allen. "He does not let

[34] *Iowa State Register,* Oct. 30; *Public Opinion,* Aug. 6; clipping from the New York *World,* Oct. 11, 1896, in Dawson Scrapbook. Hibben (*Bryan,* p. 193) gives the New York *World* of March 30, 1908, as authority for the statement that the silvermine owners contributed a total of $228,000 to the campaign, or three cents per vote polled. In June, 1900, in an exchange in the Senate between Teller and Hanna over the amount—apparently that raised in Colorado—they disagreed on the point whether it was greater or less than $100,000. *Congressional Record,* 56 Cong., 1 Sess., p. 6365. Wolcott in 1898 claimed that the Colorado contribution had been $133,000. Dawson, *Wolcott,* II, 390.

[35] Thomas R. Marshall, *Recollections* (Indianapolis, 1925), pp. 146, 147; Edith Dobie, *Political Career of Stephen Mallory White* (Stanford University, 1927), pp. 215, 216; Croly, *Hanna,* pp. 217-19; Josephson, *The Politicos,* p. 699.

down and he is not frightened by the vicious attacks upon him and his principles."[36]

It was obvious that Teller would play an important part in the campaign. When Patterson wrote that Teller could "win more votes to the Democratic ticket than any other single person," he exaggerated only insofar as the candidate himself would be more effective in that work. Teller refused a flood of invitations to speak that came not only from the West, but from New England, New York, and Pennsylvania as well, on the grounds that these regions were not debatable territory. He offered his services to the Democratic campaign committee during September and October for work in the Middle West. In the meantime he opened the campaign in the Far West with an important address at Cheyenne. Then followed several less important speeches in Colorado for the local ticket, and Teller went to Chama, New Mexico, to rest up for the campaign proper.

While Bryan was looming large in the eyes of both friends and opponents by his hitherto unequaled campaign tours back and forth across the eastern half of the country, Teller in a less spectacular fashion was covering the debatable territory, trying to win Republican votes for the Democratic ticket. He opened his campaign tour fittingly on September 7 at a record-breaking meeting at Morrison, Illinois, where he was as well known as in Colorado. From there he went to Michigan for two speeches, and then on to Washington, D. C. But he soon left for eastern Kentucky, where he was scheduled for three speeches. In spite of rainy, cold weather that made his asthma almost unbearable, he was pleased with the enthusiasm shown. He paused in Cincinnati, where he was not scheduled to speak, and found it very unfriendly to silver, but Washington Court House, Akron, and Warren, Ohio, were much better, and Teller went on to Detroit in better spirits. After the Detroit rally, he sat up until the early hours of the following morning with James E. Scripps and Milton A. McRae, unsuccessfully trying to bring the Scripps-McRae league of newspapers over to the cause. Five more meetings in southern Michigan were followed by speeches at Peoria and Joliet and a big rally at Chicago. Teller's voice was improving, and he made a speech for brother James, who was a candidate for Congress from a Chicago district. Five cities in the northern

---

[36] Aug. 27, 1896, Teller MSS.

half of Indiana were his next task. Then, after spending
October 26 at Elgin, Illinois, he went to Des Moines for two
big rallies, followed by meetings at Sioux City and Cherokee,
Iowa; and finally, on October 31, he concluded his tour with
two speeches at Sioux Falls, South Dakota—speeches Pettigrew had appealed for as absolutely necessary to the ticket
in that state.

Teller's work was aimed directly at Republican votes.
His appearances were in Republican strongholds, and invariably he was introduced by some prominent member of
that party who had left it because of its monetary plank.
Teller's hope that he could make the monetary issue clear-cut
was not to be borne out in the Midwestern campaign. Although the Eastern press was definitely for the gold standard, and brushed aside the bimetallism-by-international-
agreement argument as readily as Teller himself, in the
Middle West the campaign strategy of the Republican Party
was based upon that clause of the plank and upon the friendly record toward silver of candidate McKinley. Almost
nowhere west of Pennsylvania were the Republicans willing
to defend the gold standard frankly. They were the real
bimetallic party, ran their argument, because they proposed
to establish it by the only possible means. The free-coinage
proposal is dishonest silver monometallism. It was largely
in vain that Teller repeated his old arguments that no agreement with Great Britain was possible, for it was to her
interest to maintain the gold standard, and that the only
cure for the falling prices of an appreciating standard in the
United States was free coinage.

Although Teller discussed the monetary question in great
detail, he did not stop with that alone. He upheld the much-
criticized Democratic plank objecting to the Supreme
Court's decision on the income tax, and discussed protection,
defending his support of Bryan and the Democrats in spite
of that issue. He could not compete with Bryan as an
orator, but his speeches never failed to get a good response.[37]
Mrs. Teller, who accompanied him on the road to watch
after his health, complained to her daughter: "Mr. Teller
will talk too long in spite of all I can do. I can't blame him
so much, as whenever he tries to stop, they will ask questions

---

[37] Several of the campaign speeches are preserved. A stenographic copy of the
one at Morrison is preserved in the public library there. Others are in the Teller
MSS., and several were printed in contemporary newspapers.

and lead him on until two hours and more have passed, then follow him to the hotel and talk until late."[38]

A highly uncomfortable part of the campaign to Teller personally was the abuse he received from the opposition. It was a frequent thing to have the Republican papers herald his approach with charges that he had a large fortune invested in silver mines, from which he stood to profit handsomely under free coinage. His supporters specifically asked him to answer these charges in a few instances, and he wrote a large number of letters to newspapers to refute them where he did not speak. Other charges of holding a political rally on Sunday, and of making loans and putting a gold clause in the notes, occasioned considerable correspondence and not a little discouragement.[39]

The only hope of a Bryan victory was to carry these Midwestern states in which Teller labored. But it was clear throughout October that the election was lost, and Teller's expectation that they would be defeated did not change, although he spoke hopefully in some of his letters.

An English journalist traveling in the United States in the fall of 1896 has left what is probably the most interesting contemporary account of the election in his reports to the London *Daily Mail*. On October 7, he wrote from Chicago that the Republicans had won. Why?

> Business went further than the sound money leagues. It promised a world-shaking panic if Mr. Bryan were elected. You may say that political blackmail is no argument, but it is and the most powerful that can be urged.

Although most of the slanders of the campaign were directed against the presidential ticket, Teller suffered from personal attacks far more than ever before. The clergy was the most violent of all classes in its language, which easily surpassed the most purple passages of such Westerners as Waite. In answer to a note from Brooks Adams, Teller philosophized:

> The attacks our opponents are making on us are very irritating to those of us who know that we do not propose repudiation in any form, and would condemn a dishonest act as quickly as our detractors would. But I remember that all great movements for reform of existing abuses or for the bettering of the conditions of men, have always had just such

---

[38] Mrs. Teller to Emma Teller, Sept. 28, 1896, Tyler MSS.

[39] Teller to E. Rosewater (copy), undated; Teller to editor of *The Citizen*, Iowa City, Iowa, Aug. 6, Teller MSS.; Mrs. Teller to Emma Teller, Oct. 16, 1896, Tyler MSS.

opposition, and often from the people who had the greatest interest in the success of such a movement. I settle down and accept it as part of the battle.[40]

He had need of philosophy, for the defeat, although expected, was very great in terms of electoral votes—271 for McKinley and the gold standard to 176 for Bryan and bimetallism. All the border section which had held the balance between the East and West voted with the East. The returns on election night showed the overwhelming defeat. At the Republican headquarters in New York, related the English observer,

... white-bearded, frock-coated men were rushing about shaking hands with everybody in sight.... A little army of waiters was perspiringly trying to keep pace with the unquenchable demand for champagne. Distracted with delight the solid pillars of Sound Money could only laugh and babble, and hurry from the tape to the window and from the window back to the tape.... Passing on to the University Club, I found every member present exulting and dancing like school-boys, as a waiter read item after item of the colossal pile of victories. These fine gentlemen of New York cried for cheers for McKinley, hurled stentorian congratulations at entering friends, clasped each other around the waist by threes and fours, and waltzed round the room under the approving smiles of headwaiters.... Their dollars won it. They paid the piper; they will call the tune.[41]

All the states west of the 96th parallel had given Bryan a majority except North Dakota, Oregon, and California, where the vote was close. In states such as Colorado the Bryan majority was enormous, but his majority in South Dakota and Wyoming was very small.

The results were generally disastrous to the Silver Republicans, as the fusion tickets in most states left them in a weak bargaining position. Towne was defeated for re-election in Minnesota, although the Silver Republican candidate for governor, John Lind, ran far ahead of the presidential ticket. Except in South Dakota, where Pettigrew's slate generally won, the organization scored no victories outside the Rocky Mountain states. Congressman Hartman's re-election was the sole victory in Montana. In Idaho, Borah was defeated for Congress by a Populist, and the combination of Democrats and Populists seriously threatened Dubois' campaign for re-election to the Senate. The Silver Republican-Democratic state ticket in Colorado won, and Shafroth,

---

[40] Sept. 23, 1896 (copy), Teller MSS.
[41] G. W. Steevens, *The Land of the Dollar* (New York, 1897), pp. 165, 168, 234-36, 292-301.

the Silver Republican Congressman, and Bell, the Populist, were returned to Congress. There was almost no opposition to Teller's re-election to the Senate. When the legislature assembled in January, 1897, he was placed in nomination by the representatives of four political parties—People's, Democratic, Silver Republican, and National Silver—and seconding speeches came from three women members, a single taxer, a socialist, and the representative of the greatest "gold" district in the world, Cripple Creek. He received 92 of the 98 votes present, dangerously close, an observer remarked, to 16 to 1. The six votes against him were all Republicans. The nominating speakers called him the "Gladstone of Colorado" and "Colorado's Grand Old Man."[42]

Teller induced the legislature to pass a resolution addressed to the same body in Idaho, informing it of his re-election, and urging similar action in regard to Dubois. But it was of no value. Dubois was defeated, and a Populist elected in his stead. Dubois and Towne paid the bolter's price. Of five congressmen who had taken an active part in the bolt from the Republican Party, only two—Shafroth and Hartman—were returned to the next Congress; of the five senators, one—Teller—was re-elected, one—Dubois—defeated, and the other three—Cannon, Mantle, and Pettigrew—held over for the remainder of their terms, but did not secure re-election.[43]

---

[42] Dawson, *Teller* (1898), pp. 40-77.

[43] Allen, of Utah, and Wilson, of Idaho, did not run for re-election. Wilson was defeated for a place on the state supreme court.

CHAPTER XIX

THE LOST CAUSE
1897-98

THERE have been many lost causes in American history, and most of them have been lost by political defeat. The cause of bimetallism, however, was not vanquished by the Republican victory of 1896. Indeed, that party had declared for bimetallism by international agreement, and all over the Middle West in that campaign, Teller had been forced to meet argument that the Republicans were the true bimetallic party, while the Democrats were only silver monometallists. The cause was lost for reasons beyond the realm of politics. Great new discoveries of gold were being made through the nineties, which, together with the development of the cyanide process of refining, cheapened the cost of its production and increased the supply.

The epitaph of the cause of silver is written in the following figures for the world's production of gold stated in millions of pounds:

1890	24.62
1895	41.16
1900	52.74
1905	78.14

The production of gold was multiplied by three from 1890 to 1905.[1] The effect of this upon prices was immense. After 1895 there was no further appreciation of the value of money, and a decided inflation began to show its influence. In the United States between 1896 and 1906 prices rose about one third on an average; or, in other words, the value of money decreased by that proportion.[2] Thus the heavy yoke that the debtor class had borne from 1865 to 1895 was lifted about the time of the election of 1896 by causes over which political leaders had no control. It was replaced by an inflation movement that gave the poorer class a distinct advantage over their creditors, and a period of general prosperity followed. From the economic point of view the bank-

---

[1] L. De Launay, *The World's Gold* (New York and London, 1908), chart opposite p. 109.

[2] Between 1896 and 1906 prices rose 31 per cent according to the Labor Bureau index, 42 per cent according to Dun's index, and 42 per cent according to Bradstreet's. Irving Fisher, *The Purchasing Power of Money* (New York, 1922), p. 246. This inflation was not all due to the gold situation, but partly to the increased use of credit, and other financial and industrial conditions.

ers had failed in their struggle. Theirs was the real lost cause. The free-silver movement had as its object the replacement of the appreciating standard of value by a stable one, if possible, and by a depreciating one, if necessary. Measured on the scales of economics, it had won.

But economics is not politics. Teller stood before the public, committed to one means of checking deflation. Before that method had been applied, the condition it was intended to check had been ended, temporarily at least. What should a statesman do? Should he announce that the remedy was no longer needed? There were several reasons for not taking such a position. The most important of these was that no one had any assurance that the production of gold would continue to increase. If the South African field should suddenly play out as other fields had been known to do, the situation would be back where it was in the early nineties. It is easy for the historian to look over the development of a long period and give Olympian judgments regarding what was intelligent statesmanship and what was not, but basing one's opinion on prospective developments is a different matter.

No doubt the psychological factor had a large influence in determining Teller's later attitude. The abuse of the campaign of 1896 was not to be lightly borne, even by so mild-tempered a man as he. Teller gathered some of the worst of the denunciations and occasionally would read one into the *Record.* He quoted one from a press account of a speech of Theodore Roosevelt in 1896, in which the Illinois Democratic Convention was said to be made up of "murderers, horse thieves, burglars, libertines, crooks of all kinds—men who had been convicted of crimes ranging from pocket picking to arson."[3]

Probably these intemperate denunciations did not arouse Teller quite so much as the tone of superior morality assumed by some of the Easterners. To these, free coinage was a question of morals and not of policy, and the reason the South and West desired it was that their moral education had been defective—they wanted something that belonged to someone else. As one of the most intelligent of the contemporary observers, Albert Shaw, wrote:

It is a hard thing and a bitter thing for conscientious men who have believed that great principles were at stake to abandon a cher-

---

[3] From the St. Louis *Post-Dispatch,* Oct. 28, 1896, quoted in the *Congressional Record,* 55 Cong., 2 Sess., p. 1027.

ished cause. It is all the harder for the West and South to abandon the "16 to 1" contention for the reason that the East has never been willing to see that the silver banner has been borne in those parts of the country with a very large measure of idealism as well as gallantry —while the East has never done half justice to the strength of the logical and historical argument for the free coinage of silver at the time-honored American ratio.[4]

After the election of 1896 the Silver Republican senators were invited to join the caucus of the Republicans, but refused. Possibly the invitation was not formal, and Lodge at least was opposed to it, but there can be little doubt that there were numerous informal urgings to return.[5] There probably never was a time during the four years following 1896 that Teller would not have been welcomed back in his old party. His friends in the Senate urged him to return, but he drifted farther and farther away as lines were drawn on new issues. W. E. Chandler answered Teller's request in the summer of 1897 for a pair—an indication that he was generally against the Republicans—with this hasty note: "I will pair with you on anything where I am against your vote; and help pair you [when] I am with you. What are you doing[?] Come back my friend."[6]

Instead, the Silver Republicans continued to co-operate closely with the Populists in the lame-duck session of Congress that met after the election of 1896. Some of them, like Mantle of Montana, were strongly inclined to rejoin the old party, but the rest had rather definitely burned their bridges.

The Republican organization was under the necessity of paying its debts to those Westerners, like Wolcott and Shoup, who had held to the organization during the campaign of 1896. Wolcott used part of his political credit to get Theodore Roosevelt made Assistant-Secretary of the Navy, and was himself later to be seriously considered for the diplomatic post at London, a place for which he was admirably suited.[7] But by far the most important return would be the attempt to secure an international agreement looking toward bimetallism among the leading commercial nations, as the Republican platform had specified. There was a large number of Republican senators who were international bimetallists, and who followed Teller in their denunciation of the

[4] *Review of Reviews*, March, 1898.

[5] Frank J. Cannon and H. J. O'Higgins, *Under the Prophet in Utah* (Boston, 1911), p. 194; *Congressional Record*, 55 Cong., 1 Sess., p. 2438; Lodge to Chandler, Oct. 8, 1896, Chandler MSS.

[6] Chandler to Teller, June 7, 1897, Teller MSS.

[7] *Correspondence of Roosevelt and Lodge*, I, 245, 253; Thayer, *Hay*, II, 185.

appreciating gold standard, but were only willing to look for its remedy in international measures. Probably the most persistent and unselfish of the group was Chandler, of New Hampshire, although Hoar, of Massachusetts, and Allison, of Iowa, were definitely members of it. With unconcealed distaste, Chandler had seen the Eastern press during the campaign of 1896 make the issue definitely one of the gold standard, and treat the international agreement phase of the Republican plank as meaningless verbiage to use in the campaign in the West. All through the campaign Chandler continued to protest that the election of McKinley did not mean permanent acquiescence in the single gold standard. He wrote to Francis A. Walker, the economist:

> The course of the gold mono-metallist papers, in attempting to pervert the contest against the free coinage of silver by the United States alone, into propaganda for the single standard of gold, is mean, cowardly, and contemptible.[8]

It was this sentiment, together with the great political debt the regulars owed to leaders like Wolcott, that made the international conference idea a serious possibility, at least as far as Washington was concerned. Soon after Congress assembled in December, 1896, the Republican Senate caucus set up a committee under Wolcott's chairmanship to take steps toward carrying out the party's pledge.[9] In addition to Wolcott the committee was manned by other bimetallists such as Chandler, Carter, Hoar, and Gear. They got in touch with the President-elect, and with his approval the caucus committee sent Wolcott to Europe to feel out the British and French officials regarding possibilities for such a conference coming to some agreement.

Wolcott worked intelligently and diligently for the conference. He was already acquainted with the leaders of the European bimetallists, but that he had much expectation of success one can well doubt. It was worth working for, as even an agreement for a larger use of silver would have been a justification to Colorado and the West of his activity in 1896. There was not much interest in the United States, and the press was not inclined to take the effort seriously, even when it did not refer to it as did *The Nation* as "solemn fooling, if not worse."[10]

---

[8] Chandler to Walker, Sept. 7, 1896, Walker MSS.; Walker to Chandler, Sept. 12, 1896, Chandler MSS.
[9] John Sherman to Wolcott (copy), Dec. 30, 1896, Chandler MSS.
[10] Dec. 17, 1896.

Later Chandler brought in a bill to provide for a formal commission, which was passed and signed by Cleveland just before he left office. The Silver Republicans supported the bill but, with the exception of Mantle, predicted its failure. Dubois introduced evidence that the British considered the move "mere politics." Teller pointed to the more definite evidence that the leaders of the incoming Republican administration did not intend the proposal seriously, however honest were the beliefs of Chandler, Wolcott, and Hoar. As evidence of this, he pointed to McKinley's new Cabinet, with John Sherman as Secretary of State and Lyman J. Gage, banker and single gold-standard advocate, as Secretary of the Treasury.[11]

Soon after the election of 1896, a monetary commission had been organized by prominent gold-standard advocates and bankers. This held its sessions at Indianapolis, under the chairmanship of former Senator Edmunds. The direction of its recommendations, it soon became evident, would be the extreme demands of the banker group—the establishment of the gold standard by law, and the retirement of most of the Government paper currency and its replacement with national bank notes issued on a somewhat less secure basis than before. This was the spearhead of the bankers' demands that would have committed the country to the gold standard, and given the great banks control of the currency. It was favorably received by the metropolitan press, and undoubtedly agreed with the ideas of the new Secretary of the Treasury in all substantial particulars. But the administration wanted its tariff bill first, and was committed to the support of Wolcott's efforts, and no definite announcements were made regarding the administration's attitude toward the plan. McKinley's inaugural address merely made it clear that he would maintain the gold standard unless a satisfactory international agreement could be made.

McKinley immediately appointed the three commissioners, with Wolcott as chairman, and they went to Europe to wrestle with the problem in earnest. In the meantime, the new President called for a special session of Congress to deal with the tariff.

The new Congress presented few substantial changes from the Fifty-fourth. The House was still strongly Republican, and the Populists and Silver Republicans had the

---

[11] *Congressional Record*, 54 Cong., 2 Sess., pp. 2606-07.

balance of power in the Senate. Yet the margin of this balance had been reduced, and the Republicans lacked only two votes of a majority. There were gold-standard and protectionist Democrats, as well as Populists and Silver Republicans, who were drifting toward the administration, and it would not be difficult for the Republicans to muster a majority for any party measure on which they could maintain unity among their own members. Such would be the case in the pending tariff fight, and Cannon, who was the only Silver Republican definitely opposed to the proposed law, charged that the Senate Republican leaders "know that from some state where no Republican victory was won in the last election, will come the necessary two votes to enable them to carry a tariff here."[12]

Possibly the Utah senator, whose term only had two more years to run, was basing his charges on offers that had been made to him. At least he was later to tell that Senator Proctor had approached him to urge that he support the proposed tariff. "If you will pledge your support of the bill, we will not look elsewhere for a vote.... Anything within the 'political' power of the party to bestow you may expect. I am authorized to say that we will take care of you."[13] But it turned out that the Republicans did not need Cannon's vote. Had the opposition held together they could have refused to allow the tariff to pass, and carried out the Silver Republican threat of the year before to hold up any tariff bill that did not provide for free coinage. There was some expectation of doing this, but after the new session got under way, it was obviously impossible and probably poor strategy for the Silver Republicans in any case.[14]

Teller did not at first attend the special session which McKinley called to enact a new tariff, as personal matters and local political difficulties kept him in Colorado for a time. It was the first time that he had missed more than a few weeks of a session, and, indeed, almost the first time he had missed at all. Pettigrew wrote him that the Republicans, united under the dominance of Aldrich and Hanna, were making inducements to Mantle and to Heitfeld, Dubois' Populist successor, in an attempt to gain control of the organization of the Senate.[15] The opposition parties held to-

[12] *Congressional Record*, 54 Cong., 2 Sess., p. 2606.
[13] Cannon and O'Higgins, *op. cit.*, pp. 192, 194.
[14] F. G. Newlands to Teller, Nov. 14, 1896, Teller MSS.
[15] Pettigrew to Teller, April 12, 1897, Pettigrew MSS.

gether sufficiently so that the committees were left much as
they had been, the Republicans generally filling their vacancies, and the opposition theirs. This left the Democrat-
Populist-Silver Republicans with majorities on the key committees on appropriations and finance.

When Teller returned to Washington he announced to the
Senate that the Silver Republicans wanted a Republican
tariff so that issue would not becloud the monetary question
in 1900. He asserted that if the Republicans would bring in
a moderate measure based upon the old Republican protective ideas, he would promise them a large vote for its passage. There was a large majority of reasonable protectionists in the Senate, as all Silver Republicans and some Populists were in that group.

When the new Dingley bill came over from the House, the
Republicans on the Committee on Finance and the Republican caucus rewrote it to suit themselves. In order to secure
the necessary support for the bill, the Republicans came to
an understanding with Senator Jones, of Nevada, whose
vote was needed to report the bill from the committee and
possibly to assure its passage in the Senate. Jones held out
for substantially higher rates on wool and for a duty on
hides as the price of his support. These the Republicans
granted and strengthened their party immensely in the
Rocky Mountain states by the action. Everything was not
entirely pleasant among the Eastern and Western regular
Republicans, however, for Shoup and Carter at one time
charged the Easterners with having broken their caucus
agreement. The lack of faith in the sincerity of the administration's backing of efforts toward an international
agreement added fuel to these flames, and Carter was reported to have declared that he regretted that he had not
followed Teller out of the party the year before. But the
trouble was patched up, and schedules very favorable to
Western products were adopted.[16]

On the main issues the Silver Republicans voted with
the regulars, for the stated reason that they wanted the bill
to be satisfactory to the administration so that the question
would not complicate the monetary question in 1900. Only
on a few schedules did they make serious attempts to modify
the bill, and most of these were rates that bore heavily on
farmers as a group. After failing to get white pine lumber
put on the free list, Teller urged successfully that the duty

---

[16] St. Louis *Republic*, June 23, 24, 1897.

be reduced, only to have it raised again in the conference committee. The Silver Republicans and Populists united in support of amendments to pay bounties on exported farm products and on beet sugar, proposals that did not receive Democratic or Republican support. Probably the most serious attempt to change the bill was Senator Chilton's amendment to add to it a provision to strengthen the antitrust laws. For this Teller mustered the complete strength of the Silver Republicans, who together with the Populists and Democrats could make a majority, if Jones and Stewart, of Nevada, would stand with them. Their support of the Republicans on this amendment defeated it. Unlike Teller, Cannon, Dubois, and Pettigrew, they were extreme conservatives on most issues.

When the tariff came up for final passage Teller and Pettigrew refused to vote, as had the Silver Republicans in the House. The Populists took the same action for the most part. Cannon voted against the bill, while Mantle and Jones voted for it, and when the conference report came back, Stewart voted for it also.

Upon the conference report Teller delivered a notable speech in which he arraigned the Republican Party and its leadership in the Senate for the character of the legislation, pointing out how it favored the interests who had supported that party in the election of 1896.

> The world will never know what sums were spent and we can only arrive at the amount by examining the pending bill. . . . Upon no ground can any man account for a hundred things in this bill except upon the theory that the Republican organization, either impelled by gratitude or by that kind of gratitude which is said to be the expectation of future favors, are paying off that debt to the American manufacturers.

There was no reason for it, as there were over fifty protectionists in the Senate who would have supported a decent tariff bill. He pointed out how many of the concessions on rates that would favor the farmer had been given up by the Senate conferees without a struggle. Passion was lent to the tone of his speech by the morning's announcement that President E. B. Andrews, of Brown University, had been virtually dismissed because he refused to discontinue his advocacy of bimetallism—a dismissal that was hailed, almost without exception by the gold-standard press as wholly justified, "so rabid, so bigoted have they become that every man who does not agree with them is an anarchist. . . . " To Teller it was the crowning infamy.

The men who have had the advantages of college training, the men who have had the advantages of education have heretofore been liberal-minded men. They have believed in free thought and free speech. They have believed colleges were endowed, not to teach certain heresies, not to destroy them, but for the education and enlightenment of men, for teaching the truth. . . . This proceeding is the key to the gold-standard movement. . . . There are not ten men in the Senate who will call themselves Republicans who dare publicly denounce the infamous act. They will not do it. They, too, are afraid that their party will not share in the benefactions of the rich in the next campaign. . . .

I have not expressed my opinion of the treatment of President Andrews and other instances of the kind as I would, because language is not strong enough with me. I have not the faculty to express the indignation that swells up in. my heart when I see the un-American conduct of an old American college, and when I know it will meet the approval of the great political party with whom I have politically acted until the last year, but within whose folds I never expect again to enter. I saw in a newspaper the other day a statement to the effect that I am desirous of reentering the Republican party. Mr. President, never until it becomes a party of the people, willing to denounce any attempt at the strangulation of free thought, the debasement of colleges, and the destruction of liberty as I see is going on! When the Republican party shall take its old-time position, when it shall get back to its old principles and say, "Men are everything; dollars are nothing," then I may get back into it; but while it continues its present course and says, as it now does, "Men are nothing; dollars are everything," I have no part or lot in it, nor do I desire to have.[17]

Teller was greeted with a wild demonstration in the gallery when he concluded, but the Eastern press had stopped making an exception of the Coloradan when they denounced the silver advocates. "Mr. Teller gave many evidences of how unfair an able man may become when he falls under the influence of fanaticism," editorialized the Washington *Star*.

He has come to talk with the recklessness of a professional agitator. . . . He supported during the war the assertion of the supremacy of national authority, and yet is training with men who condemned the mere assertion of it in the Debs strike. He is a lawyer, and yet is training with men, some of whom denounce all courts as the mere tools of property and greed. And so on. . . . [18]

Shortly before the session closed, the President sent a message to Congress for the creation of a commission to

[17] *Congressional Record*, 55 Cong., 1 Sess., pp. 2846-52. Reasonably typical of the attitude of the gold press toward the Andrews case was the comment of the New York *Sun:* "If he is right, there is no use for colleges. A professor of ethics who should deliver a series of lectures on the advantages of grand and petit larceny would be no more out of place than a college president who devotes himself to preaching free silver. The question of freedom of opinion and of the free expression of opinion is not involved." *Public Opinion*, Aug. 5, 1897.
[18] July 24, 1897.

study the monetary question, and called its attention to the work of the Indianapolis conference. A large section of the press accepted the President's message as an endorsement of the financial plans of that group. Coming in the midst of Wolcott's negotiations, it could hardly have aided his efforts, for, although it was not an endorsement of that plan, it clearly indicated sympathy with it. For the British and French it created substantial doubts as to the sincerity of the United States Government in its attempts to secure international bimetallism.

Wolcott had been busy in Europe with his negotiations during and after the tariff debate, but, as was generally expected, there was little progress made. The most favorable group was the French, whose monetary system was not greatly different from that of the United States. They were willing to trade support for a conference in return for tariff concessions in the pending bill, and Wolcott agreed to work along these lines, but the Republican caucus paid small heed to what was wanted.[19] Finally, however, Wolcott worked out a tentative plan, providing that the United States and France would go over to free coinage, and the India mint would be reopened to silver, together with certain other concessions from Great Britain in the way of a larger use of silver coinage.[20] Such a limited arrangement would certainly have been opposed in the United States with hardly less vigor than free coinage had been in 1896. Finally the British put a complete end to this plan by announcing that the Indian Government refused to consider the reopening of her mint to silver coinage.

When the next session of Congress assembled in December, a number of new factors were present to influence the course of legislation. There were the ominously bad relations with Spain that were developing out of the situation in Cuba. The price of silver was lower than ever before, and grain prices, as in the fall of 1896, had been boosted by a world shortage to an unusual high. From the political standpoint the Congressional elections of the next year were the determining factor. But most important of all was the increased activity of the banking group for monetary legislation. The industrialists who had contributed heavily to the Republican campaign fund in 1896 had received their reward

---

[19] Stephenson, *Aldrich*, Chapter 10; Leon B. Richardson, in his recent *William E. Chandler* (New York, 1940), Chapter XXIV, has an excellent discussion of this.

[20] Dawson, *Wolcott*, I, 666-67.

in the Dingley tariff, and the bankers were unblushingly demanding theirs. Three months after the Republicans took office, A. B. Hepburn, formerly director of the mint and now connected with a leading New York bank, wrote to the new Secretary of the Treasury appealing for the deposit of Government funds in his bank, urging pointedly: " ... [If] you take pains to look at our list of directors you will see that we also have very great political claims in view of what was done during the canvass last year."[21] When Teller secured a copy of this letter he read it to the Senate with unconcealed pleasure, but such rewards were to be only small change.

Teller took the floor early in January to denounce the administration for its sabotage of Wolcott's work for an international agreement. Referring to McKinley's reference to the Indianapolis plan, he said:

. While the Commission was negotiating under the most delicate and trying circumstances under which men ever negotiated, the President sent to us on the 24th day of July last a message, and if there had heretofore been a possibility of success, from that moment it ceased.[22]

A few days later, Wolcott delivered an address to the Senate that was a report on his work in Europe. He testified that the President had supported the commission loyally, but laid the failure of their work partly to the statements of the Secretary of the Treasury. He reaffirmed his opposition to the gold standard, and expressed a belief that bimetallism by international agreement was still possible.

Those who agreed with Wolcott were only a small part of the Republican Party, and the plans to strengthen the gold standard had substantial pressure behind them. To head this off by forcing the members of Congress to go on record, and in this way serving notice that the recommendations of the Indianapolis commission would not be carried out, Teller assumed the offensive by introducing into the Senate a resolution similar to the Matthews resolution of 1878, declaring that all bonds of the United States were payable either in silver or gold at the election of the Government. There was nothing in the resolution that would have influenced Government policy. It merely stated the contract that was on the bond. It was meant to be a gesture of defiance to the gold-standard advocates.

---

[21] *Congressional Record*, 56 Cong., 1 Sess., p. 945.
[22] *Ibid.*, 55 Cong., 2 Sess., pp. 424-26.

It was more than a gesture of defiance as Teller worked it out. It was an attempt to make the Republicans define their position for the approaching congressional campaign, now that international bimetallism was dead. The resolution was in a more general way a repudiation of all the statements of the Treasury Department and the presidency since 1875, that there was something unsound about the silver dollar. Somewhat more subtly it was also an open declaration that there would be nothing morally wrong in the free coinage of silver at the old ratio, an argument that in the past had had few supporters in the Senate, but had been used constantly by the gold press in recent years. Congress was being asked to repudiate that argument.

Teller's decision—no doubt in close agreement with Senate Democrats and Populists—to use the old Matthews resolution involved certain other elements of strategy.[23] This resolution in 1878 had received the support of large majorities in both houses, majorities that had included a very substantial number of Republicans. Allison had then voted for it in the Senate, as McKinley had in the House. It was a resolution that Republican Congressmen would find difficulty in opposing by the cries of "repudiation" that would generally be used against it. This possibly accounts in part for the bitter character of the debate and the imputations that the advocates of the resolution were attacking the integrity and honor of the Government. After a long session of badgering questions on the Senate floor, Teller once lost his temper, and when Senator Fairbanks, of Indiana, new in the Senate and obsequious to the slightest wish of the administration, arose to inject some questions, Teller shouted, "Sit down!"

Teller admitted that the appreciation of the dollar on the gold standard seemed to have stopped, but pointed out that there was little assurance that it would not continue. Referring to the noncreditor, Teller declaimed:

> You beggar him; you destroy his opportunity . . . and then you tell us that all these things can be done, that prices may be lowered, products may be kept at a price that does not pay for production, and in the end labor must stand it all; and yet you tell us that you are doing this that the bondholder may have the bounty—not the contracted price, but the bounty—the beneficience of the Government of the United States!

23 *The Silver Knight—National Watchman*, Jan. 6, 1898.

Looking at the solid block of New England senators, who, except for Chandler, were furnishing most of the opposition, Teller pointed out that soldiers enlisted in the Union armies had done so at a contracted wage and before long the Government was paying them in depreciated greenbacks. "No New England man rose then, no New York man rose then, and said 'It is dishonest to give the soldiers 40-cent money.'" Silver money would buy as much as gold anywhere in the United States, said Teller, and why not pay it out? The only reason that the bondholders demanded gold was to discredit silver, and to make "gold the only money of ultimate redemption."[24]

The resolution passed the Senate by a vote of 47 to 32. Not only did the Democrats, Populists, and Silver Republicans vote for it, but Wolcott, Shoup, Carter, Warren, Clark, and Chandler also voted with them. Only one Democratic senator voted against the resolution. A gold-payment substitute offered by Senator Lodge was voted down 24 to 53, all the regular Republicans from the West voting against it, as well as some Easterners like Chandler and Quay. Such regulars as Allison and Burrows, of Michigan, refused to vote on the amendment. As far as the Senate was concerned, Teller's resolution had accomplished its purpose. The record was made, and the majority against the gold standard was demonstrated.

Just before the resolution passed the Senate, President McKinley had opposed it in a public address that had little influence on the Senate. The control of the House, however, was well in the hands of the administration, and after holding brief hearings at which the silver men were not allowed to present their case, it was voted down emphatically. Only one regular Republican voted for it, and only two Democrats against it. Although its defeat was a stinging blow, it accomplished one of Teller's purposes, in that it put beyond question where the Republican Party stood. "The vote in the House on the Teller resolution was just what I believed was the best that could happen for us," Senator James K. Jones wrote to Bryan.[25] It was evident that no change in the existing situation could be made in the Fifty-fifth Congress.

The resolution was not given the public attention it

[24] *Congressional Record*, 55 Cong., 2 Sess., pp. 979-80, 1022.

[25] Feb. 1, 1898, Bryan MSS. Bland later concluded that the resolution was a tactical mistake as it served as a too vigorous challenge to the gold standard forces. W. V. Byars, *An American Commoner* (Columbia, Mo., 1900), p. 249.

would have ordinarily received, because of the pressure of
other questions for the attention of the press and Congress.
The delicate relations with Spain were rapidly coming to a
crisis, and in a few months had broken out into actual war.
Before the fall campaigns were completed, the war had
ended in a series of American victories, and new problems
as well as new interests had taken the public's mind off the
monetary issue.

As soon as the war was in definite prospect, Congress
began to consider measures for raising money to meet the
new expenses of the war. In the contest over this measure,
Teller led the Silver Republicans in opposition to the bond
issue desired by the administration, arguing that the cost
of the war should be met by taxation. He attempted to add
an income tax that would be effective, and supported an
attempt to bring that question before the Supreme Court
again.[26] For the most part the attempts to add taxes on
corporations were unsuccessful, and the most substantial
victory of the free-coinage senators was the addition of a
proposal to coin the silver seigniorage now in the Treasury.
Teller did not consider it of great importance but supported
it as a means of keeping the monetary issue alive, and more
definitely drawing the line in Congress between the gold-
standard men and the bimetallists. The distinct lessening
of interest in monetary problems, evident in the press and
in the attitude of political leaders, made it a difficult task
to hold the free-coinage men together and bring them to the
support of Bryan in 1900.

What to do with the Silver Republican political organization in the Western states after 1896 had been a problem of
great concern to Teller. The simplest thing would have been
to unite with the Democrats, and this would have been
an easy way out for Teller. But it was impossible to do
that and keep any substantial number of Republicans
alienated from the administration. It was clear from the
trend in Colorado that most of the local leaders would welcome a good excuse to rejoin the national organization. To
Teller's fellow bolters, too, it was necessary to maintain their
own party. The group was clearly looking toward another
national campaign in 1900 on the monetary issue, and visualized its members as leading a substantial number of former

[26] *Congressional Record*, 55 Cong., 2 Sess., pp. 5210-15, 5274-77; *Rocky Mountain News*, May 8, 1898.

Republicans to the support of Bryan again on a free-coinage platform.

To unite the state organizations into a national party a public address was issued on Washington's birthday, 1897, urging the state organizations to designate a member of a provisional national committee, which would meet at Chicago on June 8.[27] This address was signed by Teller, Dubois, Cannon, Pettigrew, Mantle, John P. Jones, Towne, Hartman, Shafroth, and Allen. The Nevada senator here for the first time definitely associated himself with Teller's group, and withdrew such tenuous connections as he had maintained with the Populists. In fact there seems to have been no intention of maintaining the National Silver Party as an organization, and the Silver Republicans would absorb such parts of it as did not join the Democrats immediately or affiliate with the Populists. In Nevada, however, the "Silver Party" continued to be the organization of Jones, Stewart, and Newlands.

Teller did not attend the meeting at Chicago, and Towne and Dubois, who were both out of office, were in active charge. Congressman Hartman announced that the group wanted it

... distinctly understood that the organization of the silver Republican party will not be antagonistic to any of the organizations that endorse the free coinage of silver, but that we will make war with them on the common foe, the Republican party on the gold standard.

Thirty-one states and one territory were represented at the meeting, the absent ones all being from New England and the South, with the exception, if the press accounts are correct, of Nevada. Towne was elected chairman of the national committee, and a small executive committee was set up with Dubois as chairman, with power to act for the national committee when it was not in session.[28]

The committee hoped to raise about fifteen hundred dollars a month to keep the national organization operating and carrying on its organizing activities. An office was set up in Duluth with Towne in charge. It insisted on maintaining an entirely separate organization, and refused to go to the Democrats for finances. "We are not going to play second fiddle to the Democratic party,"[29] Pettigrew wrote Teller.

[27] Quoted in the *Congressional Record*, 54 Cong., 2 Sess., p. 2604.
[28] St. Louis *Globe-Democrat*, June 8, 9, 1897.
[29] June 4, 1897, Pettigrew MSS.

Towne spent a large share of his time traveling in the
Western states, making speeches and stimulating organization work. Plans were laid for the congressional elections
of 1898, which involved fusion with the Populists and Democrats wherever possible. In these movements Teller took
an active part, and advised Towne regularly as to their
propaganda and organization work. In Colorado the party
was closely identified with him personally, and the conditions
prevailing in the state organization were indicative of those
in the other Western states. After the national defeat of
1896 it had been impossible to prevent large numbers of
former Republicans from going back into the victorious
party.

The first important break had come in the fall of 1897
over the election of a supreme court judge. The Silver Republican state organization had united with the regular Republicans in support of a certain candidate, much to Teller's
disgust and over Teller's protest. Towne as national chairman refused to recognize this group, but set up a new
organization which would refuse to reunite with the regulars.[30] The new group was accepted by the large majority
of the Silver Republicans, but, encouraged by Wolcott's judicious distribution of Federal offices, the division carried over
to make a serious problem the next year.

The problem of uniting the three free-coinage parties in
any campaign was far from easy. There was a strong tendency in county and city politics for the Silver Republicans
and regulars to work together as they had before 1896, and
there were instances in Colorado where this was the principal force in reuniting the party factions.[31] Fusion on the
state ticket between two organizations is always difficult, and
among three it proved almost impossible. It was carried
through only at the expense of a great deal of ill feeling and
party bolting. Each of the three parties—Silver Republican,
Democrat, and Populist—would demand the naming of the
candidate for governor as its privilege, and labor under the
soreness of defeat if it did not get it. At the same time it
was not practicable to fuse completely with the Democratic
or Populist organizations. To the local politicians that would
mean leaving a machine which they controlled to join one
controlled by old enemies. To the voter it would mean re-

---

[30] Patterson to Bryan, Jan. 28, 1898, Bryan MSS.; Pettigrew to Towne, Dec. 9, 1897,
Pettigrew MSS.
[31] Irving W. Stanton, *Sixty Years in Colorado* (Denver, 1922), pp. 245-49.

pudiating many of the policies he had hitherto supported. Hence the threefold organization of the silver men continued.

The national officers of the three parties took advantage of the situation created by the fight over the Teller resolution, and issued statements in February calling for the union of all free-coinage supporters upon common candidates for the House of Representatives and the Senate. They pointed to the lesson embodied in the House vote as evidence that union was necessary to prevent a gold-standard majority in Congress.[32] All this activity, of course, looked toward the campaign of 1900 for another contest on the monetary question, with the free-coinage men united in support of Bryan.

The national Democratic organization was anxious to keep these forces united. Bryan appealed for fair play for the Silver Republicans and urged the Utah Democrats to support Cannon for re-election to the Senate. "I am not willing to believe," Bryan wrote Chairman Jones of the Democratic National Committee, "that Silver Republicans are so much more patriotic than Democrats that they will concede all offices to democrats if the democrats are not willing to concede any offices to the Silver Republicans."[33] Teller spent a busy summer and fall, more active in local Colorado politics than he had been for years in trying to straighten out the conflicting interests of the confusing groups.

It was arranged to hold the state conventions of the free-coinage parties in Colorado Springs at the same time in order to facilitate fusion. There was a struggle pending within the Silver Republican organization between those who wanted to carry it back to the Republican Party and those who wanted to co-operate with the other free-coinage groups. Teller had taken the leadership of the latter faction the preceding March when he declared himself unequivocally for fusion,[34] and there seemed little doubt that the rank and file would follow him. Rumors of attempts of the pro-regulars to stampede the convention against fusion with the Democrats, led the fusionists to place an armed guard in the opera house in which the convention would be held in order to prevent its seizure by the opposing factions. Early the following morning a group of men recruited in Denver

[32] Denver *Post*, Feb. 16, 1898.
[33] Feb. 21, 1898 (copy), Bryan MSS.
[34] Denver *Post*, March 28, 1898.

and led, according to the press, by certain Federal officeholders and the local sheriff, attacked the hall and gained
possession. In the accompanying gunfire one man was killed
and several were wounded.[35] The coroner's jury upheld the
legality of the conduct of the fusionists, and the anti-fusion-
ists allowed the convention to proceed in regular order.
Later in the day is was opened with a keynote speech by
Teller, who served as chairman.

The basis of fusion was that the Democrats should get
the governorship, the other parties one congressman each,
and the minor offices would be filled by the Populists and
Silver Republicans. The Silver Republicans in Teller's
group complained of this, because it gave the state administration and nearly all its patronage to the Democrats, and
left the Silver Republicans with what were, from the standpoint of party organization, decorative offices. The Democrats nominated Charles S. Thomas for governor, and the
other parties endorsed him. Shafroth, Silver Republican,
and Bell, Populist, were named for Congress.

The bolting anti-fusion faction of Silver Republicans put
a complete state ticket in the field headed by Simon Guggenheim for governor, but when the Republicans named a complete ticket headed by Henry R. Wolcott, the Guggenheim
faction withdrew in its favor. Teller was active in the
campaign, and unquestionably held the bulk of the Silver
Republican voters to the fusion ticket. With the leaders it
was different, and before the end of the campaign, Senator
Wolcott was able to boast that all but three of the sixteen
delegates and alternates who had walked out at the Republican convention in 1896 were now back supporting the regular ticket.[36]

This was one evidence of changes in the political situation in Colorado since 1896. Some of it was no doubt the
result of the distribution of Federal patronage, but more
fundamentally it was based upon returning prosperity in the
state, upon the confusion the war injected into the older
issues, and chiefly the changed economic basis of Colorado
mining. The development of the Cripple Creek gold field
and smaller ones throughout the state that were made profitable by the new methods of ore reduction had raised gold
mining from a subordinate place in Colorado to one whose

[35] The backing of the two factions is evident in the newspaper reference to them as
the "Teller-Blood" and "Wolcott-Broad" groups. St. Louis *Republic*, Sept. 8, 1898.

[36] For a time he claimed fourteen of the sixteen, but later reduced it to thirteen.
Dawson, *Wolcott*, II, 362, 391.

production came close in 1897 and 1898 to doubling the value of silver production.[37] As Silver became of less absolute and relative value, and gold became substantially more, the appeal for free coinage as a local issue lost its potency. Nevertheless the fusionists won a complete victory; Thomas became governor, and Shafroth and Bell were returned to Congress.

In the country at large the fusionists reduced the Republican majority in the House, but the administration more than made up for it by securing a substantial majority of regular Republicans in the Senate. The Silver Republicans generally did poorly. Cannon failed of re-election when the Utah legislature found itself so badly divided that it could not elect anyone. Towne came within a few votes of recapturing his old seat in Congress, and Hartman and Mantle both went out of public life when fusion with the Democratic organization failed in Montana. The only substantial victories were the return of Edgar Wilson to Congress from Idaho, and the election of John Lind as governor of Minnesota. Pettigrew's candidate for governor won, but the Republicans elected the bulk of their state ticket as they had in Minnesota.

In Colorado the results were substantial proof that the state would back Bryan on the Chicago platform in 1900. The possibility that Wolcott would succeed himself for another term in the Senate was still small, unless the fusionists split.[38] But both in Colorado and over the country it was evident that the free-coinage cause was rapidly declining, and, failing some turn in gold production and prices, it was doomed to an early death.

---

[37] The value of gold produced in Colorado exceeded that of silver for the first time since the seventies in 1897, when the relative values were: gold, $19,579,433; silver, $12,766,919. In 1898 they were: gold, $23,534,532; silver, $13,866,532. Charles W. Henderson, *Mining in Colorado*, p. 69.

[38] C. S. Thomas to Bryan, Nov. 20, 1898, Bryan MSS.

CHAPTER XX

IMPERIALISM BECOMES THE ISSUE
1897-99

FROM the beginning of the original settlements until about 1890, American history had been a process of occupying and developing territory hitherto inhabited only by Indians and wandering traders. This process was not to be checked in a matter of a few years' time without accompanying disturbances or compensatory developments. When it was announced in the census of 1890 that there was no longer a frontier of settlement, attention was called to a condition that had rapidly come into existence—namely, that almost no free land suitable for ordinary farming was now open to settlement; that large speculative profits from investment in undeveloped territory under United States laws were no longer possible; and that the restless people of the United States would hereafter have to accommodate themselves within settled communities. The problems of the closed frontier were many, but the most spectacular was the tendency to expand the nation's territorial boundaries over other settled portions of the globe.

There were many factors in America's past development favorable to such a policy. All that region west of the Mississippi River had been secured by purchase, occupation, or conquest from the hands of people and governments unable to develop it. The change had been from waste to productivity, from primitiveness to civilization, from the darkness of ignorance to the light of an educated population. Would anyone try to convince a man like Teller, who had lived through that process, that its result was not good? A chief credo of the American mentality was the ultimate good of material development under the American flag, and no one who should deny it could gain a hearing. Had there been no counterinfluences present, the closed frontier might have ushered in an era of imperialism such as a world dominated by that idea had never dreamed.

That it did not was due in a large measure to the existence in American life of certain common principles of great potency. Had expansion been merely a territorial matter, these would not have come into active influence. But it also concerned people—large numbers of people who were, by the recognition of mankind, civilized. The Americans were a young people. They had only a brief history and few traditions, but they united upon these all the emotion of a proud people. That history and that tradition were radical and revolutionary. The struggle for independence from Great Britain was always the principal subject of popular history and legend. Most schoolboys found the most attractive part of the curriculum in the story that began with the Stamp Act and ended at Yorktown. Few native-born Americans in 1900 had not declaimed as boys that speech attributed to Patrick Henry which included his revolutionary words, "Give me liberty or give me death!" Certainly everyone had heard on a Fourth of July these words pronounced with at least as much assurance as the Bible was quoted in church, "We hold these truths to be self-evident, that all men are created equal. . . . " All this praise of liberty, of the consent of the governed, and of the right of a people to rule themselves had molded people's minds in a way that would not permit any policy of unrestrained imperialism without protest.

Teller educated himself in international affairs nearly as carefully as he had upon monetary problems. Beginning with the fisheries debate in 1888, his knowledge had grown, until later debates on imperialism showed him to be one of the best-informed members of the Senate on the history of American foreign relations. He favored a vigorous foreign policy to protect American rights wherever they existed. When Cleveland issued his well-known declaration regarding the Venezuelan boundary dispute with Great Britain, Teller gave a very qualified approval. It was not our place, he held, to assume responsibility for the Latin American states.

We say . . . if those States do not deal with you as one State should with another, you may go to war with them, if necessary, to enforce their national obligations toward you . . . but you shall not take an acre of land; not because we are interested so directly in those republics, but because we are interested in this great Republic.[1]

In 1898 Teller was an expansionist. He had a firm faith, as no doubt did most of his countrymen, that American expansion would be something vastly different from that of other powers. In the controversy over the annexation of Hawaii, he had defended the acts of the Harrison administration and attacked those of Cleveland. He made a long defense of expansion, taking the opportunity to show that histori-

---

[1] *Congressional Record*, 54 Cong., 1 Sess., p. 246.

cally expansion had always been the policy of the Democratic Party, and its present members could not oppose it without repudiating their party's traditions.

His own statements of the relations of the United States to Cuba were almost a paraphrase of Jefferson's famous instructions to Livingston regarding New Orleans. He did not want a protectorate for Hawaii, either, but "an absolute incorporation," with eventual statehood. The extent and limits of his imperialism—ideas that guided all his future action—came out in that debate.

I am in favor of the annexation of those islands. I am in favor of the annexation of Cuba; I am in favor of the annexation of the great country lying to the north of us. I expect in a few years to see the American flag floating from the extreme north to the line of our sister Republics on the south. I expect to see it floating over the isles of the sea—not only these, but in the Great Gulf and in the West India sea.

This was the authentic spirit of the American frontier, but even then it was qualified by America's democratic ideology, for Teller immediately added,

If the Canadians do not choose to come to us we shall never get them. . . . I do not mean by that that I want to take an inch of territory where the people do not voluntarily come to us. I do not believe that by conquest we should take anything.[2]

Teller aided every attempt to acquire the Hawaiian Islands until they were annexed in 1898.

The event that brought about the United States' greatest step in extraterritorial expansion had been brewing for many years. Cuba had long been considered a special interest of the American people and nation. An insurrection began there in 1895 which attracted a great amount of interest in the United States, not only from the people who traded or had investments there, but from the general public. It was natural for the public to sympathize with any people struggling for independence. In the case of Cuba that sympathy was much greater, because of its nearness and the cruel methods of suppression adopted by the Spanish government, which the press played up in vivid detail. What was to be the attitude of the United States toward this contest?

Teller favored recognition of the belligerency of the rebels, and denied that it would be an act that would give

---

[2] *Congressional Record*, 53 Cong., 2 Sess., pp. 1574-79; *ibid.*, 53 Cong., 3 Sess., pp. 626-29, Appendix, pp. 200-01.

Spain any cause for complaint, much less for war. He endeavored to obtain this recognition from early in 1896 until war was declared. Teller was not favorable toward a war against Spain, and his voice was usually raised for moderation and for calm decision. When some Spanish students burned an American flag and there were those who denounced it as a national insult, Teller announced: "I have not the slightest feeling against the Spanish government ... because of the conduct of their irresponsible students."

Nevertheless, in the heat of the debate over his resolution regarding the payment of bonds in silver, Teller could and did lay the lack of sympathy of the Republican administration toward Cuba to its repudiation of the American tradition in the interest of the "salvation of dividends."[3] When the *Maine* was blown up in Havana harbor he cautioned against hasty action or judgment. "That is a matter which ... should be left alone until such time as all the facts are fully known," he told the Senate. He again used the occasion to urge recognition of Cubans' rights as belligerents.

I do not want any war, and I do not believe this proceeding ... will eventuate in war.... There are certain things we can do to indicate our sympathy with Cuba, and they are absolutely in the line of respectful treatment of Spain.[4]

But the *Maine* incident and subsequent developments made some action by the United States certain. While awaiting the expected word from the President, Teller drafted several different propositions that embodied slightly different types of action, and passed them about the Senate for comment. The one that seemed to attract most favor was one that Hoar and Spooner were later to declare they had preferred to the resolution which the Senate committee on foreign relations eventually submitted. After declaring that war existed "between the Government of Spain and the Government of Cuba," it resolved that,

Therefore the President of the United States is hereby authorized and directed to take such steps as may be necessary to terminate hostilities in the Island of Cuba and to secure to the people of that island an independent republican government by the people thereof.[5]

It will be noticed that it recognized the belligerency of the Cubans, and also left no doubt as to the establishment of an independent Cuban government.

---

[3] *Congressional Record*, 54 Cong., 1 Sess., p. 2631; *ibid.*, 2 Sess., p. 426.
[4] *Ibid.*, 55 Cong., 2 Sess., pp. 2078, 2079.
[5] *Ibid.*, 2 Sess., Appendix, p. 289.

On April 11, President McKinley, without revealing all
the facts regarding his negotiations with Spain, sent a message to Congress asking for permission to intervene in Cuba
to establish peace. Speaking of the intervention he was
asking authority from Congress to make, the President
wrote, "It involves, however, hostile constraint upon both
parties to the contest as well to enforce a truce as to guide
the eventual settlement." This seemed clearly to contemplate
opposition to the revolutionary government, and in that way
was directly antagonistic to the campaign of the friends of
Cuba. Just why it was put in this form is not entirely clear,
but McKinley was under pressure from interests which, if
any intervention occurred, would want annexation to the
United States. Furthermore, he had been opposing recognition, and this would to some extent seem more consistent
with that policy.

The Senate committee on foreign relations brought a
resolution before the Senate that did not carry out the President's wishes completely, and at the same time did not satisfy the friends of Cuban independence. The minority of the
committee brought in an amendment providing for the recognition of the Cuban Republic—the revolutionary government.

Teller vigorously supported the recognition amendment,
because, as he explained to the Senate, the President seemed
to contemplate action against the Cubans as well as against
Spain. In fact, McKinley's message had raised doubts regarding his policy toward Cuba, and in the Senate it had
become a contest between intervention with independence,
and intervention with the question of independence to be
determined in the future. No one would take a public stand
at this time for annexation. The advocates of recognition of
the Republic argued that there was no real reason against
it, unless the Government contemplated something other
than Cuban independence. Senator Berry, of Arkansas,
expressed this attitude when he told the Senate:

I cannot rid my mind of the belief that if we enter into this contest
refusing directly to recognize the Cuban Republic, there will lurk
the suspicion in the minds of the people both at home and abroad
that we mean something more than we say; that there lurks behind
this resolution an undisclosed purpose; which we will not avow....
that if we do not recognize the Cuban Republic the reason is that we
intend to impose conditions and obligations upon that republic that
they would be unwilling to assume of their own accord.[6]

_____
[6] *Ibid.*, p. 3879.

It was into this situation that Teller, urging recognition as the best means of proving the good intentions of the government, suggested that the real question might be settled by a declaratory statement that would increase the probabilities of independence whether recognition carried or not. He declared:

I want the Senate to say to the world in the most emphatic manner possible that we do not intend in any way or manner to derive benefit from this intervention. Spain is too weak and too poor to pay indemnity. I want the Senate to say that we do not intend to take that island; that whatever we may do as to some other island, as to this island, the great bone of contention, we do not intend to take it from the legally constituted authorities of the island as now established.

At the proper time, if no one else does so, I propose to offer some amendment to the joint resolution that shall make it clear to the world that it shall not be said by any European government, when we go to battle for the liberty and freedom of Cuban patriots, that we are doing it for the purpose of aggrandizement for ourselves or the increasing of our territorial holdings.[7]

The next day Teller introduced an amendment that was a complete substitute for the committee amendment plus the pending amendment for recognition of the Cuban Republic, but different in other particulars.[8] Instead of the simple demand that Spain get out of Cuba, Teller's resolution set this demand off by making the alternative to it American intervention. Possibly this was not an important difference, but to Teller it seemed to give Spain a chance to back down in such a way as to avoid war. More important than that was the qualifying clause Teller attached to the threatened intervention. The United States would intervene in its own and Cuba's interest,

... hereby disclaiming any disposition or intention to exercise jurisdiction or control over said island except for the pacification thereof—and a determination when that is accomplished to leave the government and control of the island to the people thereof.

The vote was first taken on the amendment of the minority of the foreign relations committee, adding recognition of the Cuban Republic. It was adopted by the combined votes of Democrats, Populists, Silver Republicans, and a small group of regular Republicans who had been favorable to the Cuban cause. This left the most substantial difference between Teller's substitute and the amended committee reso-

---

[7] *Ibid.*, p. 3899.
[8] *Ibid.*, p. 3954.

lution the self-denying statement quoted above, and Senator
C. K. Davis, chairman of the foreign relations committee,
after conferring with Teller and the members of his committee, agreed to add it to the resolution. Even the most
hopeful imperialist could not object to it now, as the recognition of the Cuban Republic was already in the resolution.
Davis had suggested two verbal changes in the phraseology
that were distinct improvements. "Sovereignty" was inserted before "jurisdiction," and "asserts" between "and"
and "a determination." In recasting it for a new section of
the committee resolution some other verbal changes were
made. In this form, Davis himself introduced it as a section
to the resolution. It was read in the Senate and amid cries
of "That's right!" adopted without a division.[9]

Thus amended, the resolution passed the Senate. The
House had adopted resolutions more in keeping with the
wishes of the administration, and finally forced the Senate
to recede from its demand for recognition, but did accept
Teller's resolution as a compromise. There was no argument
against it that anyone cared to make publicly. In this manner the action was taken that brought on war with Spain.

The Teller, or Fourth, Resolution, as it was destined to
be called, was unquestionably distasteful to the convinced
imperialists, because it pledged the United States to make
Cuba independent, but it represented the wishes of the public
at large at this time. The latter was sympathetic toward the
cause of Cuban independence, and was not motivated as yet
by too obvious desires for territorial expansion. Many, probably including Teller, felt that an independent Cuba would
eventually ask for annexation. Whatever its motives, the
effect of the amendment was substantial, for subsequent
developments made it adequately clear that had the promise
not been definitely made, there is every reason to believe
that Cuba would have been annexed directly to the United
States. Horatio S. Rubens gives voice to a common contemporary view when he concludes that "Cuba owes Senator
Teller the realization of her independence."[10]

[9] *Ibid.*, p. 3988; St. Louis *Globe-Democrat*, April 17, 1898. Teller reviewed the history of the resolution in 1902. *Congressional Record*, 57 Cong., 1 Sess., pp. 5801-08. Mr. Horatio Rubens states (*Liberty: The Story of Cuba* (New York, 1932), p. 341), that he rushed to Washington and suggested to Teller the necessity of the declaration. If Rubens' memory here is accurate, it certainly is faulty on the chronology of the resolution which had been introduced by Teller, before Rubens, according to his own account, reached Washington. From the Senate debate, it seems unlikely that Teller needed the suggestion. In all probability the complete resolution was largely one of the several Teller had prepared before the President's message of April 11, although the first clause was taken from the committee resolution plus the Turpie amendment.

[10] Rubens, *Liberty*, p. 342. An examination of newspaper comments reveals little interest in the Teller resolution at this time. In general, the resolutions were approved

It is easily possible to get the idea from Teller's action that he was anti-expansionist, but that is far from true. Rather, it was care for the reputation of the United States, sympathy for the Cubans, and suspicion of the motives of the administration that stimulated Teller to propose the self-denying declaration. And it is not without significance that when he did he had declared that " ... whatever we may do as to some other islands, as to this island ... we do not intend to take it."

The resolutions were followed by war. "I am going to forget that William McKinley was elected President on the Republican ticket," Teller told the Senate. "More than that, I am going to forget the class of men who stood back of him ... and I am going to stand up for every effort of his to maintain the integrity, honor, and dignity of the American people."[11]

As the war progressed with events such as Dewey's victory at Manila to stimulate enthusiasm for imperialism, the public, which had been favorable to the war as an aid to the Cuban rebels, began to revel in the phrases "imperial destiny" and "colonial empire," which the advocates of expansion had been using. A new movement to annex Hawaii was the first result. Both parties were already committed to a stand on this question, and it was obvious that two thirds of the Senate could not be secured to ratify an annexation treaty. Newlands then introduced in the House a joint resolution providing for the same action, but which required only a majority in the Senate.

Teller took a leading part in the debate, supporting annexation as he had in 1893 and 1894 on grounds of its conformity with American tradition, and especially upon the trustworthiness of the American people in administering colonial government. The vigor of his support brought the plaudits of partisan Republicans who had bestowed nothing but criticism on him since 1896.[12] Teller, Cannon, Mantle, and the Populists, Kyle and Heitfeld, joined the Republicans to pass the resolution.

as a whole. Whitelaw Reid, however, wrote the President of his deep regret over its passage, and he no doubt represented the attitude of the convinced imperialists. Royal Cortissoz, *The Life of Whitelaw Reid* (New York, 1921), II, 222. Typical of a fairly general opinion was this editorial comment from the St. Louis *Globe-Democrat* of April 18: "That utterance voices the feeling of the great majority of the American people. We want the Cubans to establish a government of their own if they desire to. But no political occurrence of the future is more certain than that Cuba will one day become part of the United States. ... Yet it will not come until the Cubans by a large majority ask for it."

[11] *Congressional Record*, 55 Cong., 2 Sess., p. 4099.

[12] *Ibid.*, p. 6156; New York *Tribune*, June 22, 1898.

Like the majority of the public, Teller's enthusiasm for
expansion seemed to grow with the progress of the war.
When this was at its height, September 8, 1898, Teller
opened the Silver Republican campaign in his state at Colorado Springs, and concluded his speech with a statement on
colonial policy which was to embarrass him in the future
more than any other speech he ever made:

I was one of those who believed that the people of Cuba were
entitled to freedom....

I say to you that we have not any doubt but what, with the consent
of the people of Cuba and Porto Rico, we are to establish a government
something on the order that we had in Colorado for fifteen years, in
which their rights as individuals will be recognized, but, beyond that,
the government will have control....

If we can put a strong hand on them and give them a good government, which they have never had, the blessings of which they will
soon realize, we shall increase the area of freedom.... The greater
question is, what shall we do with the Asiatic islands?...

There is an obligation upon us. That obligation is to see that those
people have a good government, and if they are capable of participat-
ing in it to take them in and give them the rights that we enjoyed
here [Colorado] when we were denied some of the rights of American
citizenship. Make Territories out of them. We need not make States
of them. If they should ever become affiliated with us and so assimilat-
ed with us that we can make States of them, we will make States of
them.

You can depend upon the American people to do the right thing at
the right time. You need not be afraid that we will take them in before
they are ready or that we will keep them out after they are ready to
come in....

Those islands are in the line of the great commerce of the world.
They are worth millions to us, and we can go on holding them without
any disadvantage to us.... I believe the voice of 100,000,000 men is
better than the voice of one, and I have faith in the American people,
in their intelligence, in their integrity, in their ability, and I am
willing to trust these great problems to them, and I say we shall make
no mistake if we say to them, "Here we have put our flag, here we
have buried our dead, and by the Eternal the flag shall stay while the
Union lives!"[13]

All the confusion that was present in the minds of
Americans over the new problem is evident here in Teller's
speech, and he, like most of them, was trying to eat his cake
as imperial glory and to keep it as the American dream of
freedom and liberty. It is not surprising that when Teller
became one of the most persistent opponents of the ad-

---

[13] Denver *Times*, Sept. 8, 1898; *Rocky Mountain News*, Sept. 9, 1898. Like Teller's
other speeches this one was made from notes, and the two newspaper quotations differ
slightly.

ministration's imperialistic policies its defenders would gleefully quote this speech of 1898.

After the election with its Republican victory in the Senate, the fusionists had to assume some stand on the new issues. The Democrats had committed themselves against expansion in the fight over Hawaiian annexation. Still the war and its results were popular, especially so in the West. As far as the Silver Republicans were concerned, Teller and Towne seemed agreed that they should play a waiting game, and let the Republicans announce their position first.[14] But Teller was unable to do this for long, and on the day the treaty transferring the Spanish possession to the United States was signed, he made public a statement in opposition to the current proposal of selling the Philippine Islands.

> The idea of selling the Philippines to the highest bidder is a dream. We can't do it. We are responsible to the world for order in those islands. We must give the Filipinos a chance to learn to govern themselves. Our duty goes further than saying to them, "Start a government and take care of yourself." We must aid them, and as soon as possible let them take care of their own home and municipal affairs.[15]

The Senate presented a curious mixture of groupings on the question of ratifying the treaty that on details were almost as numerous as the members themselves. Possibly without undue violence to the facts, we can point out three loose groupings. One was the administration group—Republicans for the most part. This group included such diverse persons as Lodge, who was a convinced imperialist of the type that fell in with the aggressive military theories of A. T. Mahan, and O. H. Platt, who, as a representative of conservative business interests and the McKinley administration, had opposed any aid to the Cuban rebels. This group would support ratification without condition. At the other extreme were the anti-expansionists who saw in control of foreign peoples a repudiation of all that was fine in the American tradition. Within this group were a very few conservative Republicans, such as Hoar and Hale, who had opposed recognition of Cuban belligerency and recognition of the Cuban Republic. The large part of the group, however, was composed of the more consistent defenders of the underdog, such as Vest, James K. Jones, and Pettigrew, mostly Democrats. To them, the only hope of preventing an evil imperialistic policy lay in defeating ratification of the

---

[14] Towne to Teller, Dec. 16, 1898, Teller MSS.
[15] New York *Journal*, Dec. 10, 1898.

treaty, or at least amending it so as to make the Philippines immediately independent.

Between these groups were a number of senators belonging to both parties who were favorable toward expansion on more traditional lines. They favored, in general, some kind of a protectorate policy for the new territories, with a large degree of control over local affairs in charge of the local government. There was a strong tendency for this group—to which Teller belonged—to vote with the anti-expansionists in placing restrictions in the form of reservations or accompanying resolutions about the treaty before its ratification. As the contest developed this became strategically impossible because of the administration's control of the situation. The Fifty-fifth Congress would end on March 4, and a special session of the Senate of the new Congress would, with its substantial Republican majority, quickly ratify the treaty. Joint or concurrent resolutions passed by the Senate qualifiying the ratification, or reservations added to the treaty itself, would meet speedy opposition in the House or at the hands of President McKinley. Nevertheless, the strong anti-imperialist group held out for modification or no ratification.

Before the treaty reached the Senate, the debate on imperialism began with a resolution introduced by Vest, declaring that the United States had no constitutional power to acquire territory. On December 20, Teller delivered a speech on this resolution that is a notable summary of his beliefs regarding expansion. He addressed himself first to the constitutional question, concluding that the right was "a prerogative of nationality." The principle of the Teller resolution, he held, applied to all the territories formerly Spanish and not to Cuba alone, which had been named specifically. It did not mean immediate absolute independence, but rather American assistance in establishing self-government and control by the United States of their foreign relations.

I have not felt that distrust and that fear which seem to prevail among some of our countrymen. I have more confidence in the good sense of the American people than to believe that we are about to adopt a policy of dealing with these countries that threatens the death of the Republic or even great danger to it.

Asked specifically about the Philippines, Teller replied:

I have some delicacy in suggesting what the form of government should be, because conditions may change; but I should say it is our first duty to consult the Filipinos and to aggregate in a body politic as many of them as we can who are capable of self government.

These he would give control of their local government, and he estimated that more than half the people of Luzon were capable of self-government. It would be a "moral duty" and an "obligation upon the people of the United States in their legislation . . . to keep in mind the fundamental principles which underlie free government." In regard to a possible war between the Filipino troops under Aguinaldo and the American forces in Manila, Teller observed:

> The way to avoid war is to consult these people. The way to get war is to attempt to force a government upon them by our people and not a government of their own by themselves. I am not in favor of a war on these people. I want to avoid war.[16]

This speech was the opening of Teller's efforts to bring to the support of ratification of the peace treaty all the votes in the Senate that were available, for a bitter fight was pending. He was cutting away from many of his associates on these related questions. Pettigrew was violently opposed to expansion and would fight this treaty. Dubois, although out of the Senate, was also an anti-imperialist, as were many other Populists and most of the Silver Democrats. Bryan had come out against imperialism, but urged ratification of the peace treaty in order to get the war itself out of the way, and then make a fight for independence of the Philippines. Teller's position, while similar, was not the same, for it did not include unqualified independence, and his strong support of keeping control of the Philippines at this time may well have lost him the Democratic nomination for Vice-President in 1900. This split within his own ranks Teller found very uncomfortable. Every political move of importance he had made since 1896 had been aimed at a second contest over free coinage in 1900. If these forces were to be split by the new issue, it would be a sad defeat indeed. Probably the best picture of his own mind is contained in a letter to Bryan, written a month after this speech, when the fight over ratification was bitter and close in the Senate.

> The situation here is not encouraging but I see no way to improve it at this time. Gorman is leading the fight on the ratification of the treaty with his usual tactics and seems to have captured the Democrats of the Senate. Morgan, Pettus, Faulkner, Gray and Lindsay are all the Democrats we are quite sure of, although there are some others we think will vote for the treaty. We had every reason to suppose Senator Daniel would, but of late he appears uncertain. Senator

---

[16] *Congressional Record*, 55 Cong., 3 Sess., pp. 325-30.

Faulkner has usually followed Gorman, but he assured me a few days since that he would vote for the treaty. Senator Bacon is quite inclined to support the treaty and will if some declaration can be made in the line of my speech made some time since, but the Republicans feeling that they have command of the situation and can prevent a rejection of the treaty by postponement by a vote of the Senate or by the Presidential withdrawal and re-submission, will not consent to what they profess they are in favor of.

I do not believe the treaty will be ratified before the 4th of March but it cannot be amended or rejected—this, all the opponents of it agree. If I am right about this, the President will call an extra session of the Senate and the treaty will be ratified just as soon as the Republicans want it. I am not quite sure the Republicans want to ratify it as this session. If not ratified the war goes on with the regular army consisting of 62,000 men instead of 27,000. All the pets of the administration holding positions in the Army or in positions made necessary by reasons of the existence of the war, will be kept in place, and all the advantages of the war, even if it is only a technical state of war enures to the benefit of our opponents, all of which they appreciate.

The danger of collision with the insurgents is increased by delay, but if there shall be a collision brought on by the insurgents attacking our troops, war will be carried on against them, and that, too, with the approval of the American people, for they will support the government in war even if they doubt the wisdom of its conduct. But, if the treaty is delayed and trouble arises in the Philippines or elsewhere, we are charged with it. Should there be trouble with the insurgents and we have some reverses in the Philippines, of which I think there is no great danger, our case will be still worse, for whatever befalls us it will be charged to the delay in concluding peace. Someone will figure up the great expense that the government has been put to by the delay by failure to ratify the treaty and all this will make good campaign material in 1900. But one of the worst features of the case is that if the Democratic party can be put in the attitude of continuing the war it will put the Republican party in a position to carry out the ideas of some of them at least, who wish to ignore the people of the Philippines and govern them from here, because the attitude of the Democrats on the treaty will discredit them when they attack the republican policy.

I have not written you this because I think you can change the situation here. I do not believe it can be done by anyone or by all of us.

I want to add that it appears to me that there is great danger of giving our opponents a lease of power for years to come and we certainly will if the Democrats are foolish enough to follow Gorman.[17]

Teller feared that the Democrats would prevent ratification, until an outbreak in the Philippines would put them in a position where Republican orators and newspapers could lay the blame upon them. In fact, they did not need to wait for an actual outbreak. Dolliver, of Iowa, informed the House of Representatives: "If it is necessary to use

---

[17] Jan. 20, 1899, Bryan MSS.

force in the Philippines it will be due to the almost treason-
able utterance in this Chamber, inviting a barbarous nation
to oppose the Government of the United States."[18] An outbreak furnished the final incentive to bring the treaty its
required majority. Ten Democrats, the Populists, Allen,
Butler, Harris, and Kyle, Jones, Stewart, Mantle, and Teller,
all voted with the Republicans for ratification, while two
Populists and Pettigrew voted with a majority of the Democrats against it.

Imperialism was an issue, and against Teller's fondest
wishes would become so important that it would dominate
the campaign of 1900.[19] After the contest was over, he wrote
to Sayre:

I think the Democrats made a great mistake in opposing the
ratification of the treaty, but that party lacks *leaders* just now. I think
Gorman thought he could demonstrate that he and not Bryan is the
democratic leader.[20]

The problem of holding the fusion silver parties together
until the campaign of 1900 was made much more difficult.
Furthermore, the Republican majority in the Senate after
March 4 would enable that party for the first time since repeal to force legislation through the Senate that would injure
the free-coinage cause. This possibility stimulated the gold
press to demand some legislation to carry out the monetary
plank of 1896. It is doubtful that the platform in question
promised any legislation beyond that looking toward an international agreement, but with the party control established, and interest in the monetary issue at low ebb, some
action was possible. It would be the last fight against the
gold standard in Teller's generation.

---

[18] New York *Journal*, Jan. 27, 1899. Hearst's jingo newspaper had made similar
statements earlier in the month. On Jan. 6, it pointed out that the first shot fired in
the Philippines would make "domestic oppositions to the measures of our Government
overt treason." On Jan. 11, an editorial entitled "The Traitors at Home," pointed out:
"If bloodshed shall come of all this ... it will be these unpatriotic mischief makers
[anti-expansionists] on whom the blame will rest."

[19] *Congressional Record*, 55 Cong., 3 Sess., p. 1301.

[20] Feb. 11, 1899, Sayre MSS.

CHAPTER XXI

THE LAST FIGHT FOR SILVER
1899-1901

TELLER spent the summer and fall of 1899 traveling about Colorado and the other mining states, as had been his custom during most of his years in the Senate. It was not with any expectation of victories that he looked forward to the opening of the new Congress in December, 1899. His own influence in the Senate would be weakened by the absence of Cannon and Mantle, and in the House the Silver Republicans had been reduced to two members, unless we count Newlands of Nevada as one. Prices had continued to rise and gold production to increase, and the silver cause was being forgotten. Colorado made the great gold-mining region of Cripple Creek into a separate county that year, and with unrecognized irony named it Teller County.

The immediate problem Teller faced in Congress was the monetary legislation threatened by the administration. There was no doubt that the Republican leaders had counted their votes in both houses and knew what could be enacted. House bill No. 1 provided for a close approximation of the monetary and banking legislation that the Indianapolis conference had sponsored. The Republican majority in the Senate was easily sufficient to enact it, provided they could maintain a fair degree of party unity on the question. The leaders realized that they probably could pass the House bill, but to do so would weaken the chances of re-election of the Western Republican senators. For that reason, perhaps, they reported from the finance committee a substitute that dropped most of the questionable banking features of the House bill, and prepared to make the Senate contest center principally upon the proposal to make gold the legal standard in the United States. For the most part the Republican senators refused to discuss the banking features of the House bill.

Teller led the fight against the bill in what was to be the last debate over bimetallism in his generation. It lacked the fire of former discussions, because it was realized by everyone that no return to a bimetallic standard was possible in the near future. Teller had to admit there was no immediate, but only a future, danger in the gold standard.

If the great output of gold continues for a few years the evil day will be deferred, but when it will cease—because in the history of the world it has always ceased ... there will be discovered in the business world a sliding scale toward lower prices.

In justification of their past struggles for free coinage, Teller defended the record of the silver men:

We were making our fight against the destruction of silver as money upon ... a theory that the scientific men of the world never doubted or questioned until prejudice and passion compelled them to belie history and science and declare that the quantitative theory was not a correct one. . . .

We were justified, Mr. President. Gold had been decreasing year by year for many years. Nobody knew that the great gold fields of Africa would produce what they are producing. Nobody knew that Cripple Creek ... would produce $20,000,000 in a year, with a fair prospect of doubling in the next year. Nobody knew that the Klondike would send us down twenty-five or thirty million dollars of gold and with a prospect of sending us three or four times that amount. Nobody believed that the gold product of the world would go to $300,000,000. You who contended for the destruction of silver money declared over and over again that there was gold enough and you did not want any more.[1]

Party discipline was complete except for Chandler, of New Hampshire, the most sincere of the international bimetallists, who was now throwing away his senatorial career much as Cameron had done four years before. Teller brought forward a series of amendments. One of them was for a strong affirmative declaration that the Government would work for an international agreement for bimetallism. The Republican lines held tight except for Chandler, and it was voted down. Next, Teller proposed declaratory statements of policy, first offering the Republican plank of 1892, and then the 1896 plank of the Republican Party in Ohio, but the Republicans refused them all. The committee's substitute for the House bill was adopted. Wolcott, Shoup, and other Western Republicans who had remained in the party in 1896 voted with it now on every issue, protesting that they were bimetallists and this bill was in the ultimate interest of that policy! The measure of the change in the Senate on the issue is the majority of seventeen for the bill as compared with one of fifteen for the Teller resolution of two years before.

There had not been a great deal of public interest in the

---

[1] *Congressional Record*, 56 Cong., 1 Sess., pp. 902-07, 942-48, 1340-44, 1764-71, 1819-1922, 2525.

gold-standard bill, as it was apparent to nearly all that imperialism would be the real issue of the coming campaign.
Teller hoped it would not be, and no doubt his hope guided
his judgment a great deal during the first six months of
1900. On that question he was in an embarrassing position,
which became more pronounced as the issue became more
pointed. In the first place, he was an expansionist, and as
the Democrats came more and more to oppose retention of
the Philippines, he was obviously cut off by his own opinion
and his record from complete co-operation with them. And
yet, too, in December of 1899, the Republicans in the Senate
for the most part were not openly advocating colonial
policies to which he was seriously opposed. The warfare that
had broken out in the Philippines just before the ratification
of the treaty of Paris had continued through 1899 and
showed only slight evidence of any immediate conclusion.
Unlike the more aggressive imperialists, Teller thought it
possible to come to some peaceful understanding with the
Filipinos, but, pending that, the war must go on until American control was established. When Senator Hoar asked him
if he did not think that the Teller Resolution would have
been passed if it had included the Philippines as well as
Cuba, Teller answered that it undoubtedly would have: " ...
it is one of the regrets of my life that I did not draw the
resolution broad enough to cover the present case." But he
was not yet willing to take any action that would embarrass
the administration in establishing peace there. He accused
the anti-imperialists of seeing a danger that did not exist.
He did not believe that public opinion in the United States
would support such ideas as the extreme imperialists, like
Beveridge and Lodge, were advocating.[2]

As the question of governing the new regions came
before Congress, Teller's opposition to the Republicans was
emphasized to an extent that made his alliance with the
opposition at least more comfortable. Legally he stood with
the Republicans; the Constitution did not follow the flag
until such time as Congress saw fit to extend it. He had
defended this position the year before and repeated it now
as the sound old Republican doctrine, supported by Lincoln
and opposed only by the Dred Scott decision. When the proposed government for Hawaii came before the Senate, he
appealed for more power to be given to the Islanders. He
wanted their governor to be a resident of the Islands and

---

[2] *Ibid.*, pp. 1315-16, 1333.

to have the power to appoint the judges that would man the courts. Here, as would be expected, he used his own experience under the territorial form of government to make his case. The Hawaiians, he held, were a fine, dependable people and completely capable of self-government.[3]

His position on the Foraker Act for the government of Porto Rico was similar. The people in this island were ready for self-government; they were similar in character and tradition to the inhabitants of New Mexico, and should be treated in a like manner. He did not favor making Porto Rico or the Philippines an integral part of the United States as yet, but did favor giving them charge of their local government. He introduced an amendment to permit the inhabitants of Porto Rico to govern themselves under a constitution acceptable to the President of the United States, and making the population "citizens of Porto Rico."[4]

All this opposition was to little purpose as the campaign drew nearer, and Teller began to retreat to some extent from his support of the administration in the Philippines. He had been mistaken, he told the Senate, in his belief that the administration did not intend to govern the dependencies with "imperial power."

The anti-administration senators who had voted to ratify the treaty of Paris would never have done so had they suspected that the administration would move in this imperial direction to the extent that was now evident. He would oppose the Republican Party in the approaching campaign on that issue, even if it were right on the financial question.[5]

With the silver issue dead for all immediate purposes, the tendency for the Silver Republicans to rejoin the regulars increased. The question of imperialism added drive to this, as it was clear that the Silver Republicans were not agreed, and probably the majority of them were expansionists. It would have been fairly easy for Teller to have gone back at this time, were it not for his own intellectual and emotional antagonism, and the denunciatory speeches he had made against that organization. In fact, the pressure in Colorado was great, and Wolcott was predicting that by 1902, when Teller would come up for re-election, he would either be re-elected as a Republican or not at all.[6]

---

[3] *Ibid.*, pp. 1922-24, 2180, 2187.
[4] *Ibid.*, pp. 2471-72, 2654-58, 3874-75.
[5] *Ibid.*, pp. 6514-15.
[6] Dawson, *Wolcott*, I, 271.

Teller felt keenly his lack of agreement with the Democrats on expansion, but refused to let it interfere with what had been his fixed purpose since 1896. Then, too, his long study and advocacy of bimetallism had changed his way of thinking about public questions; he had come to recognize more clearly than ever before the disguised class purposes of seemingly innocent political action, and, as between the Republicans under Hanna, and the Democrats under Bryan, he had no doubt where he belonged. He was not nearly as radical as his colleague, Pettigrew, who was now sponsoring a bill for the Government ownership of railroads, but he was still further from the legislative program of the Hanna-Aldrich leadership in the Senate. The South Dakota senator, with vast courage and considerable vindictiveness, was a constant gadfly to the administration forces, and on several occasions groups of administration senators attempted to cow him by denunciation and epithet. He even made an attack on Hanna's right to his seat in the Senate, introducing unpleasant evidence that stirred the Republican leader's anger to a white heat. On several instances Teller had rushed to Pettigrew's aid when administration leaders seemed about to squelch him, but the South Dakotan was not easily suppressed.

Shortly before the session of Congress closed for the campaign, Teller followed up one of his defenses of Pettigrew by unloosing an attack upon the armor-plate purchase feature of an appropriation bill that showed clearly how he evaluated the Republican leadership. The controversy was over the price to be paid the steelmakers for armor plate, the Senate in general insisting on one price, and Hanna, Penrose, and Elkins defending the steelmakers in their demand for a higher one. The alternative that Teller favored was to offer a certain price, and if that were not accepted, then the Government would build a plant to make its own armor plate. In spite of the opposition of some regulars, Hanna and Penrose were carrying their point. Teller declared:

The Senator's proposition is a disgraceful proposition ... it is either cowardly ... or it indicates that somewhere there is corruption.... The American people will believe, and ... I believe, that a great political organization in this country hopes to make a profit ... by giving this combine an unreasonable price.

Referring to the past dealings with the same steel companies, he described the plate they had sold the Government as "full of blow holes, filled up with grease and putty and with ashes." "If you want to give more," Teller declared looking at Hanna, "give it like men; stand up and say, 'We believe the exigencies of the party require us to yield.' "[7] Teller's reasons for staying out of the Republican Party were now clear, and he was old enough to afford the luxury of speaking his mind.

Nevertheless, the Silver Republicans as a group faced a serious problem as the election of 1900 approached. The developments of the past four years were leaving them with only two choices: join either the Republicans or the Democrats. The radicalism of the Democratic platform of 1896, irrespective of free coinage, was driving the wealthier business interests into the Republican Party in the West as in the East. Governor Thomas wrote Bryan late in 1899 to record happenings of a type not confined to Colorado alone.

I regret to say that our old friend [W. S.] Stratton has at last become joined to his idols, and is no longer with us or of us. He went to London last February, sold his mines for $11,000,000, returned to Colorado about three months ago, and is the most uncompromising single standard man imaginable. Indeed, it seems impossible in this State for any man with an independent fortune to refrain from allying himself with the republican party. It is to my mind one of the most ominous signs of the times, and means a great deal for the politics of the near future. Governor Grant, Mr. Dennis Sullivan, Captain Campbell and a number of other Democrats who were ardently with us a year ago are, if I am creditably informed, now with the opposition.[8]

In Montana the powerful copper interests, like business elsewhere, were opposed to Bryan when not to Democrats as a whole, and other large interests grouped themselves similarly.[9]

As far as national politics were concerned, the Silver Republicans and Populists were agreed upon Bryan for president again; but the sore spots that had been left by the fusion and attempted fusion in the past four years had made innumerable antagonisms that still rankled. The Western Democratic organizations not unnaturally took the cream of the offices, and in some states such as Montana and Utah refused, for the most part, to give the Silver Republicans any share in the spoils. This refusal had largely contributed to driving Dubois, Hartman, and Cannon out of

[7] Congressional Record, 56 Cong., 1 Sess., pp. 6364, 6705, 6788-90.
[8] Dec. 22, 1899, Bryan MSS.
[9] Thomas H. Patterson to Bryan, Sept. 13, 1898, June 9, 1899, Bryan MSS.

public life, and a vast number of lesser lights back into the
Republican Party. "The treatment of their allies in these
north-western States by the Democracy is very trying on the
rank and file," Dubois had written Bryan after the election
of 1898.[10]

Teller had already resolved all doubts as to what his
organization in Colorado would do, although the old problem
of fusion on the state ticket was threatening to disrupt
it badly. Late in April there was a meeting in Denver of
Silver Republican delegates from the state, and A. M. Stevenson wired Teller for the group, asking for suggestions
for resolutions and indicating that one would surely be
passed against fusion on the state ticket without getting the
governorship for their party. In a fairly direct sense it was
an ultimatum on the part of some of the Silver Republicans
that without a larger share of offices on the fusion ticket they
were going to rejoin the regular Republicans. Teller's suggestions were unmistakable:

> Considering our former position and the course of the Republican
> party in the present Congress on financial matters we cannot think of
> any alliance with that party. To operate separately is to aid them
> indirectly. The resolutions should be strong for our financial position;
> condemnatory of the Republican party's course during this session and
> favorable to the fusion of all silver forces on fair and just terms.

Later in the day he again telegraphed, stating he did
not think it "advisable to make any specific demand upon
the Democratic party for position with threats."[11]

In order to save his organization nationally Teller appealed to Bryan for assistance. He detailed instances of the
refusal of the Democratic organization in Denver to co-
operate with the Silver Republicans and Populists.

> The complaint that is made in Colorado against the democrats is
> made in every state where there is a silver republican organization.
> We are told that the democrats of Colorado do not intend to unite with
> the silver republicans or populists but to put a ticket in the field and
> that we can support it or not as we please. . . . That this class is largely
> composed of cheap politicians or democratic boodlers who have repub-
> lican money in their pockets is quite true, and it is equally true that
> men like Governor Thomas are for fusion, as are the rank and file. The
> chances are that these politicians will control the conventions and de-
> feat fusion. . . . I am assured by Colorado democrats in whom I have

---

[10] Dec. 19, 1898, Bryan MSS.

[11] Clippings from the Denver *Times*, March 24, 1900, Dawson Scrapbook; Stevenson
to Teller, April 26, Teller to Stevenson (copy), April 27, 1900, Teller MSS.

full confidence that there will be no fusion unless you make the democratic rank and file understand that you desire it.... I want to add that whatever is done should be done early.[12]

A large faction of the Populists was threatening to have its own presidential ticket in the field, and on every consideration it was desirable that some gesture of conciliation, like the vice-presidential nomination, be made by the Democrats. If the contest were going to be over the same issues as in 1896, that would not be difficult, and even the trust question would not complicate it, but the expansion issue would, and did. "If Teller had not made his absurd speech on expansion," Chairman Jones of the Democratic National Committee wrote to Bryan regarding the vice-presidential nomination, "I would believe him to be the best man, but that shuts him out of course."[13] A campaign against expansion would be made to look foolish if one of the candidate's speeches could be quoted for it as Teller's could. Pettigrew wrote Dubois:

Teller is an expansionist, and of course will be of no value in this campaign. I would not have him in my State for any sum of money and you had better avoid him also. He is a dear splendid old fellow, but he does not agree with us on anything but silver.[14]

While Pettigrew exaggerated the difference within the group—for the only substantial difference was on expansion—still it was obvious that Teller's usefulness to the fusion campaign in 1900 would not be very great outside of Colorado.

Eventually those who wanted to conciliate the smaller of the silver parties attempted to secure the vice-presidential nomination for Charles A. Towne. Although there was danger that his nomination would emphasize the silver issue to a degree that was strategically undesirable, that danger was not too great, for he had taken an active part in the public discussion of expansion that put himself in the same position as Bryan.

The Populist National Convention would meet earlier than the others, and whatever action was to be taken needed to be outlined before it met. It was to meet in Sioux Falls, Pettigrew's home, and the South Dakota senator had become very active in the affairs of that party in his state,

[12] March 10, 1900, Bryan MSS.
[13] Nov. 24, 1899, Bryan MSS.
[14] March 8, 1900, Pettigrew MSS.

which was not distinct from the Silver Republican. The Silver Republicans, the Populist leaders in Washington, and many Democrats were favorable toward Towne's nomination on the same ticket with Bryan, but the strategy of naming him at Sioux Falls was questioned by many; for if it were done and the Democrats named someone else it would create the same difficulties that the separate vice-presidential nomination of the Populists had in 1896.[15]

At Sioux Falls were gathered nearly all of the important leaders of the Populists: Weaver, Simpson, Patterson, and Senators Allen, Butler, and Pettigrew. A platform was adopted, and Bryan nominated for president without a break in the procedure. On the crucial question of the vice-president three plans were presented: to nominate a candidate; to nominate a list of five acceptable candidates for the information of the other two conventions; or to leave the nomination to a committee. Patterson, chairman of the convention, Weaver, Allen, and Simpson all favored the committee procedure, and Towne had advised some of his friends that he considered it the most desirable. But the demand for a nominee of their own on the part of the delegates, supported by Pettigrew and Butler, was too strong for the majority of the leaders, and the alternatives were voted down. Towne was nominated on the first ballot; for even those who did not want a nomination preferred Towne to any other of the several candidates.[16]

The Republican National Convention met next, with Wolcott serving as temporary chairman, and renominated McKinley, with Theodore Roosevelt as his running mate.

The Democratic and Silver Republican conventions were scheduled to meet in Kansas City on July 4. The Eastern Democrats had been exercising their influence upon Democrats everywhere to drop the silver issue and make the campaign on imperialism and anti-trust legislation. Their compromise was to have the convention endorse the Chicago platform in general terms, and not mention silver specifically. Bryan was opposed to this, as were most of the Western Democrats, but harmony talk to reunite the conservatives to the party was potent as the conventions met. When Teller arrived in Kansas City on July 2, with that discussion in the air, he announced that failure to make a

---

[15] Pettigrew to Towne, Feb. 14, 18, May 1, 1900, Pettigrew MSS.; Kansas City *Times*, May 7, 1900.

[16] Kansas City *Times*, May 9-12, 1900; Fred Emory Haynes, *James Baird Weaver* (Iowa City, 1919), pp. 391-94.

definite declaration would result in "utter defeat" in the election.[17]

On July 4, the Silver Republicans convened, with a large number of delegates from surrounding states, and good-sized delegations from most of the Western states. In all, "upwards of 1,000 delegates" were in attendance.[18] Teller served as temporary chairman of the convention and delivered a long address on the political situation and the financial question. He was named to head a committee to "present" Towne's name to the Democratic convention for the vice-presidential nomination.

A platform was next reported to the convention from its committee on resolutions. This brief document, as platforms go, stated the party's position for bimetallism, endorsed a graduated income tax, direct election of senators, civil service reform, anti-trust laws, statehood for the Territories, the initiative and referendum, and national aid for reclamation projects. It expressed sympathy for the Boers in their struggle against Great Britain, denounced the Porto Rican tariff, declared it favored applying the principle of the Teller Resolution to the Philippines, and that it "observed with satisfaction" the growing sentiment toward public ownership of utilities. It was a more radical document than the Democratic platform, and it indicated how far the group had moved away from the parent Republican Party. It was adopted by acclamation. There had been trouble, it seems, only over the plank on imperialism, the Westerners not wanting the strong denunciation the Easterners supported. As finally phrased, it read:

> Our creed and our history justify the nations of the earth in expecting that wherever the American flag is unfurled in authority, human liberty and political freedom will be found. We protest against the adoption of any policy that will change, in the thought of the world, the meaning of our flag. We insist that it shall never float over any vessel or wave at the head of any column directed against the political independence of any people or any race.[19]

In the meantime, the committee to present Towne's name to the Democratic convention was not having an easy time. Harmony was the spirit of the Democratic gathering. Towne had substantial support there; in fact, he had more

---

[17] New York *Daily Tribune*, July 3, 1900.

[18] Kansas City *Star*, July 7, 1900. Teller's temporary chairmanship of the Silver Republican convention gave a chairmanship to each of Colorado's leading politicians. Patterson, Wolcott, Teller, and Thomas all served as either temporary or permanent chairmen of each of the four conventions: Populist, Republican, Silver Republican, and Democrat.

[19] St. Louis *Republic*, July 6, 1900.

pledged delegates than anyone else when the convention began. "It is Towne against the field. And the chances are in favor of the field," Walter Williams summarized in the Kansas City *Times* on July 5, noting that the Democratic leaders were strongly inclined to name someone who would appeal to factions not friendly to Bryan. After the Eastern delegates rather gracefully accepted a direct reaffirmation of the monetary plank of 1896, the desire to name a ticket more acceptable to them increased and worked against Towne.

While this was still hanging fire in the Democratic convention, Teller placed Bryan in nomination for the presidency in the Silver Republican convention, and he was chosen unanimously. That convention then adjourned until the afternoon to await the action of the Democratic meeting upon the vice-presidential nomination. On the first ballot the Democrats named Adlai E. Stevenson, who had been vice-president in Cleveland's second administration. The Silver Republican delegates returned to their convention hall in an ugly temper. All the bitterness that had carried over from the attempts at fusion during the past four years now came to the surface. When a delegate placed Stevenson in nomination for vice-president, he was howled down by cries of "We want Towne!" A delegate nominated him, and a chorus of seconds rose from the floor of the convention. At this juncture Teller arrived on the platform and took the floor. He faced the howling delegates with an appeal to reason. Such a procedure would repeat the Populist fiasco of 1896, and destroy the effectiveness of the campaign.

We have been disappointed; we have been aggrieved; but let us act with deliberation.... No man living should stand in the way of this cause.... This is not a scramble for place, but a fight for liberty. Who is Charley Towne, or any other man?

He pleaded in vain; they were not inclined to listen, and he was howled down in the convention of the party he had fathered. He was an old man, tired and hoarse with much speaking, and could no longer fight as he once had. Towne arrived and took Teller's place for a similar plea, and finally a motion by Dubois to leave the question of the vice-presidential nomination to the national committee carried.[20] The convention was over.

[20] Kansas City *Star*, July 7; Kansas City *Times*, July 7; New York *Daily Tribune*, July 7, 1900; William Jennings Bryan, *The Second Battle* (Chicago, 1900), pp. 9-38, 239-48.

The next day the committee nominated Stevenson, and selected Teller with two others as the organization's representatives upon the Democratic National Committee. Later Towne withdrew as the nominee of the Populists.

There was a hard prospect ahead of Teller in Colorado, made more difficult by the defeat of Towne, and by the evident fact that the Silver Republicans were bound for eventual union with the Democrats. In August, A. M. Stevenson, who had been a loyal supporter of Teller since the bolt of 1896, announced that he was going over to the regulars, and with him went the others who would not be reconciled to permanent opposition.[21] Stevenson's rejoining the Republicans was symptomatic of the drift of the state. Wolcott would be up for re-election in the next legislature, and he was bending all his energy to carry the state, supported by unusual aid from the administration, which wanted to carry the state for McKinley only slightly more than it wanted Wolcott to retain his seat.

The fight over the Senate position complicated the fight of the fusion forces. The Democratic leaders in the state were almost without exception candidates for the place, and that made them opponents of any fusion with the Silver Republicans and Populists; for fusion would probably mean that Thomas M. Patterson would be Wolcott's successor. Patterson was still classifying himself as a Populist, but his work in keeping the pro-silver forces together and in bringing them success had earned for him the reward of the senatorship. Some of the Democrats had begun early to lay grounds for a straight ticket in the state that would permit one of them to go to the Senate.[22]

The conventions of the three groups were held at the same time in Denver, but after conference committees from each convention had met, the Democratic committee held out for fusion only on their own terms, which the Populists and Silver Republicans refused. When this impasse was reached, Teller and Patterson demanded recognition in the Democratic convention, took the platform, and pled for fusion on a basis fair to the smaller parties. In a remarkable political reversal, the Democratic delegates repudiated their own leaders and agreed to accept the terms the smaller parties offered. The Democrats were to have the governor

---

[21] Denver *Post*, Aug. 13, 1900.

[22] Thomas J. Maloney, to Bryan, Sept. 29, 1899, Bryan MSS.; C. S. Thomas to Dawson, no date, 1900, Teller MSS.

and auditor, and the Silver Republicans and the Populists the remaining places.[23] Teller's own account of the convention was related to Dawson immediately afterwards:

We have had a three days convention and after much tribulation we have secured a fusion that I believe is quite acceptable as was the fusion of 1898. . . . Mr. Patterson and I appeared before the democratic convention and made speeches in behalf of fusion and the rank and file took the case out of the hands of the Committee and against the wishes of Thomas, Hughes, Adams, and Maloney gave to us the fusion that we proposed. . . . The vote was more than two to one in favor of our proposition which was a victory of the rank and file over the bosses and indicates very plainly that the democrats of this state are for fusion and that too on fair terms. Say to Mr. Bryan that I do not think there is any possibility of the republicans carrying either the state ticket or the legislature.

"It was a hard fight Tom," the assistant secretary added at the bottom of the letter, "& if it had not been for the Senator [we] would have lost."[24]

Teller was not available for speeches outside of Colorado, for a better reason than that his record on expansion was not in line with the Democratic platform, and that was that the contest in Colorado required all his ability and energy. The Republican campaign committee sent into the state its leading campaigners, headed by Theodore Roosevelt and including several Republican members of the Senate. More important than these perhaps, it sent the former Kansas Populist, Peffer, and Senator William M. Stewart, of Nevada, both recently returned to the bosom of the Republican Party. Supported by abundant campaign funds and the local candidates they made a strenuous contest.[25]

Wolcott saw clearly as did the others that he could not win, nor carry Colorado for McKinley either, but a strong showing would put the Republicans in a position to contest the state two years hence, and on that Wolcott centered his party's campaign. Teller never worked harder. He wrote on September 24:

The last three weeks have been busy ones. I have done more political figuring and caucus work than I have done in all of my political service and I am sick of it. Our fusion is all right, our candidates on the whole are all right, a few might have been improved, but we can elect the ticket.[26]

[23] Kansas City *Star*, Sept. 13, 1900.
[24] Teller to Dawson, Sept. 13, 1900, Teller MSS.
[25] Teller to Dawson, Sept. 30, 1900, Teller MSS.
[26] Teller to Dawson, Teller MSS.

As far as the campaign was concerned Teller stuck to national issues, and tried to keep the financial question uppermost. He declared in opening the campaign:

If there is a man in the United States today who comes near to Abraham Lincoln, that man is William J. Bryan. . . . I say Bryanism is Americanism and if we could have less Hannaism and more Bryanism we should be better off.[27]

The Republicans denied that there was any financial question, and talked expansion and "Our boys in the Philippines."[28] The miners at Victor, Colorado, refused to let Lodge, Roosevelt, and Wolcott speak, and violence marked the balloting in Denver.

The fusion ticket won in Colorado, but by greatly reduced majorities, re-electing Shafroth and Bell to Congress and winning a safe majority in the legislature. Over the nation Bryan was defeated by greater majorities than in 1896. Utah, Wyoming, South Dakota, Kansas, Nebraska, and Washington, states that had voted for him four years before, now were carried by McKinley. Hanna secured his personal revenge on Pettigrew by defeating him badly in South Dakota. Chandler, the lone Eastern silver supporter in the Senate, also went down to defeat.

There were some compensations. Patterson was elected to the Senate in place of Wolcott, and although Teller's personal relations with the latter had stayed on very friendly terms, the result must have gratified the senior statesman. Dubois, now with the united support of the fusionists in Idaho, was elected to the Senate over Shoup. Towne received a small windfall when, on the death of Senator Davis, Governor Lind appointed him to the United States Senate for a few brief days. These were the only consolations.

One thing was certain. There was no longer any purpose in maintaining the Silver Republican Party. Those former members who would not co-operate with the Democrats had already drifted back into the Republican fold. The issue upon which it was founded had become of so little significance that it was futile to keep up a separate organization. Had it been a personal matter with Teller, the Silver Republicans would not have maintained a separate party as long as they did. As long as the Western and Southern elements maintained control of the Democratic Party, it was as much

[27] Dawson Scrapbook.
[28] Denver *Republican*, Oct. 9, 1900; Dawson, *Wolcott*, I, 282-84, II, 414-21.

in line with his own policies as the Republican Party had ever been. Republican policies on most questions that had come up since 1896 had served to alienate Teller further from that party. The Silver Republican platform of 1900 was much closer to the Democratic and Populist than it was to the Republican, even on issues other than finance. As far as Colorado was concerned, Teller had been on reasonably friendly terms with the Democratic leaders since 1896. They had supported him for the presidency at Chicago in 1896, and Towne for the vice-presidency at Kansas City in 1900. More than that, the state convention of 1900 had proved that the local leaders of the Democrats would follow Teller readily, and he had no reason to fear that he would lose the support of any organization by ending the pretense of maintaining a separate party. It was from every angle the sensible move to make.

When the Fifty-sixth Congress ended on March 4, 1901, an address to the Silver Republicans was issued, setting forth the advisability of uniting permanently with the reformed Democratic Party. It was signed by Dubois, Towne, Cannon, Hartman, Shafroth, and Senator George Turner, of Washington, in addition to Teller. Teller also announced that when Congress reassembled he would take a seat on the Democratic side. Commented the Washington *Star:*

He will look a little out of place there for a while. . . . From his old seat he has delivered many a scathing arraignment of the democratic party, and within the hearing of some of the men with whom he is now to touch partisan elbows. So when from his new seat he fires back on his old friends the spectacle will be interesting.[29]

----

[29] March 9, 1901. There is a copy of the address in the Teller MSS.

CHAPTER XXII

BACK TO THE DECLARATION OF INDEPENDENCE
1901-03

NEITHER inwardly nor outwardly was there any marked change in Teller's life after transferring his party membership. That the Tellers became less active socially, and soon gave up their house in Washington and began to live in one of the hotels, was largely a result of their age and the absence of their children. Their social intercourse continued to be with their older friends, most of whom were Republicans, and many of whom were interested in the same causes to which Mrs. Teller devoted herself. Mrs. Teller continued her activities in the Methodist Episcopal Church, serving as president of its home missionary society for several years, and devoting considerable time to a newsboys' home in Baltimore. She was still, as she had been in the eighties, "in charitable work the head and front at the Capital."[1] As their older personal friends passed out of Washington life there were fewer social affairs in their home. Possibly it was somewhat old-fashioned in its atmosphere in the Washington after 1900, but it did attract the attention of observers. One woman visitor in the capital who was taken to call on Mrs. Teller, published an account of the visit:

I mention this call for there I encountered a different atmosphere from any I have yet met with. Such repose, such dignity, so much cordiality, and withal the utmost simplicity. I stayed a long, long time, and then was loath to leave, for I have never, since I came to Washington, been in a house where I felt more thoroughly at home, or which reminded me of the best one meets in England.[2]

Teller's office in the Capitol, which he held as a chairman of one of the less important Senate committees, was the "Washington headquarters for Coloradans," and in it during an average legislative day one would see nearly everyone from the state who was in Washington.[3]

Teller's political career after 1900 presents a sharp contrast to the earlier part. It was not only that his partisan associates were changed, but in a large measure his influence was gone also. The Republican majorities in both Senate

---

[1] Chapin, *American Court Gossip*, p. 227.
[2] Clipping in the Tyler MSS.
[3] Denver *Post*, Dec. 20, 1903. Clipping in the Dawson Scrapbook.

and House beginning in 1899, were continued throughout the rest of his senatorial career. Never, while he was in the Senate as a Democrat, was that party to be in the majority. Consequently no important committee chairmanships—the reward of long service for the majority—with the consequent attachment of the chairman's name to legislation were to fall to his lot. More deeply influential was the change in the character of the Senate itself. The safe Republican majorities revived the power of that party's caucus, and Senate legislation became in a large measure Republican caucus action, and the function of the minority became almost wholly one of criticism.

Teller's interests in legislation also shifted back somewhat toward purely local and sectional problems. Even the colonial policy on which he continued to be very active was in a sense an extension of his interest in the Western territories. From one standpoint he was in a much more satisfactory position than he had been in the past few years. Patterson's election to the Senate had given Teller a colleague who enjoyed the active political work in Colorado, and that together with the formal union of the Silver Republicans and Democrats would leave Teller free of the most bothersome part of a senatorial career.

With the single exception of Teller, Patterson was the only important political leader in Colorado who had been active before statehood. He had been a territorial delegate to Congress in 1875 and 1876, and a member of the House in 1877 and 1878. From then until 1901 he had not held public office, but his activity had not decreased, and the purchase and editorship of the *Rocky Mountain News* had served to increase this influence and to sharpen his sense of political values. Generous, warm-hearted, and somewhat quixotic, Patterson was an uncompromising foe of all privilege and corruption in public life. Since 1890 he and Teller had seen eye to eye on almost all public questions, but Patterson, possibly because he had been out of office, was far more ready to rush to the aid of the underprivileged, no matter where the contest might be or what its character was. Although the junior senator had come to the United States from Ireland as a young lad without resources, he had acquired a substantial fortune from the practice of criminal law and from fortunate investments. If his wealth influenced his orientation on public questions, it is not evident either in his own career or the conduct of the *News*. Not only did he sup-

Thomas M. Patterson—nicknamed "Old Perplexity"—Colorado senator and editor of the embattled *Rocky Mountain News.*

port the Colorado Populists, but he was the one uncompromising supporter of labor in his state in the numerous and bloody wars that labor fought against the forces of the mine owners and at times against the Government.

He was in close agreement with Teller on almost every question that was to come before Congress, and he brought to their support great courage and considerable eloquence. His support was inclined to be so enthusiastic that he threw caution to the winds, and as a result was frequently caught in an uncomfortable legislative situation, which opponents were not slow to utilize.[4] "Old Perplexity," his journalistic enemies in Colorado termed him, making sport of the owlish appearance given his face by the heavy glasses his myopia necessitated, and in Washington and in the Eastern Republican press he replaced Pettigrew as the butt of many denunciations of the anti-imperialists. He was unselfishly loyal to Teller, and rendered him invaluable aid in Colorado politics.

More and more, too, Teller's local interests were being cared for by Dawson, who, as his secretary, answered and signed a large amount of his mail and carried on a large political correspondence in his own name. Teller treated him well, trusted him implicitly, and Dawson responded with loyalty and unselfish service. It was a rare understanding that had developed between the reserved Senator and the warm, friendly secretary, and the association of the two had strengthened the Senator politically a great deal.[5] Some years before, Teller had added Clarence Northrup to his staff as an assistant secretary, and he, too, continued to be a faithful aid to both Teller and Dawson as long as the former was in the Senate.

After 1900, anti-imperialism came very definitely to replace bimetallism as the paramount issue in Teller's senatorial career. Yet his shift was slow, for when he first addressed the Senate on the question in 1901, he stated that he saw it as the duty of Congress to maintain the army in the Philippines as long as the administration desired. But he coupled this support with a denunciation of its policy in governing the island, and the character of the warfare being carried on there. "I take back what I said two years ago," he told the Senate. "Imperialism has come; it is there in its worst form.[6]

[4] Mary Fonda Adams, "Thomas M. Patterson: Some Aspects of His Political Career" (unpublished thesis, University of Colorado Library, 1933).

[5] E. M. Ammons, "Thomas F. Dawson," *Colorado Magazine* I (Nov., 1923), 3-8.

[6] *Congressional Record*, 56 Cong., 2 Sess., pp. 535-36.

The administration sponsored the Spooner Amendment to the army appropriation bill, establishing the unquestioned legal power of the President in governing the islands to grant franchises, to dispose of public lands, and the other necessary powers for capitalistic exploitation. It was too obvious in its purposes, however, and in that form the Democrats would not have let it pass in that session. Consequently, the majority radically modified it to limit the power of granting franchises to certain necessary types for a short period, and the granting of public lands was practically prohibited.[7] From the standpoint of personal rights, the amendment was still vicious in the eyes of the anti-imperialists. But attempts to change this were unsuccessful. Hoar's proposal promising eventual independence was overwhelmed by a large majority. Teller's milder suggestion promising local self-government was defeated by a slightly smaller majority. The Coloradan then presented an amendment taken from the Act of 1812 establishing Missouri Territory, that would guarantee to the Filipinos certain fundamental civil rights, but it was defeated by a vote of 23 to 41.

The issue was sending Teller back to the history of the American Revolution, and there was a great deal of its spirit in his opposition. On the question of passage of the revised amendment, Teller took the floor to read from the resolutions passed by the Continental Congress during the Revolution. "To say it now I have no doubt is treason, but it was patriotism and good law then." He did not overlook the Tory argument at that time, and, without making any personal applications, he quoted it at some length, and commented. "If there is not a familiar sound that we have heard for the last ninety days, then I have not ears to hear."[8] Unsatisfactory as the bill was, Teller informed the Republicans that the opposition would not insist that it go over to the next Congress, as the concessions the majority had made on the economic features were worth taking. In this rather innocuous form, as far as real exploitative power was concerned, the Spooner Amendment was adopted.

When the administration's Philippine tariff was before the Senate, Teller renewed his attacks of the year before upon the conduct of the army in the Philippines. In answer

---

[7] José S. Reyes, *Legislative History of America's Economic Policy Toward the Philippines* (New York, 1923), pp. 138-44.

[8] *Congressional Record*, 56 Cong., 2 Sess., 3107, 3137-40.

to the objections of Senator Lodge, Teller declared: "Every man who stood here and complained of the attitude of this government, who stood for what this country has always stood for, has been practically charged with treason." No crime committed by the American Government in the Philippines could be too great but that the same senators would defend it. He introduced evidence to show that the intention of the American imperialists in governing the Philippines was to imitate the British and Dutch in the Far East, and make no concessions to the principles of democracy. He confessed:

As an American, I cannot feel happy over the defeat of ... American arms. But I cannot but respect the people who believe that we are attempting to subject them and put upon them a government and a system of civilization that they dislike.... After all the man who, when he thinks his home is assailed, stands in front of it with his gun is a model of excellency the world over.

He proceeded to relate the evidences of brutality in the Philippines, and thereafter, as long as it was an issue, he continued to do so. He returned again and again to the history of America's revolution, to the resolutions of the Continental Congress, and to the debates in the British Parliament at the time of the Revolution. These he used to compare with the relations between the Philippines and the United States Government, and to appeal to the old American sentiments. He drew a parallel between the British use of Indians against the Colonists and the use of the Macabees in the Philippines against the other Filipinos. He pointed to the rapid spread of syphilis in the United States as a result of the occupation of the Philippines by American troops, and asked the imperialists if the results would be worth the cost. He singled out the disrepute the entire adventure left upon the American principles of democracy, as the worst result of the adventure.

Teller sponsored two amendments to the Philippine tariff. One attempted to put in effect in those islands the "Constitution and the laws of the United States which are not locally inapplicable." The second was a declaratory statement that it was not the intention to annex the Philippines "as an integral part of the United States," but merely to help them establish a government to control their local affairs, and eventually to give them independence. To that end the second amendment declared that the United States would at all times co-operate with the "peaceably disposed inhabitants." Both of these were voted down by an almost solid party vote.[9]

The Philippine government bill was brought up later when the warfare in the islands was nearly over. Although Teller had attacked its expected political features in the debate over the tariff, his emphasis now was on the economic clauses of the bill, particularly upon its provisions for the disposal of the public lands. Teller did not call it, as Patterson did, a bill "to make easy the exploitation of the Philippine Islands by American capital and American capitalists," but he pointed out that the provision allowing a corporation to acquire as much as five thousand acres of public land was there merely to facilitate its exploitation by outside capital. In this case it would encourage the development of large absentee-owned sugar plantations, which were not in the interest of the Filipino and would be directly competitive with American growers. If the committee did not drop the proposal, he threatened to force a direct vote on an amendment to eliminate it. He also pointed out that grants to individuals of one hundred and sixty acres was not in accordance with conditions prevailing in the Philippines, and that these might better be reduced to forty acres. Similar protests in the Senate and the press forced the Senate committee to make both changes, but the House replaced the provision for corporation grants, and in conference it was left in after a reduction of half in the acreage a corporation could acquire from the government.[10]

Teller was at his best in the debates over the Philippines, and next to Hoar, who as an otherwise regular Republican was in a strong position, he probably offered the most effective opposition to the imperialists. In one sense his record was a handicap, and in each debate some Republican senator would read from Teller's speeches of 1898 as an answer to his argument, but the Colorado senator had little difficulty showing that his position at the two periods was not fundamentally inconsistent.[11] The fact that he had been an expansionist, and still was in favor of the United States managing the foreign affairs of the Philippines, gave his opposition to the policies of the administration greater force with a large portion of the Senate and the public.

[9] Ibid., 57 Cong., 1 Sess., pp. 1064-69, 1519-23, 1576-83, 1640-53, 2023-25.

[10] Ibid., pp. 5212-15, 6228.

[11] Ibid., pp. 5216-20; Washington Star, May 13, 1902.

It can easily be overlooked that the opponents of imperialism had scored substantial victories in these legislative contests. The restrictions they put upon acquisitions of public land by corporations tended to prevent the development of exploitative economic relationships that are the essence of imperialism, and the imperialists never ceased to complain about that limitation.[12] The defense of civil rights for the natives, added to these economic measures, kept alive the cause of Philippine independence, and makes it an attainable goal today, as the tariff favors to Philippine producers make them obvious competitors of the American farmer.

The attitude of the majority of Congress on the Philippines, Porto Rico, and Hawaii, is evidence of what would have happened to Cuba, had not the Teller Amendment been added to the resolutions that brought on the war. Even in spite of this definite promise there was a growing sentiment among the imperialists in favor of the retention of Cuba as a permanent possession of the United States. The resolution was subject to a great deal of public criticism. President McKinley was represented in 1901 as having "always disapproved" of it.[13]

The attitude of most imperialists after 1900 was that the adoption of the resolution had been a serious error, but it was a promise that must be kept. Beveridge was less inclined to take that view and he advocated retention, as did a substantial part of the Republican press. It would seem that a promise as definite as that made in 1898 could not be dodged by any sort of circuitous reasoning, but it is apparent that large sections of public opinion were prepared to justify ignoring it. On February 6, 1901, the New York *Tribune* argued:

If then, the Teller resolution respecting Cuban independence were an error, it would neither be wise nor just to persist in maintaining it. The course of prudence and honor would lie frankly in admitting the error, and in atoning for it by doing now the thing that should have been done at the outset.[14]

It was this evident sentiment that led General Gómez, while visiting in the United States that summer, to declare,

---

[12] W. Cameron Forbes, *The Philippine Islands* (Boston and New York, 1928), I, 323-24.

[13] *The Nation*, Feb. 6, 1901.

[14] See also the editorial on February 3, 1901, and Russell H. Fitzgibbon, *Cuba and the United States, 1900-1935* (Menasha, Wis., 1935), pp. 70, 74, 107.

"Had it not been for this promise and the repeated reminders of it which the administration has received, Cuba would now be annexed to the United States."[15]

Teller's interest in Cuba had grown with time. He served on the Senate committee on relations with Cuba as long as it was in existence. In the spring of 1900 he had gone to Havana with Platt and Aldrich for a brief investigation of conditions, and had returned convinced of the wisdom of independence. But the attitude of his colleagues in the Senate and the press roused in his own mind doubts as to whether independence would be achieved. He took occasion several times in the last session of the Fifty-sixth Congress, before any legislation was submitted, to warn the Senate of the trend of press opinion.

We hear rumblings now that the plighted faith of this Government with reference to Cuba is to be abandoned, and that Cuba, like the Philippines, is to be a dependency and not an independent government.[16]

But the administration, whatever its wishes, had no stomach for a direct repudiation of the pledge, and some definite steps would have to be taken soon to define the relations of that island to the United States after the new Cuban government was set up. The Republicans on the Cuban committee began to hold conferences among themselves on this question, and late in the session brought out their plan as the Platt Amendment to the army appropriation bill.

To most observers the Platt Amendment looks like a very parsimonious payment of the promise in the Teller resolution. It provided that the Cuban government should make a part of its constitution, and embody in a "permanent treaty with the United States," certain provisions. The most important of these gave the United States the right to intervene in Cuba for the preservation of the island's independence, for the "maintenance of a government adequate for the protection of life, property, and individual liberty," and for the discharge of obligations imposed on the United States by the Treaty of Paris.

Teller declared that the Republican proposals were not "so savage" as he had feared. He did not think that they would destroy Cuban independence or seriously curtail it.

---

[15] *Public Opinion*, July 18, 1901.

[16] *Congressional Record*, 56 Cong., 2 Sess., p. 2009.

He did not claim that the Platt Amendment was wholly inconsistent with the Teller resolution, but rather based his opposition to it on the grounds that it would needlessly wound the sensibilities of the Cubans.[17] He proposed as an amendment, the elimination of the phrase "protection of life, property, and individual liberty" as a justification of intervention, a change that would have eliminated the most imperialistic feature of the entire proposal. It was defeated by a vote of 21 to 43 in the Senate and the entire committee amendment adopted.[18]

One cannot deny, and Teller never did, that the Platt Amendment represented even more independence for Cuba than Teller had desired when he introduced the Fourth Resolution. Although the pledge is specific, Teller never intended much more than local self-government, and the imperialists missed one of their best arguments against Cuban independence when they failed to use Teller's own statements in an attempt to prove that the resolution never meant that.

The erection of the independent Cuban government over a year later was hailed with delight by the anti-imperialists, and even by the moderate expansionists in the Senate. Almost without exception they credited its successful achievement to the effect of the Teller Amendment, and complimented its author in words which it is seldom the fate of a senator to hear from his colleagues. Senators Hale, Cullom, and Spooner in turn made laudatory speeches. Senator Hoar, who started the compliments, doubted "whether any man who has sat in this Chamber since Charles Sumner died, or whether all who sit here now, put together, have done a more important single service to the country than he did in securing the passage of the resolution which pledged us to deal with Cuba according to the Declaration of Independence."

Teller modestly denied that the amendment represented any particular forethought on his part. He stated that he had not expected any promise was necessary to make the American Government give the Cubans their independence, and that he was thinking chiefly of the European situation when he introduced it. On the other hand, he complimented the administration for carrying out the pledge.

---

[17] *Congressional Record*, 56 Cong., 2 Sess., p. 3091.

[18] *Ibid.*, pp. 3146, 3149. Teller's legal opinion of the Platt Amendment was that it did not impair the sovereignty of Cuba; for she could always amend her constitution if she wished.

I glory in the act of the administration in finally putting into operation the Republic of Cuba. I think it is a great thing, and I think it is worth boasting of ... that we have put back of us the cry of greed and avarice, which would have induced us to forget ... our obligation under a solemn promise ... made ... to all mankind.[19]

There was an unquestioned acknowledgment of legislative achievement in the whole affair for Teller, and the praises of the many who desired the same end could not have been unpleasant to him.

But the Cuban question was then before the Senate in a different way, and it presented a more complicated problem to Teller. During the winter of 1901 and 1902, a large amount of publicity was current in the United States favoring either complete reciprocity or mutual percentage reductions of tariff rates between Cuba and the United States. Naturally, where no other interests were involved, imperialists would favor such an arrangement. Largely this reduction would concern the tobacco and sugar growers, and when President Roosevelt got behind the proposal, Teller began an intensive study of the question.

Sugar had recently become a local interest in Colorado. From an insignificant production value of $100,000 in 1899, it had increased to $3,600,000 in 1901.[20] When the discussion of sugar-beet production had begun in Colorado, Teller had been inclined to doubt its feasibility, and indeed up to this time had not been counted as any champion of the industry. So well-known was his attitude that he had to take the floor of the Senate on April 26, 1902, to deny a statement that he had declared that the sugar producers of Colorado did not need any duty for their protection.

To defeat the demand for reciprocity Teller planned an investigation to expose the selfish groups promoting it. Shortly before the House reciprocity bill was sent to the Senate, he introduced a resolution for this investigation, asking that the committee find out whether or not it was true that the sugar trust had acquired the Cuban crop for the current year, and to what extent it had extended its ownership over the Cuban cane lands. This passed the Senate, in a restricted form.[21]

Thus, while the Senate committee on relations with Cuba was considering the House bill, it was also conducting the

---

[19] *Congressional Record*, 57 Cong., 1 Sess., pp. 5801-08.
[20] *Ibid.*, p. 2467.
[21] *Ibid.*, pp. 4423, 4667.

investigation Teller had forced upon it. These hearings were conducted in May and June, and when they were over Teller had proved very definitely these points: that since the war, the American Sugar Refining Company and certain corporations it controlled had acquired a vast area of cane lands, and was making it into plantations; that the sugar industry in Cuba was largely in the hands of foreign capitalists—American and European; that the effective propaganda agencies for the reciprocity proposal had been financed partly by money supplied by Leonard Wood from Cuban government funds he was administering as governor general, and partly by Havemeyer, the head of the sugar trust.[22]

The evidence of the Wood and Havemeyer support of the propaganda campaign was the blow that killed the bill in that session of Congress. The whole situation was complicated by a lack of unity on the question in the Republican Party. The administration was supporting the measure, and a large number of Republicans in Congress from sugar-producing sections up for re-election in the fall were opposing it. Before the House had passed the bill, these Republicans had helped to remove from it the provision especially desired by the sugar trust, the "differential" on refined sugar. If this could not be replaced, the trust would lose most of its interest in the bill, as would also those members of the Senate who supported it. Whether Platt and Aldrich could put it back in the Senate was doubtful, so divided were the members of the Republican caucus in that body. Republicans from sugar-producing sections were not going home to the fall campaign with the record of having voted with the sugar trust to lower the tariff on one of the few products of the farm that it benefited. The other Republicans seemed to lack enough interest in the House bill without the differential to unite with the Democrats to pass it, as they could easily have done.

President Roosevelt tried to save the situation by sending to Congress, a few days after Teller's exposure, a special message, urgently demanding the bill. But it was too late. When the President's message was read, Senator Bailey

---

[22] The most essential parts of the testimony are printed in *Senate Documents*, 57 Cong., 1 Sess., No. 434; Washington *Star*, May 5, 6; Kansas City *Star*, June 11; St. Louis *Globe-Democrat*, June 12; *Public Opinion*, June 19, 1902. Apparently James E. Campbell secured the evidence that Teller used to show Wood's connection with financing the propaganda. Campbell to Teller, May 24, 1902, Teller MSS.

remarked, "I believe I will not do it, but I feel inclined to move to refer the message to the Republican caucus."[23]

Just before the session closed, Teller delivered a speech summarizing the evidence that had been brought out before the committee, and stating his position. He was not strongly opposed to a 20 per cent reduction, as that would not hurt the beet growers except as an entering wedge to drive the tariff down still further. He would co-operate with the Republicans to reduce the tariff rates on all products—the beet grower did not ask for any special favors!

Senator Platt, chairman of the committee, tried to reply for the majority, but his answer was little more than the threat that, without reciprocity, conditions in Cuba would force the United States to annex the island. "That is a baby cry," Teller replied, "if I may say so without being offensive. It is childish."[24] The contest had set the Democratic slogan for the Congressional campaign. The Republicans dared not touch a tariff rate that favored a trust.

Although Teller was busy on a host of minor legislative matters after 1900, nearly all those to which he gave substantial aid related more or less directly to colonial and foreign policy. He had taken a leading part in the fight against Hanna's plan for a ship subsidy. He had helped lead the unsuccessful fight in the Senate for a constitutional amendment for the direct election of senators.[25] In general, he had voted with the Democrats, but not always. He joined the majority of the Republicans to vote for the Spooner proposal to make Panama the first choice for the site of the isthmian canal. In the midst of the Philippine debate he had given the administration unqualified praise for the enunciation of the open-door policy in China.[26] He was still an independent more than a partisan, but certainly he was far from a supporter of the Republican Party.

If we except the defense of the tariff on sugar, Teller's and Patterson's opposition to imperialism was not very popular in Colorado. The now active Republican press was busy there as it was elsewhere in the country labeling as "traitors" all opponents of the administration's policy in the Philippines. In May, the Denver *Republican* was trying

---

[23] *Congressional Record*, 57 Cong., 1 Sess., p. 6720.

[24] *Ibid.*, pp. 7506-13.

[25] *Congressional Record*, 56 Cong., 2 Sess., pp. 2471-72, 4027; *ibid.*, 57 Cong., 1 Sess., pp. 2820-24, 5953, 5954; *The Nation*, Feb. 14, 1901.

[26] *Congressional Record*, 57 Cong., 1 Sess., p. 1646.

The Denver *Republican's* caricature of Patterson's and Teller's attack
on imperialism in 1902.

to stimulate the assembling of mass meetings over the state to protest against the senators' "despicable" conduct regarding the Philippines. "Modern copperheads," it editorialized.[27]

Still a considerable portion of the Republican Party in the state wanted Teller back in it, partly to counterbalance Wolcott's power, and partly to strengthen it with the voters. Vice-President Roosevelt was in Colorado in the summer of 1901 to attend the twenty-fifth anniversary celebration of statehood, and Teller introduced him to an enthusiastic audience in Colorado Springs. When McKinley was shot a month later and Roosevelt became President, he considered for a time a reversal of partisan policies in the state that contemplated attempting to win Teller back by taking his advice on appointments. The Federal appointments in the state, which had been completely Wolcott's since 1896, were creating trouble for the party, as they usually do when one faction controls them, and some well-publicized weak appointments had helped to make them a minor scandal. Looking toward strengthening the party in the state, Roosevelt felt out the possibilities, suggested by anti-Wolcott factions, of an understanding with Teller. Lodge, who knew from his experience in the Senate that Teller would not give the Republicans any help, did his best to prevent any change, and if the President made any such efforts, they had no noticeable influence. Certainly there is no probability that Teller ever seriously considered a return.[28]

The election of 1902 in Colorado proved to be the forerunner of Teller's bitterest campaign for the Senate. It would seem that in the light of his almost unanimous election in 1897, a re-election in 1903 would not be difficult. Even as late as August 28, Patterson wrote Newlands that although the dissensions in the Democratic ranks made the election of the Democratic ticket doubtful, he regarded Teller's re-election as a "certainty." But Wolcott had laid his political plans well, and, aided by the Republican trend over the country, he himself was in a strong position to come back. The Republican Party in Colorado had become simply a patronage machine when the Silver Republicans left it in 1896. Between that time and 1902 its control of the Federal offices, together with the vast influx of new population in the prosperous years about 1900, had given it an effective vote-

[27] May 14-17, 1902.
[28] *Correspondence of Roosevelt and Lodge*, I, 495, 497, 509.

getting organization that could compete on equal terms with the remnants of the combined silver parties. The Democratic Party, at least in Denver, was of the same general character. Teller had always taken pains to steer as clear of Denver politics as possible, for the character of many of its leaders was that of machine politicians the country over. "I am going to Central on Saturday if I can get away & *next week* I will get out of Denver if I have to go to Alaska or the North Pole," Teller wrote Sayre in 1899, in what was typical of his attitude when the Denver political pot was brewing.[29] Money was playing an ever larger part in Colorado campaigns, and offices were considered legitimate objects of purchase. But the Silver Republican and Populist parties had created a large body of independent voters who were attracted by personalities rather than by political labels. Consequently, reputable headliners were more necessary than usual to carry any ticket filled with organization nominees. It was such a situation that gave the older leaders such as Teller, Patterson, and Shafroth strength with the machine politicians.[30] T. J. O'Donnell was placed in charge of a campaign to ensure that the Democratic and Populist state conventions declared for Teller, in order to bind their candidates for the legislature. An appeal was issued based on the necessity of preventing the Denver organization from controlling the convention and preventing such action. The response was flattering.

When the state conventions met, there was no doubt that the voters and the press of the fusionist groups were united in support of Teller's re-election to the Senate. Both the Democratic and Populist conventions "vied with each other in paying homage to Colorado's Grand Old Man," and pledged him their support for re-election. In his address to the Democratic group, Teller made his confession of faith:

I believe that today the Democratic party stands for the best interests of all the people while the Republican party stands for the interests of a few, and for this reason I have chosen, after deliberation extending over a period of six years, to give my adherence to the party of the people. Not only ... do I stand with the Democratic party on the subject of coinage, but upon many other vital points, such as imperialism, the trusts and national elections.[31]

[29] May 24, 1899, Sayre MSS.

[30] Walter L. Wilder, Robert Wilbur Steel, *Defender of Liberty* (Denver, 1911), pp. 24-26, 75.

[31] T. J. O'Donnell to J. N. Ashley, Aug. 8, 1902; Thos. F. O'Mahoney to O'Donnell, Aug. 15, 1902, O'Donnell MSS.; *Rocky Mountain News*, Sept. 11, 1902.

He probably regretted as the campaign drew nearer that the provision for the direct election of senators that he had been urging in the last several Congresses had not been adopted, for it was clear that his chances for re-election would have been better had he not had to carry along such a large number of questionable candidates for the legislature, running at least partly on local issues. In fact, the personal element was so strong in his favor that Wolcott stayed out of the state during the campaign in order to play down the senatorial race as much as possible.

Colorado, never given to pollyanna campaigns, had seen few that were marred with as many corrupt practices as that of 1902, and neither party organization seems to have been handicapped by moral scruples. The Republicans won, electing their candidate for governor, James H. Peabody, and two of the three congressmen the new apportionment had given the state, and leaving Shafroth with only a slight majority in the other district. Had the senatorial contest turned upon the results of this election entirely, a Republican would have been chosen. What seemed to be a Republican victory, on the face of the returns, was, however, more than offset by the holdover members of the state senate who had not been up for re-election. These, with the members of the two houses elected in 1902, gave the Democrats a majority of ten on a joint ballot.

The Republicans were not willing to abide by the returns, and freely predicted that when the contests were settled, their party would have a majority on a joint ballot. More confusion was added to the situation by the fact that the Republicans were not united on a candidate, and many of the Republican legislators were bitterly anti-Wolcott. Among the Democrats, too, there was considerable fishing about in troubled waters, for a small group of them proved to be open to influence before the contest was over. The *Post* and *Republican* kept repeating charges that the older Democratic leaders such as Thomas, Adams, and C. J. Hughes, were actively trying to manipulate the situation to secure the replacement of Teller by one of themselves.[32] In view of this situation it is clear that had the Republicans been able

---

[32] The *Post* insisted that Patterson planned a "conspiracy" to defeat Teller, which certainly was not true. There is no real contemporary evidence against the others either, and the charges were no doubt aimed at disrupting the Democratic lines in the legislature. Dawson Scrapbook. T. J. O'Donnell made specific charges against C. J. Hughes in 1908, and submitted considerable evidence. O'Donnell to C. B. Ward, Oct. 22, 1908, O'Donnell MSS.

to unite on Wolcott they could have elected him; for, among
other things, the control of both Federal and state patronage
put them in an advantageous position to provide for, at
least, the absence of a few Democratic members of the
legislature.

To make the most of this, the national leaders called on
the local Republicans to unite. President Roosevelt and
Senator Hanna, chairman of the National Republican Committee, issued appeals for a Republican senator. A large
number of Colorado businessmen united in an appeal for
the election of Wolcott, if a Republican were chosen.[33]

When the legislature assembled, the Republicans, still
not united on a candidate, made it clear that they would
attempt to secure a majority by unseating Democratic members of the lower house, where they already had control.
When they had unseated six Democrats, enough to give them
a majority of two on a joint ballot, the Democratic-controlled
Senate unseated two Republican senators and delivered an
ultimatum that for every other Democratic House member
unseated, they would unseat one Republican senator. That
process was checked, for although the Senate would soon
have run out of Republicans to unseat, the factions within
the Republican group could not agree upon any more
removals.

Next, the Republican minority of the Senate met sepa-
rately with the Republican lieutenant governor and constituted their own senate with the addition of enough contestants to give them a majority. The legislature was by that
time in complete anarchy with armed guards and thugs
everywhere. An appeal was finally made to the governor for
the militia to preserve order, and the affair became a national scandal.

The Republican majority in the House was blocked at
every other turn, for any vote on a joint ballot with the
regular Senate would give a Democratic majority. Finally
the anti-Wolcott Republicans and the Democrats voted to
adjourn over the days on which they were required by law
to vote for a senator. Still a legal election would take place
if the Democratic members of the House went over to the
regular Senate, for together they would make a majority
of all still unseated members.

After several delays as one Democratic member after

[33] Denver *Republican*, Jan. 4, 10, 11, 1903.

another was induced to disappear, Teller was elected by a unanimous vote of the Democratic majority of the legislature.[34] According to a local newspaper report, during the deadlock when one Democrat or another was holding up the election, Teller ordered the party leaders to "call for second choices and if you can find one Democrat upon whom enough Democrats can agree to elect him, then I will withdraw."[35] But no such agreement was possible, as Ammons declared in a letter to Dawson:

It was interesting—too much so to be comfortable, but I believe a large majority of the people are glad the result is Teller. . . . Whatever lingering hopes anyone may have had at the outset, everyone learned as the contest progressed that it must be Teller or nobody, and when that became certain all the leaders felt it must be a Democrat, and notwithstanding the reports of treachery, which personal dislike to certain leaders caused to be published, there was in my opinion perfect good faith on the part of all leaders. Senator Teller's conduct was perfectly admirable. He refused to entertain stories of bad faith and prevented criticism when members of his own party seemed to block his election. He had many staunch supporters in the legislature who would listen to no proposition that included his withdrawal and when that possibility was talked on Friday evening before the election many of them asked me to go to him and urge him under no circumstances to do so—that defeat in his support might be at least honorable, but that no other course could be. I had a talk with him late that evening and was able to make a satisfactory report. One thing I do not know—how they finally got Madden; and I do not care.[36]

It must be added that when Wolcott issued his statement testifying to the legality of the election, he stated in great detail charges of fraud against the Democrats and the Republicans opposed to his election, but generously exempted the victor. "Senator Teller is in no sense a party to the frauds."

After the election there was a reception for Teller in the Brown Palace Hotel, where some thirty-five hundred friends and leaders from over the state came to offer congratulations. The press reported extensive rejoicing in Washington both in Congress and in the departments where among the personnel Teller had many friends and admirers.[37]

One incident turned up later to mar his unquestioned pleasure in his re-election. The Republicans saw that they

[34] Dawson, Wolcott, I, 297-316; Thomas, "Fifty Years," p. 929; Rocky Mountain News, Jan. 20-26; Denver Republican, Jan. 2-26, 1903; Teller to Bela S. Buell (copy), Feb. 11, 1903, Teller MSS.

[35] Denver Republican, Jan. 25, 1903.

[36] Jan. 29, 1903, Teller MSS.

[37] Rocky Mountain News, Jan. 26, 29, 1903; St. Louis Republic, Jan. 20-25, 1903.

had good grounds for a contest against Shafroth, and prepared to carry it before the Republican-controlled Congress.
Shafroth, aware of their intentions, went over the evidence
himself, and quickly saw that they had a good case and
would likely unseat him, although a partisan contest could
be made against it. He therefore resigned his office, without
letting it come to a contest, on the grounds that a fair count
would have given his opponent a majority. There was a
small flurry of hopeful expectation among the Republicans
in Colorado that Teller might do likewise, but as the specific
majorities on which Shafroth based his resignation would
not make any change in Teller's election by the legislature,
they made no real demand.[38]

---

[38] Earl [B. Coe] to Dawson, Nov. 14, 1903; Denver *Post* to Teller, Feb. 16; Dawson
to Denver *Post* (copy), Feb. 18, 1904, Teller MSS.

CHAPTER XXIII

DEFENDER OF THE CONSTITUTION
1903-05

DURING the contest in the legislature over Teller's re-election, the attempt to bring about the ratification of the Cuban reciprocity treaty had been renewed. With the congressional election past it was easier to secure legislative support from Republican congressmen. From the vantage point of Denver, Teller saw no pressing reason for continuing the opposition. Even the Colorado sugar interests were very hesitant about antagonizing the American Sugar Refining Company. Anticipating that the treaty would be ratified before he returned, Teller sent his instructions to Dawson:

Get me a pair against it. You may not be able to get more than one but that will do. The Sugar men here are afraid of Havemeyer. I *do not* care if it passes but I will not vote for it.[1]

But it was not ratified, and when Teller returned to the Senate he aided in securing further postponement. Now, for the first time, he made a defense of beet sugar as a deserving infant industry, and again held up the propaganda campaign as one inspired by the sugar trust and other foreign investors in Cuba to promote the exploitation of the island. He read the Republicans their platform and campaign textbook of 1900 with its pledges of protection for sugar.[2] It was a fight he had long since given up as lost, but maintained it for the purpose of warding off future attacks. The approval carried with only eighteen votes in opposition.

Before Cuban reciprocity was out of the way, the "seizure" of Panama had become the central theme of senatorial debate. The proposals to construct an interoceanic canal had interested Teller. When it was first seriously discussed in the Senate, he began to study the question in the same way he did all the problems in which he developed an interest. Engineering projects, whether railroads, bridges, or irrigation systems, had always fascinated him. As he was to say later, he read everything that had been written on the subject of an interoceanic canal. Added to his study

---

[1] Jan. 10, 1903, Teller MSS.
[2] *Congressional Record*, 58 Cong., 2 Sess., pp. 37-46, 66-72, 254-57.

was the practical experience he had gained in building the
Colorado Central Railroad, in mining, and in irrigating his
two Colorado farms. He delighted in talking to engineers.
His correspondence with Captain Berthoud, chief engineer
of the old Colorado Central, who, incidentally, had been assistant engineer on the construction of the Panama Railroad
in 1851 and 1852, is filled with references to technical matters in which they were both interested. Among his most
enjoyable friendships he counted that with James B. Eads,
who built the Mississippi River jetties and the great bridge
over the Mississippi River at St. Louis.

Out of his study and discussions with engineers, Teller
came to several conclusions as to how the canal should be
built, and these he maintained tenaciously to the end of his
life: it should be built by the government and not by a
private corporation; it should be built large enough to serve
the purposes of commerce for many years and to accommodate the largest ships that would be built; it should be a
sea level canal; and it should be under the complete
control of the United States.[3] All these ideas came out in
his discussion of the proposal in the eighties, and because
they were not followed in the plans that came before the
Senate in that and the next decade, he voted against all canal
bills—being in most cases in a minority of less than ten, and
on some occasions in a minority of two or three. Most senators then were like Dubois, who said he found it easier to
vote for the bills than to explain why he voted against them.[4]
Teller had always favored a canal, but always opposed the
specific projects brought up—"one-horse canals," he called
them—as of no value. Later he was able to say truthfully of these early projects, "there is not a Senator on this
floor to-day who would vote for one of them if it were here
for his approval or disapproval."[5] On several occasions he
pointed out that advocates of particular bills had insufficient
data on which to act intelligently, and that they vastly un-
derestimated the cost and the time necessary for completing
a canal. In 1899 he estimated the canal would take at least
ten years to build and would cost not less than $400,000,000,
but that it was worth that and more. A few years later he

---

[3] *Congressional Record*, 50 Cong., 1 Sess., pp. 1493-94; *ibid.*, 50 Cong., 2 Sess., p.
547; *ibid.*, 52 Cong., 2 Sess., pp. 1531, 1572; *ibid.*, 54 Cong., 4 Sess., pp. 1434-37; *ibid.*,
55 Cong., 3 Sess., pp. 749-53.

[4] Dunn, *From Harrison to Harding*, I, 364.

[5] *Congressional Record*, 58 Cong., 2 Sess., p. 2247.

reduced this time to not less than eight years and raised the cost estimate to half a billion. Most of the plans, he insisted, contemplated a canal that was too small. While he did not oppose Nicaragua in 1899, he wanted Panama investigated also. In 1902 he voted for the Spooner amendment, which preferred the Panama route, if the administration could make satisfactory arrangements.[6]

It was not the building of the canal, but the "seizure" of Panama that brought the administration and Teller into opposing factions, which corresponded in general with those on other aspects of imperialism. Nothing that happened during Roosevelt's presidency excited Teller's antagonism as much as his action in Panama. President Roosevelt and Secretary of State John Hay negotiated an agreement with Colombia for a canal right-of-way across the Isthmus of Panama. This treaty was ratified by the United States Senate but rejected by the Senate of Colombia. Between the encouragement of the owners of the rights to the earlier French project on the Isthmus, and hope of assistance from the United States, a quiet revolution was staged in the state of Panama and its independence declared. Interference of the military forces of the United States prevented Colombian forces from attempting to put down the rebels. The new government was recognized by the United States with unprecedented haste. Immediately a canal treaty was negotiated with the new republic and presented to the Senate for ratification.[7]

That the country and Congress were eager to accept this affront to international decency can only be accounted for by a fairly wide acceptance of the high-flown imperialism of Mahan and Beveridge, and by the effective way in which President Roosevelt stated the issue as a choice between the highly popular isthmian canal or submission to "inefficient bandits." These beliefs were not confined to Republicans, and as Congress assembled there was widespread pressure upon Democratic senators to ratify the Panama treaty. The Louisiana legislature unanimously instructed the senators from that state to vote for it. Such an important leader of Democratic opinion as Clark Howell, of the Atlanta *Constitution*, proclaimed its justification:

---

[6] *Ibid.*, 55 Cong., 3 Sess., pp. 749, 752, 2302; *ibid.*, 58 Cong., 2 Sess., pp. 2246, 2247; *ibid.*, 59 Cong., 1 Sess., p. 342.

[7] Perhaps the best brief statement is Tyler Dennett, *John Hay* (New York, 1933), pp. 364-83.

The simplest observer of popular temper in this country can not mistake how the American people feel about this matter. They approve what has been done to date, they want and mean to have the canal, and they will visit their wrath upon whatever man or party may defeat their wishes.[8]

The few senators who took the unpopular side of opposition girded themselves for the debate. In this Teller took a prominent part, assuming the leadership in presenting the violation of international law involved.[9] In answer to Lodge's labored defense of the legality of the administration's action, Teller presented a refutation that stripped the action to its bare bones of aggression.[10] His own appeal was to the American concepts of justice, to observance of international law, and to American constitutional principles. Colombia had acted within her constitutional rights, and the United States should respect them.

I am more anxious that the Government of the United States should go before the world as an honest, law-abiding, justice-loving nation, than I am that it should glory in the greatest work of human hands. It will not do to say that it is in the interest of civilization, and thus acquit ourselves of a violation of international law. You have no right to take Colombia's land in the interest of civilization. That . . . is a robber's claim. It is a doctrine that might makes right. We want it, and therefore we take it.

Before he had finished with the matter, he was thundering warnings like a national Jeremiah, a role that his increased years seemed to encourage.

National morality is as essential as individual morality; national justice as individual justice; national righteousness as individual righteousness, and in my judgment, a nation can no more transcend the great laws of God and man with impunity than can individuals. There will come condign punishment, although it may be generations before it is felt. Step by step violations of constitutional, of international law, lead you farther and farther away from the great principles upon which the Government was founded and which can only be maintained by strict adherence thereto.[11]

Teller voted and worked fruitlessly against the ratification of the treaty with Panama, and never ceased to denounce the action of the administration in regard to it. His judgments regarding events and international law then are

[8] Literary Digest, Jan. 2, 1904.

[9] M. A. DeWolf Howe, Portrait of an Independent: Moorefield Storey (Boston, 1932), pp. 232-33.

[10] Congressional Record, 58 Cong., 2 Sess., pp. 796-805, 828-36, 966-68

[11] Ibid., pp. 835, 836.

squarely in accordance with present-day interpretations.[12]

With this question decided against him—there were only fourteen votes against ratification—Teller returned to the question of the canal. In general he supported all appropriations for it. Frequently he urged that the canal was not large enough and that it should be a sea-level canal. Increased cost on such an important project, he held, was not a serious objection. His arguments for the sea-level canal were largely based upon the susceptibility of a lock canal to attack, and the extreme difficulty of enlarging or repairing a lock canal while it was in use. With the lock system accepted, he repeatedly urged that the locks be increased and the canal deepened. Virtually the last important speech he made in the Senate was to return to these ideas and repeat his convictions regarding them.[13] Two years after he ceased to be a senator, he pointed to the approaching completion of the canal as "the great achievement of the decade."[14]

The seizure of Panama was followed by another Caribbean involvement that brought Teller again into direct opposition to the administration. This was the enunciation of the expansion of the Monroe Doctrine later to be called the Roosevelt Corollary, and its application to the Dominican Republic in 1905.

In fact, it is clear that Roosevelt planned to make an agreement with the Dominican Republic, giving the United States a substantial control over its revenues and other affairs which would bring it under much more direct control of the United States than was Cuba under the Platt Amendment. To avoid possible disapproval by the Senate, the President planned to evade submitting it to that body by calling the agreement something other than a treaty. After it was signed, indirect newspaper reports carried its terms. Teller immediately inserted one of these accounts in the *Record*, and challenged the power of the administration to bind the United States by any treaty, protocol, or contract without ratification by the Senate. It is clear from the evidence now available that this attack caused Roosevelt to order that the provisions be changed to include postponing its

---

[12] Dennett, *op. cit.;* H. C. Hill, *Roosevelt and the Caribbean* (Chicago, 1927), pp. 37-67.

[13] *Congressional Record,* 58 Cong., 2 Sess., pp. 2246-47; *ibid.,* 59 Cong., 1 Sess., pp. 388-93. 8540-45; *ibid.,* 60 Cong., 1 Sess., p. 1518; *ibid.,* 60 Cong., 2 Sess., pp. 2076-77, 3621-28. It is interesting that Berthoud agreed with Teller in his preference for a sea-level canal, and wrote him approvingly after reading an account of the Senator's speech of Feb. 4, 1908. E. L. Berthoud to Teller, Feb. 9-10, 1908, Teller MSS.

[14] Clipping from the Denver *Post,* May 26, 1911, in Tyler MSS.

taking effect until ratified by the United States Senate, although for publicity's sake he told his journalistic partisans that Teller had "had a pipe dream."[15]

Later, when the agreement was before the Senate, Teller sponsored a resolution demanding copies of the instructions of the agents who had negotiated it.[16] This time he found himself on the side of a temporary majority, as many Republican members objected either to the agreement, or to the attempt of the President to ignore the Senate. The entire policy involved in the Corollary was denounced by Teller as contrary to good foreign policy. "It is no part of our duty to go out as missionaries lifting up other people."[17] As the treaty could not be ratified, Roosevelt put part of its terms in force on a temporary basis, and a year later submitted a new treaty which went a considerable distance toward meeting the objections that had been raised to the first one. Although opposed by the great majority of Democratic senators, it was ratified, and the Dominican Republic joined Cuba and Panama as protectorates. However, the opposition had taught the President that he could not successfully add to this group on his own volition alone, and that the control established could not be as complete and unchallengeable as he wished.

It is impossible to estimate the total influence the opposition exercised in softening the harshness of American rule on subject peoples. Outside of the case of Cuba, which was a standing argument for self-government, it may not have been of great importance. But it did some things. In the case of Cuba it handicapped all attempts in the United States to turn the protectorate status into a complete dependency. It kept alive, to some degree, the old spirit of revolutionary radicalism in America. It protected the natives against many laws that would have worked against their interests by making economic exploitation easy, such as the land laws in the Philippines. It secured for them a greater measure of self-government than they would otherwise have secured. And, finally, it helped to keep alive in all the regions the hope of complete independence, or at least of greater local self-control.

Teller's opposition to President Roosevelt never became

---

[15] The evidence is well stated in W. Stull Holt, *Treaties Defeated by the United States Senate* (Baltimore, 1933), pp. 213-28.

[16] *Congressional Record*, 59 Cong., 1 Sess., pp. 16-30.

[17] *Ibid.*, pp. 1475-78.

personal, although he increasingly objected to the President's tendency to ignore legal forms and practices. Particularly he disliked the worshipful adulation that made the President's partisans in the Senate, especially Lodge, rush to his defense in everything he did or wanted. A senator, Teller thought, should be above sycophancy, and had his own position and dignity to maintain.

Teller's instinctive reaction against Roosevelt's adventuring, as well as his own growing anti-imperialism, made the Senator modify some of his earlier enthusiasms. Before 1898 he had been a big-navy advocate, and in 1900 had told the Senate, "I have voted for every proposition to build ships since we began to increase the Navy. I intend to do so until we reach the limit."[18] But Roosevelt's requests were found too large for his judgment, and by the end of his senatorial career Teller was voting against them. His opposition to increasing the size of the standing army involved no such inconsistency with his past record. He regularly ridiculed the idea that a large army was needed for national defense. A professional soldiery was a danger to republican institutions. This idea grew with him, and, in 1908, he commented:

[If] you double the army ... you will probably have some incentive on the part of a large number of people to get up a difficulty, if possible with some nation so that they may be useful and that the avenues of preferment and distinction may be open to them.[19]

About the only administration action that received Teller's unmeasured praise was Roosevelt's work in settling the anthracite coal strike. There, Teller informed the Senate, Roosevelt had shown "patience and good temper" in forcing the operators from their uncompromising stand.[20]

Teller's objection to Roosevelt's lack of respect for legal and constitutional principles in dealing with foreign affairs found a counterpart in Governor Peabody's violations or constitutional forms in suppressing the labor unions in the Colorado mining areas. Beginning in 1903 and extending into 1904, the Western Federation of Miners was in a death struggle with the mine owners of most sections of Colorado. Strikes against wage cuts, and sympathy strikes, with more than normal violence from both sides, were the result of the

---

[18] Ibid., 56 Cong., 1 Sess., p. 5495.
[19] Ibid., 60 Cong., 1 Sess., p. 4475.
[20] Ibid., 57 Cong., 2 Sess., p. 215.

aggressive tactics of that organization and of the determination of the Mine Managers' Association to drive the unions out of the state. News from Colorado in the Eastern press during the spring and summer of 1904 was almost entirely of violent labor conflict.

In their efforts to drive out the unions, the mine owners and their "Citizen's Alliance" conducted an organized campaign in which they had full co-operation from Governor Peabody. The latter obligingly declared Teller County, where the union was strongest, in a state of insurrection and rebellion. The state militia moved in, and, co-operating with the other agencies of the mine owners, conducted a vigorous campaign to drive out the union and its leaders. It refused to heed the processes of the civil courts.

All the usual means of suppression were used to the fullest extent as the unionist forces weakened under the double attack from state government and mine owners. That it was not worse was due chiefly to the fearless work of Teller's colleague, Patterson, who, in contrast to the remaining Denver newspaper owners, kept before Colorado the case for the miners and the violations of law and justice that were being practiced against them. In a sense it was a vain effort, as in the end the union was driven from the important mining centers, and its members were black-listed over most of the state.

The climax of the affair was the explosion at Independence Station where thirteen nonunion miners were killed. The Western Federation immediately offered a high reward for information regarding the guilty persons. But its cause was ruined by the success with which the owners were able to fasten the murders upon the union. In spite of Patterson's plea for reason, the corporate triumvirate—the militia, the Citizens' Alliance, and the Mine Managers' Association—immediately followed the explosion with a systematic wrecking of all union organizations and property. Deportations, the forced resignation of local officials by threats of violence and their replacement with agents of the Mine Managers' Association, the stirring up of mob violence, and the raiding of newspaper offices and arresting of their employees were some of the many weapons brought to bear upon the union.[21] Generally, in the country over, as well as in Colorado, there was little criticism at first, so well had the publicity of the

---

[21] Stone, *Colorado*, I, 860-71; *Literary Digest*, May 7, June 4, 18, 25, 1904.

Berryman, in the Washington *Post* combines Colorado politics in 1905
with Teller's attack on Roosevelt's foreign policy.

explosion labeled the union as its perpetrator. Commented the *Literary Digest* after surveying press opinion the country over:

> The subsequent hunting down and exile of unionists by the militia, and forced resignations of local officials, by threat of the rope, have been regarded by the newspapers without a word of protest.[22]

In the defense of civil liberties Patterson rendered the miners every assistance. He introduced a resolution in the Senate for a Federal investigation; he assisted in bringing cases into court to bring a measure of constitutional procedure into the war. Even when the State Supreme Court decided for the power of the militia against the civil courts, he did not give up. Most important of all, perhaps, he helped commit the Democratic Party in the state to opposition to the illegal and unconstitutional methods which were being used to defeat the Union.

In all this, Teller gave him valuable, although somewhat legalistic, support. When the cause was the blackest, Teller wrote a careful statement of the rights of organized labor, which Patterson published on the front page of the *News*.[23]

It was an appeal to middle-of-the-road opinion to support constitutional principles. Although cautiously legal, it was emphatic upon the main point. Fair-minded people, he held, must concede labor its legal rights to organize and to strike. Although unions must be voluntary and have no right to keep others from working, their rights of organizing were clearly legal. Such mutual-benefit organizations, he declared, were as "old as history," and had greatly benefited labor. The suppressions against them that were being practiced were "gross violations of rights secured by the constitution of the state." Governor Peabody's action was illegal and unwise, and the militia was legally bound to respect the state courts. As to the State Supreme Court's decision upholding the power of the military as against civil processes, he declared:

> My professional education and long professional life as a lawyer have made me exceedingly conservative when I come to speak of decisions of courts ... and I shall content myself with saying that I do not believe the decision of the court can be supported upon principle or

---

[22] June 18, 1904.

[23] July 24, 1904. See also C. P. Connolly, "Conspiracies of Capital and the Courts," *Pacific Monthly*, Sept., 1908. On July 15, the *News* had published an essay by Teller's youngest brother, James, on "The Decadence of the Spirit of Liberty," which was a defense of civil liberties with examples of their violation by the state government and vigilantes in the current strikes.

precedent, and the court will have the distinction of being the only court in this broad land of ours that has ever made a decision of that character.

His denunciation of the vigilantism of the state government and the Citizens' Alliance was the kind of appeal that would carry weight with any citizen of democratic sentiments.

Patterson was not to escape unscathed. The common ramifications of ownership furnished an opportunity for the mineowners to attack his two papers, and soon his chief advertisers, the department stores of Denver, began to boycott him. Patterson met this straight-on, published the names of the boycotters, and urged friends of the freedom of the press to boycott the stores in retaliation. Teller wrote a letter for Patterson to publish in which he also denounced the boycott and praised the *News*.

No paper in the West has been so consistently and earnestly loyal to the best interests of its own state as has *The Rocky Mountain News*. ... No one can overestimate the importance of an unpurchasable and untrammeled press.[24]

The controversy over the rights of labor in Colorado merged into the fall campaign and gave Teller an issue such as he had not enjoyed on a state question for many years. It was fortunate that it did, for national politics in 1904 had little comfort for the now discredited silverites. Bryan's two defeats had left him under a cloud as a possible Democratic candidate for president, and with him most of his friends and supporters. There was no other candidate who had a chance of winning—unless we concede that Senator Francis M. Cockrell had such a chance—in whose victory Teller would take any personal satisfaction. No doubt he took pride in the public announcements of two old friends, ex-Senator Blair, of New Hampshire, Republican, and ex-Senator Butler, of North Carolina, Populist, that Teller, himself, would be an ideal candidate—the "strongest" the Democrats could nominate.[25]

The Democratic National Convention chose Judge Alton B. Parker as its candidate with the support of part of the Colorado delegation. After he was named, a telegram from him was presented to the convention in which he repudiated

24 *Rocky Mountain News*, June 17-22, 1904; Adams, "Patterson," pp. 95-96.
25 Clippings from the Washington *Post*, Dawson Scrapbook.

the silver planks of the last two platforms. Although Teller had long since given up any idea that it was politically possible to re-establish the free coinage of silver, it must have given him moments of perplexity to contemplate himself supporting a gold-standard Democrat of the Cleveland tradition.

After Parker's nomination, a reporter sought out Teller for an interview. He tried to turn the question by praising the vice-presidential nominee, Henry Gassaway Davis. When challenged with a direct question he replied:

> Personally, I do not know Judge Parker, but I know a great many people who do know him, and from them I had formed a very high opinion of him long before he was mentioned as a candidate. I do not believe that at any time in the history of the country it has been so important to make a change in administrations as it is today. I believe Judge Parker will give the country a safe, conservative administration, and while I know that he is a gold standard man, and have known that since 1896, I have no hesitation in supporting him and I believe, all things considered, it was the best nomination the party could have made.[26]

But his real interest was in the state campaign. The Republicans renominated Governor Peabody and defended his suppression of the miners' union; the Democrats put their best foot forward by naming former Governor Alva Adams and made Peabody's record in the labor war the main issue. Teller, like Patterson, found himself happier urging this point of view from the stump than he did the election of Parker. It was also necessary strategy, for against the colorful Roosevelt, liberal and progressive, albeit imperialistic, it was useless to urge Parker's claims in Colorado. Consequently, for the first time since he had gone to the Senate, Teller reversed his usual procedure of ignoring local issues and talking national policies; this time he talked the violations of constitutional principles involved in the suppression of the union. His plea for Adams was for a governor who would adhere to the law, observe the constitution, and not use the power of the state government to suppress the rights of one group of citizens for the profit of another. As usual, he closed the campaign with an enthusiastic meeting in Central City.[27]

Roosevelt swept the country, including Colorado. The Republican state ticket was carried along on the tide, and

---

[26] *Rocky Mountain News*, July 15, 1904.
[27] *Ibid.*, Nov. 8, 1904.

all except Governor Peabody won. The latter ran behind the President in essentially all precincts. On the face of the returns, Adams had a plurality of from ten to twelve thousand, and his was the only state-wide Democratic victory, a result of the Democrats' courageous opposition to Peabody's war on labor, the credit for which belonged more to Patterson than to anyone else.

Teller's comment on the national results was optimistic. He wrote Dawson:

> When you come to look at his [Roosevelt's] vote it is not so wonderful as it looked at first as his vote is not more than the natural increase in his party vote, but Parker's vote shows a loss over Bryan in 1896 that is quite surprising. The fact is the democratic party is pretty badly demoralized & it will not improve under the guidance of John Sharp Williams Sheean & Taggart. I can stand Roosevelt if we can get rid of Peabody here.[28]

But it was rapidly becoming doubtful that they could get rid of Peabody in Colorado. The Republicans were claiming fraud, and indeed there had been fraud—Democratic fraud in Denver and Republican fraud state wide—but nowhere as outrageous as in the areas where the Mine Managers' Association had taken over the government. So threatening was the danger that Adams would be kept out of the governorship by some means that neither Teller nor Patterson left Denver when Congress opened. Teller wrote to Dawson that conditions were far from satisfactory:

> The Republicans mean, if they can to seat Peabody not because he is a Republican but because the Corporations can use him & they fear they cannot use Adams. If it is necessary to do so I have no doubt Peabody will call out the militia. . . . I am disgusted at some Democrats & more so at the Republicans. If all the men who ought to be in the penitentiary could be sent there we would need a dozen new ones.[29]

There were good reasons for being disgusted at some Democrats, as it seemed apparent that there were those who were none too anxious to see Adams as governor. These were generally credited as being the leaders of the machine in Denver, which was at outs with Patterson. With considerable truth Patterson had been accusing them of being closely allied with Colorado utility interests and their willing agent in corrupting the Denver government. In the city elections of 1904, Patterson had supported the Republican

---

[28] Teller to Dawson, Dec. 8, 1904, Teller MSS.
[29] Dec. 6, 1904, Teller MSS.

candidate for mayor in an effort to break the power of the city Democratic organization. Although there had been complete co-operation in the state campaign, now that it was over, there were rumors that pressure was being brought upon the organization to aid in unseating Adams.[30]

Patterson and Teller saw Adams inaugurated in the regular way. Then the Republican-controlled legislature began an investigation of the election. Frauds were proved on both sides, but final decision turned upon other considerations. Apparently with some aid from the Denver machine, a strange compromise was agreed upon. Adams was unseated, and Peabody declared elected. Immediately after the latter was sworn in he resigned in accordance with the terms of that agreement. This permitted Republican Lieutenant Governor Jesse F. McDonald to succeed to the governorship.[31]

This result, climaxing a disastrous election, was far from encouraging, and Teller became less and less active in state politics. Patterson, however, like the crusader he was, turned his energies toward driving the Denver machine out of politics. He included the State Supreme Court in his slashing criticisms and was soon cited for contempt. With a legal staff which included Teller, Charles S. Thomas, and other Democratic leaders, he met the citation by the answer that the charge was true. The Attorney General declared that such an answer admitted the contempt, and the truth or falsity of the charge was immaterial. The court accepted this view, found Patterson guilty, and fined him a thousand dollars. However good the court's law was, it was exceedingly bad politics, as it avoided a trial on the merits of the charges. Patterson had undoubtedly scored a great victory and for "a few days was the most popular man in the State." Undismayed when the United States Supreme Court threw out his appeal, Patterson renewed his fight on selfish corporate control of government, and its agent, the Denver machine.[32] Through his newspapers and on the stump he laid the charges of utility domination and corruption against it and every Democrat who co-operated with it. He was able to exclude it from any part in the management of the party at the state convention of 1906, although its control in Den-

---

[30] Thomas, "Fifty Years," p. 936.

[31] Stone, *Colorado,* I, 444.

[32] Thomas, "Fifty Years," p. 938; Adams, "Patterson," pp. 112-17; Denver *Republican,* Nov. 21, 30, 1905.

ver was still unquestioned. As a result, that campaign lacked its effective support, and the Democrats, hurt also by the independent candidacy of Judge Ben Lindsey for governor, lost again.[33] But the machine came back, and even if helpless out-state, it maintained itself in Denver against all the efforts which Patterson could bring against it.

---

[33] Lindsey and his attempts at reform in Denver seem to have had encouragement from both Patterson and Teller for a time. When the names of the two senators were used to awe him into suppressing a report exposing graft, he appealed to them directly, and received his first real encouragement by being told to "go ahead and show up the grafters regardless of party." Lincoln Steffens, *Upbuilders* (New York, 1909), p. 231. Lindsey himself criticized Willard Teller and his partner, C. C. Dorsey, as active members of the railroad lobby. Willard Teller was still attorney for the Union Pacific. Ben B. Lindsay and Harvey Jay O'Higgins, *The Beast* (New York, 1910), p. 243.

CHAPTER XXIV

THE WEST AND STATES' RIGHTS
1905-08

TELLER'S last years in the Senate were not his most successful politically, but, in spite of illnesses that kept him absent a great deal, they were the most satisfactory personally. This was due to the growing respect with which he was generally regarded. These were years when the Senate was under attack. The muckrakers had discovered it and placed it under a microscope. More than that, the progress of the proposal to make it a popularly elected body made it a subject of frequent and unflattering study. Through all these Teller came with flying colors, generally acknowledged as one of the few who most nearly upheld the "best traditions of the Senate."[1] No one now suggested that he was a "railroad" senator, as they might easily have done when he went to Washington in 1876. The new progressives found him an ally on all but a few questions, and treated him as one.

Because he would be within a few months of seventy-nine years of age if he lived to complete his term, he was included in much of the comment about the "old men" who made up the Senate. They were old men. When Mr. Dooley announced that the entrance of Beveridge into the Senate at the age of eight had reduced "th' average age iv that body to ninety-three," he was satirizing this condition. In 1903, seventeen of the ninety members were past seventy years of age, including Pettus, of Alabama, who was past eighty.[2] Death soon decreased this number substantially. Hoar, Quay, O. H. Platt, Pettus, and Morgan all passed away before the end of 1907, and when Allison died the next year there was no one left in the Senate who had been there when Teller arrived in 1876. The Coloradan made one of his rare jokes on the Senate floor in 1908 when he denied an imagined suggestion that he had been a member of the upper house in 1814.[3]

---

[1] George H. Haynes, *The Election of Senators* (New York, 1906), p. 93. This was a study made by a panel consisting of one administrative official, a member of the House, an expert investigator, and two Washington correspondents. Private expression of the same tenor includes James K. Jones to Dawson, Dec. 14, 1904: "I regard him as one of the strongest, best and ablest men I have known in public life." Teller MSS.

[2] Washington *Post*, Feb. 15, 1903.

[3] *Congressional Record*, 60 Cong., 1 Sess., p. 2881.

All this was saddening in the light of his own few years remaining. Although his mother had but recently died at the advanced age of ninety-four, the death of Willard Teller in 1905 was a direct reminder that his own career was about over. But there were compensations even for this eventuality. "Colorado's Grand Old Man" was no mean title, and its use was fairly general even in opposition newspapers. His unusual ability in committee work could now find an outlet in the more important Senate committees, especially those on finance, rules, and appropriations, which were his regular assignments during these years. Then, after the complete failure of the conservative Democrats to make a respectable showing with Parker, the progressives and the old silver faction were rapidly regaining control of the national organization. It must have been exceedingly comforting personally not to be considered an anachronism, even if one had to admit many years. To the last, Teller dressed in the black frock coat of an earlier period, and his manner of speaking reminded one observer of an old-fashioned preacher.[4] Nevertheless, he could read that some of the press correspondents regarded him as evidence of the modern trend in the Senate. Writing in 1906, Charles Willis Thompson observed that the old Senate of orators was rapidly passing:

> Senatorial ability now finds its expression in the silent mastery of men, the chess-playing with senators for pawns, of Aldrich; the sturdy common sense and directness of the late Mark Hanna, which achieved results with no circumlocution and no eloquence; the businesslike and downright speeches of Teller.... The ability may be as great, the results are as great, but the method is different.[5]

Another correspondent was even more comforting:

> There has never been a man in public life more honest and faithful, and more true to his convictions and the courage to express them, than Henry M. Teller.... He is now 75 years of age, but at this writing is a young old man and does good work for his constituents and his country. He has a lovely disposition and is extremely popular, and everybody admires and respects him for his intellectual qualities and his honesty of purpose in all his legislative efforts.[6]

As far as national politics was concerned, Teller had been exceedingly pessimistic about accomplishing anything of value after the Republican victory of 1904. "Whatever

---

[4] O. O. Stealey, *Twenty Years in the Press Gallery* (New York, 1906), p. 460.
[5] *Party Leaders of the Time* (New York, 1906), p. 59.
[6] O. O. Stealey, *op. cit.*, p. 437.

the republican party wants to do it will do," he wrote his secretary. "The President is now the party and what he wants to do his party will do & profess to be pleased with doing it."[7] Judging by what Roosevelt had wanted the past three years, the future did not look very promising. He also found the domination of the Senate by the oligarchy of Republican leaders unsatisfactory, although among this group were some—such as Allison and Platt—who were among his most intimate friends. That Teller's last years in the Senate were better years than he anticipated was due solely to the growing progressivism of the country and of President Roosevelt.

In his own growth, the President was responding to a surge of public sentiment, based upon the pioneer work of the Populists and now fed by the muckrakers and younger progressive leaders, such as La Follette, Folk, and Cummins. As he sensed the trend, he unconsciously shifted into a position to lead, if not the vanguard, at least the second rank of progressives. Here was a happier circumstance for the Bryan Democrats of the nineties; it gave some presidential encouragement to the policies they favored, and, more important, perhaps, it split the Republican unity in Congress so that members of the minority could again exercise some positive influence on legislation. So impressed was Patterson with the change that in January, 1906, he praised the President's recent policies to the Senate, including his participation in the Algeciras Conference, and the Santo Domingo treaty, as well as his fight for railroad rate regulation.[8]

Teller never found it possible to say a kindly word for Roosevelt's foreign policy, but the new tone of his domestic policy pleased him nearly as much as it did Patterson. It made railroad rate regulation possible, and Teller found that congenial. When Roosevelt came to the front with proposals to strengthen the law in 1904, 1905, and 1906, most of the Democrats in the Senate were delighted, partly because the South and West wanted such a law, but also because it set the administration's declared policy in direct opposition to what the Republican Old Guard in the House and Senate desired. Senator Tillman wrote to former Senator Chandler:

---

[7] Teller to Dawson, Dec. 8, 1904, Teller MSS.
[8] Washington *Post*, Feb. 1, 1906; Adams, "Patterson," p. 160.

The coming session of Congress promises to be interesting and perhaps fruitful of surprises. It all depends on your man Teddy. If he means business on the rate-making programme he laid down last year, we Democrats—all the patriots who are left—will have an opportunity to help use the big stick on recalcitrant Republican heads.[9]

The essence of the contest was between the Old Guard senators proper, who under various guises were doing their best to prevent any effective rate regulation, and those Western and Southern senators who wanted the Interstate Commerce Commission to have power to set rates that were no higher than necessary to pay a low return on the investment involved. The apparent contest was over broad versus narrow court review, which meant that the first group, accepting the necessity of satisfying the public clamor with legislation, worked for that which would permit conservative federal courts to suspend and later reverse the rates set by the commission, and the second group worked for a law that would permit as little interference with the commission by the courts as was constitutionally possible. At first the President worked with the Democratic and Republican senators in the second group, but after a time accepted as his own a compromise policy that conceded enough to the Old Guard senators of his own party to restore Republican harmony and pass a Republican bill. Unquestionably it marked a great advance in regulation, but not as much as such progressives as the President himself had originally desired.

Teller made his main contribution a defense of the legality and practicality of forbidding the courts from issuing interlocutory orders suspending rates set by the commission. The commission's "order should stand until such time as the court shall, upon final investigation, and final determination, decide otherwise."[10] The Old Guard opposition to this never admitted, of course, that its objection was based upon the fear that such a restriction would make the commission's rate-making effective; but rather it was pitched upon the high moral ground that such restrictions upon the powers of the court violated essential constitutional principles.

After the President had retreated, the Republican compromise was embodied in the Allison amendment, and received virtually unanimous Republican support. This en-

---

[9] Oct. 19, 1905. Quoted in Stephenson, *Aldrich*, p. 279.
[10] *Congressional Record*, 59 Cong., 1 Sess., pp. 4283, 6315.

abled Teller to strip the disguise from the Old Guard's constitutional camouflage by pointing out that it should be against the compromise also, as it "violated" the same sacred principle that had guided it in its declared opposition earlier. The only difference, he insisted, was one of degree and not of principle. As for himself, he approved the principle of restricting the court's power and consequently approved the Allison amendment even if it did not go as far as he wished.

Teller voted consistently with the most extreme group of those who wished effective rate regulation, even voting for the La Follette proposal to evaluate the properties of the roads for use as a basis for rates. He pointed out that the Republican compromise was under the direction of the very Old Guard that was an enemy of the legislation, and it was handing a "gold brick" to the people who, "after two or three years of effort to get redress under this bill" will find that they have to fight for new legislation all over again. He was glad to vote for it because it was better than the old law and "infinitely better" than the House bill.[11]

Teller never became intensely interested in the politics of the progressive movement as he had been in more purely Western questions or imperialism. In fact, his last years in the Senate, when progressivism was popular, were marked by a reabsorption in the policies that he had been interested in when he first came to the Senate: public lands, Indians, and the territories. Greatest of these was public lands.

Francis G. Newlands, now a member of the Senate, and an old associate in the silver fight, was taking the lead in reorganizing the land system in such a way as to bring about a planned system in the West, financed and controlled by the Government. This included the abandonment of many of the old *laissez-faire* pioneer land practices, as well as a substantial surrender of local self-control. Had these matters first come up about 1890, it seems probable that Teller's opposition to all features of these changes would not have been as intense or indeed even present, but Western experience with forest reserves had not been conducive to willing acceptance of its expansion. The reservations set aside under the law by Cleveland and McKinley had included areas of land in Colorado that were unwooded and useless for the purpose indicated. The intrusion of these federally controlled areas within a state created no end of serious prob-

---

[11] *Ibid.*, pp. 6677, 6883, 7080-91.

lems. Conflicts with local people whose land bordered or was surrounded by the reserve, and with local government units were numerous, and because of the remoteness of Washington almost impossible to adjust except after the passage of considerable time. Then, as the system expanded, and more and more of a state's undeveloped territory was permanently removed from the possibility of supporting a population, it came home with considerable force that a state's growth was being permanently limited, with a check to the regular increase in real-estate values that Americans had always known. It is little wonder that Teller, conditioned by Western experience as he was, reacted rather violently against the entire idea, and began to defend states' rights like a prewar Democrat.

On several occasions after 1900 he arose in the Senate to defend the land laws as revised in 1891. When at the opening of certain Indian reservations it was proposed to place the land on sale and use the proceeds for reclamation in the arid regions, Teller objected and defended the Homestead Act, with the one reservation that the commutation right, which had been restricted in the early legislation, should now be abolished. That was sufficient to ensure that real settlers got the land. "Any man who goes upon one of those quarter-sections of land and makes a home there is entitled to the land without paying a single cent for it."[12] In one instance, at least, he succeeded in making this change, but as the attack on the land laws become more intense, bills to repeal all laws granting free land to settlers were brought before the Senate. This had been met by a typical speech from Teller in the spring of 1904, defending the current system of granting free lands to settlers. The real attack on the system then, he pointed out, came from a well-financed lobby in Washington maintained by land-grant railroads with large land areas of their own for which they were anxious to find a good market. The public lands should be devoted to the creation and maintenance of a land-owning citizenry.

I am one of those who believe that the strength and hope of this nation is with the men who till the soil and who own the soil they till. I have heard a great deal said about the man who follows the plow. Mr. President, the man who follows the plow on some other man's land is a serf. If he follows it on his own he is a freeman, and he becomes a good citizen.[13]

---

[12] *Congressional Record*, 57 Cong., 1 Sess., p. 4913; *ibid.*, 58 Cong., 2 Sess., pp. 4917-24.

[13] *Ibid.*, 58 Cong., 2 Sess., pp. 5679-88; *ibid.*, 59 Cong., 1 Sess., p. 6055.

During these debates Teller denied that there was any public sentiment in Colorado favorable to the sale of public lands to finance irrigation works. When the Newlands Act was passed he wanted to protect the state's control of the irrigation systems established, a position which he had long urged.[14] He was no doubt influenced in part by the controversies between Colorado and its eastern neighbors, Kansas and Nebraska, over Colorado's right to use the water in the eastward-flowing rivers; but whatever the combination of causes, he gave only qualified support. In fact, as the Federal Government moved in the direction of greater control over waterways, Teller went the entire distance of the states' rights champion and denied its constitutional authority over such water. It had merely a "franchise" to use the water for shipping, and could not go into the business of irrigation or power production.[15]

But against the policy of forest reserves there were no qualifications to the Coloradan's opposition: "I will join with anybody for the protection of forests in any method that does not outrage the people of the States where they are located," he had declared in 1898, but by the time he left the Senate he was insisting that it was a matter for state jurisdiction.[16] In the meantime, Roosevelt's expansion of reserves had increased their proportion of Colorado's area to over one fifth of the total.

Most of all, Teller resented the currently popular denunciations of the avariciousness of the American pioneer for using and destroying his timber. To make the crime more ignoble, Teller quoted Senator Dolliver as saying in a typical denunciation, "It was based upon greed and avarice and the love of money." Teller answered:

My father was a settler and he cleared up a farm; my grandfather cleared up a farm, and all my neighbors cleared up farms. . . . Is anybody justified in saying that the men who cleared up those farms and made homes are guilty of a crime of such stupendous magnitude because they did not have the foresight to save their pine timber and did not wait forty or fifty years that it might be sold to somebody who came after them. . . . I have great admiration for the men who went

---

[14] *Ibid.*, 56 Cong., 2 Sess., pp. 1564-66.

[15] Arthur B. Darling, ed., *Public Papers of Francis G. Newlands* (Boston, 1932), II, 197-203; *Congressional Record*, 58 Cong., 2 Sess., pp. 1634-35.

[16] *Congressional Record*, 55 Cong., 2 Sess., p. 3511. After he left the Senate, he followed up this constitutional argument by a pamphlet in which he presented evidence that the national government could not attach unusual conditions when it disposed of public lands or water rights which would impair the sovereignty of states. *State Control of Water*. 24 pp. N.p., n.d.)

into the timber and made homes.... I cannot rid myself of the idea that a home on a piece of land is infinitely better than a piece of unbroken timber.[17]

His greatest criticisms were aimed at the manner in which the reserves were administered,[18] possibly because this was easier to attack, and partly because the policies of Roosevelt's Secretary of Interior, E. A. Hitchcock, were as a whole exceedingly unpopular. It was not for nothing that one congressman told a Gridiron Club banquet that when Hitchcock resigned "there wasn't a dry throat west of the Mississippi."[19]

Over two years after Teller retired from the Senate, he told the public lands convention in Denver, "I favor putting the public lands in the hands of the people as fast as possible. There has never been a landlord in the history of the world as oppressive as a national landlord."[20]

Regarding Indians, Teller's interest and activity continued, even to the extent of accepting membership again on the Committee on Indian Affairs, the "most difficult and troublesome and unsatisfactory" committee in the Senate in his opinion. He continued his support of Indian education, including Government support of the church schools where there were no other adequate educational facilities.[21] As far as the Senate was concerned, he was the great advocate of education as the solution of the Indian problem. "The children of all the Indian schools have shown just as much ability as the white children of the same age," he asserted in 1901, and testified that he had employed Indians on his farm in Colorado and they were excellent workers. "There is virtue in all classes of people and the Indian has his share of it."[22]

Regularly he followed the committee bills onto the Senate floor, defending provisions already in the bill, and submitting amendments that the committee had not approved. Besides the encouragement of education, these had two main purposes, to protect the tribal status of the Indian and to protect the title to his land as long as it was in any way legally

[17] *Congressional Record*, 60 Cong., 1 Sess., pp. 6064-66.

[18] Walter Andrew Voss, "Colorado and Forest Conservation" (unpublished thesis, University of Colorado, 1931), pp. 58-59.

[19] Arthur W. Dunn, *Gridiron Nights* (New York, 1915), p. 185.

[20] Clipping from Denver *Times*, Sept. 29, 1911, in Dawson Scrapbook; also *Speech of H. M. Teller*, 20 pp. (N.p., n.d.)

[21] *Congressional Record*, 54 Cong., 2 Sess., pp. 2040-45; *ibid.*, 56 Cong., 1 Sess., pp. 3831-48, 3880-89, 5937.

[22] *Ibid.*, 56 Cong., 2 Sess., p. 1373; *ibid.*, 60 Cong., 1 Sess., p. 2647.

possible. In both cases, he seldom got as much as he asked, but usually got something. It is not surprising that he occasionally declared, "I told you so," in regard to the working out of the severalty policy of the Dawes Act. He frequently cited evidence that the Dawes Act was making a landless Indian as soon as the restriction was removed. Tribal ownership, he insisted, should continue, and with it the other social and political tribal conditions, at least until the Indians themselves asked to have the status changed.[23]

His objection to extending citizenship to the Indian under the Dawes Act was vindicated when the Burke Act of 1906 was passed to prevent the worst of evils which had resulted from that provision. Sometimes the rulings of the Department of the Interior came in for criticism, and occasionally for correction by legislation. In spite of this fine, unselfish work of many years, Teller was powerfully moved by the increasingly sad condition of the Indian. In 1908 he testified as to the inadequacy of his own work:

> I have made every effort I could from time to time to benefit their condition. I acknowledge my dereliction, Mr. President. I believe I could have done better. I believe I ought to have done better. I propose, so far as I can, to do better in the little time that I shall serve in the Senate.[24]

With the admission of the omnibus states of the Northwest in 1889 and 1890, Teller's interest in the territories had lessened for a time, but never disappeared. The present states of Arizona, New Mexico, and Oklahoma were still under a territorial form of government. Toward legislation for these areas he was always active. His interest was not only political, for he and Hal Sayre had acquired a farm near Yuma in Arizona Territory, and by 1904 were greatly interested in the speculative possibility of raising Algerian dates there for market.[25]

Essentially, however, it was the old contest for statehood over again with little new in the arguments presented. The most bitterly contested bill had been before the Senate in the short session of 1903. This proposal had been to admit all three as states: Oklahoma, New Mexico, and Arizona. Although the Republican Party had pledged itself to this

[23] *Ibid.*, 57 Cong., 1 Sess., p. 7503; *ibid.*, 59 Cong., 1 Sess., pp. 2975-76, 3061-62, 3122, 5788-92, 5807-10.

[24] *Ibid.*, 58 Cong., 1 Sess., pp. 3061-62, 3275-76; *ibid.*, 60 Cong., 1 Sess., p. 2425.

[25] Teller to Sayre, Jan. 14, 1904, Sayre MSS.

action in its platform of 1900, and it had enough votes to pass it in the Senate, still the Old Guard oligarchy killed the bill by a filibuster. The Republican-controlled Senate Committee on Territories had traveled hurriedly through the area the summer before, and recommended against admission. In fact, the chairman, Beveridge, was committed against statehood before the "investigation" started and had already set in motion propaganda on a national scale against it.[26]

As the main problem was to secure a vote, Teller had stayed out of the debate, making the opponents who were filibustering the bill keep the floor. Once, however, the reflections upon the residents of New Mexico in speeches against the bill and in the committee report brought him to his feet to defend Westerners of Mexican descent. "They are infinitely better than the people you are admitting from Europe today," he declared. The real basis of the objections made to these people was that they continued to speak Spanish. "Did you ever see a race that was worthy of the consideration of mankind that did not have an attachment to the tongue which they had in their youth?" he inquired. And what was wrong with Spanish? "It is a written language. It is an old language. It is a beautiful language. Any man who can speak it well can express every sentiment and every thought of which he is capable as beautifully as in any other known language. . . . Why should they abandon it?" This was only an ostensible reason for opposition, he insisted; the real reason was fear of increasing the power of the West in national affairs. "You are keeping them out because you are afraid of their influence."[27] This was the sum of Teller's speech on the question, although he followed the speeches of the opposition closely, interjecting a question now and then to make clear the reality of the opposition and the nature of the filibuster.

A week later he was following a long, dilatory speech by Senator Depew, a humorous rehash of most of the argument against admission. It did not make Teller comfortable, because most of it was a depreciation of Western country and Western people. Finally, the New York senator brought out the suggestion that small states should resist any addition to their number, otherwise it might bring on a revolution by the great states because they could not find the

---

[26] Claude G. Bowers, *Beveridge and the Progressive Era* (Cambridge, 1932), pp. 193-94.

[27] *Congressional Record*, 57 Cong., 2 Sess., pp. 1891-92.

means of expressing their desires in a Senate controlled by the small states. With this Teller lost his usually controlled temper:

I cannot hear with much patience the threat of revolution in this country. New England, with its twelve Senators in this body [nearly all of whom were against the bill] has not as many people as has the State of New York. Has this Government ever suffered ... by the small States of New England being represented in this body? I say here and I want to say to the Senator, that he does not represent any-body in this country when he talks about breaking up the form of government. ... I have listened to a good deal of nonsense, and I have listened without protest during this debate to a good deal that I consider beneath the dignity of the Senate; but I could not listen to what the Senator from New York has said without saying here ... that I resent the insult ... from the Senator. ... [28]

The gallery applauded, and Depew's speech was a wreck.

When closure was proposed to force a vote on the bill Teller refused to support it. But after Aldrich succeeded in displacing the statehood bill with his banking bill just before the end of the session, the Colorado senator helped filibuster that to death in retaliation, as Aldrich had been the real power behind the filibuster of the statehood bill. And in doing so he took occasion to pay his respects to Aldrich and the other senators from the small states. "Why is it?" he asked regarding their opposition. "It is because you are afraid of the power of the West in this body. That is the plain English of it." Only one of the twelve senators from the tiny New England states, he pointed out, was favorable to the bill. As usual they were a "solid phalanx" in the Senate.

I am inclined to think that our New England friends feel that in the course of time New England may lose the supremacy that she had in this body. Her twelve senators will be insignificant in number com-pared with a membership in the Senate of 96.

As for Aldrich's charge that Teller was engaged in a filibuster, why deny it? "How did you get the divine right to filibuster? ... Is it because you are a majority?"[29]

In 1906, the contest was resumed on Beveridge's bill to admit Oklahoma and to unite the territories of New Mexico and Arizona and admit them as one state. The real issue was whether Arizona and New Mexico should come in as

---

[28] *Ibid.*, 57 Cong., 2 Sess., Appendix, pp. 93-113; New York *Tribune*, Feb. 18, 1903.
[29] *Congressional Record*, 57 Cong., 2 Sess., pp. 2972-75.

one or two states. For this proposal Beveridge presented one
of the orations for which he was famous. Teller followed
with his usual factual statement that deflated most of the
"oratory" that had preceded him. The Indiana senator's
evidence, he pointed out, was highly questionable, being bare
assertion for the most part. The people of the territories
did not want that bill, and everyone knew it. The telegrams
Beveridge had introduced to prove its popularity had all
come, Teller charged, in response to requests and meant
nothing at all. Instead of being a "crowning glory" to the
men who voted for the proposal, it would be a "crowning disgrace."[30] It passed, and Oklahoma entered the Union, but
Arizona voted down the union plan and the two territories
were not admitted as states until after Teller had retired
from the Senate.

During these debates, Teller had not forgotten Alaska.
Fighting for a territorial status for that region, he seldom
neglected to include her in the group of eventual states,
arguing that she would soon be ready for statehood. On all
matters which related to the region—schools, railroads,
fisheries, land laws, natives, and mining laws—he was exceedingly active.[31]

As the technical aspects of government had always interested Teller, especially so after his experience in the
Department of the Interior, he continued his activity in the
direction of desired changes. In 1902 he had pleaded for a
better status in the civil service for employees of the census
bureau who were being let out as their work was completed.[32]

When the creation of a Department of Commerce was
under consideration, Teller objected to the separation of
statistical bureaus in different departments, and advocated
one bureau with a permanent head not subject to change
with administrations.[33] His interest in this work was also
shown in his attaching an amendment to the census bill to
have an assistant director who should be a trained statisti-
cian.[34] He gave substantial aid to the establishment of new
bureaus in whose work he had confidence, such as the Bureau

---

[30] *Ibid.*, 59 Cong., 1 Sess., pp. 3576-77.

[31] *Ibid.*, 56 Cong., 1 Sess., pp. 3929-34, 4214-20, 4374-76; *ibid.*, 58 Cong., 2 Sess., pp.
3914-17; *ibid.*, 59 Cong., 1 Sess., p. 4853; Mack, "Stewart," pp. 132-37; *Selections from
the Correspondence of Roosevelt and Lodge*, II, 1-2.

[32] *Congressional Record*, 57 Cong., 1 Sess., p. 1789.

[33] *Ibid.*, 57 Cong., 1 Sess., pp. 767-68.

[34] *Ibid.*, p. 1802.

of Plant Industry in the Department of Agriculture.[35] Like
most of his colleagues, he continued to support the Civil War
pension system. Rather surprisingly for one who had been
such an ardent advocate of the Star Routes, he opposed the
establishment of the rural free delivery system.[36] He was
ill and absent when the vote was taken on seating Republican
Senator Smoot, opposed because of his intimate connection
with the Mormon church, but was paired for his right to his
seat.[37] In the spring of 1908, he followed through the new
penal code with many suggestions for change, some of which
were adopted. Later that year, a resolution came before the
Senate to recognize Mother's Day, and he moved that it be
laid on the table. "It seems to me puerile."[38]

When Teller had recourse to an argument against the
policies that were opposed to Western sentiment, during
these latter years, he usually fell back upon the Constitution
and states' rights. Essentially this was because the issue,
especially that of forest reserves, was going against him,
and states' rights is usually the nearest refuge of a loser.
But with Teller it marked another tendency that developed
with age: to return to his legal training and background
for argument and for ideas. His speeches became more
legalistic; he discussed the constitutionality of proposals
more frequently. Even when he was looking for political
issues this was evident.[39] These states' rights statements
are in striking contrast to his nationalism in, say 1865, if
we go back to our earliest record of his ideas on the subject.

In anticipation of the approaching election of 1908, Teller's contribution was the theme of Roosevelt's tendency to
ignore the constitutional division of power between the state
and nation, and among the three branches of the Government:

Mr. President, nobody will sneer me down by saying there is no
danger of executive interference or executive changes in the system
of this Government. That has always been the cry of all men who
want to exercise arbitrary power. Buckle ... declared that power
exercised by classes had never been exercised but what it was ultimately abused. I believe that is the history of mankind. . . . there is not

---

[35] B. T. Galloway, "The Genesis of the Bureau of Plant Industry" (typed manuscript, June 30, 1926, loaned by James C. Malin).

[36] *Congressional Record*, 55 Cong., 2 Sess., p. 4616; *ibid.*, 58 Cong., 2 Sess., p. 2351.

[37] *Ibid.*, 59 Cong., 2 Sess., p. 3429.

[38] *Ibid.*, 60 Cong., 1 Sess., pp. 1534-35, 5971-72.

[39] As chairman of the program committee for the Public Land Convention of 1907,
Teller's agenda centered the question almost entirely upon constitutional issues. See
printed copy of agenda dated May 29, 1907.

anything that will so degrade the human being as an exercise of arbitrary and unjust power. Buckle might have added...that there was no history of the arbitrary exercise of executive power by an individual in which he did not ultimately demand more power....[40]

On his seventy-eighth birthday, May 23, 1908, Teller addressed the Senate, formally summing up his objections to the trend of government under Roosevelt. He deplored the growing rarity of debate on the Constitution in the Senate, and the President's tendency to ignore that document. He discussed the proper relation of the state and national government, praising Marshall's decision in *Gibbons* vs. *Ogden*, and suggested the desirability of having it read and discussed in the Senate on a stated day each year, as Washington's Farewell Address was read and discussed. His plea was for the preservation of local government with all the rights stated in the Constitution "to be construed not strictly, but honestly."[41]

One serious decision had to be made by Teller in the spring of 1908. Would he again be a candidate for the Senate? Democratic Party leaders in Colorado were extremely polite, at least pretending that he could have a renomination if he desired it. There can be little doubt that he did want it badly, but in the end could not bring himself to ask for it. His advanced age made it seem obviously unjust for him to continue. More than that, his ill-health and frequent absences from the Senate during the previous two years made it obvious that it would not look well to demand another term. On the other hand, he was not in the same position as he had been in 1896, when he had contemplated retiring. His age now made it highly improbable that he could earn a comfortable living from the practice of law. Moreover, his mines and other investments were in poor shape. In fact, he had been trying for the past several years to dispose of these and reduce or clear away his indebtedness. But his efforts had been fruitless, and only a few pieces of property had been sold to satisfy pressing obligations.[42] In spite of this, the fact had to be faced; he could not ask for a re-election with dignity. He announced to his friends first, and later publicly, that he was not a candidate for re-election.

[40] *Congressional Record*, 60 Cong., 1 Sess., p. 2967.

[41] *Congressional Record*, 60 Cong., 1 Sess., pp. 6792-99.

[42] Teller to Dawson, Aug. 19, 1908, Teller MSS. Teller to Sayre, Feb. 7, Oct. 21, 1907; H. G. Shuck to Sayre, Oct. 20, 1907, Sayre MSS.

"I am seventy-eight years old and it is time I should leave public life."[43]

After this decision was made, the serious problem of who should be his successor had to be met. The Republican legislature had elected Simon Guggenheim as Patterson's successor in January, 1907, an election that was generally hailed as simply more evidence that the Senate was becoming a club of millionaires. To the militant progressives in Colorado, Guggenheim was the "smelter trust senator." He voted with the Republican Old Guard in the Senate, remained on good terms with Teller, and made no use of the position for personal advantage. In the meantime, his philanthropies in Colorado did something to belie the charges made against him there.[44]

The ability of the Republicans to elect a senator at that time had been due partly to the increased popularity of the party in Colorado under Roosevelt's national leadership, but chiefly because of the serious split between the Speer organization in Denver and Patterson. This bitter warfare, in which by every standard of political decency Patterson was in the right, boded ill for the party in 1908, as Mayor Speer was dominant in Denver, where one third of the total vote was cast. A Democratic split might easily give the state to the Republican candidate for president, and also result in a Republican senator as Teller's successor.

As Teller returned home from Washington in June, 1908, the national situation was more to his liking than it had been for many years. It was clearly evident that Bryan would again be named the Democratic candidate for president at the national convention, this time to be held in Denver. Nothing could vindicate Teller's own career like the election of the Nebraska commoner. Although the latter had made what was, perhaps, a political error in endorsing the Government ownership of railways, and Teller had written him protesting against it, there had been otherwise no disagreement between the two men since they had first known each other.[45]

---

[43] *Rocky Mountain News*, June 10, 1908.

[44] Thomas, "Fifty Years," p. 937. The Denver *Post*, which had become a vindictive enemy of both Patterson and Guggenheim by 1908, published an anonymous letter (Oct. 11, 1908) charging that Guggenheim had offered Teller $100,000 to resign from the Senate when he was ill in 1904. Admitting that Teller had denied that any such offer had been made, the writer threatened to publish a list of names of persons who knew the facts. A search of the file of the *Post* does not indicate that it was more than a threat.

[45] Bryan to Teller, Dec. 5, 1906 (?), Teller MSS.

The national conventions went through as scheduled, with Denver outdoing itself in entertaining the Democrats. The platform and Bryan were everything Teller could have wished. The only serious problem in Colorado now was whether or not the Democrats could present a united front for the national and state tickets. The Speer machine controlled the vote in Denver beyond all question, and Patterson's battle cry was, "No compromise!"

Hot undercover contests were on for the Democratic nominations for the state offices and the designation for United States Senator to succeed Teller. For the latter designation, in which Teller was most interested, T. J. O'Donnell was receiving the support of Patterson, and Charles J. Hughes the support of the Speer organization. Both were appealing for support as ardent disciples of "Colorado's Grand Old Man."

O'Donnell appealed for support on the basis of his work for Teller's re-election in 1903, and invited correspondents to write Teller for confirmation. "I hope you will spread this news among the people of Mesa County," he wrote a supporter, "for I know that Senator Teller is regarded as almost a resident and citizen of the county, and is very strong there as he is, and deservedly, everywhere."[46]

It is clear that the Democratic National Committee was seriously alarmed over the situation in Colorado, for unity was necessary to carry the state for Bryan. It does not appear that Teller was active in any way, before September. He wrote Dawson:

I think that the outlook for Bryan in the West is good, but he must carry something more than the West to be elected. I wish he may be elected but it is not as hopeful as I wish. The laboring people are not likely to know what is for their interest at least they never have. The democracy of Colorado is in a bad way and so are the Republicans.

As for the senatorial race, he did not think the Democrats could carry the legislature because of the large number of Republican members of the state senate who held over, and his successor in all probability would be a Republican.[47]

Teller went to the state convention at Pueblo as a delegate from Gilpin, announcing that he favored John Shafroth for governor. He was given a seat on the speakers' platform.

46 To T. B. Arbuckle, Aug. 18, 1908. See also letter to John Dempsey, Aug. 17, 1908. Carbons, O'Donnell MSS.
47 Aug. 8, 19, 1908, Teller MSS.

There, as in the June convention, the Patterson delegates were refused seats, although the Speer group which was seated was far from popular with the other delegates. This defeat of Patterson was a fatal blow to O'Donnell, as he was among those refused a seat. Charles S. Thomas, former governor, and Teller seem to have taken upon themselves the rôles of peacemakers, trying to fix up a compromise which would get a united party in the campaign. Apparently a deal was made in which Speer's organization was to have certain minor state offices and Hughes would be designated for the senatorship. After the knockdown fight over the seating of contested delegates, Teller was "called out" in the old-time Little-Kingdom-of-Gilpin way. He got up reluctantly and expressed regret that he was compelled to say anything. Then followed an appeal for majority rule and harmony.

> Party government is necessary to success. You cannot carry on a party without unification.... I agree with everyone who wants harmony, but don't want to fight my own friends. Let us support Bryan. He is on the highest plane, moral and political, of any man who has been before the people in a generation.

After he had finished, a message was read from Bryan addressed especially to Patterson and Speer and appealing for harmony in the convention and campaign. When the nomination for senator came before the convention, Thomas nominated Hughes and Teller supported him. Although there was considerable dissatisfaction evident, it carried overwhelmingly. John Shafroth was named for governor and the remainder of the ticket completed, with the Speer organization getting little besides the senatorship. Whatever its defects, the slate was good enough to secure substantial support from Republican progressives.[48] The convention adjourned with its compromise slate, but not complete harmony. Patterson refused to support Hughes, as did O'Donnell, and it was so persistently reported during the campaign that Teller was dissatisfied at the prospect of Hughes as his successor that the Senator had to issue a public endorsement: "I have known him for many years and have been associated with him in important litigation.... I consider him an ideal candidate."[49]

---

[48] *Rocky Mountain News*, Sept. 8-14, 1908; Denver *Republican*, Sept. 8-13, 1908; Denver *Post*, Sept. 8-13, 1908; interviews with C. S. Thomas, August, 1930; Thomas, "Fifty Years," p. 939.

[49] Denver *Post*, Sept. 27, 1908. When asked to help in the campaign, O'Donnell refused. Hughes, he insisted, was the head of the public utilities and would be their

There can be little doubt that the last was a considerable exaggeration. Had he been able to select his successor freely, Teller's preference, it seems likely, would have been for Thomas, Shafroth, Adams, or O'Donnell. But he wanted Shafroth to be governor, and he wanted Bryan to carry the state. He got all these wishes. But Bryan's carrying of Colorado was an empty victory in the face of Taft's large vote elsewhere. Teller summed it all up in a post-election letter to Bryan:

I knew that the great interests that have controlled the government for several years past were not going to lose control of the government or the business interests of the country without a determined fight. I knew they would resort to those disgraceful measures of 1896 and subsequent thereto to frighten the plain voter by threats of panic and disaster if you were elected. It may seem incredible that such a condition can exist, but when a man's daily wages stand between his family and starvation, we can hardly wonder that he shall say I will take no chances for my little ones, and thereupon votes as his master dictates.

We did well in Colorado. We have control of all departments of the State government and I will have the pleasure of having a good strong man as my successor, one of whom our people may well be proud and who will be of service to the State and to the Nation.[50]

senator. "If I could, like the Senior Senator, gulp down the whole nauseating mess and say I liked it, there would be no difficulty." That Hughes had been behind the efforts to defeat Teller in 1903, he presented evidence and charges. "I know that Senator Teller is either too innocent or too astute to admit that he believes Mr. Hughes was disloyal and Senator Teller had no opportunity to become personally cognizant of the facts. . . . Guggenheim smells sweet and clean in comparison with such uncircumcized, unrepetant and uncrucified political malefactors." O'Donnell to Charles B. Ward, Oct. 22, 1908, O'Donnell MSS.

[50] Nov. 23, 1908, Bryan MSS.

CHAPTER XXV

WINDING UP A SENATORIAL CAREER
1908-09

WITH the election of 1908, Teller's public career was
nearly at an end. He returned to the short session of
Congress to make his farewells and valedictory. He seemed
anxious to leave his attitude on questions clearly expressed.
Consequently, he rose frequently to state his views on his
favorite subjects. He argued against closure; he defended
most other senatorial traditions; and he upheld again the
constitutional division of powers among the three branches
of the Federal Government, and between the state and national governments.[1] He restated his defense of the pioneer,
and more specifically the Colorado pioneer and his use of
timber on the public lands. He boasted:

> We have made some return for this depredation on the timber. We
> have built a civilization not inferior to any other civilization on the
> American continent or on the face of the earth. These hardy miners
> and these few scattered ranchmen ... established a school system that
> has never been excelled in usefulness by any school system ever es-
> tablished on the American continent.... There has never been a race
> bill in the State, and the schools have been open to black men and
> white and red men alike. There has never been a segregation of
> any class of pupils—Chinamen, Japanese, negroes, Indians or anybody
> else—and today the wildest Indian can walk into one of our schools ...
> and become a student, and he is not required to pay a single sou for
> the privilege. That could not be done if Mr. Pinchot's system of
> managing the forests had existed. The country would still be the home
> of the coyote and the panther and the bear.... We do not need the
> fostering hand of the National Government. We want its hand taken
> off.... [The] forest reserves in Colorado have been an unmitigated
> curse and not a blessing.[2]

In the last few days of the session he indulged in the
unusual luxury of killing two bills by filibuster—one, a new
forest reserve bill, the other, a bill to establish a federal
bureau of mines. His opposition to the last, as to the first,
was on his now favorite ground that the national government
was getting too much power over local affairs.

Teller's senatorial career was over on March 4, 1909,
just as Theodore Roosevelt left the White House to make
room for William Howard Taft. Except for rare meetings

---

[1] *Congressional Record*, 60 Cong., 2 Sess., pp. 3747-59.
[2] *Ibid.*, pp. 3224-25.

of the monetary commission, he was through with Washington, which had been his real home for the past thirty-three years. After a farewell reception by five hundred Masonic brethren and their ladies, the Tellers returned to Colorado.[3] There was no reason for returning to the decaying Central City, so they went to Denver to live with their widowed daughter, Emma Teller Tyler. In Denver was Teller's brother James, twenty years his junior, and soon to become a member of the state supreme court. Here also was the Senator's youngest son Bruce, who was engaged in the practice of law. In other parts of Colorado were the eldest son Harrison and brother Addison and his family. Except for his sisters still at Morrison, all his close relatives were in Colorado, and he had returned to spend his last years among them.

One important public duty still remained to keep Senator Teller in the public eye to some extent—the monetary commission which had been set up by Congress in the Aldrich-Vreeland Act of 1908. Teller's connection with this is important only as it relates to his long fight for a bimetallic monetary standard. It will be remembered that he had helped filibuster the original Aldrich banking bill to death in the spring of 1903, in retaliation for the Republican filibuster of the statehood bill. At that time Teller had bid farewell to bimetallism for his own generation.

I know that the theory which some of us have advocated for the treatment of gold and silver on a ratio established by law is not now attainable.... Nobody expects to revive that now.[4]

The panic of 1907, which was hard on Teller's own personal resources, had brought home to him as to others the immediate need of banking reorganization. Late that year he wrote to Hal Sayre:

Just what will happen in the future, nobody seems able to tell. I have, myself, been very optimistic in this matter and have believed it would be only temporary, but so many people think it is liable to continue and grow worse, that I am somewhat doubtful of my own judgment in the matter.[5]

On the floor of the Senate he spoke with more assurance, blaming the panic on speculation and defending the action

---

[3] Clipping from the Washington *Star*, March 15, 1909, in Dawson Scrapbook.
[4] *Congressional Record*, 57 Cong., 2 Sess., p. 2697.
[5] Dec. 17, 1907, Sayre MSS.

of the Secretary of the Treasury and the banks. As an emergency measure, he advocated the bill recently reported by the committee on finance, of which he had long been a member.[6] This bill, called the Aldrich bill after the chairman of the committee, was designed to provide for the issue of additional currency in times of financial stress like that just past. Teller did not agree to all of its provisions, but he supported it upon the floor of the Senate as the "only measure ... that will in any manner meet the emergency that may possibly come." He opposed amendments substantially changing the national banking system, on the grounds that this was not the time to do that. He vigorously but unsuccessfully supported Senator Bailey's amendment—in fact, introduced it as Bailey was absent—providing for the substitution of government paper money for the proposed bank currency, and voted with the majority to pass the bill.[7] The House returned a different bill providing for the issuance of currency based upon commercial paper, to which Teller was strongly opposed. He urged the defeat of the amended bill. The asset currency feature, he declared, was far worse than the much derided subtreasury plan of the Populist Party. He saw no immediate danger; for, as he truly predicted, the banks would never take advantage of the provisions of the bill to any large extent. He protested against any interest charge upon Government deposits in banks. That led, he knew, to insecure loans and unstable banks. The Senate, he said, did not know enough about banking to enact important legislation regarding it. He told the senators that once when John Bright had been asked if he understood the currency question he had replied that he did not, but understood that "some people" did. Teller testified:

After thirty-odd years of experience in public life, I do not believe the latter part of his answer is correct. I really do not know of anybody who understands the currency question, unless he himself is to be the judge. If you leave it to his neighbor, he will decline to admit it.[8]

Before the end of the session a compromise between the House and Senate bills was finally passed, with Teller voting against it.

Included in the Aldrich-Vreeland Act, as the compromise was called, was a provision for a monetary commission to

---

[6] *Congressional Record*, 60 Cong., 1 Sess., pp. 1025, 2031.

[7] *Ibid.*, pp. 1025-31, 3856, 3861, 4019-25.

[8] *Ibid.*, pp. 7109-12.

study the entire banking problem and suggest legislation to Congress. Teller was appointed as one of the Democratic members of the commission. When his senatorial term ran out on March 4, 1909, his membership would have ceased automatically had not special provision been made to continue him as a member. This was highly important to Teller in at least one way. It continued his salary for three years beyond the end of his senatorial term. As he was badly in need of the income, this was exceedingly welcome, and it is not unlikely that his friends in the Senate had this as their chief purpose in keeping him a member.[9]

Teller was anxious to play an active part in the work of the commission, if only because his retirement from the Senate had left him little to do. But he refused from the first to accompany those who went to Europe for a personal investigation of national banking systems there. He considered that a "junket" without real purpose, as these banking systems were adequately described in the available literature. Besides, he believed an American system had to fit vastly different conditions and should not be modeled upon those in Europe.

As far as the few hearings that were held by the commission were concerned, the Coloradan played an active part in the examinations.[10] It does not appear that he had anything to do with the actual plan which was presented to Congress in January, 1912, except in the negative way that it had to meet his ideas substantially or he would not sign it.[11] That this proposal—largely the work of the large bankers—did meet his favor is evident in his oft-quoted remark when he signed it, that he considered his approval one of the most important acts of his life.[12] It might have been, had the plan been enacted into law. But the fate which had identified Teller with lost financial causes dogged his footsteps to the end. The Democratic National Convention of 1912 pronounced against it. Only as it served in a small way as a model for the later Federal Reserve Act did it influence American financial history.

[9] Washington *Post*, Feb. 28, 1909; Teller to Emma Teller Tyler, Dec. 20, 1908, Tyler MSS.

[10] *Senate Document*, No. 404, 62 Cong., 1 Sess.; Denver *Republican*, July 15, 1908. The statement in David S. Barry, *Forty Years in Washington* (Boston, 1924), p. 206, is obviously inaccurate.

[11] Paul M. Warburg, *The Federal Reserve System* (New York, 1930), I, 61; A Piatt Andrew to author, April 23, 1930.

[12] *Commercial and Financial Chronicle*, Jan. 13, 1912; Henry Parker Willis, *The Federal Reserve System* (New York, 1923), p. 77; Stephenson, *Aldrich*, Chapter 24.

CHAPTER XXVI

COLORADO'S GRAND OLD MAN
1909-14

FROM 1909 to 1914 Teller lived in Denver, relieved of his only occupation and subject to the ills of old age. That he could not tear himself away from national politics was evident in the careful scrutiny he made daily of newspapers and of the *Congressional Record*, as though he stayed in the realm of the living only in order not to miss the daily drama recorded by the press.[1] He had a desk in the office of the successors to his and Willard's old law firm downtown in Denver, and spent about half his day there reading, visiting, and looking after his personal affairs. It was dull business after his years in the Senate, and he often wished he were back where he had lived most fully. "I would not give the life I have lived for another," he told a reporter in 1912, "but I only wish I might be seventy again, and who knows, I suppose I would be back in the Senate with my old cronies. I stayed there until I felt I no longer did justice to the people."[2]

Teller was soon adjusted to a new daily routine that began with rising anywhere between five and six o'clock and caring for his beloved roses. After breakfast he walked or went by streetcar to his downtown office. There he spent a long forenoon, looking after the details of his property and visiting with old friends, especially the old settlers who had known him when the Little Kingdom had been in its glory. At late noon he returned home to dine, and spent the remainder of the afternoon reading and puttering in the garden.

Honors came to him that were pleasurable. He was asked to give the commencement address at Colorado University in June, 1909. He responded with "The Duties of Citizenship in a Representative Government."

"I want you men and women to take the politics of this State out of the low condition in which it sometimes is found. . . . Politics is nothing but the theory of government

---

[1] He even wrote Dawson to have the advance sheets of the decisions of the Supreme Court sent to him. "I think that I know pretty near what the law is but sometimes I differ from the Supreme Court & want to know what they think about it." May 21, 1909, Teller MSS.

[2] Clipping from the Denver *Republican*, May 24, 1912, Tyler MSS.

under which we live, and it ought to be your ambition to put this State in a condition where mental and moral worths would control. . . . Will you do it?"[3]

He was presented afterward with another honorary degree to add to those he already had from Alfred and Denver universities. Someone gathered a long series of fullhearted tributes from his colleagues in the Senate and published them in the *Central Christian Advocate*.[4] He accepted an invitation to address the Public Lands Convention in 1911, and used the opportunity to review his ideas on that subject.[5]

Religion was of some consolation to him. Although he had withheld himself from any close identification with organized religion until he was past seventy, he had then joined the church of which his wife and his parents had long been members. The death of his son-in-law, Dr. G. E. Tyler, in 1902 had affected him powerfully, as he was strongly attached to the young man. Shortly thereafter at a church meeting in Central City, he had been moved for the first time in his life to give public testimony of his faith. This he did and became a member of the Methodist Episcopal Church.[6]

He continued to find intense satisfaction in the trend of public affairs, as the Democrats seemed obviously headed for an early return to national power. When the party won scant control of the House in the election of 1910, Teller gave out an enthusiastic interview, and declared that he would live to see a Democrat—perhaps Woodrow Wilson—in the White House.[7] Later, as the campaign of 1912 approached, he declared himself for Champ Clark for the Democratic nomination.[8] When Senator Hughes died in office in 1911 there was at least one voice which urged that Teller be sent back to his old place in the Senate.[9]

The campaign of 1912 found the Senator ill but intensely interested, and the election vindicated his own career to him in a way that was very satisfactory. Wilson in the White House, Bryan in the State Department, and Democrats in

---

[3] Clipping from the Denver *News*, June 9, 1909, in Dawson Scrapbook.

[4] Sept. 1, 1909. Clipping in Tyler MSS.

[5] Denver *Post*, Sept. 29, 1911; the speech was published in pamphlet form.

[6] Wilbur Fletcher Steele, in *The Christian Advocate*, Aug. 19, 1909; B. T. Vincent, *Address Delivered at the Funeral Services of Henry Moore Teller* (Denver, 1914).

[7] Clippings from New York papers of Nov. 11, 1910, Tyler MSS.; also Denver *Post*, May 26, 1911.

[8] Clipping from the Denver *Republican*, May 24, 1912, Tyler MSS.

[9] Denver *Post*, Feb. 2, 1911.

Thomas F. Dawson, for many years Senator Teller's secretary
and aide.

control of both House and Senate—these were comforting events for the old man to contemplate. And political affairs in Colorado were as satisfactory. Shafroth and Thomas were to be the new team from Colorado in the Senate, and Elias M. Ammons, Dawson's partner who had named his oldest son after Teller, was the new governor. Even Dawson was provided for by becoming executive secretary of the United States Senate. Truly, Teller could feel that he had been one prophet who had lived long enough to be honored in his own household and his own lifetime, however late.

The Denver papers continued to seek out and publish his opinions on public questions as long as he lived. His birthdays were occasions for public congratulations. The day he became eighty-two the Denver papers asked for interviews, and one received his recipe for living:

> Don't drink: whiskey is the curse of the United States.
> Don't smoke; it is expensive, both as to health and pocketbook.
> Marry early, if you can, but better late than never—marry sometime. Bachelors are an abomination; they are no real good to themselves or to the community.
> Rise early; work hard; sleep well and plentifully; eat moderately.
> Spend the first hour of your day thinking of the hours to come and of the hours past, resolving to do much and to remedy the mistakes of yesterday—then keep your resolution.[10]

When one reporter asked if he had written his autobiography, he replied, "That's just what I have not done. My record is my life; I must stand or fall by that before posterity."[11]

On February 23, 1914, after a long period of intermittent illness, Henry M. Teller died. Colorado outdid herself to pay her respects to the man she had honored and who had honored her for so long. The body lay in state in the rotunda of the Capitol, and then was moved back to the Tyler home at the request of Mrs. Teller. The funeral was in charge of the Masonic fraternity. An early Central City pastor of the Methodist church, long active in Colorado, delivered the funeral oration, and burial was made in Denver.

Governor Ammons now proposed that Colorado place a bust of its Grand Old Man in one of Colorado's two places in the statesmen's hall of fame, Statuary Hall at Washington. The idea was widely approved, and then quickly for-

---

[10] Denver *Republican*, May 24 ,1912, in Dawson Scrapbook.
[11] Interview with Frances Wayne, James H. Teller Scrapbook.

gotten.[12] Colorado had newer interests than those with which Teller's generation had been concerned.

But Colorado had a morbid interest in the financial affairs of her pioneers, developed, no doubt, by the great wealth of some, and by the strange bequests of others. If one may judge from the Denver press, the Colorado public awaited expectantly the probating of Teller's will to see how it would register upon the financial scales. If it anticipated that he would leave a fortune because his real-estate holdings spread from Chicago to California, it was disappointed. Like many other Westerners, Teller had died land-poor, made so by the panic of 1907, the decline of Gilpin County, and his own mismanagement during his later years. The estate showed assets of $131,000 and liabilities of $126,000. Among the liabilities was an unusual proportion of notes guaranteed for others, the Senator's most expensive charity.[13]

The epitaph Teller might well have chosen for himself is one he had used in eulogizing Richard Parks Bland: "He was an honest man, a patriot, an American statesman of the best type."[14]

---

[12] Clippings from Dawson Scrapbook; Denver *News*, Feb. 24, 1914.

[13] Clipping from the Denver *Post*, April 18, 1914, in Dawson Scrapbook; several financial statements in the Sayre MSS. Some small provisions had been made for the Teller children before the Senator's death.

[14] *Congressional Record*, 51 Cong., 1 Sess., p. 3971.

BIBLIOGRAPHY

MANUSCRIPT COLLECTIONS

Teller MSS. A group of letters to Teller and his penciled drafts of letters to correspondents, in the Library of the State Historical Society of Colorado at Denver. It includes Teller's letters to Thomas F. Dawson from 1882 to 1909.

Teller-Orahood MSS. In addition to a number of letters from H. M. and Willard Teller to Harper Orahood, all previous to 1878, this collection includes many letters to H. M. Teller. Most of the latter concern the Colorado Central Railroad. In addition there are many other manuscripts—legal briefs, account books, canceled checks—concerning the Teller brothers' businesses in Central City. The collection was found by James F. Willard in the old Teller law office in Central City, and is now a part of the Historical Collection of the University of Colorado Library.

Teller Letters. This collection contains a complete file of the letters to Teller for 1877 and 1878. Included also are a few drafts of Teller's own letters. These are cited here as Letters to distinguish them from the Teller Manuscripts. Western Collection, Denver Public Library.

Tyler MSS. This contains a small but very valuable group of letters from Teller to his wife and daughter, and an equally valuable group of letters to Teller. Many press clippings, a short diary of Mrs. Teller's, and other family documents are also included.

William B. Allison MSS. An enormous collection of little help in this study. State Historical, Memorial, and Art Department, Des Moines, Iowa.

Wharton Barker MSS. Library of Congress.

William Jennings Bryan MSS. Library of Congress.

William N. Byers Letterbooks. Historical Collection, University of Colorado Library.

William E. Chandler MSS. Library of Congress.

Henry L. Dawes MSS. Library of Congress.

James A. Garfield MSS. Library of Congress. (Use of copies of letters from Colorado leaders only.)

Walter Q. Gresham MSS. Library of Congress.

Frank Hall MSS. State Historical Society of Colorado.

R. B. Hayes MSS. Hayes Memorial Library, Fremont, Ohio.

Samuel J. Kirkwood MSS. State Historical, Memorial, and Art Department, Des Moines, Iowa.

Samuel J. Kirkwood Letterbooks. State Historical Society of Iowa.

John A. Logan MSS. Library of Congress.

Justin S. Morrill MSS. Library of Congress.

Francis G. Newlands MSS. Yale University Library. (A. B. Darling, custodian.)

Thomas J. O'Donnell MSS. Historical Collection, University of Colorado Library.

R. F. Pettigrew MSS. Pettigrew Museum, Sioux Falls, South Dakota.

F. W. Pitkin Letterbook. State Historical Society of Colorado.

Hal Sayre MSS. Historical Collection, University of Colorado Library.

William M. Stewart MSS., Nevada State Historical Society, Reno, Nevada.
Francis A. Walker MSS. Library of Congress.

UNPUBLISHED REMINISCENCES

Dawson, Thomas F., "The Personal Side of Senator Teller," State Historical Society of Colorado.
Dawson, Thomas F., "Teller and Wolcott in Colorado Politics," State Historical Society of Colorado.
Hawley, J. W., "Diary," State Historical Society of Colorado.
Teller, Mrs. H. M., "Senator Teller as a Young Man," State Historical Society of Colorado.
Teller, James H., "Reminiscences," State Historical Society of Colorado.
Tyler, Mrs. Emma Teller, "Recollections," in the author's possession.
Withrow, Chase, "Reminiscences," State Historical Society of Colorado.

GOVERNMENT DOCUMENTS

Congressional Globe, 39th to 41st congresses.
Congressional Record, 44th to 60th congresses.
Senate Journal, 44th to 60th congresses.
Senate Reports, 44th to 60th congresses.
Annual Report of the Secretary of the Interior, 1880 to 1887, in *House Executive Documents*, No. 1, Part 5, 46th to 50th congresses.
Decisions of the Department of Interior and General Land Office, Vols. I-III, Washington, 1882-85.
Colorado, *General Laws*, 1st to 4th Legislative Sessions.
Colorado Supreme Court, *Reports*.

UNPUBLISHED THESES AND OTHER STUDIES

Adams, Mary Fonda, "Thomas M. Patterson, Some Aspects of His Political Career," University of Colorado, 1933.
Cooper, Esther F., "The Genesis and Application of the Dawes Act," State University of Iowa, 1924.
Fuller, Leon W., "The Populist Regime in Colorado," University of Wisconsin, 1933.
Galloway, B. T., "The Genesis of the Bureau of Plant Industry," typed manuscript, 1926.
Lunsford, Lena Mae, "The History of the Domesticated Reindeer in Alaska," University of Missouri, 1933.
Mack, Effie Mona, "William M. Stewart," University of California, 1930.
Mock, Samuel Donald, "Railroad Development in the Colorado Region to 1880," University of Nebraska, 1938.
Perrigo, Lynn Irwin, "A Social History of Central City, 1859-1900," University of Colorado, 1936.
Scheidler, Lawrence John, "Silver and Politics, 1893-1896," University of Indiana, 1936.
Silveus, Marian, "The Antecedents of the Campaign of 1896," University of Wisconsin, 1933.
Spiva, Agnes E., "The Utes in Colorado," University of Colorado, 1929.
Voss, Walter A., "Colorado and Forest Conservation," University of Colorado, 1931.

White, Forest Lowell, "The Panic of 1893 in Colorado," University of Colorado, 1932.

NEWSPAPER CLIPPINGS

Dawson Scrapbooks, Library of the State Historical Society of Colorado. Vol. 61, pp. 1-175 is devoted specifically to Teller.
James H. Teller Scrapbook, Mrs. B. O. Edgerton, Denver.
J. H. Randall Morgue, Historical Collection, University of Colorado.
Mrs. S. J. Kirkwood Scrapbook, State Historical Society of Iowa.

NEWSPAPERS AND PERIODICALS

Atlanta *Constitution*
The Cherokee Advocate
Chicago *Daily Tribune*
Colorado Republican and Mountain Herald
Commercial and Financial Chronicle
Colorado Tribune (Denver)
Denver *Daily Times*
Denver *Daily Tribune*
Denver *Republican*
Denver *Post*
Denver *Weekly Times*
Gunnison (Colorado) *Daily Review Press*
Harper's Weekly
The Independent
Iowa State Register
Kansas City *Star*
Kansas City *Times*
The Literary Digest
Miner's Register, variously titled *Daily Miner's Register* and *Daily Central City Register* (Central City, Colorado)
Mining Journal (Blackhawk, Colorado)

Minneapolis *Journal*
The Nation
National Watchman
New Orleans *Times*
New York *Journal*
New York *Sun*
New York *Tribune*
The News and Courier (Charleston)
Omaha *World-Herald*
The Outlook
Public Opinion
Raleigh *News and Observer*
Review of Reviews
The Rocky Mountain News (Denver)
St. Louis *Globe-Democrat*
St. Louis *Post-Dispatch*
St. Louis *Republic*
The Silver Knight-National Watchman
Sterling (Illinois) *Republican and Gazette*
Washington *Post*
Washington *Star*
Whiteside Sentinel (Morrison, Illinois)

BOOKS AND ARTICLES

"Address of the People of Colorado to the People of the United States," leaflet (Denver, 1893).
Alfred University, *General Catalogue of Matriculates and Graduates of Alfred University, 1836-1869* (Westerly, R. I., 1896). Part II contains "A Memorial of President William Colgrove Kenyon," by Jonathan Allen.
Allen, A. A., *Life and Sermons of Jonathan Allen* (Oakland, California, 1894).
Ammons, E. M., "A Tribute to Thomas F. Dawson," *Colorado Magazine,* I (1923), 3-8.
Andrews, E. B., *The United States in Our Own Times* (New York, 1912).
Arnett, A. M., *The Populist Movement in Georgia* (New York, 1922).

Baker, James H., and Hafen, LeRoy R., *History of Colorado* (Denver, 1927), 3 vols.

Bancroft, F., *Speeches, Correspondence, and Political Papers of Carl Schurz* (New York, 1913), 6 vols.

Bancroft, F., and Dunning, W. A., *Reminiscences of Carl Schurz* (New York, 1918), 3 vols.

Bancroft, H. H., *History of Nevada, Colorado, and Wyoming* (San Francisco, 1890).

Barnard, Harry, *"Eagle Forgotten"; the Life and Times of John Peter Altgeld* (Indianapolis, 1938).

Barnes, James A., *James G. Carlisle* (New York, 1931).

Beardsley, Isaac H., *Echoes From Peak and Plain* (Cincinnati and New York, 1898).

Beer, Thomas, *Hanna* (New York, 1929).

Bemis, Edward W., "The Silver Situation in Colorado," *Review of Reviews*, Sept., 1898.

Bent, Charles, *History of Whiteside County* (Morrison, Ill., 1877).

Berry, David S., *Forty Years in Washington* (Boston, 1924).

Bishop, Joseph B., *Theodore Roosevelt and his Time* (New York, 1920), 2 vols.

Bowers, Claude G., *Beveridge and the Progressive Era* (Boston, 1932).

Bowles, Samuel, *Across the Continent* (Springfield, Mass., 1865).

Bryan, William J., *The Memoirs of William Jennings Bryan* (Philadelphia, 1925).

———, *The First Battle* (Chicago, 1896).

———, *The Second Battle* (Chicago, 1900).

Bullock, Charles J., *Essays on the Monetary History of the United States* (New York, 1900).

Burrell, James, "History of Gilpin County," in W. B. Vickers, *History of Clear Creek and Boulder Valleys* (Chicago, 1880).

Byars, W. V., *An American Commoner* (Columbia, Mo., 1900).

Caldwell, Robert G., *James A. Garfield* (New York, 1931).

Cannon, Frank J., and O'Higgins, Harvey J., *Under the Prophet in Utah* (Boston, 1917).

Chapin, Mrs. E. N., *American Court Gossip* (Marshalltown, Iowa, 1887).

Chidsey, D. B., *The Gentleman from New York* (New Haven, 1935).

Clark, Champ, *My Quarter Century of American Politics* (New York, 1920), 2 vols.

Clark, Dan Elbert, *Samuel Jordan Kirkwood* (Iowa City, Iowa, 1917).

Colorado Directory of Mines (Denver, 1879).

Connelley, W. E., *Life of Preston B. Plumb* (Chicago, 1913).

Connolly, C. P., "Conspiracies of Capital and the Courts," *Pacific Monthly*, XX (1908), 279-93.

Crawford, Samuel J., *Kansas in the Sixties* (Chicago, 1911).

Croly, Herbert, *Marcus Alonzo Hanna* (New York, 1912).

Cullom, Shelby M., *Fifty Years of Public Service* (Chicago, 1911).

Curtis, Francis, *The Republican Party* (New York, 1904).

Cushman, Frank, and Waterman, J. P., *The Gold Mines of Gilpin County* (Central City, Colo., 1876).

Dale, E. E., "History of the Ranch Cattle Industry in Oklahoma," *Annual Report of the Americn Historical Association*, 1920, pp. 307-22.

BIBLIOGRAPHY 397

Dale, E. E., *The Range Cattle Industry* (Norman, 1930).

Darling, Arthur B., ed., *The Public Papers of Francis G. Newlands* (Boston, 1932), 2 vols.

Davis, C. C., *Olden Times in Colorado* (Los Angeles, 1916).

Davis, C. C., and Alderson, W. A., *The True Story of Ramona* (New York, 1914).

Davis, W. A., *History of Whiteside County, Illinois* (Chicago, 1908), 2 vols.

Dawson, Thomas F., *Life and Character of Edmund Oliver Wolcott* (New York, 1911), 2 vols.

――, *Senator Teller* (Washington, 1923).

――, *Senator Teller: A Brief Account of his Fifth Election to the United States Senate* (Washington, 1898).

De Launay, L., *The World's Gold* (New York and London, 1908).

Democratic National Conventions, *Official Proceedings*, 1900 to 1908.

Dennett, Tyler, *John Hay* (New York, 1933).

Dennis, Alfred P., *Adventures in American Diplomacy* (New York, 1928).

Dewey, Davis R., *Financial History of the United States* (New York, 1924).

――, *National Problems 1885-1897* (New York, 1907).

Dill, R. G., *The Political Campaigns of Colorado* (Denver, 1895).

Dobie, Edith, *The Political Career of Stephen Mallory White* (Stanford University, 1927).

Dodge, G. M., *How We Built the Union Pacific Railway* (n.p., n.d.).

Donaldson, Thomas, *The Public Domain* (Washington, 1884).

Dubbs, Henry A., "The Unfolding of Law in the Mountain Region," *Colorado Magazine*, III (1926), 113-32.

Dunn, Arthur W., *From Harrison to Harding* (New York, 1922), 2 vols .

――, *Gridiron Nights* (New York, 1915).

Eckenrode, Hamilton J., *Rutherford B. Hayes* (New York, 1930).

Ellis, Elmer, "Colorado's First Fight for Statehood," *Colorado Magazine*, VIII (1931), 23-30.

――, "The Silver Republicans in the Election of 1896," *Mississippi Valley Historical Review*, XVIII (1932), 519-34.

Fish, Carl R., *Civil Service and the Patronage* (New York, 1904).

Fisher, Irving, *The Purchasing Power of Money* (New York, 1922).

Fisher, Willard, "Coin and His Critics," *Quarterly Journal of Economics*, X (1896), 185-208, 324-40.

Fitzgibbon, Russell H., *Cuba and the United States 1900-1935* (Menasha, Wis., 1935).

Fitz-Mac [James McCarty], *Political Portraits* (Colorado Springs, 1886).

Foraker, Joseph B., *Notes on a Busy Life* (Cincinnati, 1916), 2 vols.

Forbes, W. Cameron, *The Philippine Islands* (Boston and New York, 1929), 2 vols.

Fossett, Frank, *Colorado: Its Gold and Silver Mines* (New York, 1880).

Fuess, Claude M., *Carl Schurz, Reformer* (New York, 1932).

Fuller, Leon W., "Governor Waite and His Silver Panacea," *Colorado Magazine*, X (1933), 41-47.

Glasson, William H., *Federal Military Pensions in the United States* (New York, 1918).

Goodykoontz, Colin B., "The Exploration and Settlement of Colorado," in *Colorado: Short Studies of its Past and Present* (Boulder, Colo., 1927).

Greely, A. W., *Handbook of Alaska* (New York, 1925).

Gresham, Matilda, *Life of Walter Quintin Gresham* (Chicago, 1919), 2 vols.

Hafen, LeRoy R., *The Overland Mail* (Cleveland, 1926).

Hall, Frank, *History of Colorado* (Chicago, 1889-95), 4 vols.

Hay, John, *Letters and Diaries of John Hay* (Washington, 1908).

Haynes, F. E., *James Baird Weaver* (Iowa City, 1919).

Haynes, George H., *The Election of Senators* (New York, 1906).

Henderson, Charles W., *History of Mining in Colorado* (Washington, 1925).

Hibbard, Benjamin H., *A History of the Public Land Policies* (New York, 1924).

Hibben, Paxton, *The Peerless Leader* (New York, 1929).

Hicks, John D., *The Populist Revolt* (Minneapolis, 1931).

Hill, Howard C., *Roosevelt and the Caribbean* (Chicago, 1927).

Hinton, R. J., "Irrigation and Legislation," *Belford's Magazine*, Oct., 1890.

Hoar, George F., *Autobiography of Seventy Years* (New York and London, 1903), 2 vols.

———, "The Fate of the Election Bill," *The Forum*, April, 1891.

Hollister, O. J., *The Mines of Colorado* (Springfield, Mass., 1876).

Holt, W. Stull, *Treaties Defeated by the United States Senate* (Baltimore, 1933).

Howard, M. W., *The American Plutocracy* (New York, 1895).

Howbert, Irving, *Memories of a Life Time in the Pike's Peak Region* (New York, 1925).

Howe, George F., *Chester A. Arthur* (New York, 1934).

Howe, M. A. DeWolf, *Portrait of an Independent: Moorefield Storey* (Boston, 1932).

Hoxie, Robert F., "The Silver Debate of 1890," *Journal of Political Economy*, I (1893), 535-87.

Hütter, Jean Paul, *L'Incidence Economique De La Frappe De Monnaie D'Argent Aux Etats-Unis* (Paris, 1938).

———, *La Question De La Monnaie D'Argent Aux Etats-Unis* (Paris, 1938).

Indian Rights Association, *Fifteenth Annual Report of the Executive Committee* (Philadelphia, 1898).

Ise, John, *The United States Forest Policy* (New Haven, Conn., 1920).

Jessupp, Philip C., *Elihu Root*, 2 vols. (New York, 1938).

Josephson, Matthew, *The Politicos*, 1865-1896 (New York, 1938).

Karsner, David, *Silver Dollar* (New York, 1932).

Keasby, L. M., "The New Sectionalism—A Western Warning," *The Forum*, Jan., 1894.

Lake Mohonk Conference of Friends of Indians and Other Dependent Peoples, *Twenty-ninth Annual Report* (1911).

Lauck, W. Jett, *The Causes of the Panic of 1893* (Boston, 1907).

Laughlin, J. Lawrence, *The History of Bimetallism in the United States* (New York, 1896).

Leupp, Francis E., *The Indian and His Problem* (New York, 1910).

———, "Personal Recollections of Thomas B. Reed," *The Outlook*, Sept. 3, 1910.

Lindsey, Ben B., and O'Higgins, Harvey J., *The Beast* (New York, 1910).

Lodge, H. C., ed., *Selections from the Correspondence of Theodore Roosevelt and Henry Cabot Lodge* (New York, 1925), 2 vols.

McCall, Samuel W., *Thomas B. Reed* (Boston, 1914).

McCormack, Thomas J., ed., *Memoirs of Gustave Koerner* (Cedar Rapids, Iowa, 1909).

McElroy, Robert, *Grover Cleveland* (New York and London, 1923), 2 vols.

McKenzie, F. A., *The Indian* (Columbus, Ohio, 1908).

McLaughlin, James, *My Friend the Indian* (Boston and New York, 1910).

McMechen, Edgar Carlisle, *Life of Governor Evans* (Denver, 1924).

Marshall, Thomas M., *Early Records of Gilpin County* (Boulder, Colo., 1920).

———, "The Miners' Laws of Colorado," *American Historical Review*, XXV (1920), 426-39.

Marshall, Thomas R., *Recollections* (Indianapolis, 1925).

Merriam, Lewis, *The Problem of Indian Administration* (Baltimore, 1928).

Mills, Enos A., *The Story of Estes Park* (Estes Park, 1911).

Moorehead, Warren K., *The American Indian in the United States* (Andover, Mass., 1914).

Mott, T. Bentley, *Myron T. Herrick* (Garden City, 1929).

Nankivell, John H., *History of the Military Organizations of the State of Colorado, 1860-1935* (Denver, 1935).

Nevins, Allan, *Grover Cleveland* (New York, 1932).

———, *Letters of Grover Cleveland* (New York, 1933).

Nichols, Jeannette P., "The Politics and Personalities of Silver Repeal in the United States Senate," *American Historical Review*, XLI 1935), 26-53.

Noyes, Alexander D., *Forty Years of American Finance* (New York, 1909).

Oberholtzer, E. P., *History of the United States* (New York, 1926), 5 vols.

Odell, Ruth, *Helen Hunt Jackson* (New York, 1939).

Olcott, Charles S., *The Life of William McKinley* (Boston and New York, 1916), 2 vols.

Oliver, John W., *A History of Civil War Pensions, 1861-1885* (Madison, Wis., 1917).

Orcutt, W. D., *Burroughs of Michigan and the Republican Party* (New York, 1927), 2 vols.

Paxson, F. L., "The Territory of Colorado," *American Historical Review*, XII (1906), 60-61.

Peake, Ora B., *The Colorado Range Cattle Industry* (Glendale, Calif., 1937).

Peck, H. T., *Twenty Years of the Republic* (New York, 1907).

Pelzer, Louis, *The Cattlemen's Frontier* (Glendale, Calif., 1936).

Pettigrew, R. F., *Imperial Washington* (Chicago, 1922).

Platt, T. C., *The Autobiography of Thomas Collier Platt* (New York, 1918).

Poor, Ben Perly, *Reminiscences of Sixty Years in the National Metropolis* (Philadelphia, 1886), 2 vols.

Portrait and Biographical Album, Whiteside County (Chicago, 1885).

Pratt, J. W., *Expansionists of 1898* (Baltimore, 1936).

Pratt, Richard Henry, *The Indian Industrial School* (Carlisle, no date).

Pringle, H. F., *Theodore Roosevelt* (New York, 1931).

Proceedings of the Grand Commandery of the Knights Templar of Colorado at its Thirty-ninth Annual Conclave (Denver, 1914).

Proceedings of the Grand Lodge of Free and Accepted Masons of the Territory of Colorado, Reports 1 to 15 (Central City and Denver).

Pyle, J. G., *The Life of James J. Hill* (Garden City, 1917), 2 vols.

Republican National Convention, *Official Proceedings,* 1876 to 1896.

Reyes, José E., *Legislative History of America's Economic Policy Toward the Philippines* (New York, 1923).

Rhodes, James Ford, *The History of the United States from the Compromise of 1850* (New York, 1919), 9 vols.

Richardson, Albert D., *Beyond the Mississippi* (Hartford, Conn., 1869).

Richardson, Leon B., *William E. Chandler, Republican* (New York, 1940).

Richmond, George Q., "The Men With Whom I've Smiled," *Colorado Magazine,* I (1924), 145-51.

Robinson, William A., *Thomas B. Reed, Parliamentarian* (New York, 1930).

Rosser, Charles M., *The Crusading Commoner* (Dallas, 1937).

Rubens, Horatio S., *Liberty: The Story of Cuba* (New York, 1932).

The Rushford Centennial (Rushford, New York [?], 1908 [?]).

Russell, Charles Edward, *These Shifting Sands* (New York, 1914).

Russell, Henry B., *International Monetary Conferences* (New York, 1898).

Sageser, A. B., *The First Two Decades of the Pendleton Act* (Lincoln, 1935).

Sayre, Hal, "Early Central City Theatricals and Other Reminiscences," *Colorado Magazine,* VI (1929), 47-53.

Sebert, William L., and Stevens, John F., *The Construction of the Panama Canal* (New York and London, 1915).

Sherman, John, *Recollections of Forty Years in the House, Senate, and Cabinet* (Chicago, 1895), 2 vols.

Simkins, Francis B., *The Tillman Movement in South Carolina* (Durham, 1926).

Smiley, Jerome C., *History of Denver* (Denver, 1903).

———, *Semi-Centennial History of the State of Colorado* (Chicago, 1913).

Smith., T. C., *The Life and Letters of James Abram Garfield* (New Haven, 1921), 2 vols.

Sparks, E. E., *National Development* (New York and London, 1907).

Stanton, Irving W., *Sixty Years in Colorado* (Denver, 1922).

Stanwood, Edward, *American Tariff Controversies in the Nineteenth Century* (Boston, 1903), 2 vols.

———, *James Gillespie Blaine* (Boston, 1905).

Stealey, O. O., *Twenty Years in the Press Gallery* (New York, 1906).

Steevens, G. W., *The Land of the Dollar* (London, 1897).

Steffens, Lincoln, *Upbuilders* (New York, 1909).

Stephenson, Nathaniel W., *Nelson W. Aldrich* (New York, 1930).

Stewart, William M., *Reminiscences* (New York, 1908).

Stone, W. F., *History of Colorado* (Chicago, 1918), 3 vols.

Stryker, L. P., *Andrew Johnson* (New York, 1929).

Taylor, Bayard, *Colorado: A Summer Trip* (New York, 1867).

Teller, James H., *The Battle of the Standards* (Chicago, 1896).

Thayer, W. R., *Life and Letters of John Hay* (Boston, 1915), 2 vols.

Thomas, Charles S., "Fifty Years of Political History," Chap. XVII
in Vol. III of *History of Colorado*, edited by James H. Baker and
LeRoy R. Hafen (Denver, 1927).

————, "The Pioneer Bar of Colorado," *Colorado Magazine*, I (1924),
193-204.

Thompson, Charles Willis, *Party Leaders of the Time* (New York,
1906).

Underwood, Oscar W., *Drifting Sands of Party Politics* (New York,
1928).

Vincent, B. T., *Address Delivered at the Funeral Services of Henry
Moore Teller* (Denver, 1914).

Walker, Francis A., *International Bimetallism* (New York, 1896).

*War of Rebellion, A Compilation of the Official Records of the Union
and Confederate Armies*, Series III, Vol. I.

Washburne, Charles B., *The Life of John W. Weeks* (Boston, 1928).

Webb, Walter P., *The Great Plains* (Boston, 1931).

Weinberg, A. K., *Manifest Destiny* (Baltimore, 1935).

Wellborn, Fred, "The Influence of the Silver Republican Senators,
1880-1891," *Mississippi Valley Historical Review*, XIV (1928),
462-72.

Welles, Gideon, *The Diary of Gideon Welles* (Boston and New York,
1911), 3 vols.

White, William A., *Masks in a Pageant* (New York, 1928).

Wikoff, Peter, "The Bench and Bar of Denver and Colorado," *Magazine of Western History*, IX (1889), 608-10.

Wilder, W. L., *Robert Wilbur Steele* (Denver, 1911).

Willard, James F., "The Gold Rush and After," in *Colorado: Short
Studies of its Past and Present* (Boulder, Colo., 1927), pp. 101-21.

————, "J. B. Chaffee," in *Dictionary of American Biography* (New
York, 1929), III, 590.

Williams, C. R., ed., *Diary and Letters of Rutherford B. Hayes* (Columbus, Ohio, 1922-26), 5 vols.

————, *The Life of Rutherford B. Hayes* (Boston and New York,
1914), 2 vols.

Woodward, C. Van, *Tom Watson, Agrarian Rebel* (New York, 1938).

Wright, Dunham, "A Winter in Estes Park with Senator Teller,"
The Trail, July, 1920.

Young, Frank C., *Echoes from Arcadia: The Story of Central City*
(Denver, 1903).

INDEX

Abolition, 21, 23, 24, 44, 62
Adams, Alva, 180, 349, 363-65, 384
Adams, Brooks, 284
Adams, Henry, 218, 239
Aguinaldo, E., 317
Alaska, 173-74, 378
Aldrich, Nelson W., 190, 200, 233, 292, 324, 342, 345, 368, 377
Aldrich-Vreeland Act, 368-87
Alfred Academy, 22-24
Allen, W. V., in debate on Purchase Act repeal, 224, 225; introduces resolution for investigation of treatment of Coxey's army, 232; letters to, 239, 281; follows Teller's lead, 252; for fusion of state organizations, 301; votes for ratification of peace treaty, 319; at Populist National Convention, 328
Allison Amendment, 370
Allison, William B., 125, 133, 181, 240, 243, 290, 298, 299, 367, 369
Altgeld, John P., 267, 271
American Bimetallic League, 237, 247
Ammons, E. M., 208, 253, 351, 391
Andrews, E. B., 294
Angelica (New York), 26
Anthony, Susan B., 24
Anthracite Coal Strike, 359
Armour, C. L., 57-58
Arthur, Chester A., supported by Colorado delegation for vice-president, 120; becomes president, 132; selects new Cabinet members, 133-34; social functions under, 136-37; Teller's estimate of, 137-38; opens parts of Indian reservations by executive order, 142; concurs on land grant patents, 150; problem of securing Republican nomination for, 156; Teller's support of, 157; mentioned, 140, 175
Atlanta *Constitution*, 355

Bacon, A. O., 318
Bailey, Joseph W., 345, 387
Baker, Jehu, 181
Baring Brothers, 204
Barker, Wharton, 244, 248
Bayard, Thomas F., Sr., 163
Belford, James B., 90, 93, 111
Bell, John, 32
Bell, John C., 219, 286, 304-05, 333
Bemis, Edward W., 221
Bennet, Hiram P., 62-64
Berry, James H., 310
Berthoud, E. L., 79, 354
Beveridge, Albert J., 250, 322, 341, 355, 376, 377-78
Bimetallism, Republican National Convention of 1896, 17-18, 250-63; Bland-Allison bill, 125-26; issue in Colorado campaign of 1888, 181-82; Teller's theory of, 184-87; dissatisfaction with the Bland-Allison Act, 187-88; issue in the campaign of 1888, 188; the Sherman Purchase Act, 188-93; silver senators and the Force bill, 197-201; the Purchase Act and the campaign of 1892, 206-12; the contest over repeal of the Purchase Act, 213-28; free coinage becomes the national issue, 229-32, 237-47; move to create a united silver party, 247-48, 252-57, 261-62, 265-73, 302-05,

325-31; attempt to unite cause of free coinage with protection, 248-49; in the Republican Convention of 1897, 250-63; in the Democratic Convention of 1896, 265-73; attempts to unite free-coinage factions on Bryan, 274-82; in the campaign of 1896, 280-86; cause of the decline of the issue, 287-89; attitude of Republican Party after 1896, 289-92, 294-300, 320-22; Teller Resolution declaring bonds payable in silver or gold, 297-300; decline of free-coinage issue, 305, 320, 325; Gold Standard Act, 320-22; in campaign of 1900, 326-34; in campaign of 1904, 362-63; Teller's farewell to, 386
Blaine, James G., heads Half-Breed faction in Congress, 111-12, 120, 156; Colorado support of, 157-58; as possible Republican presidential nominee in 1892, 205; announces he is not a candidate, 206; loses nomination, 209-11; mentioned, 114, 180, 181, 196
Blaine, Mrs. James G., 210
Blair Bill, 177, 193
Blair, Henry W., 195, 362
Bland-Allison bill, 125, 184, 187
Bland, Richard P., starts move to pass free-coinage bill, 206; in the Purchase Act repeal contest, 219; leading Democratic presidential nominee, 255; Teller on nomination of, 269; candidate at the 1896 Chicago convention, 270-72; Teller's eulogy of, 392; mentioned, 266
Boise, Horace, 269-72
Borah, William E., 278, 285
Bowen, Thomas M., 155, 182
Bowles, Samuel, 60
Breckinridge, John C., 32
Bright, John, 387
Bromwell, H. P. H., 90-91
Brooklyn *Eagle*, 237
Brown, Arthur, 242
Brown, John, 31
Bruce, Harriet, wife of H. M. T., meets H. M. T., 26; marriage of, 41
Bruce, Packard, father of Mrs. H. M. T., 26
Bryan, William J., asks for copies of Teller's speech, 208; opposes repeal of Purchase Act, 219; nominated for president, 271-77; in campaign of 1896, 278-85; writes to Chairman Jones, 303; letter from Teller to, 317; letter from Gov. Thomas to, 325; letter from Dubois to, 326; Teller appeals for assistance from, 326; letter from Jones to, 327; Populist National Convention, 1900, nominates, 328; Democratic National Convention, 1900, nominates, 330, defeated in 1900, 333; supported by Teller in 1908 campaign, 381-84; mentioned, 266, 268, 299, 300, 305, 319, 324, 362, 390
Buchanan, James, 117
Burke Act, 375
Burrows, Julius C., 299
Butler, Marion, 242, 276, 319, 328, 362
Byers, William N., 94, 105

Cameron, John D., 111, 134, 200, 201, 239, 248, 249
Cameron, Simon, 42

DUE